Fodor's 2002

P9-DCS-240

Cancún, Cozumel, Yucatán Peninsula

Fodor's Travel Publications • New York, Toronto, London, Sydney, Auckland
www.fodors.com

CONTENTS

MAPS

Circled letters in text correspond to letters on the photographs. For more information on the sights pictured, turn to the indicated page number **ⓐ** on each photograph.

DESTINATION CANCÚN, COZUMEL, YUCATÁN PENINSULA

Well within living memory, the Yucatán Peninsula was a backwater of Mexico, overgrown by jungle and exceptionally hard to get to (not that it mattered to most people). Things are different now. Government-backed development, for the most part judicious, has created a Yucatán of sun, surf, unspoiled nature, shopping, nightlife, fine dining, and sundry other pleasures that can recharge your batteries. One pleasure special to the area is the splendor of Maya ruins like those at El Castillo, a pyramid at Chichén Itzá. Stripped of creepers, the ancient monument inspires awe—just as the Yucatán, stripped of its own creepers, now inspires boundless fascination and fun.

Where *nada* stood 30 years ago, Mexico's most popular destination now welcomes millions annually to more than 100 lushly landscaped hotels, most crowding a slim, 14-mile-long barrier island called the ⓓ**Hotel Zone.** The fun here

CANCÚN

comes in all varieties, from outdoorsy to raucous to culturally enriching. With the Caribbean on one side and Laguna de Nichupté on the other, water sports are a major draw—windsurfing, fishing, snorkeling on a coral reef just offshore. So are clear, turquoise vistas and soft white sand, like that gracing the "front yard" of the ⓒ**Hyatt Regency Cancún.** You won't be as happy to feel soft white sand between your toes at the ⓐ**Pok-Ta-Pok Golf Club,** one of the first-rate courses in the Hotel Zone, but views of sea and lagoon will more than repay you, and there's a small Maya ruin on the 12th hole, just to remind you where you are. When the sun sets, Cancún gets down. Club-hopping and tequila-sampling attract throngs of merrymakers

ⓐ 42

from happy hour until almost dawn. The dining scene offers choices galore—Cajun, Italian, Japanese, American, and more. You can in fact spend your vacation in Cancún only marginally aware of being in Mexico. But what a pity that would be. Even without leaving the Hotel Zone you can enjoy the Ⓑ**Ballet Folklorico de Cancún,** featuring dances from across Mexico. If you venture farther afield, on the mainland in Ⓔ**El Centro,** downtown Cancún, you'll find real Mexican-Maya flavor. Markets like Ki Huic, the largest, are full of indigenous crafts and food. And you're only a day trip from the superb Maya ruins at Chichén Itzá and Tulum, where ancient developers built for the ages.

Ⓒ 36

Ⓓ 25

Ⓔ 21

Isla Mujeres is just a few miles from Cancún by boat. But it's light-years away in temperament, a laid-back counterpart to the big resorts' flash. Except when ferries disgorge cargoes of shoppers, Isla gives you more elbow room on the same

white-sand beaches, with the same great diving, for much less money. A stroll on Ⓐ**Avenida López Mateos** leads to the island's lovely cemetery. Take in the views along Ⓑ**Laguna Makax,** where pirates once lay in wait for treasure ships on the Spanish Main. The waters of Ⓒ**El Garrafón National Park** offer an introduction to the colorful world just offshore.

ISLA
MUJERES

COZUMEL

Mellower than Cancún, hipper than Isla Mujeres, gentle Cozumel appeals to visitors who want a bit of both worlds. Most of all, though, it lures divers. Cozumel's reefs—especially off Ⓑ**Playa de Palancar**—are among the finest, and the island is a star among those who go under in wet suits. Knowing a good thing, the government now protects large areas of reef and land as national parks. The showpiece is Ⓐ Ⓓ**Parque Chankanaab,** where you can meet a Maya Chacmool beneath the waves or a golden iguana resplendent by the lagoon. Cozumel's ruins aren't monumental, but they still impress; those at Ⓒ**San Gervasio** deserve a visit. Reef, ruins, and retailers can fill your days here, but there's good news for night owls, too: Cozumel rocks.

A 140

CARIBBEAN COAST

South of Cancún, golf carts and tennis shops disappear and the number of acres of beach per visitor skyrockets. And what beaches. Along the Riviera Maya, as the area is called, strands are dazzling and white and the waters azure and turquoise, perfect not only for sun worshippers and snorkelers, but also for birders, beachcombers, and anyone else who likes his ocean clear and his seascapes dominated by nothing taller than the local jungle. Lodgings come in every style, from bungalows and campgrounds to glitzy resorts. There is even a Cancún-in-the-making, ©**Playa del Carmen,** where dining options are plentiful and the nightlife goes on until the wee hours.

Mostly, however, the Caribbean coast is about great natural beauty. At the huge ⓓ**Sian Ka'an Biosphere Reserve,** a UNESCO showcase and a magnet for ecotourists, you can see the Yucatán as it was when the Maya ruled. To see the grandeur of ancient Maya civilization itself, visit the great stone faces at Ⓐ**Kohunlich.** Or make the pilgrimage to Ⓑ**Tulum,** truly a ruin with a view, or to grand Ⓔ**Cobá,** where you can mix aerobics with archaeology on the Nohoch Mul pyramid. Mixing and matching pleasures are the charm of this region: Explore in a jeep and serendipity will be your navigator; the next day, just beach yourself, serene and sunscreened, and peace will be your reward.

©▷117

ⓓ▷133

Ⓔ▷131

11

MÉRIDA AND THE YUCATÁN

Ⓐ 158

Ⓑ 171

If the ancient Maya call to you, they're calling from here. The ruins in Yucatán State are unsurpassed and include world-famous Ⓑ**Chichén Itzá,** the first Maya ruin to be excavated and still the most familiar, as well as the understated, elegant Uxmal. Of course, the Maya never left the Yucatán. Indeed, it's an open question whether the Mexicans truly got in. Maya culture is strong and vibrant. In some villages, Maya is the language of choice; in a few, it's the only option. The old gods receive their due, and even Catholic holidays such as the Ⓒ**Day of the Dead** can have a pagan feel to them when Yucatecans are doing the celebrating. All this makes Mérida, the state capital, a fascinating base from which to explore: Maya meets colonial here, weaving a rich visual and cultural tapestry. Once wealthy, and still lovely in places, as evidenced by

Ⓒ 152

the Ⓐ**Palacio Municipal,** Mérida has endearing quirkiness and charm (and traffic fumes and noise). The dining scene is cosmopolitan, the shopping and museums those of a sophisticated city. The nightlife holds its own, too. And two hours west of town the flamingo-watching is superb.

Ⓐ➤ 208

Mellow in general, Yucatecan life is at its mellowest in this flat, rural state. Here the Maya imprint remains strong. In Ⓑ**Becal,** artisans still weave traditional hats known as *jipis*. And ancient ruins are numerous, architecturally diverse, and richly detailed. In Campeche City it's the Spanish colonial heritage that's most

CAMPECHE

palpable, notably at Ⓐ **Fuerte San José,** whose cannons forced pirates to think twice about stopping, and ensured a night's sleep for the residents of Ⓓ**Calle 59,** one of many streets with lovely old buildings. Southern Campeche is primeval rain forest, now protected as the Ⓒ**Calakmul Biosphere Reserve,** where jaguar, puma, and ocelot still stalk their prey amid tangled vegetation and more than 100 species of orchid.

Ⓑ➤ 215

Ⓒ➤ 223

Ⓓ➤ 207

FODOR'S
CHOICE

Even with so many special places in Cancún, Isla Mujeres, Cozumel, and the Yucatán Peninsula, Fodor's writers and editors have their favorites. Here are a few that stand out.

ARCHAEOLOGICAL SITES

Ⓓ **Chichén Itzá.** This best-known Maya ruin was the most important city in the Yucatán from the 11th to the 13th centuries. ☞ p. 171

Cobá. Once a central city–state in the Maya domain, this site has long languished in its lush, tropical setting. Only about 5% of its more than 6,000 structures have been excavated. ☞ p. 131

Ⓔ **Edzná.** Archaeologists believe that this remote and remarkably intact ruin played a crucial transitional role in Maya architectural development. ☞ p. 216

Uxmal. The lovely Uxmal style includes ornate stone friezes, intricate cornices, and soaring arches. ☞ p. 178

BEACHES

Ⓙ **Akumal.** Shells, crabs, and migrant birds fill long stretches of this popular section of the Caribbean coast. The tranquil coves are ideal for swimming and snorkeling. ☞ p. 125

Playa Norte. A white sand beach on the northern tip of Isla Mujeres, Playa Norte is both scenic and social. ☞ p. 60

Xcalak Peninsula. One of the Caribbean coast's still-remote spots, this peninsula is lush with mangrove swamps, tropical flowers, and wildlife. ☞ p. 137

NATURE RESERVES AND NATURAL BEAUTY

Isla Contoy. An unspoiled island preserve off the coast of Isla Mujeres, Isla Contoy is especially notable for its birds; more than 70 species pass through in fall. ☞ p. 69

Laguna de Bacalar. Sea and fresh water mix to produce stunning hues in this "Lake of Seven Colors," Mexico's second largest lake. ☞ p. 138

Ⓖ **Loltún Caves.** This largest of the many limestone caverns that honeycomb the central Yucatán Peninsula has colorful rock formations as well as pictographs left by the Maya, who lived here for thousands of years. ☞ p. 182

Parque Natural Río Lagartos. One of the biggest colonies of flamingos in North America rests here. ☞ p. 190

Ⓑ **Sian Ka'an Biosphere Reserve.** At this 1.3-million-acre preserve you can see half-submerged Maya ruins in mangrove canals and bird-watch for exotic species in the jungle. ☞ p. 133

SHOPPING

Los Cinco Soles, Cozumel. Cruise-ship passengers with limited time find a bonanza of well-priced clothing and crafts here. ☞ p. 99

Mercado de Artesanías "García Rejón," Mérida. This handicraft market is a stellar source for hammocks, Panama hats, and other Yucatán souvenirs. ☞ p. 156

Ⓕ **Mercado Municipal, Mérida.** The best general market in the Yucatán sells everything from live birds and food to intricate local crafts. ☞ p. 157

DINING

Ⓗ **La Bella Epoca, Mérida.** This gracious former mansion indulges diners with platters of Middle Eastern specialties as well as well-prepared French and Yucatecan fare. $–$$ ☞ p. 159

La Cocay, Cozumel. The name is Maya for firefly. Meals here are some of the most innovative and flavorful on Cozumel. $–$$ ☞ p. 87

Marganzo, Campeche. The food at this popular, low-key place typifies the distinctive seafood dishes known as *estillo campechano* (Campeche style), served all over Mexico. $–$$ ☞ p. 211

Sasha's Bistro, Cancún. At his don't-miss bistro, chef—owner Alexander (Sasha) Rudin melds Asian and European flavors to serve up some of

the Riviera Maya's most innovative fare. $–$$ ☞ p. 30

Velazquez, Isla Mujeres. This quintessential palapa-style eatery is right on the beach. Don't be misled by the simple, rustic setting; here you'll find the best seafood on the island. $ ☞ p. 63

LODGING

Presidente Inter-Continental Cozumel. A great water-sports center, a beach with fine snorkeling, and bright, contemporary-style rooms make it the best bet for luxury on Cozumel. $$$$ ☞ p. 90

Ⓒ **Ritz-Carlton Cancún.** Facilities and restaurants are superb in this classy Cancún link in the international chain. $$$$ ☞ p. 35

Casa del Balam, Mérida. This lovely hotel recalls a more genteel time, its lobby court-yard adorned with a black-and-white tile floor, ironwork, a fountain, and arcades. $$$ ☞ p. 163

Ⓐ **Na Balam, Isla Mujeres.** Rooms here are attractive in their simple, folk-art fashion, and their proximity to sea and sand is hard to beat. $$$ ☞ p. 64

Calakmul Cabanas, Campeche. Along the Río Bec route, the cabanas, both rustic and elegant, are tucked away in the forest on the edge of the Calakmul Biosphere Reserve. $$ ☞ p. 224

AFTER HOURS

Ⓘ **Azucar, Cancún.** Locals and visitors of all ages gather at this hot nightspot for the best live salsa in Cancún. ☞ p. 41

Dady'O, Cancún. Though it's been around for a while, this is still the place to come if you need a cure for Saturday Night Fever. ☞ p. 41

Joe's Lobster House, Cozumel. Beginning about 9 PM, live rollicking reggae and hot salsa spice up the music menu into the wee hours. ☞ p. 93

1 CANCÚN

The rhinestone of Mexico's Caribbean coast, Cancún is Mexico's biggest dazzle-for-dollar destination. The Hotel Zone is lined with high-rise resorts, glitzy discos, air-conditioned malls, and gorgeous beaches. For a taste of the real Mexico, go downtown, where you can sample Yucatecan specialties at casual eateries.

Updated by
Shelagh
McNally

FLYING INTO CANCÚN, you see nothing but green treetops for miles. It's clear from the air that this resort was literally carved out of the jungle. When development began here in the early 1970s, the beaches were deserted except for birds and iguanas. Now luxury hotels, shopping malls, and restaurants line Cancún's oceanfront. More vacationers come here than to any other part of Mexico, and many come again and again for the white-sand beaches, crystalline turquoise waters, sizzling nightlife, numerous restaurants, and the proximity of Maya ruins throughout the Yucatán peninsula.

Cancún has two very different sides. On the mainland is the actual Ciudad Cancún (Cancún City), the commercial center that is also informally known as El Centro. The other half, the Zona Hotelera (Hotel Zone), is the tourist mecca. The Zone is actually a 22½-km (14-mi) barrier island off the Yucatán Peninsula. A separate northern strip called **Punta Sam,** north of Puerto Juárez (where the ferries to Isla Mujeres depart), is sometimes considered part of the Zone and is unofficially referred to as the Northern Hotel Zone. Both areas have been designed to please average American tastes: most people speak English, and there are fast-food outlets, brand-name stores, and cable TV. Shopping, eating, and lounging in the year-round tropical warmth are the main activities. (The sun shines an average of 240 days a year, reputedly more than at almost any other Caribbean spot. Temperatures linger at about 80°F.) At night you can enjoy a variety of activities, such as knocking back tequila slammers at a bar, listening to great music at clubs, watching folkloric dance performances, and sampling Yucatecan food.

But there is more to Cancún than plopping yourself down under a *palapa* (thatch roof). Downtown offers a more authentic glimpse into the sights and sounds of Mexico. For diving and snorkeling, the reefs off Cancún and nearby Cozumel, Puerto Morelos, and Isla Mujeres are among the best in the world. Cancún also makes a relaxing base for venturing to the stupendous ruins of Chichén Itzá, Tulum, and Cobá, remnants of the area's rich Maya heritage.

As for Cancún's history, not much was written about it before its birth as a resort. The Maya people did settle the area during the Late Preclassic era, around AD 200, and remained until the 14th or 15th century, but little is known about them. Other explorers seem to have overlooked the barrier island—it doesn't appear on early navigators' maps. It was never heavily populated, perhaps because its terrain of mangroves and marshes (and resulting swarms of mosquitoes) discouraged settlement. Some minor Maya ruins were discovered in the mid-19th century, but archaeologists didn't get around to studying them until the 1950s.

In 1967, the Mexican government, under the leadership of Luis Echeverría, commissioned a study to pinpoint the ideal place for an international Caribbean resort. The computer chose Cancún, and the Cinderella transformation began. At the time the area's only residents were the three caretakers of a coconut plantation. In 1972 work began on the first hotel, and the island and city grew from there.

As is typical of any tourist resort area, Cancún first attracted the jet set, gradually welcoming less affluent tourists. Today the Zona Hotelera alone has more than 25,000 hotel rooms, many filled with package-tourists and college students, particularly during spring break, when hordes of tanned young bodies fill the beaches and restaurants.

But Cancún's success has not come without a price. Its lagoons and mangrove swamps have been polluted; a number of species, such as conch and lobster, are dwindling; and parts of the coral reef are dead. And although the beaches still appear pristine for the most part, an increased effort will have to be made in order to preserve the physical beauty that is the resort's prime appeal.

Pleasures and Pastimes

Archaeological Sites

Cancún is dotted with the vestiges of a Maya settlement from 900–1520. Magnificent Chichén Itzá and Tulum are easy day trips from the resort.

Beaches

The Mexican government might have designed the resort, but nature provided its most striking features—its cool, white, porous limestone sand and clear turquoise waters. Except for the tip of Punta Cancún, Cancún Island is one long beach. The windward beaches that fringe the Bahía de Mujeres have the calmest water and are ideal for water sports and swimmers of all levels. The east coast faces the open sea; the waves are bigger here, and there are serious currents and riptides. The more popular beaches, such as Playa Chacmool and Playa Tortugas, have restaurants, bars, and sports facilities. On the less trafficked eastern strand, Playa Delfines has spectacular views. All beaches are federal property and are open to everyone.

Dining

One of the best things about Cancún is its diversity of restaurants. Many present a hybrid cuisine that combines fresh fish from local waters, elements of Yucatecan and Mexican cuisines, and a fusion of French, Italian, and American influences. Fiesta dinners are a weekly staple at many hotels, so you can sample a variety of Mexican favorites without venturing out. If you enjoy high drama at dinner, there are places where waiters artistically prepare meals table-side or mix flaming cocktails with great flourish.

Lodging

There are more than 25,000 hotel rooms in Cancún and well over 110 hotels. The resort's architecture, especially in the Hotel Zone, tends to be a cross between Mediterranean style and a developer's interpretation of Maya style. In many cases the combination yields an appealing, if kitschy, look. Typical Mediterranean structures—low, solid, rectangular, with flat, red-tile roofs; Moorish arches; and white stucco walls covered with exuberantly pink bougainvillea—take on palapas and such ornamental devices as colonnettes, latticework, and beveled cornices. Inside are contemporary-style furniture and pastel hues.

Boulevard Kukulcán is the main thoroughfare, on which most of the hotels are located. It is a two-lane road, artfully landscaped with palm trees, sculpted bushes, waterfalls, and tiered pools. The hotels pride themselves on delivering endless opportunities for fun. Water sports, marinas, golf, tennis, kids' clubs, fitness centers, spas, shopping, entertainment, dining, and tours and excursions are all offered, along with warm Mexican hospitality and attentive service. Of course, you pay for all of this—the Hotel Zone can be quite expensive. Downtown is more modest, and local color far outweighs resort facilities.

Nightlife

Cancún is a party town. From early evening to dawn the whole Zone pulses with music. Salsa, reggae, hip-hop, mariachi, jazz, classical, disco, rock and roll—it's all here. Such local discos as Coco Bongo and

La Boom give you the chance to dance the night away, while ubiquitous American chain entertainers such as the Hard Rock Cafe and Pat O'Briens offer both food and music. Many hotel lobby bars have two-for-one drink deals at happy hour, and bar-hopping in the big resorts is a great way to check out the different hotel interiors. To see how the locals party, head to the Latin clubs. For a taste of old Mexico, take in the Folkloric Ballet dinner show at the convention center. Or dine and dance under the stars aboard the *Cancún Queen* or the *Columbus.*

Water Sports

Cancún is one of the water-sports capitals of the world and, with the Caribbean on one side of the island and the still waters of Laguna Nichupté on the other, it's no wonder. The most popular activities are snorkeling and diving along the coral reef just off the coast, where schools of colorful tropical fish and other marine creatures live. If you want to view the mysterious underwater world but don't want to get your feet wet, a glass-bottom boat or "submarine" is the ticket. Cancún also offers opportunities to fish, sail, jet-ski, parasail, or wind surf.

EXPLORING CANCÚN

Cancún's Zona Hotelera is a small island shaped roughly like the numeral seven. The top extends east from the mainland into the Caribbean; the Punta Cancún–Punta Nizuc strip has a slight north–northeast arc. Hotel development began at the north end (close to the mainland), headed east toward Punta Cancún, and then moved south to Punta Nizuc. At the south end of the Hotel Zone, the road curves west toward the highway and airport. Downtown Cancún—El Centro—is 4 km (2½ mi) west of the Hotel Zone on the mainland.

A system of lagoons separates the Hotel Zone from the mainland. Nichupté, the largest (about 29 square km, or 18 square mi), contains both fresh and salt water. Bojórquez is nestled inside the northeastern elbow. Laguna Río Inglés is south of Nichupté. Bahía de Mujeres lies north of the Zone; the bay, which is 9 km (5½ mi) wide, separates Cancún from Isla Mujeres.

Boulevard Kukulcán is the main drag in the Hotel Zone, and because the island is so narrow—less than 1 km (½ mi) wide—you can see both the Caribbean and the lagoons from either side of it. Regularly placed kilometer markers alongside Boulevard Kukulcán indicate where you are. The first marker (Km 1) is near downtown on the mainland; Km 20 lies at the south end of the Zone at Punta Nizuc. The area in between consists entirely of hotels, restaurants, shopping complexes, marinas, and time-share condominiums. It's not the sort of place you can get to know by walking, although there is now a bicycle–walking path that starts at the Cancún Convention Center in Punta Cancún and ends downtown. The last half of the path parallels a grassy strip of Boulevard Kukulcán decorated with reproductions of ancient Mexican art, including the Aztec calendar stone, a giant Olmec head, the Atlantids of Tula, and a Maya Chacmool (reclining rain god).

South of Punta Cancún, Boulevard Kukulcán becomes a busy road, difficult to cross on foot, punctuated by steeply inclined driveways that turn into the hotels, most of which are set at least 100 yards from the road. The lagoon side of the boulevard consists of scrubby stretches of land alternating with marinas, shopping centers, and restaurants. Because there are so few sights, there are no orientation tours of Cancún: just do the local bus circuit to get a feel for the island's layout.

When you first visit El Centro, the downtown layout might not be self-evident. It is not based on a grid but rather on a circular pattern. The whole city is divided into districts called Super Manzanas (abbreviated Sm), each with its own central square or park. The main streets curve around the manzanas, and the smaller neighborhood streets curl around the parks in horseshoe shapes. Avenida Tulum is the main street—actually a four-lane road with two northbound and two southbound lanes. The inner north and south lanes, separated by a meridian of grass, are the express lanes. Along the express lanes, smaller roads lead to the outer lanes, where local shops and services are located. This setup makes for some amazing traffic snarls, and it can be quite dangerous crossing at the side roads. Instead, cross at the speed bumps placed along the express lanes that act as pedestrian walkways.

Avenidas Bonampak and Yaxchilán are the other two major north–south streets that parallel Tulum. The three major east–west streets are Avenidas Cobá, Uxmal, and Chichén. They are marked along Tulum by huge roundabouts, each set with a piece of sculpture.

Numbers in the text correspond to numbers in the margin and on the Cancún map.

A Good Tour

Cancún's scenery consists mostly of its beautiful beaches and crystal-clear waters, but there are also a few intriguing historical sites tucked away among the modern hotels. In addition to the attractions listed below, two modest vestiges of the ancient Maya civilization are worth a visit, but only for dedicated archaeology buffs. Neither is identified by name. On the 12th hole of Pok-Ta-Pok golf course (Boulevard Kukulcán, Km 6.5)—the name means "ball game" in Maya—stands a ruin consisting of two platforms and the remains of other ancient buildings. And the ruin of a tiny Maya shrine is cleverly incorporated into the architecture of the Hotel Camino Real, on the beach at Punta Cancún.

You don't need a car in Cancún, but if you've rented one to make extended trips, start in the Southern Hotel Zone at **Ruinas del Rey** ① and **San Miguelito** ②, drive north to **Yamil Lu'um** ③, and then stop in at the **Cancún Convention Center** ④, home to a small anthropology and history museum, before heading west to **El Centro** ⑤.

Sights to See

❹ Cancún Convention Center. This strikingly modern venue for cultural events is the jumping-off point for a 1-km (½-mi) string of shopping malls that extends west to the Presidente Inter-Continental Cancún. In the convention-center complex itself, **Inter Plaza** contains 15 restaurants, 21 boutiques, a bank, and several airline offices.

The **Instituto Nacional de Antropología e Historia** (National Institute of Anthropology and History; ☎ 9/883–0305), a small museum on the ground floor of the convention center, traces Maya culture with a fascinating collection of 1,000- to 1,500-year-old artifacts collected throughout Quintana Roo. Looking through it is a great way to spend a rainy afternoon. Admission to the museum is about $3 (free Sunday); it's open Tuesday through Sunday 9–7. Guided tours are available in English, French, German, and Spanish. ⊠ *Blvd. Kukulcán, Km 9,* ☎ *9/883–0199.*

❺ El Centro (Downtown Cancún). Markets, instead of malls, offer a glimpse into a more provincial Mexico. The main street, **Avenida Tulum,** is easily recognizable for the huge seashell sculpture in the roundabout, which adds drama to the city when lit up at night. Many restau-

TO PUNTA SAM

TO ISLA MUJERES

Puerto
Juárez

**CANCÚN
CITY**

Av.
Bonampak

Av.
Uxmal

Av. López Portillo

Av. Yaxchilán

Av. Tulum

Blvd. Kukulcán

Bahía de Mujeres

*Laguna
Morales*

Av. Cobá

Aviary
Park

**Playa
Linda**

**Playa
Langosta**

**Playa
Tortugas**

Punta
Cancún

*Laguna
Bojórquez*

**Playa
Chac Mool**

HOTEL

Av. Tulum

*Laguna
Nichupté*

Blvd. Kukulcán

ZONE

**Playa
Marlin**

Caribbean Sea

**Playa
Ballenas**

*Laguna
Río
Inglés*

**Playa
Delfines**

N

KEY

Ferry

Paseo   Kukulcán

Punta
Nizuc

TO TULUM

0		2 miles
0		3 km

Cancún Convention Center **4**	Instituto Nacional de Antropología e Historia **4**	San Miguelito **2**
El Centro **5**	Ruinas del Rey **1**	Yamil Lu'um **3**

rants and shops are along this street, including **Ki Huic,** the largest crafts market in Cancún. If you're looking for shopping bargains, however, the parallel **Avenida Yaxchilán** usually has better prices, particularly in the Mercado Veintiocho (Market 28). Just off Avenidas Yaxchilán and Sunyaxchén, this is the hub of downtown, filled with shops and restaurants frequented by locals.

**NEED A
BREAK?**   If you're looking to satiate your sweet tooth and learn about Mexican pastries at the same time, **Le Bombón** (⊠ Av. Xel-há 71, in front of San Francisco de Asís at Mercado Veintiocho, ☎ 9/887–1317) is the place to come. Although it's actually a bakery, you can buy slices of cake to take away or eat at the stand-up counter. The cakes are remarkably fresh and sinfully delicious. It's open 10–8 Monday through Saturday.

🔺 ❶ **Ruinas del Rey** (Ruins of the King). Large signs on the Zone's lagoon side, roughly opposite the Playa de Oro and El Pueblito hotels, point out these small ruins, which have been incorporated into the Caesar Park Beach & Golf Resort complex. First entered into Western chronicles in a 16th-century travelogue, then sighted in 1842 by American explorer John Lloyd Stephens and his draftsman, Frederick Catherwood, the ruins were finally explored by archaeologists in 1910, though excavations did not begin until 1954. In 1975 archaeologists, along with the Mexican government, began the restoration of the Ruinas del Rey and San Miguelito.

Del Rey may not be particularly impressive when compared to major archaeological sites such as Tulum or Chichén Itzá, but it is the largest ruin in Cancún, and it's definitely worth a look. Dating from the 3rd to 2nd century BC, del Rey is notable for its unusual architecture: two main plazas bounded by two streets—most other Maya cities contained only one plaza. The pyramid here is topped by a platform, and inside its vault are paintings on stucco. Skeletons interred both at the apex and at the base indicate that the site may have been a royal burial ground. Originally named Kin Ich Ahau Bonil, Maya for "king of the solar countenance," the site was linked to astronomical practices in the ancient Maya culture.

Now its only residents are iguanas, which lounge sleepily in the mid-afternoon sun. The grounds are covered with flowering trees, creating a cool, tranquil refuge that's a stark contrast to the zooming traffic just outside the gates. If you don't have time to visit the other major sites, this one will give you an idea of what the ancient Maya cities were like. ⊠ *Blvd. Kukulcán, Km 17,* ☎ *no phone.* ⊡ *About $3, free Sun.* ☉ *Daily 8–5.*

🔺 ❷ **San Miguelito.** On the east side of Boulevard Kukulcán are the remains of a Maya site—a very small stone building, about the size of a shack, with a number of columns each about 4 ft high. Local archaeologists have plans to do more work on this site. ⊠ *Blvd. Kukulcán, Km 16.5,* ☎ *no phone.* ⊡ *Free.*

🔺 ❸ **Yamil Lu'um.** A small sign at the Sheraton directs you to a dirt path leading to this site, which stands on the highest point of Cancún—the name Yamil Lu'um means "hilly land." Although it comprises two structures—one probably a temple, the other probably a lighthouse—this is the smallest of Cancún's ruins. Discovered in 1842 by John Lloyd Stephens, the remains date from the late 13th or early 14th century. ⊠ *Blvd. Kukulcán, Km 12,* ☎ *no phone.* ⊡ *Free.*

BEACHES

Cancún Island is one long, continuous beach. By law the entire coast of Mexico is federal property and open to the public. In reality, hotel security guards discourage locals from using the beaches outside hotels. Some all-inclusive hotels distribute neon wristbands to guests, and only people wearing the bands are allowed to use the facilities. Those without a wristband are not actually prohibited from being on the beach—just from entering or exiting via the hotel. Everyone is welcome to walk along the beach, as long as you get on or off from one of the public points. Unfortunately, these points are often miles apart. One way around the situation is to find a hotel open to the public, go into the lobby bar for a drink or snack, and afterward go for a swim along the beach. This usually eliminates any problems with hotel security.

Most hotel beaches have lifeguards, but, as with all ocean swimming, use common sense—even the calmest-looking waters can have currents and riptides. Overall, the beaches on the windward stretch of the island—those facing the Bahía de Mujeres—are best for swimming; farther out, the undertow can be tricky. *Don't* swim when the red or black danger flags fly (swimmers ignoring these warnings have been known to drown); yellow flags indicate that you should proceed with caution; green or blue flags mean the waters are calm.

Two popular public beaches, **Playa Tortugas** (Km 7) and **Chacmool** (Km 10), have restaurants and changing areas, making them especially appealing for vacationers who are staying at the beachless downtown hotels. Be careful of strong waves at Chacmool, where it's tempting to walk far out into the shallow water. South of Chacmool are the usually deserted beaches of **Playa Marlin** or **Playa Ballenas** (between Km 15 and Km 16) and **Playa Delfines** (between Km 20 and Km 21), noted for its expansive views. Swimming can be treacherous in the rough surfs of Ballenas and Delfines, but the beaches are breezy, restful places for solitary sunbathing.

Be sure to protect yourself from the intense tropical sun. The sea breeze can trick you into thinking it's much cooler than it really is, but you can burn *badly* in fewer than 20 minutes during peak sunlight hours (11–3). Wear a hat, use sunscreen or sunblock, and avoid prolonged exposure.

DINING

With more than 1,200 restaurants in Cancún, finding the right dining spot might be the hardest work you do while on vacation. Both the Hotel Zone and downtown have plenty of great places to eat. There are some pitfalls: restaurants that line noisy Avenida Tulum often have tables spilling onto pedestrian-laden sidewalks with gas fumes and hordes of people detracting from the romantic outdoor-café ambience. In the Hotel Zone, restaurants often cater to what they assume is a tourist preference for bland food.

One key to eating well in Cancún is to find the local haunts, most of which are in the downtown area. Parque de las Palapas, just off Avenida Tulum, is where locals go for expertly prepared Yucatecan-style food. Farther into the city center, you can find the freshest seafood and other traditional Mexican fare at Mercado Veintiocho. Dozens of small restaurants there serve great food at reasonable prices.

Large breakfast and brunch buffets are among the most popular meals in the Hotel Zone. With prices ranging from $3 to $15 per person, they are a good value—eat on the late side and you won't need to eat again until dinner. They are especially pleasant at palapa restaurants on the beach.

Unless otherwise stated, restaurants serve lunch and dinner daily.

What to Wear

Dress is casual in Cancún, but many restaurants do not allow bare feet, short shorts, bathing suits, or no shirt. At upscale restaurants, pants, skirts, or dresses are favored over shorts at dinnertime.

CATEGORY	COST*
$$$$	over $30
$$$	$21–$30
$$	$10–$20
$	under $10

per person for a main course at dinner

Hotel Zone

$$$$ ✕ **Club Grill.** The dining rooms of Cancún's Ritz-Carlton are the hands-down favorite for exceptional food and romantic dining. Everything is quietly elegant: rich wood trimmings, fresh flowers, tall windows overlooking a courtyard fountain. Classic dishes have been given a distinctly Mexican flavor. The sautéed foie gras with caramelized mango is a good starter, followed by the bean and lentil soup with *habañero* chili. If you're having trouble deciding, try the tasting menu, a selection of dishes paired with wines. Don't forget the wickedly delicious desserts. Cynthia Davis, one of Cancún's top jazz vocalists, entertains nightly. ✉ *Blvd. Kukulcán (Retorno del Rey 36)*, ☎ *9/885–0808. AE, MC, V. No lunch.*

$$$–$$$$ ✕ **Ruth's Chris Steak House.** With its cream-color interior and stained-glass accents, this restaurant goes beyond what you'd expect at your typical neighborhood steak house. The steak here—whether fillet, porterhouse, or rib eye—is so tender it can be cut with a fork. The blackened tuna and barbecue shrimp are also well prepared, and the accompanying wine list is excellent. ✉ *Kukulcán Plaza, Blvd. Kukulcán, Km 13.5*, ☎ *9/885–3301. AE, MC, V.*

$$–$$$$ ✕ **Côté Sud.** Dining is relaxed and stylish in this main restaurant of Le
★ Meridien hotel. Decorated with fresh green-and-taupe plaids, white linen, and contemporary table settings, it offers spectacular views of the ocean. The menu features dishes from France's Provence region with creative twists, such as duck breast in a potato *galette* (a flat cake) and lavender sauce or rack of lamb Moroccan style. Fresh fish is grilled to perfection, and the bread is baked daily on the premises. A dessert called "The Fifth Element"—a chocolate extravaganza designed to look like the planet Mars, dripping with strawberry sauce—has become the most-talked-about dessert in the Hotel Zone. All of this is complemented by an extensive wine list and an attentive staff that cares about the details. ✉ *Le Meridien, Blvd. Kukulcán, Km 14 (Retorno del Rey 37)*, ☎ *9/881–2260. AE, DC, MC, V.*

$$–$$$$ ✕ **Mikado.** Sit around the *teppanyaki* tables and watch the utensils fly as showmen chefs prepare steaks, seafood, vegetables, and rice. The beef is exceptional, the sushi fresh, and the curries hot. The menu includes Japanese classics as well as Thai specialties. Feast on the delicious Thai spring rolls, *negimaki* (rib eye and green-onion roll), or *tendon* (shrimp and vegetable tempura). The pad thai and curries are also amazing. ✉ *Marriott Casa Magna, Blvd. Kukulcán, Km 14.5*, ☎ *9/881–2000. DC, MC, V. No lunch.*

$$–$$$$ ✕ **The Plantation House.** Clever decor re-creates the plantation era of the Caribbean in this handsome eatery. The well-furnished lounge resembles that of an elegant house; downstairs, tables dressed in crisp white linen overlook the lagoon and mangroves. White-gloved waiters and live piano music add to the refined atmosphere. All of the islands are represented in a variety of inspired dishes—have a taste of St. Maarten with duck medallions in green-pepper sauce, or visit St. Lucia in the fillet of beef with a two-wine sauce. Traveling has never been so delicious. ✉ *Blvd. Kukulcán, Km 10.5*, ☎ *9/883–1433. Reservations essential. AE, MC, V. No lunch.*

$$–$$$ ✕ **Blue Bayou.** The first Cajun restaurant in Mexico, Blue Bayou was an immediate success that continues to be popular with locals and visitors alike. Five levels of intimate dining areas are decorated in wood, rattan, and bamboo against a backdrop of cascading waterfalls and a tropical garden. Specialties include Cancún jambalaya, blackened grouper, herb crawfish Louisiana, plantation duckling, and chicken Grand Bayou. There is live jazz every night and dancing on the weekends. ✉ *Hyatt Cancún Caribe, Blvd. Kukulcán, Km 10.5*, ☎ *9/883–0044. Reservations essential. AE, DC, MC, V. No lunch.*

Cancún Hotel Zone Dining and Lodging

$$–$$$ ✕ **Casa Rolandi.** The secret to the success of this elegant sister to the Pizza Rolandi chain is its creative handling of the Swiss–northern Italian cuisine. Be sure to try the carpaccio *di tonno alla Giorgio* (thin slices of fresh tuna with extra-virgin olive oil and lime juice), the homemade lasagna, or the ravioli *neri ripieni d'arargosta* (black ravioli stuffed with lobster). With such appetizers as puff bread from a wood-burning oven and a huge salad and antipasto bar you may never make it to the main course—which would be a shame. Soft lighting, a beautiful setting, and exceptional service create an atmosphere both cool and serene. ⊠ *Plaza Caracol, Blvd. Kukulcán, Km 8.5,* ☎ 9/883–2557. AE, MC, V.

$$–$$$ ✕ **La Dolce Vita.** This grande dame of Cancún eateries consistently produces excellent variations on classic Italian dishes, such as green ribbons of pasta with lobster medallions and *boquinete dolce vita* (snapper, shrimp, and mushrooms in a puff pastry). Add the candlelit tables, lace tablecloths, soft live music, and pretty furniture, and you have a romantic evening. The atmosphere is enhanced by an incredible view of Laguna Nichupté, especially during full moons. ⊠ *Blvd. Kukulcán, Km 14.5, across from the Marriott hotel,* ☎ 9/885–0161. AE, MC, V.

$$–$$$ ✕ **Lorenzillo's.** Named after a 17th-century pirate, this is one of the handsomest waterfront restaurants in the Hotel Zone. Built on the lagoon underneath a giant palapa roof, its indoor–outdoor terrace is the perfect spot to watch the sunset. It has its own lobster farm, so the delicacy is offered year-round and is fresh—not frozen like at so many other restaurants. Also good are the "Treasure Chest" (shrimp stuffed with lobster) and *los pirates* (beef medallions in a three-peppercorn sauce). ⊠ *Blvd. Kukulcán, Km 10.5,* ☎ 9/883–1254. AE, MC, V.

$–$$$ ✕ **The Captain's Cove.** One of the few Zone eateries open at 7 AM, this spot under the giant palapa on Laguna Nichupté serves hearty, delicious breakfasts at unbelievably low prices. In the evening the menu focuses on lobster, shrimp, and crab. ⊠ *Blvd. Kukulcán, Km 16.5,* ☎ 9/885–0016. AE, MC, V.

$–$$$ ✕ **Iguana Wana.** This upbeat, contemporary Mexican café decorated with art from around Mexico offers an extensive, inexpensive all-you-can-eat breakfast buffet along with special vegetarian and children's menus. During the day, televised sports provide the entertainment; in the evening, there's live music. Choose from the extensive "zizzling" fajitas menu or from the "wana grill." There is also a tempting selection of beers and tequilas. ⊠ *Plaza Caracol, Blvd. Kukulcán, Km 8.5,* ☎ 9/883–0829. AE, MC, V.

$–$$$ ✕ **Maria Bonita.** Here is authentic Mexico in food, music, and atmo-
★ sphere. This delightful restaurant overlooking the water is divided into sections named after three states of Mexico: Jalisco, Michoacán, and Oaxaca. The menu includes food from these areas, as well as other Mexican specialties. Worth trying are the various mole dishes, such as chicken almond mole (with chocolate, almonds, and chilies), *la dona* (poblano chilies stuffed with lobster and mushrooms), or any of the various Tex-Mex or grilled entrées. The menu, which explains the different chilies used by the kitchen, makes this a great place to learn about Mexican cuisine. Attentive service matches the wonderful food. ⊠ *Hotel Camino Real, Punta Cancún, Blvd. Kukulcán, Km 9,* ☎ 9/848–7000. AE, MC, V. No lunch.

$–$$$ ✕ **La Sirenita.** Experience the best of Cancún at this romantic beach-
★ front restaurant in the Hilton Cancún Beach & Golf Resort. Executive chef Elmer Komagata has successfully blended the flavors of East and West for spectacular gourmet Asian cuisine. Watch the waves crash, listen to the trio of singers play guitar, and enjoy sublime oysters, mussels, sushi, sashimi, beef tenderloin, tempura, or grilled fish. The dessert menu is divine, the coffee heavenly. A soft blue decor of ceramic shells and carved pillars enhances the whole dreamy experi-

ence. Service is excellent. During full moons, you can dine right on the beach under the stars. ⊠ *Hilton Cancún, Blvd. Kukulcán, Km 17 (Retorno Lacandones),* ☎ *9/881–8000 ext. 8399. AE, MC, V.*

$$ ✕ **Cambalache.** This Argentine steak house is renowned for mouthwatering, tender, juicy steaks served in a boisterous atmosphere. Other highlights include suckling pig on a stick, salads, and a well-stocked bar. Meat eaters are not likely to come away disappointed. Vegetarians, on the other hand, may wish to go elsewhere—the only vegetables on the menu are side dishes. ⊠ *Forum-by-the-Sea, Blvd. Kukulcán, Km 9.5,* ☎ *9/883–0897. AE, MC, V.*

$$ ✕ **La Destileria.** Be prepared to have your perceptions about tequila
★ changed forever at this combination restaurant–tequila museum. Tables are centered on a huge antique still from a tequila distillery. Enjoy one of 100 tequilas to taste, or try the amazing margaritas (be warned—you may never again be able to enjoy cheap tequila drinks). The tasty, traditional northern Mexican food (served by seriously charming waiters) includes *sopa de elote* (spiced corn soup) and *pescado con flor de calabaza* (fish with pumpkin flowers). The title of the dessert menu, "Favorite Sins," says it all. Afterward, you can drop by the restaurant's tequila shop and pick up your favorite brand. ⊠ *Blvd. Kukulcán, Km 12.65 (across from Kukulcán Plaza),* ☎ *9/883–1087. AE, MC, V.*

$$ ✕ **Tony Roma's.** If you love ribs, this is the place to eat them. Baby back ribs are the specialty and are melt-in-your-mouth tender. Also available are thick, juicy steaks and freshly prepared Caesar salads. Sports lovers may appreciate the cable feeds and well-stocked bar. ⊠ *Blvd. Kukulcán, Km 11.5,* ☎ *9/883–0084. AE, MC, V.*

$–$$ ✕ **Cenacolo.** Italian art and stained glass fill the relaxed interior of this
★ charming neighborhood restaurant, where musicians serenade you throughout your meal. Outside is a bustling, plant-filled patio overlooking Boulevard Kukulcán. The food is consistently excellent, especially the salad of mixed greens, the ricotta ravioli, the lasagna with béchamel, and the sliced filet mignon in balsamic vinegar. The staff spoils you completely. ⊠ *Kukulcán Plaza, Blvd. Kukulcán, Km 13.5,* ☎ *9/885–3603. AE, MC, V.*

$–$$ ✕ **El Mexicano.** This fun, lively restaurant seats 300 for a folkloric dinner show (nightly at 8) in a room resembling the patio of a hacienda. Although touristy, it does try to serve authentic Mexican cuisine; the menu offers a number of family recipes. Try the *huachinango a la Veracruzana* (snapper in the Veracruz style, with tomatoes, olives, and sweet chili) or the *carne asada la Tampiqueña* (thin fillets of seared beef served with chilies). Traditional T-bone steaks are also good. With mariachis serenading you while you eat, this is not the place for a quiet, romantic dinner. ⊠ *Blvd. Kukulcán, Km 11.5, next to Plaza Caracol,* ☎ *9/883–2220. DC, MC, V.*

$–$$ ✕ **Modern Art Café.** Here's your chance to dine in an art gallery. Everything at this café is for sale: the sculptures, paintings, carvings—even the chairs. The artwork changes every three to four months, so the only thing that always looks the same is the ceiling, which is decorated with colossal palettes and paintbrushes. The menu is a hybrid of international dishes that don't always live up to its ambitions. Still, it's worth going to look around and enjoy one of the exotic cocktails—especially the martinis. At 9 PM there is a passionate performance of flamenco dance and music, with no cover. ⊠ *La Isla Shopping Village, Blvd. Kukulcán, Km 12.5,* ☎ *9/883–4511. AE, MC, V.*

$ ✕ **100% Natural.** Looking for something light and healthy? Head to one of these cheery open-air restaurants, done up with plenty of plants and modern Maya sculptures. The menus emphasize soups, fruit and veggie salads, fresh fruit drinks, and other nonmeat items, though egg dishes, sandwiches, grilled chicken and fish, and Mexican and Italian specialties are also available. The branch at Plaza Terramar is open around the clock. *Hotel Zone:* ✉ *Plaza Terramar, Blvd. Kukulcán, Km 8.5,* ☎ *9/883–1184;* ✉ *Kukulcán Plaza, Blvd. Kukulcán, Km 13.5,* ☎ *9/885–2903;* ✉ *Forum-by-the-Sea, Blvd. Kukulcán, Km 9.5,* ☎ *9/883–1180; Downtown:* ✉ *Av. Sunyaxchén 62,* ☎ *9/884–3617;* ✉ *Plaza las Americas, Av. Tulum, Sm 4,* ☎ *no phone. Reservations not accepted. AE, DC, MC, V.*

$ ✕ **Studebaker Bar & Grill.** The Fonz would be right at home in this 1950s–'60s theme diner centered on the golden era of the Studebaker car. The grill produces some of the best hamburgers around (the "Avanti" burger is not to be missed) and thick, cold shakes. ✉ *Hotel Baccará, Blvd. Kukulcán, Km 11.5,* ☎ *9/883—2077. AE, MC, V.*

Downtown

$$–$$$ ✕ **La Habichuela** (The Green Bean). Once an elegant home, this en-
★ chanting, much-loved garden restaurant is decorated with local trees, flowers, and plants and accented by Maya sculpture. The garden, lit up at night, is bewitching. In the 24 years since the Pezzotti family took over, there have been very few unhappy customers. Don't miss the famous *crema de habichuela* (a rich, cream-based seafood soup) or the *cocobichuela* (lobster and shrimp in a light curry sauce served inside a coconut). The grilled seafood, chicken, and steaks are also sensational. Finish off your meal with Xtabentun, a Maya liqueur made with honey and anise. ✉ *Av. Margaritas 25, Sm 22,* ☎ *9/884–3158. AE, DC, MC, V.*

$$–$$$ ✕ **Lacanda Paolo.** Southern Italian cuisine is brought to new heights
★ of excellence in this sophisticated, innovative restaurant—considered by many to be the best Italian in Cancún. Don't even think of passing up the black pasta in calamari sauce, or the penne with basil and tomato sauce. Also delicious are the steamed lobster in garlic sauce and the lemon fish. Flowers, artwork on the walls, and attentive service combine for an atmosphere that's old-world warm without being fussy. ✉ *Av. Uxmal 35, Sm 3,* ☎ *9/887–2627. AE, DC, MC, V.*

$$–$$$ ✕ **Perico's.** Zany and eclectic, this restaurant–bar is a big hit with travelers. Bar stools are topped with saddles, caricature busts of political figures line the walls, and waiters dressed as *zapatas* (revolutionaries) serve flaming desserts. The Mexican menu is passable, but the real draw is the party atmosphere that begins nightly at 7 when the mariachi and marimba bands play and everyone jumps up to join the conga line. Your reward for galloping through the restaurant and nearby streets is a free shot of tequila. ✉ *Av. Yaxchilán 61,* ☎ *9/884–3152. AE, MC, V.*

$$–$$$ ✕ **Rosa Mexicano.** At one of Cancún's prettiest Mexican colonial–style restaurants, colorful paper banners and piñatas hang from the ceiling, and waiters dress as *charros* (Mexican cowboys). Yes, it's touristy, but at least it's tastefully done. For extra romance, reserve a table on the candlelit patio. Savory appetizers include *nopalitos* (cactus strips sautéed with corn, cilantro, and cheese). Specialties are *filete Rosa* (beef and onions in a tequila–orange sauce) and *camarones al ajillo* (shrimp sautéed in olive oil and garlic, with chili peppers). ✉ *Calle Claveles 4,* ☎ *9/884–6313. AE, DC, MC, V. No lunch.*

$$ ✕ **El Pescador.** This is a restaurant geared toward tourists, and the long lines attest to how popular it remains. With its lively atmosphere, palapa roof, and open-air patio, which looks out onto the street, it's a good place to watch all the action. Heavy hitters on the menu include red snapper broiled with garlic, charcoal-broiled lobster, Creole-style shrimp, and stone crabs. ✉ *Av. Tulipanes 28, Sm 22,* ☎ *9/884–2673. Reservations not accepted. AE, MC, V.*

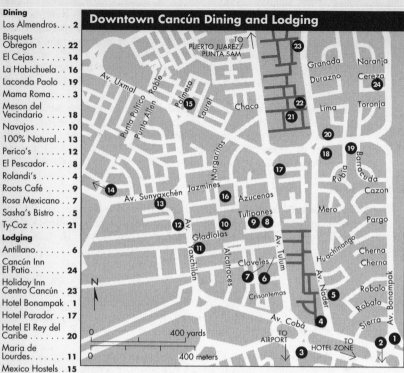

Downtown Cancún Dining and Lodging

$-$$ ✕ **El Cejas.** In the heart of the bustling, lively Mercado Veintiocho, this
★ is a neighborhood restaurant with an international reputation. The
seafood is the freshest there is and it's cheaper than in the Hotel Zone.
If you've had a wild night, try the *vuelva la vida*, or "return to life" (conch,
oysters, shrimp, octopus, calamari, and fish with a hot tomato sauce).
Equally wonderful is the ceviche and hot, spicy shrimp soup. ⊠ *Mercado Veintiocho, Av. Sunyaxchén,* ☎ 9/887–1080. AE, DC, MC, V.

$-$$ ✕ **Mama Roma.** This popular restaurant chain—designed like a ware-
house and decorated with 1950s Italian memorabilia—offers a wide
selection of fresh pasta, pizza, and other delights. Try the thin-crust
salmon pizza or the black-mushroom spaghetti. There is a large cocktail, wine, and beer menu, which you can enjoy at the long bar. The
breakfast menu includes cheese omelets, egg fettuccine, and cannelloni.
There's a second location in the Hotel Zone at Forum-by-the-Sea. ⊠
Plaza las Americas, Av. Tulum, Sm 4 and 9, ☎ 9/887–4520; Hotel Zone:
⊠ *Forum-by-the-Sea, Blvd. Kukulcán, Km 9.5,* ☎ 9/883–1862. AE,
MC, V.

$-$$ ✕ **Mesón del Vecindario.** This sweet little restaurant tucked away from
the street resembles an A-frame house in the woods. The menu specializes in all kinds of cheese and beef fondues along with terrific salads, fresh pasta, and baked goods. Breakfasts are hearty and economical.
It makes a pleasant change from the usual downtown fare. ⊠ *Av. Uxmal
23, Sm 3,* ☎ 9/884–8900. AE.

$-$$ ✕ **Sasha's Bistro.** Dinner at this not-to-be-missed bistro is an experi-
★ ence you're not likely to forget. Owner Alexander (Sasha) Rudin, a Swiss
master chef, knows how to play up the subtleties of his ingredients.
He serves the most original and inspired menu found in Cancún (or
anywhere along the Riviera Maya)—a fusion of Asian and European
flavors—and the presentation is as artful as the food. The menu changes
monthly so it's always fresh, but Sasha is so accommodating you can

virtually custom-order your food. Past masterpieces have included grilled lamb chops in a pecan and macadamia crust over Moroccan couscous, ahi tuna parfait with two caviars, and tempura duck tenderloins over sticky rice. The back room is a smoking lounge where Sasha's own brand of cigars is available along with the perfect drink. ⊠ *Av. Nader 118, Sm 3 (at Av. Mojarro),* ☎ *9/887–9105. MC, V. Closed Sun. and Mon. No lunch.*

$ ✕ **Los Almendros.** Illustrations take some of guesswork out of the to-
★ tally Yucatecan menu at this modest spot. Specialties include lime soup and *poc chuc* (Yucatecan pork marinated in a sour-orange sauce with pickled onions), *papadzules* (tortillas piled with hard-boiled eggs and drenched in a pumpkin-seed sauce), and *pollo pibíl* (chicken baked in banana leaves). The staff has that genuine Yucatán warmth often missing in the larger places. This is the best introduction to Maya food in these parts. ⊠ *Av. Bonampak and Sayil, opposite the bullring,* ☎ *9/ 887–1332. AE.*

$ ✕ **Bisquets Obregon.** With its cheery colors, two levels of tables, and
★ sit-down luncheon counter, this cafeteria-style spot is *the* place to have breakfast downtown. Begin your day with hearty Mexican classics such as *huevos rancheros* (eggs sunny-side up on tortillas, covered with tomato sauce) or *huaraches* (thick tortillas with a variety of toppings). There is fresh-squeezed orange or carrot juice, but do try the *cafe con leche* (coffee with hot milk)—just watching the waiters pour it is impressive. The place opens early (7 AM). ⊠ *Av. Nader 9,* ☎ *9/ 887–6876. MC, V.*

$ ✕ **Navajos.** Just behind the Parque de las Palapas, this outdoor restaurant serves simple, light food. Breakfast features yogurt, sweetbreads, and fruit plates. Lunch and dinner offerings include soups, sandwiches, and salads, all fresh and filling, with daily specials offered at great prices. The decor, as the name suggests, honors Native Americans. It's a great place to watch all the action in this busy downtown neighborhood. ⊠ *Av. Alcatraces 18,* ☎ *9/887–7269. AE, MC, V.*

$ ✕ **Rolandi's.** The wood-burning ovens are in clear view at this bright red-and-yellow sidewalk eatery, another success in the Rolandi story. There are 15 varieties of pizza to choose from—if you can't make up your mind, try the delicious *che* pizza, with three different types of cheese. Homemade pasta dishes are also on the menu. Delivery to your hotel is available. ⊠ *Av. Cobá 12,* ☎ *9/884–4047. MC, V.*

$ ✕ **Roots.** This classy little café also doubles as Cancún's best jazz club. Listen to local musicians jam while enjoying fresh salads, soups, sandwiches, and pastas. ⊠ *Av. Tulipanes 26, Sm 22,* ☎ *9/884–2437,* FAX *9/ 884–5547. DC, MC, V. Closed Sun. and Mon.*

$ ✕ **Ty-Coz.** Just behind the Commercial Mexicana and across from the bus station on Avenida Tulum, this restaurant has the best sandwiches in town, prepared on freshly baked bread and sold at reasonable prices. The soups are excellent as well. ⊠ *Av. Tulum, Sm 2,* ☎ *no phone. No credit cards.*

LODGING

You might find it bewildering to choose among the variety of hotels in Cancún, not least because brochures and Web sites make them sound—and look—alike. For luxury and amenities, the Hotel Zone is the place to stay. If proximity to downtown is a priority, you probably want to stay in the north end. Many of the malls are within walking distance, and taxis downtown and to the ferries at Puerto Juárez cost less than from hotels farther south. If you prefer something more secluded, there is less development at the south end.

For the most part the downtown hotels don't offer anything near the luxury or amenities of the Hotel Zone properties. They will, however, give you the opportunity to stay in a popular resort without paying resort prices, and many places have free shuttle service to the beach. Downtown hotels are also closer to Ki Huic, Cancún's crafts market, and restaurants that are more authentic—and less costly—than those that are in the Zone.

Expect minibars, satellite TV, laundry and room service, private safes (check to see if there is an extra charge for safe use), and bathroom hair dryers in hotels in the $$$$ category; in addition, almost every major hotel has suites, rooms for people with disabilities, no-smoking rooms, an in-house travel agency and/or a car-rental concession, guest parking, water-sports facilities, hair salon and spa, fully equipped gymnasium, and a daily schedule of planned games and activities for guests. Unless otherwise noted, all hotels have private baths.

Boutique hotels have been springing up; these small luxury hotels usually have no more than 30 rooms, each individually decorated. Boutique hotels cater to smaller crowds and offer individual services and amenities.

Many hotels now have all-inclusive packages. For the best rates, book these ahead of time with a travel agent. In keeping with this trend, many properties are also offering theme-night parties complete with food, beverages, activities, and games. Mexican, Italian, and Caribbean themes seem to be the most popular. Take note, however, that the larger the all-inclusive resort, the blander the food is likely to be. (It's difficult to provide gourmet fare when serving hundreds of people.) For fine dining, you may need to leave the grounds.

Price categories are based on nondiscounted rates in the peak winter season, December to early May. For most of the hotels, it's best to make reservations at least one month in advance and up to three months in advance for the Christmas season. Many of the larger chain hotels also offer special Internet deals, with room rates dropping considerably when reserved on line.

CATEGORY	COST*
$$$$	over $200
$$$	$120–$200
$$	$50–$120
$	under $50

All prices are for a standard double room, excluding 12% tax.

Punta Sam

North of Puerto Juárez (where the ferries leave to Isla Mujeres), this mostly residential area is being developed into the Northern Hotel Zone. For now it remains quieter than the actual Hotel Zone or downtown but still offers a variety of services.

$$$ ⊞ **Blue Bay Club Cancún.** Nestled between the ocean and mangroves on a long, narrow strip of beach, this comfortable all-inclusive resort caters to families. Rooms are spacious with king-size beds, kitchens, pull-out sofas, and private terraces. Half of the rooms overlook the ocean; the others look out over both the water and the mangroves. A wide range of water activities is available, as well as bicycling, tennis, basketball, a gym, and a huge theater and disco. For guests desiring more privacy, some rooms by the mangrove trees offer the feel of a private residence. Guests are also welcome to use the facilities at Blue Bay Getaway, the sister hotel in the Hotel Zone, however children aren't allowed at that property. A complimentary shuttle bus operates between Punta Sam and the Hotel Zone. ⊠ *Cancún Carretera Punta Sam, Km 3.5, Punta Sam 77500,* ☎ *9/881–7900,* FAX *9/883–0904,* WEB *www.blue-bayresorts.com. 100 rooms. 3 restaurants, 3 bars, air-conditioning, pool, 2 tennis courts, basketball, gym, dance club, theater, car rental. AE, DC, MC, V.*

$$ 🏨 **Chalet Maya.** These gorgeous waterfront bungalows are on the vir-
★ gin beaches of Isla Blanca—9 km (5½ mi) north of Punta Sam. With no phones or televisions, the hotel has been designed for maximum privacy and relaxation. Bungalows have two rooms, each individually decorated with features like hand-carved sculptured headboards created by local artist Leticia Sansores Cota. The total effect is a tranquil and artistic setting in which to enjoy the magnificent beach. A charming on-site restaurant offers moderately priced and delicious meals. The hotel can make arrangements for bird-watching trips to nearby Isla Contoy and snorkeling or fishing trips out to the reef. ⊠ *Isla Blanca, Km 9, Punta Sam 77500,* ☎ *9/850–4610,* FAX *9/850–4819,* WEB *www.chalet-maya.com. 20 rooms. Restaurant, air-conditioning, pool, dock, boating. MC, V.*

The Hotel Zone

$$$$ 🏨 **Avalon Grand Resort.** Completed in 2001, this beautiful resort shares facilities with the Baccará, which is a few doors down; both properties are run by Yucatan Resorts. A dramatic staircase entrance leads to the all-inclusive suites, which are decorated with Mexican art, ceramics, textiles, and furniture. Choose a suite with a beach or lagoon view. Some of the rooms don't require meal-plan participation. ⊠ *Blvd. Kukulcán, Km 12, 77500,* ☎ *9/883–2077,* FAX *9/883–2173,* WEB *www.yucatanresorts.com. 138 suites. 2 restaurants, lobby lounge, sports bar, air-conditioning, 2 pools, hair salon, gym, beach, baby-sitting, business services, meeting room, car rental. AE, DC, MC, V.*

$$$$ 🏨 **Baccará.** Each suite of this gorgeous Yucatan Resorts property, a
★ perfect example of a boutique hotel, is decorated differently, with a variety of Mexican paintings, sculptures, ceramics, textiles, and furniture. All have fully equipped kitchens, living and dining rooms, and private hot tubs that overlook either the ocean or the lagoon. Downstairs is a lobby and beach bar centered on an artfully designed pool area. You can dine at the elegant Avanti restaurant or grab a hamburger downstairs at Studebaker's. The attentive staff adds to the hotel's warmth. ⊠ *Blvd. Kukulcán, Km 11.5, 77500,* ☎ *9/883–2077 or 800/713–8170,* FAX *9/883–2173,* WEB *www.yucatanresorts.com. 34 rooms. 3 restaurants, 3 bars, air-conditioning, pool, beach, car rental. AE, DC, MC, V.*

$$$$ 🏨 **Fiesta Americana Cancún.** A perennial favorite, this hotel has everything going for it: perfect location, gracious service, beautiful decor, and good restaurants. It's been designed to resemble a Mexican village, with brown and yellow color schemes. The public areas have been decorated with marble from Mexico, which is offset by Guadalajara stained glass. The rooms have rattan furniture, marble floors, colorful rugs, and decorative art. All face the calm northern waters of Bahía de Mujeres (one of the best beaches for swimming). On the premises is a fine Italian restaurant, Barola, as well as the Chulavista Café, which serves breakfast. ⊠ *Blvd. Kukulcán, Km 9.5 (Box 696), 77500,* ☎ *9/881–1400 or 800/343–7821,* FAX *9/881–1401,* WEB *www.fiestaamericana.com. 236 rooms, 16 suites. 3 restaurants, 3 bars, air-conditioning, pool, barbershop, hair salon, spa, health club, beach, baby-sitting, car rental, free parking. AE, DC, MC, V.*

$$$$ ⊞ **Hilton Cancún Beach & Golf Resort.** Hilton has taken over the for-
★ mer Caesar Park Beach & Golf Resort, combining the best of the old
with the best of the new. The lobby has been refurbished in cheerful
Caribbean colors, and the rooms brightened up in yellows and greens
that complement the terra-cotta floors and rattan furniture. All rooms
have a balcony or terrace with an ocean view; some have views of the
resort's championship 18-hole, par-72 golf course across Boulevard
Kukulcán. Seven lavish, interconnecting pools wind through palm-dot-
ted lawns, ending at the magnificent beach. For total luxury consider
staying at the Beach Club, with its 80 oceanfront villas. During the day,
Spices restaurant serves excellent international fare. In the evening enjoy
incredible Asian fare at the romantic seaside restaurant, Sirenita. The
hotel staff's warmth and efficiency are bonuses. ⊠ *Blvd. Kukulcán,
Km 17 (Retorno Lacandones), 77500,* ☎ *9/881–8000,* FAX *9/881–
8082,* WEB *www.hilton.com. 426 rooms, 4 suites. 3 restaurants, 3 bars,
lobby lounge, air-conditioning, 7 pools, hair salon, hot tubs, sauna,
18-hole golf course, 2 tennis courts, aerobics, gym, beach, shops, children's programs (ages 4–12), car rental. AE, DC, MC, V.*

$$$$ ⊞ **Hyatt Cancún Caribe Villas & Resort.** One of Cancún's first luxury
hotels, this crescent-shape, intimate resort retains the special qualities
that made it a standout when it first opened. The lobby is done in white
marble and furnished with rattan furniture in pale colors. The seven-
story tower has 139 oceanfront rooms decorated with contemporary
Mexican accents: colorful stenciled borders on the walls, tile floors,
light wood furniture, curtains and bedspreads in dusty pinks and pale
green prints. Beach-level rooms have gardens. For the ultimate in privacy try one of the 28 beachfront rooms. Each has two levels, with the
option of a fully equipped kitchen or a dining–living room area. Be
sure to eat at least once at the Blue Bayou restaurant. ⊠ *Blvd. Kukulcán, Km 10.5, 77500,* ☎ *9/883–0044 or 800/633–7313,* FAX *9/883–
1514,* WEB *www.hyatt.com. 173 rooms, 28 villas. 3 restaurants, 2 bars,
air-conditioning, 3 pools, hair salon, hot tubs, 3 tennis courts, jogging,
beach, dock, shop. AE, DC, MC, V.*

$$$$ ⊞ **Marriott Casa Magna.** Sweeping grounds lead up to this eclectically
designed six-story hotel. The 44-ft-high lobby is set with Roman-style
arches, large windows, crystal chandeliers, hanging vines, and contemporary furniture. Rooms are decorated in a rose, mauve, and earth-
tone color scheme with tile floors and soft rugs. All have ocean views
and most have balconies; corner suites have enormous terraces. Three
restaurants overlook the handsome pool area and the ocean. In the
evening, sit back and watch the chefs perform at Mikado, the hotel's
fine Japanese steak house. ⊠ *Blvd. Kukulcán, Km 14.5, 77500,* ☎ *9/
881–2000 or 888/236–2427,* FAX *9/881–2085,* WEB *www.marriott.com.
414 rooms, 36 suites. 3 restaurants, bar, air-conditioning, hair salon,
hot tubs, sauna, 2 tennis courts, health club, beach, dock, shops. AE,
DC, MC, V.*

$$$$ ⊞ **Meliá Cancún.** A sheer black marble wall and a waterfall flank this
boldly modern version of a Maya temple. The ultrachic atrium has lush
tropical flora dappled with sunlight, which floods in from corner windows and a pyramid skylight overhead. Ivory, dusty-pink, and light-
blue hues softly brighten rooms (all with private balconies or terraces),
and ivory-lacquered furniture and wall-to-wall carpeting make them
opulent. This is one of the largest hotels in the area and houses a convention center and six meeting halls—don't come expecting an intimate ambience. ⊠ *Blvd. Kukulcán, Km 16, 77500,* ☎ *9/885–1114,*
FAX *9/885–1963,* WEB *www.solmelia.es. 794 rooms, 64 suites. 5 restaurants, 3 bars, air-conditioning, 2 pools, spa, 9-hole golf course, tennis
court, health club, paddle tennis, volleyball, beach, baby-sitting, convention center, travel services, car rental. AE, DC, MC, V.*

$$$$ ⊞ **Meliá Turquesa.** Little sister to the Meliá Cancún, this striking hotel resembles a pyramid. The rooms on one side have awesome views of the lagoon; those on the other side have ocean views. Rooms are decorated with white wicker furniture and soft pastels; all have private terraces. The pool is quite large and includes a small "island" with a palapa. There's another palapa on the beach, which is lovely. The staff is attentive, personable, and friendly, making for a pleasant stay. ⊠ *Blvd. Kukulcán, Km 12, 77500,* ☎ *9/881–2500,* FAX *9/881–2501,* WEB *www.solmelia.es. 414 rooms, 36 suites. 2 restaurants, 3 bars, air-conditioning, 2 pools, hair salon, 2 tennis courts, paddle tennis, volleyball, beach, shops, laundry service, meeting rooms. AE, DC, MC, V.*

$$$$ ⊞ **Le Meridien.** The architecture of this refined yet relaxed resort hotel
★ is updated Art Deco with subtle Maya influences; there's lots of wood, glass, and mirrors. High on a hill, the property offers rooms with spectacular views, furnished tastefully in French provincial style. The many thoughtful extras—a complimentary shopping bag, different temperature in each of the three swimming pools—make a stay here special. The Spa del Mar is the best in the area, offering the newest European techniques and state-of-the-art equipment, along with a modern gym that overlooks an outdoor hot tub and waterfall. The spa is open to the public for a modest fee, so it's worth a visit even if you're not a hotel guest. Gourmet dining can be found at the wonderful Côté Sud. ⊠ *Blvd. Kukulcán, Km 14 (Retorno del Rey, Lote 37), 77500,* ☎ *9/881–2200 or 800/543–4300,* FAX *9/881–2201,* WEB *www.meridiencancun.com.mx. 213 rooms, 28 suites. 3 restaurants, 2 bars, air-conditioning, 3 pools, hot tub, spa, 2 tennis courts, gym, beach, shops, children's programs (ages 4–12). AE, MC, V.*

$$$$ ⊞ **Presidente Inter-Continental Cancún.** It's hard to miss the striking yellow entrance of this hotel, five minutes from Plaza Caracol. Inside, lavish marble with accents of Talavera pottery decorates the hotel throughout. It has a quiet beach and a waterfall in the shape of a Maya pyramid by the pool. Larger-than-average rooms are done in royal blue or beige color schemes with light wicker furniture and area rugs on stone floors. Rooms on the first floor have patios and outdoor hot tubs. The suites offer contemporary furnishings, in-room video equipment, and spacious balconies. ⊠ *Blvd. Kukulcán, Km 7.5, 77500,* ☎ *9/883–0200 or 800/327–0200,* FAX *9/883–2515,* WEB *www.interconti.com. 290 rooms, 6 suites. 2 restaurants, bar, air-conditioning, 2 pools, hair salon, hot tubs, tennis court, gym, beach, shops. AE, MC, V.*

$$$$ ⊞ **Ritz-Carlton Cancún.** Ultraposh, ornate, and sumptuous, the Ritz ra-
★ diates old-world elegance. The lobby, richly appointed with thick carpets, plush furniture, and European and American antiques and oil paintings, evokes the Ritz atmosphere so strongly that you may forget you are in Mexico. Rooms are decorated in shades of teal, beige, and rose; all offer wall-to-wall carpeting and large balconies overlooking the Caribbean. Travertine marble bathrooms are fitted with telephones and separate tubs and showers. The hotel's elegant restaurants, especially the Club Grill and Fantino (which serves northern Italian dinners), are standouts. ⊠ *Blvd. Kukulcán, Km 14 (Retorno del Rey 36), 77500,* ☎ *9/885–0808 or 800/241–3333,* FAX *9/885–1048,* WEB *www.ritzcarlton.com. 365 rooms, 40 suites. 3 restaurants, 2 bars, air-conditioning, 3 pools, hot tub, spa, 3 tennis courts, health club, beach, pro shop, shops. AE, DC, MC, V.*

$$$$ ⊞ **Sheraton Cancún Resort & Towers.** At this two-hotels-in-one Sheraton there are 304 "designer" rooms, all with spectacular views of the ocean or lagoon. The Resort-building lobby has a contemporary black, white, and beige color scheme; rooms mirror the modern design with sleek furnishings. The adjacent Tower building is newer and quieter. Done in soft Caribbean colors, the 167 rooms in the Tower all have private balconies facing the ocean. The main pool is surrounded by in-credible gardens with lush grass, exotic flowers, and verdant palm trees. On the grounds is the small Maya ruin Yamil Lu'um. Several rooms overlook the ruin. ⊠ *Blvd. Kukulcán, Km 12.5, 77500,* ☎ *9/883–1988 or 888/625–5144,* FAX *9/885–0204,* WEB *www.sheraton.com. 471 rooms. 4 restaurants, 3 bars, 2 pools, hair salon, 4 tennis courts, health club, beach, shops, children's programs (ages 4–12). AE, MC, V.*

$$$$ **Westin Regina Resort Cancún.** On the southern end of the Hotel Zone on Punta Nizuc, this low-rise hotel is more secluded than many other properties in the area. The lobby is dramatic, with sculptures and art-work displayed against vivid pink or blue backdrops. The lobby bar overlooks the equally stylish restaurant and both have stunning ocean views. Rooms are even more elegant; cozy beds are dressed in soft white linens, oak tables and chairs rest against blue walls, and pale marble floors extend to balconies overlooking the pool and ocean. This is one of the few hotels with direct access to both a 1,600-ft beach and La-guna Nichupté. For added privacy consider staying at its Royal Beach Club, a separate area on the grounds that has 48 rooms. ⊠ *Blvd. Kukul-cán, Km 20, 77500,* ☎ *9/848–2400 or 888/625–5144 in the U.S.,* FAX *9/885–0296,* WEB *www.westin.com. 278 rooms, 15 suites. 4 restaurants, 3 bars, 5 pools, 2 tennis courts, health club, beach, children's programs (ages 4–12). AE, MC, V.*

$$$ **Gran Caribe Real Resort.** This beach resort has all-inclusive pack-ages geared to families. The lobby and restaurants are bright and lux-urious with stained-glass windows, hanging plants, and elegant furniture. Sunny, efficient, and comfortable, the suites all have ocean views. There is plenty to keep you busy: a gym and spa, a game room, ten-nis courts, two pools, water-sports equipment, theme-party nights, pool aerobics, scuba lessons, day trips, and even an open-air theater. The facilities and programs for children are among the best in Can-cún. As a guest, you can also use the facilities at the two sister hotels, Costa Real Hotel & Suites in Cancún and Porto Real Resort in Playa del Carmen. Be warned: this is not the place for peace and quiet. ⊠ *Blvd. Kukulcán, Km 5.5, 77500,* ☎ *9/881–7399,* FAX *9/881–7399,* WEB *www.real.com.mx. 466 rooms, 34 suites. 2 restaurants, 2 bars, 2 pools, spa, 2 tennis courts, gym, beach, dock, theater, video games, shops, children's programs (ages 2–12). AE, MC, V.*

$$$ **Hyatt Regency Cancún.** A cylindrical 14-story tower with the Hyatt trademark—a striking central atrium filled with tropical greenery and topped by a sky-lighted dome—affords a 360-degree view of the sea and the lagoon. Soothing blue, green, and beige tones prevail in the rooms. There's also an enormous two-level pool with a waterfall. Cilantro, the hotel's pretty waterfront dining room, serves a good breakfast buffet. This Hyatt is close to the Convention Center and several shopping malls. ⊠ *Blvd. Kukulcán, Km 8.5, 77500,* ☎ *9/883–0966 or 800/233–1234,* FAX *9/883–1438,* WEB *www.hyatt.com. 300 rooms. 2 restaurants, 3 bars, air-conditioning, pool, health club, beach, recreation room. AE, MC, V.*

$$$ **Krystal Cancún.** Its location along Punta Cancún places this hotel in the heart of the Hotel Zone, within walking distance of three major shopping malls and dozens of restaurants. The lobby is split level, with marble pillars leading to two towers where the rooms are located. All rooms have ocean views and are modestly furnished in earth tones with contemporary furniture. While the beach is small, there are three spa-cious pools with poolside service. The hotel houses four restaurants, as well as the popular Christine disco. ⊠ *Blvd. Kukulcán, Km 9, Lote 9, 77500,* ☎ *9/883–1133 or 800/232–9860,* FAX *9/883–1790,* WEB *www.krystal.com.mx. 322 rooms. 4 restaurants, 4 bars, air-condi-tioning, pool, hot tub, sauna, 2 tennis courts, gym, beach, shops, dance club. AE, DC, MC, V.*

$$$ ⊡ **Omni Cancún Hotels & Villas.** This pink 10-story hotel surrounded by smaller villas has a pleasant, relaxed atmosphere. It also offers lots of flexibility, with an all-inclusive option or European-plan rates if you prefer to eat outside the grounds. The lobby is cozy but modern with marble floors, sea-green and pink color schemes, and tasteful wood furniture—a scheme that continues into the rooms. The more expensive rooms have balconies; all have either ocean or lagoon views. Highlights of the hotel include three restaurants, three snack bars, a three-level pool, a fitness center, and a spa. ⊠ *Blvd. Kukulcán, Km 16.5, 77500,* ☎ *9/881–0600,* FAX *9/885–0259,* WEB *www.omnihotels.com. 331 rooms, 15 villas. 3 restaurants, 2 bars, 3 snack bars, air-conditioning, pool, 2 tennis courts, gym, beach, dock, shops. AE, DC, MC, V.*

$$$ ⊡ **Park Royal Pirámides Cancún.** One of the most charming hotels in
★ Cancún, this twin pyramid property has a lobby that's compact but well laid out, with cool beige furnishings. Rooms are decorated in sea and sunset colors, and original artwork (some of it created with local sand) hangs on the walls. Standard suites have two double beds and full baths; Ambassador suites have fully equipped kitchens, living–dining rooms, three double beds, and full baths. Selected suites also have private Jacuzzis and terraces either facing the lagoon or the ocean. The beachside presidential suite has a remarkable view of the Maya ruin Yamil Lu'um next door. The property has two pools joined by a waterfall, a lovely beach, and a well-stocked, reasonably priced grocery store. ⊠ *Blvd. Kukulcán, Km 12.5, 77500,* ☎ *9/885–1333,* FAX *9/ 885–0113,* WEB *www.piramidescancun.com.mx. 232 rooms, 54 suites. Restaurant, bar, grocery, air-conditioning, 2 pools, gym, beach, shops, children's programs (ages 4–12), travel services. AE, MC, V.*

$$$ ⊡ **El Pueblito Beach Hotel.** Built on a hill, this all-inclusive resort is designed with clusters of guest rooms in tri-level units. Pathways lined with tropical foliage lead to terraced pools with waterfalls and stone archways; there's also a long, separate water slide for children. Rooms, which are large for the price, have marble floors and simple rattan furnishings; a few have kitchenettes. This is a good choice for families, as the rooms are spacious and comfortable. Ask about the European plan, which excludes meals and can lower the cost of the room. ⊠ *Blvd. Kukulcán, Km 17.5, 77500,* ☎ *9/885–8800,* FAX *9/885–0731. 348 rooms. 3 restaurants, bar, air-conditioning, kitchenettes (some), 5 pools, tennis court, beach, shops, travel services. AE, MC, V.*

$$$ ⊡ **Villas Tacul.** These 23 villas on 5 acres of land—including their own stretch of beach—are a great place to set up housekeeping. The grounds are beautifully landscaped with well-trimmed lawns, flowering shrubs, and trees. Inside, highlights include red-tile floors, authentic Mexican colonial–style furniture, wagon-wheel chandeliers, and tin-work mirrors. All villas have kitchens and from two to five bedrooms, making them ideal for families or couples traveling together. For an extra charge you can have a housekeeper who cleans and serves breakfast. There are also some less expensive rooms available without kitchen facilities. ⊠ *Blvd. Kukulcán, Km 5.5, 77500,* ☎ *9/883–0000 or 800/ 842–0193,* FAX *9/883–0349,* WEB *www.villastacul.com.mx. 23 villas. Restaurant, bar, air-conditioning, pool, 2 tennis courts, basketball, beach. AE, DC, MC, V.*

$$ ⊡ **Holiday Inn Express.** Within easy walking distance of the Pok-Ta-Pok golf course, this clean, pleasant hotel was built to resemble a Mexican hacienda—but with a pool instead of a courtyard at its center. Rooms are decorated in bright blues and reds with modern furniture and have either patios or small balconies that overlook the pool and deck. While not luxurious, it's perfect for families in which Dad wants to golf, Mom wants to shop, and the kids want to hit the beach. A complimentary shuttle bus takes guests to the shops and beaches five minutes away; taxis are inexpensive alternatives. ⊠ *Paseo Pok-Ta-Pok, 77500,* ☎ *9/883-2200,* FAX *9/883-2532,* WEB *www.holidayinncancun.com.mx. 119 rooms. Restaurant, air-conditioning, pool. AE, MC, V.*

$$ ☶ **Suites Sina.** These economical suites are in the heart of the Hotel Zone in front of Laguna Nichupté and close to the golf course. Each suite is equipped with comfortable furniture, kitchenette, dining–living room with sofa bed, balcony or terrace, television, and double beds. Outside is a central pool and garden. Perhaps the best deal in the Hotel Zone, these suites are particularly affordable if you rent for a few weeks or share with someone. ⊠ *Club de Golf, Calle Quetzal 33, 77500,* ☎ *9/883–1017 or 877/666–9837,* FAX *9/883–2459,* WEB *www.cancunsinasuites.com.mx. 33 suites. Air-conditioning, kitchenettes, pool. AE, MC, V.*

$$ ☶ **Sun Palace.** This adults-only, all-inclusive resort is set up like a camp. Daily planned activities are posted in the lobby, and activity coordinators direct guests toward game rooms, tennis courts, exercise and water-sports equipment, the pool, and a 40-person hot tub with its own waterfall. Rooms have ocean views but no balconies or room service. Included in the package are day tours, scuba lessons, food, and beverages. Guest also have access to all the sister resorts, including Beach Palace and Cancún Palace. If you book this resort through a travel agent or over the Internet, you're likely to get the best price. ⊠ *Blvd. Kukulcán, Km 20, 77500,* ☎ *9/885–1555 or 877/505–5515,* FAX *9/885–2425,* WEB *www.palaceresorts.com. 227 rooms, 19 suites. 3 restaurants, air-conditioning, pool, hot tub, 3 tennis courts, gym, Ping-Pong, beach, billiards, recreation room. AE, MC, V.*

Downtown

$$ ☶ **Antillano.** On the main strip, this beautifully maintained hotel
★ stands out from the others in its league. Each room is fitted with wood furnishings, one or two double beds, a sink area separate from the bath, red-tile floors, and a small television. There is a cozy little lobby bar and decent-size pool. The quietest rooms are those facing the interior—avoid the noisier rooms that face Avenida Tulum. ⊠ *Av. Tulum at Calle Claveles, 77500,* ☎ *9/884–1532,* FAX *9/884–1878,* WEB *www.hotelantillano.com. 48 rooms. Bar, air-conditioning, pool, shops, babysitting. AE, DC, MC, V.*

$$ ☶ **Cancún Inn El Patio.** This charming inn has the feel of an old Mexican residence. The entrance leads off a busy street into a central patio, landscaped with trees, flowers, and a lovely tiled fountain. Off to one side is a comfortable dining–living room. Upstairs, large, airy rooms are furnished with Spanish-style furniture and Mexican photos and ceramics. Downtown attractions are within walking distance, and the helpful owners, who live on site, can direct you to the best spots in the area. ⊠ *Av. Bonampak 51, Sm 2-A, 77500,* ☎ *9/884–3500,* FAX *9/884–3540,* WEB *www.cancun-suites.com. 18 rooms. MC, V.*

$$ ☶ **Holiday Inn Centro Cancún.** This is the place to stay if you want to
★ pay modest rates and be near the restaurants and shops but still have luxury hotel amenities. The attractive, pink, four-story building is reminiscent of a hacienda and houses modern rooms with mauve and blue color schemes and appealing Mexican touches, like ceramics and textiles. All rooms overlook a large pool surrounded by tropical plants. Its sister hotel, Margaritas Cancún, at Avenida Yaxchilán 41 (☎ 9/884–9333), also downtown, has prettier rooms with balconies and the same amenities and is a little less expensive. ⊠ *Av. Nader 1, Sm 2, 77500,* ☎ *9/887–4455 or 800/465–4329,* FAX *9/884–7954,* WEB *www.holidayinn.com. 246 rooms. 2 restaurants, 2 bars, air-conditioning, pool,*

hair salon, tennis court, gym, nightclub, coin laundry, travel services, car rental. AE, DC, MC, V.

$$ **Hotel Bonampak.** Named after one of the famous Maya ruins, this comfortable hotel is on the edge of the Hotel Zone, just minutes away from the beach by bus or taxi. The bullring and open-air markets are within walking distance. Rooms are basic, with a rose and taupe color scheme. There are no patios or terraces, but the windows do look out onto the medium-size pool and garden below. Each floor has a large, bright, airy sitting area. The staff is quite helpful. Salad lovers can find sustenance at the Ensalada Rico restaurant, right on the premises. ✉ *Av. Bonampak 225, 77500,* ☎ FAX *9/884–0280 or 9/887–3158. 80 rooms. Restaurant, air-conditioning, pool, laundry service, free parking. AE, MC, V.*

$$ **Hotel El Rey del Caribe.** A marvel in downtown Cancún, El Rey del
★ Caribe has been designed to have zero impact on the environment, in part by using solar energy for electricity, a water recycling plan, and special composting toilets. And its luxuriant garden, which blocks the heat and noise of downtown, makes it an oasis. Hammocks hang poolside, and wrought-iron tables and chairs are placed throughout the grounds. Rooms are on the small side but are pleasant and have convenient kitchenettes. The hotel is within walking distance of all downtown shops and restaurants. ✉ *Avs. Uxmal and Nader Sm 2-A, 77500,* ☎ *9/884–2028,* FAX *9/884–9857,* WEB *www.reycaribe.com. 26 rooms. Kitchenettes, pool, hot tub. AE, MC, V.*

$ **Hotel Parador.** At this heart-of-the-city hotel, rooms are strung along two long, narrow courtyards that lead back to a pool, a grassy sunning area, and a palapa bar. The functional, modern rooms have two double beds, showers, and cable television. This hotel is popular with spring breakers. ✉ *Av. Tulum 26, 77500,* ☎ *9/884–1922,* FAX *9/ 884–9712,* WEB *www.hotelparador.com.mx. 66 rooms. Restaurant, bar, air-conditioning, pool, baby-sitting, laundry service. AE, MC, V.*

$ **Maria de Lourdes.** This budget hotel offers a lot of luxury for ex-
★ tremely reasonable rates. Basic rooms are furnished with two queen-size beds, television, and bath. A well-maintained, decent-size swimming pool is surrounded by tables, where guests gather to play cards and chat. The staff is as amiable as the surroundings. It's within walking distance of shops and restaurants along Tulum. ✉ *Av. Yaxchilán 31, 77500,* ☎ *9/884–4744,* FAX *9/884–1242. 50 rooms. Restaurant, bar, pool. MC, V.*

$ **Mexico Hostels.** Four blocks from the main bus terminal and open
★ 24 hours, this hostel is absolutely *the* cheapest place to stay in Cancún. The pleasant, clean space offers beds (four per room), private lockers, access to a full kitchen, a lounge area, and Internet access. Those who want to sleep outdoors can share a space with 20 others under a palapa roof. ✉ *Calle Palmera 30 (off Av. Uxmal, beside the BMW dealership), 77500,* ☎ *9/887–0191 or 212/699–3825 ext. 7860,* WEB *www.mexicohostels.com. 50 beds. No credit cards.*

NIGHTLIFE AND THE ARTS

The Arts

The **Casa de Cultura** (✉ Prolongación Av. Yaxchilán, Sm 21, ☎ 9/884–8364) hosts local cultural events, including art exhibits, dance performances, plays, and concerts, throughout the year.

Festivals

Cancún's **Jazz Festival** is an annual weeklong event in late May that draws a huge international crowd from the United States, South America, and Europe. The Cancún Hotel Association (☎ 9/884–7083) can provide information about this popular gathering.

Each fall the city of Cancún hosts the **Caribbean Culture Festival.** Artists and musicians from all over the Caribbean come to participate in a series of events that range from dance to music to poetry readings. There are also exhibits by Latin American painters and sculptors. The real draw, however, is the variety of salsa music performed. Consult your hotel for details.

Film

Most movies that play in Cancún are Hollywood blockbusters shown in English with Spanish subtitles, although some of the more popular movies are now being dubbed into Spanish. Look for "En Español" displayed alongside the title on the marquee or in newspaper listings. The clerk usually tells you when you are buying a ticket for a Spanish movie instead of an English one. All children's movies are dubbed in Spanish.

In the Hotel Zone, **Cinemas Kukulcán** (✉ Plaza Kukulcán, Blvd. Kukulcán, Km 13.5, ☎ 9/885–3021) has two small screens. There are two **Cinemark** theaters (✉ Forum-by-the-Sea, Blvd. Kukulcán, Km 9.5; ✉ La Isla Shopping Village, Blvd. Kukulcán, Km 12.5, ☎ 9/883–0576), one with two large screens at Forum-by-the-Sea and the other with five large screens at La Isla Shopping Village.

Downtown, the **Cinepolis** at Plaza las Americas (✉ Av. Tulum, Sm 4 and 9, ☎ 9/884–4056) has 12 large screens—the largest location and widest selection in all of Cancún. **Tulum Plus** (✉ Av. Tulum 10, Sm 2, ☎ 9/884–3451) is a small movie theater with six large screens and cheaper prices than at many other newer theaters. It gives the traditional Mexican half-time intermission and has great snacks.

Performances

The **Ballet Folklórico de Cancún** performs Monday through Saturday at the convention center (✉ Blvd. Kukulcán, Km 9, ☎ 9/883–0199). This popular ballet folklórico dinner show has upbeat music and dances from across Mexico. Cocktails are at 6:30; dinner, a typical Mexican buffet, is at 7; and the dance production goes on at 8. Tickets are $50. Every weeknight the **Teatro de Cancún** (✉ El Embarcadero, Blvd. Kukulcán, Km 4, ☎ 9/849–4848) presents two shows: *Voces y Danzas de Mexico* (*Voice and Dance of Mexico*), a colorful showcase of popular songs and dances from different cities in Mexico, as well as *Tradución del Caribe* (*Caribbean Tradition*), which highlights the rhythms, music, and dance of Cuba, Puerto Rico, and other Caribbean destinations. Tickets for each performance are $29. Downtown the nightclub **Backstage** (✉ Av. Tulipanes 30, Sm 22, ☎ 9/887–9106) offers a gay cabaret and floor show Tuesday to Sunday.

Nightlife

Nightlife happens all over Cancún and in a wide variety of places. Many restaurants do double duty as party centers; discos offer music (sometimes taped, sometimes live) and light shows; and most nightclubs have live music and dancing. Sometimes the lines between the three get blurred.

Dinner Cruises

AquaWorld's **Cancún Queen** (✉ AquaWorld Marina, Blvd. Kukulcán, Km 15.2, ☎ 9/885–2288) is the only paddle wheeler in Mexico. It offers cruises of the lagoon, complete with a three-course dinner, starting at $65. The 62-ft galleon **Columbus** (✉ Royal Yacht Club, Blvd. Kukulcán, Km 16.6, ☎ 9/883–1488) offers Lobster Dinner Cruises at sunset (5 PM) and star cruises at 8 PM. *Pirate's Night* (✉ Playa Langosta Dock, Blvd. Kukulcán, Km 5.5, ☎ 9/883–1488) offers trips to Treasure Island and a buffet dinner. Children under 12 are half price. The modern sailboat is decked out like a pirate ship, the crew like pirates. Reservations are recommended for all dinner cruises.

Discos

Cancún wouldn't be Cancún without its glittering discos, which generally start jumping about 10:30. **La Boom** (✉ Blvd. Kukulcán, Km 3.5, ☎ 9/883–1152) is always the last place to close; it has a video bar with a light show and regular weekly events. The scene's grande dame is **Christine** (✉ Krystal Cancún Hotel, Blvd. Kukulcán, Km 9, Lote 9, ☎ 9/883–1793), which puts on an incredible light show. The wild, wild **Coco Bongo** (✉ Blvd. Kukulcán, Km 9.5, across the street from Dady'O, ☎ 9/883–0592) has no chairs, and everyone dances on the spot or on top of the tables. **Dady'O** (✉ Blvd. Kukulcán, Km 9.5, ☎ 9/883–3333) has been around for a while but is still very "in" with the younger set. Next door to Dady'O, **Dady Rock** (✉ Blvd. Kukulcán, Km 9.5, ☎ 9/883–3333) draws a high-energy crowd with live music, a giant TV screen, contests, and food specials. **Fat Tuesday** (✉ Blvd. Kukulcán, Km 6.5, ☎ 9/882–2676), with its large daiquiri bar and live and taped disco music, is another place to go and dance the night away. The **Liquid Club** (✉ Blvd. Kukulcán, Km 9.5, Party Center, ☎ 9/883–3147) is a high-energy disco with high-tech lighting and sound. **Ma'Ax'O** (✉ Blvd. Kukulcán, Km 1.5, ☎ 9/883–5599), in La Isla Shopping Village, is a club–bar with the latest music and a wild dance floor. In La Isla Shopping Village, **Myth/El Alebrije** (✉ Blvd. Kukulcán, Km 1.5, ☎ 9/883–4525) has fantasy decorations and continual laser shows but a small dance floor. At **Pravda** (✉ Blvd. Kukulcán, Km 8, ☎ 9/883–5705), clubbers can find the latest in progressive, psychedelic trance and lounge music. To help you get in the mood, try the killer cocktails with Russian vodka. **Up and Down** (✉ Hotel Oasis, Blvd. Kukulcán, Km 15.5, ☎ 9/885–0867) holds foam parties popular with spring-breakers.

Music

To mingle with locals and hear great music for free, head down to the **Parque de las Palapas** (✉ bordered by Avs. Tulum, Yaxchilán, Uxmal, and Cobá). Every Friday night at 7:30 there is live music that ranges from jazz to salsa to Caribbean.

Azucar (✉ Hotel Camino Real, Blvd. Kukulcán, Km 9, Punta Cancún, ☎ 9/883–7000) showcases the very best Latin American bands. Go just to watch the locals dance (the beautiful people don't turn up here until *really* late) and enjoy the hot salsa. Proper dress is required—no jeans or sneakers. **Batacha** (✉ Hotel Miramar Misión, Blvd. Kukulcán, Km 9.5, ☎ 9/883–1755) is a terrific, down-to-earth spot for Latin American and Mexican music, as well as a great place to practice your salsa moves—there's always a local willing to offer you tips. The **Blue Bayou Jazz Club** (✉ Hyatt Cancún Caribe, Blvd. Kukulcán, Km 10.5, ☎ 9/883–0044) has nightly jazz in the lobby bar. **El Camarote** (✉ Avs. Uxmal and Nader, ☎ 9/884–3218) offers bohemian-style and alternative music. The classy downtown **Roots Bar** (✉ Av. Tulipanes 26, near Parque de las Palapas, ☎ 9/884–2437) is the place for jazz, flamenco, blues, and modern Brazilian music.

Restaurant Party Centers

While the food at the following restaurants is usually quite good, the real draw at each spot is the nightly parties that usually have live music until dawn.

At **Carlos 'n' Charlie's** (⊠ Blvd. Kukulcán, Km 5.5, ☎ 9/883–0846) zany waiters perform on stage with live rock bands. **Mango Tango** (⊠ Blvd. Kukulcán, Km 12.5, ☎ 9/883–0303) has a Las Vegas–style dinner-theater show with Caribbean music and dance. **Pat O'Briens** (⊠ Blvd. Kukulcán, Km 11.5, ☎ 9/883–0418) brings the New Orleans party scene to the Zone with live rock bands and its famous cocktails. **Señor Frog's** (⊠ Blvd. Kukulcán, Km 12.5, ☎ 9/883–1092) is known for its crazy souvenir drinks.

OUTDOOR ACTIVITIES AND SPORTS

Bullfighting

The Cancún **bullring** (⊠ Blvd. Kukulcán at Av. Bonampak, ☎ 9/884–8372 or 9/884–8248), a block south of the Pemex station, hosts year-round bullfights. A matador, charros, a mariachi band, and flamenco dancers entertain during the hour preceding the bullfight (from 2:30 PM). Tickets cost about $40. Fights are held Wednesday at 3:30.

Golf

The main course is at **Pok-Ta-Pok** (⊠ Blvd. Kukulcán, between Km 6 and Km 7, ☎ 9/883–1230), a club with fine views of both sea and lagoon; its 18 holes were designed by Robert Trent Jones, Sr. The club also has a practice green, a swimming pool, tennis courts, and a restaurant. The greens fees are $70 ($55 after 2 PM); electric cart, $25; clubs, $15; caddies, $20; and golf clinics, $25 per hour. Playing hours are 6–6 (last tee-off is at 4). There is an 18-hole championship golf course at the **Hilton Cancún Beach & Golf Resort** (⊠ Blvd. Kukulcán, Km 17, ☎ 9/881–8016); greens fees are $95 ($75 for hotel guests), carts are included, and club rentals run from $20 to $30. The 18-hole executive course (par 53) at the **Hotel Meliá Cancún** (⊠ Blvd. Kukulcán, Km 12, ☎ 9/885–1160) forms a semicircle around the property and shares its beautiful ocean views. The greens fee is about $20. There is a mini-golf course at **Cancún Palace Hotel** (⊠ Blvd. Kukulcán, Km 14.5, ☎ 9/885–0533).

Go-Carts

About a 20-minute ride south of Cancún, **Karting International Cancún** is a great place for speed demons. The Honda-engine go-carts reach speeds of up to 120 km (70 mi) per hour on the racetrack. There's a smaller track with slower carts for children. Your choice of cart and track determines the price, which is by the hour. If you don't have a car to get here, a taxi ride should run about $10 to $15. ⊠ *Cancún–Puerto Morelos Hwy./Hwy. 307, Km 7.5,* ☎ *9/882–1275.* ☉ *Daily 10–10.*

Health Clubs

Most deluxe hotels have health clubs. Check them out carefully, as some are quite small and not open to the public. For a club downtown with good equipment and trainers, try **Body's Aerobics Studio** (⊠ Av. Nader 54, ☎ 9/884–0634).

Running

If the idea of jogging in the intense heat of Cancún sounds appealing, there is a 14-km (9-mi) track that extends along half the island, running parallel to Boulevard Kukulcán from the Punta Cancún area into Cancún City. Every December the city puts on an international marathon called the **Most Beautiful Marathon in the World.** The route goes through both the Hotel Zone and downtown. For more information contact the Mexico City office at 5574–1065 or the United States office at 813/985–5050.

Water Sports

There are lots of ways to get your adrenaline going while getting wet in Cancún. You can find places to go parasailing (about $35 for eight minutes); waterskiing ($70 per hour); or jet-skiing ($70 per hour, or $60 for Wave Runners, double-seated Jet Skis). Paddleboats, kayaks, catamarans, and banana boats are readily available, too.

El Embarcadero, at Playa Linda, is the largest marina complex and is where most water tours depart. At the dock you can find the Garrafon Ferry, the Isla Mujeres Tour Boat, the Captain Hook Galleon, the Nautibus, Aquabus, and HeliTours. Inside the complex are Xcaret ticket booths, an artist's flea market, various snack bars, and the Teatro Cancún, where nightly performances are given.

Aqua Fun (⊠ Blvd. Kukulcán, Km 16.5, ☎ 9/885–2930) maintains a full-service marina with large fleets of water toys such as Wave Runners, Jet Skis, speedboats, kayaks, and windsurfers. **AquaWorld** (⊠ Blvd. Kukulcán, Km 15.2, ☎ 9/885–2288, FAX 9/885–2299), a full-service marina, rents boats and water toys to thousands of people a day. **Parque Nizuc** (⊠ Blvd. Kukulcán, Km 25, ☎ 9/881–3030) is the area's newest marine park. Your entry fee includes a visit to Baxal-Há, a snorkel area that's home to gentle sharks and manta rays; and Wet n' Wild, a water theme park offering seven water slides and a chance to see dolphins at Atlántida, an interactive dolphin aquarium. There is an extra charge to swim with the dolphins. Visitors are asked not to bring food or beverages into the park. If you would like to swim with the dolphins or feed some sharks without leaving the Hotel Zone, head over to the **Interactive Aquarium** (⊠ Blvd. Kukulcán, Km 12.5, ☎ 9/884–8487), at La Isla Shopping Village. Prices start at $40 for a half-hour dip with the dolphins, $19.95 sans dolphins.

FISHING

Some 500 species of tropical fish, including sailfish, wahoo, bluefin, marlin, barracuda, and red snapper, live in the waters adjacent to Cancún. Deep-sea fishing boats and gear may be chartered from outfitters starting at about $350 for four hours, $450 for six hours, and $550 for eight hours. Charters generally include a captain and first mate, gear, bait, and beverages. The following all have charter boats for deep-sea fishing at competitive prices: **Aqua Tours** (⊠ Blvd. Kukulcán, Km 6, ☎ 9/883–0227); **Barracuda Marina** (⊠ Blvd. Kukulcán, Km 14, ☎ 9/885–3444); **Marina del Rey** (⊠ Blvd. Kukulcán, Km 15.5, ☎ 9/883–0554); and **Mundo Marina** (⊠ Blvd. Kukulcán, Km 5.5, ☎ 9/883–0442).

MARINAS

There are a number of marinas throughout the Hotel Zone, all offering a variety of services. They include the following: **Aqua II** (☎ 9/884–1057); **Aqua Fun** (☎ 9/885–2930); **Aqua Tours** (☎ 9/883–0400); **AquaWorld** (☎ 9/885–8300); **Barracuda** (☎ 9/885–3444); **Cancún Marina Club** (☎ 9/883–2165); **Club Lagoon** (☎ 9/883–3109); **Embarcadero Cancún** (☎ 9/849–7344); **Kin-Ha** (☎ 9/883–2377); **Manglar** (☎ 9/885–1808); **Marina del Rey** (☎ 9/885–0273); **Mundo Marina** (☎ 9/883–0554); **Scuba Cancún** (☎ 9/883–5846); and **Solo Buceo** (☎ 9/883–3979).

SNORKELING AND SCUBA DIVING

Snorkeling is best at Punta Nizuc, Punta Cancún, and Playa Tortugas, although you should be especially careful of the strong currents at the last. You can generally rent gear for $10 per day from many of the scuba-diving places, and most hotels and resorts have their own gear for rent. If you've brought your own snorkeling gear and want to save money, take a city bus down to Club Med and walk along the resort's beach for less than 1 km (½ mi) until you get to Punta Nizuc.

Barracuda Marina (✉ Blvd. Kukulcán, Km 14, ☎ 9/885–2444) has a two-hour Wave Runner jungle tour through the mangroves, which ends with snorkeling at the Punta Nizuc coral reef. The $38.50 fee includes snorkeling equipment, life jackets, and refreshments.

Scuba diving has gained in popularity in Cancún. A word of caution about one-hour "resort" courses offered as freebies by the resorts: this does not prepare you to dive in the ocean, no matter what the high-pressure concession operators tell you. A one-hour lesson in a controlled environment such as a pool differs vastly from one in the open ocean. If you have caught the scuba bug, invest in a few more lessons and prepare yourself properly so you can enjoy the experience. Remember that scuba-diving accidents can be fatal.

The secret of a good scuba company is personal attention, which is more often found at the smaller companies. Ask to meet the dive master and check out the company's equipment and certifications thoroughly. **Scuba Cancún** (✉ Blvd. Kukulcán, Km 5, ☎ 9/883–1011) specializes in diving trips and offers NAUI, CMAS, and PADI instruction. It's operated by Luis Hurtado, who has more than 35 years of experience. **Solo Buceo** (✉ Blvd. Kukulcán, Km 9, ☎ 9/883–3979) offers two-tank dives for $50 with NAUI, SSI, and PADI instruction. The outfit goes to Cozumel, Akumal, Xpu-ha, and Isla Mujeres. Extended diving trips are available from $180.

SHOPPING

Resort wear and handicrafts are the most popular purchases in Cancún, but the prices are higher than in other cities and the selection is limited. If your vacation includes visits to other Mexican locales, it's best to postpone your shopping spree until then. Still, it is possible to find Mexican specialties such as handwoven textiles, leather goods, and jewelry handcrafted from silver and local coral. Cancún is most noted for luxury items. Many stores are "duty-free," selling designer goods at reduced prices, sometimes as much as 30%–40% off the usual retail price.

A note of caution about tortoiseshell products: the turtles from which they're made are an endangered species, and it is illegal to bring tortoiseshell into the United States and several other countries. Simply refrain from buying anything made from tortoiseshell. Also be aware that there are some restrictions regarding black coral. You must purchase it from a recognized dealer.

Throughout Mexico you often get better prices by paying with cash (pesos or dollars) or traveler's checks. This is because Mexican merchants frequently tack the 3%–6% credit-card company commission on to your bill. If you can do without plastic, you may even get the 12% sales tax lopped off. If you are just window-shopping, use the phrase "*Sólo estoy mirando, gracias*" (*so*-lo ess-*toy* mee-*ran*-do, *gras*-yas; I'm just looking, thank you). This will ease the high-pressure sales pitch that you invariably get in most stores.

Most prices are fixed in shops, but bargaining is expected at markets. Never settle for the offered price. Start by offering half the price, and let the haggling begin. Shopping around is a good idea, too, because the crafts market is very competitive. And always examine merchandise closely: some "authentic" items—particularly jewelry—might be poor imitations.

In Cancún, shopping hours are generally weekdays 10–1 and 4–7, although more and more stores are staying open throughout the day rather than closing for siesta between 1 and 4. Many shops keep Saturday morning hours, and some are now open on Sunday until 1. Shops in the malls tend to be open weekdays from 9 AM or 10 AM to 8 PM or 10 PM.

Shopping Districts, Streets, and Malls

Shopping can be roughly categorized by location: mall or market. The *centros comerciales* (shopping malls) in Cancún are as well kept as similar establishments in the United States or Canada. Fully air-conditioned, they sell just about everything: designer clothing, beachwear, sportswear, jewelry, music, video games, household items, shoes, and books. Some even have the same terrible mall food that is standard north of the border. Prices are generally—but not always—higher than in the shops and markets downtown.

While mall shopping is more orderly, market shopping is more colorful. Stores are jumbled together in a chaotic fashion with the beautiful beside the ugly, quality alongside junk. Shopping is lively, and time-consuming—try out your bargaining skills to pick up some real deals.

Downtown

There's a wide variety of shops downtown along Avenida Tulum (between Avenidas Cobá and Uxmal). **Fama** (⊠ Av. Tulum 105, ☎ 9/884–6586) is a department store that sells clothing, English reading matter, sports gear, toiletries, liquor, and *latería* (crafts made of tin). The oldest and largest of Cancún's crafts markets is **Ki Huic** (⊠ Av. Tulum 17, between Bancomer and Bital, ☎ 9/884–3347), which is open daily from 9 AM to 10 PM and houses about 100 vendors. **Mercado Veintiocho** (Market 28), just off Avenidas Yaxchilán and Sunyaxchén, is a popular market filled with shops selling many of the same souvenir items found in the Hotel Zone but at half the price. **Ultrafemme** (⊠ Av. Tulum and Calle Claveles, ☎ 9/885–1402) is a popular downtown store that carries duty-free perfume, cosmetics, and jewelry. It also has branches in the Hotel Zone at Plaza Caracol, Plaza Mayafair, Kukulcán Plaza, and La Isla Shopping Village.

Plaza las Americas (⊠ Av. Tulum, Sm 4 and 9, ☎ 9/887–3863) is the largest shopping center in downtown Cancún. Its 50-plus stores, three restaurants, eight movie theaters, video arcade, fast-food outlets, and three large department stores will—for better or worse—make you feel right at home.

Hotel Zone

There is only one open-air market in the Hotel Zone. **Coral Negro**, next to the convention center, is a collection of about 50 stalls selling crafts items. It's open daily until late evening. Everything here is overpriced, but bargaining does work.

Flamingo Plaza (⊠ Blvd. Kukulcán, Km 11.5, across from the Hotel Flamingo, ☎ 9/883–2945) is a small, high-tech plaza beautifully decorated with marble. Inside are a few designer emporiums, duty-free shops, an exchange booth, sportswear shops, and two boutiques selling Guatemalan imports.

Forum-by-the-Sea (⊠ Blvd. Kukulcán, Km 9.5, ☎ 9/883–4425) is a sparkling, three-level entertainment–shopping plaza in the Zone. Cancún's biggest selection of cinemas, brand-name stores, and restaurants is here, all in a circuslike atmosphere.

The glittering, ultratrendy, and ultra-expensive **La Isla Shopping Village** (✉ Blvd. Kukulcán, Km 12.5, ☎ 9/883–5025) is on the Nichupté Lagoon under a giant canopy. A series of canals and small bridges is designed to give the place a Venetian look. In addition to a wide range of shops, the mall has a marina, an aquarium, a disco, restaurants, and movie theaters. You won't find any bargains here, but it's a fun place to window-shop.

Kukulcán Plaza (✉ Blvd. Kukulcán, Km 13, ☎ 9/885–2304) is a mall that never seems to end, with around 130 shops (including Benetton and Harley Davidson boutiques), 12 restaurants, a bar, a liquor store, a bank, a three-screen cinema, bowling lanes, and a video arcade. The plaza is also notable for the many cultural events and shows that take place in the main public area.

Leading off Plaza Caracol is the oldest and most varied commercial center in the Zone, **Mayafair Plaza** (✉ Blvd. Kukulcán, Km 8.5, ☎ 9/883–2801). Mayafair has a large open-air center filled with shops, bars, and restaurants, including El Mexicano. An adjacent indoor shopping mall is decorated to resemble a rain forest, complete with replicas of Maya stelae.

The largest and most contemporary of the malls, **Plaza Caracol** (✉ Blvd. Kukulcán, Km 8.5, ☎ 9/883–2961) is north of the convention center. It houses about 200 shops and boutiques, including two pharmacies, art galleries, a currency exchange, and folk art and jewelry shops, as well as a café and restaurants. Boutiques include Benetton, Bally, Gucci, and Ralph Lauren, with prices lower than those of their U.S. counterparts. You can rest your feet upstairs at the café, where there are often afternoon concerts, or enjoy a great meal at one of the fine restaurants.

Specialty Shops

Galleries

The **Renato Dorfman Gallery** (✉ Avs. Sunyaxchén and Yaxchilán 63, Sm 25, ☎ 9/887–4615; ✉ La Isla Shopping Village, Blvd. Kukulcán, Km 12.5, ☎ 9/883–0359 or 9/883–5573) carries Dorfman's original pieces as well as his hand-carved replicas of Maya art and stelae. The **Modern Art Café** (✉ La Isla Shopping Village, Blvd. Kukulcán, Km 12.5, ☎ 9/883–4511) is decorated with a revolving exhibit of works by local and international artists, all for sale. The **Iguana Wana** restaurant (✉ Plaza Caracol, Blvd. Kukulcán, Km 8.5, ☎ 9/883–0829) displays a small collection of art for sale. The **Huichol Collection** has three locations: Plaza Kukulcán (✉ Blvd. Kukulcán, Km 13, ☎ 9/883–6078), Plaza Caracol (✉ Blvd. Kukulcán, Km 8.5, ☎ 9/883–5059), and La Isla Shopping Village (✉ Blvd. Kukulcán, Km 12.5, ☎ 9/883–5025). Each store sells handcrafted beadwork and embroidery made by the Huichol Indians of the West Coast. You can also watch a visiting tribe member doing this amazing work.

Grocery Stores

The few grocery stores in the Hotel Zone tend to be expensive. It's better to shop for groceries downtown. Major supermarkets downtown include **Comercial Mexicana** (✉ Avs. Tulum and Uxmal, across from the bus station; Av. Kabah at Av. Yaxchilán, Sm 21, ☎ 9/880–9164); a **Costco** (✉ Av. Kabah at Av. Yaxchilán, Sm 21, ☎ 9/881–0250); and **Sam's Club** (✉ Av. Cobá, Sm 21, Lote 2, ☎ 9/884–1383). Other stores include **Chedraui** (✉ Av. Tulum, Sm 22; Plaza las Americas, Av. Tulum, Sm 4 and 9, ☎ 9/887–2111) and **San Francisco de Asís** (✉ Av. Tulum 18, ☎ 9/884–1155; ✉ Mercado Veintiocho, Avs. Yaxchilán and Sunyaxchén).

CANCÚN A TO Z

To research prices, get advice from other travelers, and book travel arrangements, visit www.fodors.com.

ADDRESSES

In Cancún addresses, "Sm" stands for Super Manzana. All neighborhoods are labeled with an Sm number (Sm 23, Sm 25, etc.). Each Sm has its own park or square, and the area streets are fashioned around the park.

AIR TRAVEL TO AND FROM CANCÚN

Aeroméxico flies nonstop to Cancún from Houston, Miami, and New York. American has nonstop service from Dallas and Miami. Continental offers daily direct service from Houston. Mexicana's nonstop flights are from Los Angeles, Miami, and New York. From Cancún, Mexicana subsidiaries Aerocaribe and Aerocozumel fly to Cozumel, the ruins at Chichén Itzá, Mérida, and other Mexican cities.

➤ AIRLINES AND CONTACTS: **Aerocaribe** (☎ 9/884–2000 downtown; 9/886–0083 airport). **Aerocozumel** (☎ 9/884–2000 downtown; 9/886–0162 airport). **Aeroméxico** (☎ 9/884–3571). **American** (☎ 9/904–6000). **Continental** (☎ 9/886–0006). **Mexicana** (☎ 9/887–4444 or 9/883–4881).

AIRPORTS AND TRANSFERS

Cancún International Airport is 16 km (9 mi) southwest of the heart of Cancún and 10 km (6 mi) from the southernmost point of the Hotel Zone.

➤ AIRPORT INFORMATION: **Cancún International Airport** (✉ Cancún–Puerto Morelos Hwy./Hwy. 307, Km 9.5, ☎ 9/886–0073).

AIRPORT TRANSFER

The public-transport options are taxis or *colectivos* (vans); buses are not allowed into the airport due to an agreement with the taxi union. A counter at the airport exit sells colectivo and taxi tickets; prices range from $15 to $40, depending on the destination. Getting back to the airport for your departure is less expensive; taxi rates to the airport range from about $15 to $22. Hotels post current rates. Be sure to agree on a price before getting into the taxi.

BOAT AND FERRY TRAVEL

From Playa Linda, Plaza Caracol, and Playa Tortuga on Cancún, you can take a shuttle boat to the main dock at Isla Mujeres. Municipal ferries carry vehicles and passengers between Cancún's Punta Sam and Isla's dock. (*See* Chapter 2 for more information about boat travel to and from Isla Mujeres.)

Aquabus, a water-taxi service in the Hotel Zone, travels from the hotels to various restaurants and shops; a one-way fare is $3.

➤ WATER-TAXI INFORMATION: **Aquabus** (☎ 9/883–3155).

BUS TRAVEL TO AND FROM CANCÚN

First-class buses arrive at the downtown bus terminal from Mexico City; first- and second-class buses come from Puerto Morelos, Playa del Carmen, Tulum, Chetumal, Cobá, Valladolid, Chichén Itzá, and Mérida. Local public buses take Route 8 to Puerto Juárez and Punta Sam for the ferries to Isla Mujeres (or you can take a taxi from the bus station to Puerto Juárez for about $2).

➤ BUS INFORMATION: **Bus terminal** (✉ Avs. Tulum and Uxmal, ☎ 9/884–1378 or 9/884–3948).

BUS TRAVEL WITHIN CANCÚN

Public buses run between the Hotel Zone and downtown from 6 AM to midnight; the cost is 5 pesos. There are designated bus stops—look for blue signs with white buses in the middle—but you can also flag down drivers along Boulevard Kukulcán. The service is frequent and quite reliable. Buses from the Zone do not go into downtown Cancún but will drop you off anywhere along Avenida Tulum when you indicate you would like to get off the bus. From there you can catch a connecting bus that takes you into the downtown area. Taking the bus can save you a considerable amount of money on taxis, particularly if you are staying in the Hotel Zone. The buses are filled with a variety of people, and the driver often plays his favorite music as he barrels along the boulevard.

CAR RENTAL

Cars are available at Cancún International Airport or from any of a dozen agencies in town. Most of the agencies have several locations in the area: Avis, Thrifty, and Localiza Rent a Car have five each; Hertz has nine; and National has seven. The telephone numbers given here are for the airport locations.

Most rental cars are standard-shift subcompacts and Jeeps; air-conditioned cars with automatic transmissions should be reserved in advance (though bear in mind that some smaller car-rental places have only manual-transmission vehicles). Rates average around $55 per day but can be as high as $75 daily if you haven't reserved a car; you can save a great deal on a rental by booking before you leave home. It's also a good idea to shop around. In addition to the rental agencies, the Car Rental Association can help you arrange a rental.

➤ MAJOR AGENCIES: **Avis** (✉ Cancún International Airport, ☎ 9/886–0222). **Hertz** (✉ Cancún International Airport, ☎ 9/884–1326). **National** (✉ Cancún International Airport, ☎ 9/886–0152). **Thrifty** (✉ Cancún International Airport, ☎ 9/886–0333).

➤ LOCAL AGENCIES AND CONTACTS: **Car Rental Association** (☎ 9/884–2039). **Executive** (✉ Av. Yaxchilán 160, Sm 20, ☎ 9/884–2699). **Econorent** (✉ Avs. Bonampak and Cobá, ☎ 9/887–6487). **Localiza Rent a Car** (✉ Av. La Costa 128, Sm 30, ☎ 9/887–3109). **Zipp Rental Cars** (✉ Baccará Hotel, Blvd. Kukulcán, Km 11.5, ☎ 9/883–2077).

CAR TRAVEL

Driving any kind of vehicle in Cancún is not for the faint of heart. Traffic moves at a breakneck speed; adding to the danger are the many one-way streets, traffic circles (*glorietas*), sporadically working traffic lights, ill-placed *topes* (speed bumps), numerous pedestrians, and large potholes. Be sure to observe speed limits in the Hotel Zone and downtown. The traffic police are quite vigilant and eager to hand out tickets. In addition, car travel becomes expensive, as it entails tips for valet parking as well as gasoline and rather costly rental rates.

Although driving in Cancún is not recommended, you might want a car to explore the surrounding areas on the peninsula. The roads are excellent within a 100-km (62-mi) radius. (*See* Car Travel *in* Smart Travel Tips A to Z.)

Route 180 runs from Matamoros at the Texas border through Campeche, Mérida, Valladolid, and into Cancún. The trip from Texas can take up to three days. Route 307 runs south from Cancún through Puerto Morelos, Tulum, and Chetumal, then into Belize. There are few gas stations on these roads, so keep your tank full. Route 307 has two Pemex stations between Cancún and Playa del Carmen. When approaching any village, town, or city, watch out for the numerous speed bumps—hitting them at top speed can ruin your transmission and tires.

COMPUTERS ON THE ROAD

If you are traveling with your laptop, watch it carefully. The biggest danger, aside from theft, is the constantly fluctuating electricity, which will eventually damage your hard drive. Invest in a surge protector that can handle the frequent fluctuations in voltage—the standard plug-in strip you use at home won't do. It's best to leave repairs until you are back home.

CONSUMER PROTECTION

The Consumer Protection Agency may help you with hassles with companies or consumer goods.
➤ CONTACTS: **Consumer Protection Agency** (✉ Av. Cobá 9, 2nd floor, Sm 22, ☎ 9/884–2369).

EMBASSIES AND CONSULATES

The consulates in Cancún operate with skeleton staffs, and for complicated problems you need to contact the offices in Mérida. The U.S. Consulate, in the Hotel Zone, is open weekdays 9–1; the Mérida offices are open weekdays 7:30–4.

The Canadian Consulate is open daily 11–1. Should you have an emergency when the embassy is closed, contact the Canadian Embassy in Mexico City.
➤ CANADA: **Consulate** (✉ Plaza Caracol 11, 3rd floor, ☎ 9/883–3360; 01–800/706–2900 emergencies, FAX 9/883–3232). **Embassy** (☎ 015/724–7900 in Mexico City).
➤ UNITED STATES: **Consulate** (✉ Plaza Caracol, 3rd floor, ☎ 9/883–0272; ✉ Blvd. Montejo 453, Mérida, ☎ 9/925–5011; 9/845–4364 after-hours emergencies).

E-MAIL

Many hotels have complimentary Internet service for guests; a number of places in Cancún offer access for a small fee. Compu Copy, in the Hotel Zone, is open daily 9–9. Downtown, the Internet Café is open Monday through Saturday 11–10, and Infonet is open daily 10 AM–11 PM. Rates are about $3.50–$5 per hour.
➤ SERVICES: **Compu Copy** (✉ Kukulcán Plaza, Blvd. Kukulcán, Km 13, ☎ 9/885–0055). **Infonet** (✉ Plaza las Americas, Av. Tulum, Sm 4 and 9, ☎ 9/887–9130). **Internet Café** (✉ Av. Tulum, Sm 2, behind Comercial Méxicana, across from the bus station, ☎ 9/887–3167).

EMERGENCIES

In case of medical emergency, the safest bet is the American Medical Centre, run by Drs. Michael and Lisa McFall, from the United States.

Cancún has a lot of pharmacies. Among those that offer delivery service are Canto, Farmacia Cancún, and Paris (all downtown) and, in the Hotel Zone, Roxsanna's. Paris delivers around the clock.
➤ DOCTORS AND DENTISTS: **American Medical Center** (✉ Blvd. Kukulcán, Km 8, ☎ 9/883–1001; 9/883–0113; 9/887–1455 pager, PIN 10844).
➤ EMERGENCY SERVICES: **Emergencies** (☎ 06). **Fire Department** (☎ 9/884–9480). **Highway Police** (☎ 9/884–2445). **Immigration Office** (☎ 9/884–1749). **Municipal Police** (☎ 9/884–1913). **Red Cross** (✉ Avs. Xcaret and Labná, Sm 21, ☎ 9/884–1616). **Traffic Police** (☎ 9/884–0710).
➤ PHARMACIES: **Canto** (✉ Av. Yaxchilán 35, ☎ 9/884–9330). **Farmacia Cancún** (✉ Av. Tulum 17, ☎ 9/884–1283). **Paris** (✉ Av. Yaxchilán 32, ☎ 9/884–3005). **Roxsanna's** (✉ Plaza Kukulcán, Kukulcán Blvd., Km 13, ☎ 9/885–0860).

LODGING

The Cancún Hotel Association can provide information on area lodging but *not* reservations.

➤ CONTACTS: **Cancún Hotel Association** (✉ Av. Ign. García de la Torre, Sm 1, Lote 6, 77500, ☎ 9/884–2853 or 9/884–5895, FAX 9/884–7115).

MAIL AND SHIPPING

The post office (*correos*) is open weekdays 8–5 and Saturday 9–1; there's also a Western Union office in the building and a courier service. Bear in mind, however, that postal service to and from Mexico is extremely slow and may take four weeks or more. Avoid sending or receiving parcels—and never send checks or money through the mail. Invariably they are stolen.

You can receive mail at the post office if it's marked "Lista de Correos, Cancún, 77500, Quintana Roo, Mexico." If you have an American Express card, you can have mail sent to you at the American Express Cancún office, which is open weekdays 9–6, Saturday 9–1.

➤ SERVICES: **American Express** (✉ Av. Tulum 208, at Calle Agua, ☎ 9/881–4020 or 01–800/502–0600). **Post office** (✉ Av. Sunyaxchén at Av. Xel-há, ☎ 9/884–1418). **Western Union** (✉ Av. Sunyaxchén at Av. Xel-há, ☎ 9/884–1529).

MEDIA

NEWSPAPERS AND MAGAZINES

You can pick up many helpful publications at the airport, malls, tourist kiosks, and many hotels. Indeed, you can't avoid having them shoved into your hands. Most are stuffed with discount coupons offering some savings. The best of the bunch is *Cancún Tips*, a free pocket-size guide to hotels, restaurants, shopping, and recreation. Although it's loaded with advertising, the booklet, published twice a year in English and Spanish, has some useful information as well as some discount coupons. The accompanying *Cancún Tips Magazine* has pleasant, informative articles about local attractions. The *Mapa Pocket Guide* is handy for its Hotel Zone map and local contact information, if you can get past all the ads and perforated coupons for Xcaret—the people who own the park publish this guide. *Passport Cancún* is for serious coupon junkies only.

MONEY MATTERS

Generally, banks in Cancún are open weekdays 9–5, with money-exchange desks open 9–1:30. Downtown locations are along Avenida Tulum; some of the larger banks have branches in the Hotel Zone as well. All have automatic teller machines that dispense Mexican money. The ATMs at the smaller banks are often out of order, but the larger banks generally have working machines. If your PIN (personal identification number) has more than four digits, you may have trouble using the ATMs. Also, don't delay in taking your card out of the machine. ATMs are quick to eat up cards, and it takes a visit to the bank and a number of forms to get them back. If your transactions require a teller, go early to avoid long lines.

Banamex, which has offices downtown and in the Hotel Zone, can exchange or wire money. Other banks include Bital, Banca Serfin, Banco del Sureste, Bancomer, Inverlat, and Santander Mexicano.

➤ BANKS: **Banamex** (✉ Av. Tulum 19, next to City Hall, ☎ 9/884–6402; ✉ Plaza Terramar, Blvd. Kukulcán, Km 37, ☎ 9/883–3100). **Banca Serfin** (Downtown: ✉ Av. Cobá at Av. Tulum, ☎ 9/884–4850; ✉ Plaza Kukulcán, Blvd. Kukulcán, Km 9 Hotel Zone, ☎ 9/881–4809).

Bancomer (Downtown: ⊠ Av. Tulum 20, ☎ 9/884–4400; Hotel Zone: ⊠ Plaza El Parián, Blvd. Kukulcán, Km 9.5, next to the convention center, ☎ 9/883–1128). **Banco del Sureste** (⊠ Avs. Yaxchilán and Sunyaxchén, ☎ 9/884–4991). **Bital** (Downtown: ⊠ Av. Tulum 15, ☎ 9/881–4113; Hotel Zone: ⊠ Plaza Caracol, Blvd. Kukulcán, Km 8.5, ☎ 9/883–4652). **Inverlat** (⊠ Av. Tulum 26, ☎ 9/884–3130). **Santander Mexicano** (Downtown: ⊠ Av. Tulum 173, ☎ 9/884–0629; Hotel Zone: ⊠ Plaza Lagunas, Blvd. Kukulcán, Km. 8.5, ☎ 9/883–0148).

MOPED TRAVEL

Mopeds are extremely dangerous, and you risk your life using one in either the Zone or downtown. If you have never ridden a moped or a motorcycle before, *this is not the place to learn*. Mopeds rent for about $25 a day; you are required to leave a credit-card voucher for security. You should receive a crash helmet, which by law you must wear. Read the fine print on your contract; companies will hold you liable for all repairs or replacement in case of an accident and will not offer any insurance to protect you.

TAXIS

Taxi rides within the Hotel Zone cost $5–$7; between the Hotel Zone and downtown, $8 and up; and to the ferries at Punta Sam or Puerto Juárez, $15–$20 or more. Prices depend on distance, your negotiating skills, and whether you pick up the taxi in front of a hotel or decide to save a few dollars by going onto the avenue to hail one yourself (look for green city cabs). Most hotels list rates at the door; confirm the price with your driver *before* you set out. If you lose something in a taxi or have questions or a complaint, call the Sindicato de Taxistas (☎ 9/888–6985).

TELEPHONES

Most hotels charge the equivalent of between 50¢ and $1 for each local call you make from your room. In addition, there is usually a hefty service charge on long-distance calls, and it can add up quickly. In order to make a phone call—local or long distance—from any public phone, you must purchase a Ladatel phone card, sold in blocks of about $3, $5, $10, and $20. An alternative to the phone card is the *caseta de larga distancia*—the long-distance telephone office. There are offices in Plaza Kukulcán, Plaza Mayafair, and Plaza Caracol; the offices have specially designed booths where you take your call after the number has been dialed by a clerk. A service fee of $3.50–$5 is added on top of the steep long-distance charge. The booths do, however, offer more privacy and comfort than many public-phone booths.

INTERNATIONAL CALLS

For calls to the United States or Canada, dial 001, followed by the area code and number. To make a collect call, dial 090 for the international operator.

LOCAL CALLS

For local calls, the 8 of Cancún's 98 area code must be dialed first. The change was made in order to accommodate a growing number of telephone lines. Bear in mind that some of the older printed material on Cancún does not reflect this change and shows the telephone written in the old style.

LONG-DISTANCE CALLS

For long-distance calls within Mexico, dial 01, followed by the area code (sometimes called the city code) and number.

TOURS

BOAT TOURS

Day cruises to Isla Mujeres are popular. They generally include snorkeling, shopping downtown, lunching at an open-bar buffet, and listening to music or lounging at Playa Norte. Plenty of tour operators offer such trips. Captain Hook runs an Isla Mujeres day tour that departs at 10 AM from the pier in front of Fat Tuesday, on Boulevard Kukulcán, and returns at 5 PM; it costs about $55. Dolphin Discovery sails daily from Playas Langosta and Tortugas to the company's dock on Isla Mujeres; its program includes an instruction video, a 30-minute swim session with the dolphins, and time to explore the island. Tickets start at $75. Riviera Holiday Cruises offers a three-day, two-night cruise from Cancún to Havana for $150.

➤ FEES AND SCHEDULES: **Captain Hook** (✉ Blvd. Kukulcán, Km 4.5, ☎ 9/883–3736). **Dolphin Discovery** (☎ 9/883–0777 or 9/883–0779). **Riviera Holiday Cruises** (✉ Calle Tierra 15, Local E, Sm 4, ☎ 9/884–7743, WEB www.rivieraholidaycruises.com).

ECOTOURS

While many claim to have ecological tours, few outfits actually deliver truly ecological experiences in authentic jungle settings. An exception is Reserva Ecológica El Edén, which was established in 1990 by one of Mexico's leading naturalists, Arturo Gómez-Pompa, and his nephew, Marco Lazcano-Barrero. The 500,000-acre reserve, 48 km (30 mi) northwest of Cancún, is dedicated to research for biological conservation in Mexico. It offers excursions for people interested in experiencing the reserve's wetlands, mangrove swamps, sand dunes, savannas, and tropical forests. "Eco-scientific" tours include bird-watching, animal-tracking, stargazing, crocodile ecology, and cenote and archaeological explorations. Prices include transportation between Cancún and the reserve, one to two nights' accommodation at La Savanna Research Station, meals, cocktails, guided nature walks, and all tours. Two-day, one-night excursions start at $235 per person, three-day, two-nights at $315.

➤ FEES AND SCHEDULES: **Reserva Ecológica El Edén** (✉ A.P. 308, Cancún, Quintana Roo 77506, ☎ FAX 9/880–5032, WEB maya.ucr.edu/pril/el eden/Front.html).

PLANE TOURS

Promocaribe flies one-day tours between Cancún and Guatemala City, continuing on to Flores and the ruins at Tikal. A round-trip fare of $267 includes all ground transfers, departure taxes, entrance to ruins, a tour guide, and lunch.

➤ FEES AND SCHEDULES: **Promocaribe** (✉ Plaza Centro, Av. Nader 8, Local 309, Sm 5, ☎ 9/884–4741, WEB www.promocaribe.com).

SUBMARINE TOURS

Nautibus, a "floating submarine," has a 1½-hour Caribbean-reef cruise. At press time, departures were set at 9:30, 11:30, 1, and 3, but times often change, so double-check in advance. The $30 price includes music and drinks. You buy tickets and board at the El Embarcadero Marina, at Playa Linda.

➤ FEES AND SCHEDULES: *Nautibus* (☎ 9/883–2119).

TRANSPORTATION AROUND CANCÚN

Motorized transportation of some sort is necessary, as the island is somewhat spread out. Public bus service is good, and taxis are relatively inexpensive.

TRAVEL AGENCIES

American Express, Aviomar, Intermar Caribe, and Mayaland Tours all offer day trips. You can shop around for the best price or call the Travel Agency Association for further information.

➤ Local Agent Referrals: **Travel Agency Association** (✉ Plaza México, Av. Tulum 200, Suite 301, ☎ 9/887–1670, FAX 9/884–3738).

➤ Local Agents: **American Express** (✉ Av. Tulum 208, ☎ 9/884–2001). **Aviomar** (✉ Av. Yaxchilán 82, ☎ 9/884–8831). **Intermar Caribe** (✉ Av. Tulum at Av. Cobá, ☎ 9/884–4266). **Mayaland Tours** (✉ 225 Party Center, Blvd. Kukulcán, Km 9, ☎ 9/883–0679).

VISITOR INFORMATION

The Mexican Ministry of Tourism has a toll-free 24-hour English-language help line for visitors.

➤ Tourist Information: **Mexican Ministry of Tourism help line** (☎ 01–800/90392). **State Tourism Information Center** (✉ Av. Tulum 23, ☎ 9/884–8073). **State Tourism Office—Quintana Roo** (SECTUR; ✉ Government Palace, Av. Tulum, ☎ 9/884–0437).

2 ISLA MUJERES

Only 8 km (5 mi) across the bay from
Cancún, Isla Mujeres is an ocean away in
attitude, as sleepy and unassuming as its
neighbor is outgoing and flashy. Snorkeling,
exploring the remnants of the island's past,
eating fresh seafood, and lazing under a
thatched roof is about as lively as it gets.

Updated by
Shelagh
McNally

SLA MUJERES (*ees*-lah moo-*hair*-ayce) has a magic of its own that seems to defy change. It makes this tiny, fish-shape island 8 km (5 mi) off Cancún a tranquil alternative to its bustling western neighbor. Only about 8 km (5 mi) long by 1 km (½ mi) wide, Isla has flat sandy beaches on its northern end and steep rocky bluffs to the south.

The name means "Island of Women," although no one is exactly sure who dubbed it that. Many believe it was the ancient Maya, who used the island as a religious center for worshiping Ixchel (ee-*shell*), the Maya goddess of rainbows, the moon, and the sea, and the guardian of fertility and childbirth. Another popular legend has it that the Spanish conquistador Hernández de Córdoba named the island when he landed here in 1517 and found hundreds of female-shape clay idols dedicated to Ixchel and her daughters. Others say the name dates from the 17th century, when Isla was a haven for buccaneers and smugglers. Pirates would stash their women here before heading out to rob the high seas.

After its popularity waned with brigands, Isla settled into life as a quiet fishing village. In the 1950s it became a favorite vacation spot for Mexicans. Americans discovered it shortly afterward, and in the '60s Isla became well known among hippies and backpackers. As Cancún grew so did Isla. During the late 1970s, the number of day-trippers coming over from the mainland increased, bringing Isla's hotel, restaurant, and shop owners more business than ever. Boatloads were streaming off the ferries for quick lunches followed by frenzied shopping, and thus the island became a small-scale tourist haven.

Like the rest of the area, Isla is being developed, but it manages to keep its character as a peaceful retreat with its own local history and culture centered on the sea. And it continues to be a favorite of people who prefer such seaside pleasures as scuba diving, snorkeling, and relaxing on the beach to spending time in Cancún's fast-food joints and rollicking discos. Isleños largely wish to continue the legacy of the late Ramon Bravo, the shark expert, ecologist, and filmmaker who had fought to preserve the island's ecology so that Isla would remain a peaceful, authentically Mexican getaway. (He died in 1998.)

Pleasures and Pastimes

Beaches
The island's finest and most popular beach is Playa Norte, where you can wade far out in placid waters or relax at congenial palapa (thatchroof) bars with drinks and snacks. At sunset the view here is spectacular. Playa Paraíso and Playa Lancheros on the western shore are both pleasant spots for swimming and sunning. On Sunday both these beaches are filled with locals enjoying their day off.

Bird-Watching
About 45 minutes north of Isla Mujeres, Isla Contoy (Isle of Birds) is a national wildlife park and bird sanctuary. The tiny island is a beautiful, unspoiled spot with sand dunes, mangroves, and coconut trees. It's a favorite of birders, who come to see the 70-plus local species.

Dining
Food on Isla Mujeres is what you would expect on a small island: plenty of fresh grilled lobster, shrimp, conch, and fish. It also offers pleasant variations on pasta, pizza, steak, and sandwiches. Bright mornings, sweet fruits, fresh coffee, and baked goods make breakfast on Isla a treat.

Fishing

Billfish (such as marlin and bonefish) are a popular catch in spring and early summer. The currents around Isla make for fine fishing, and the island is something of a magnet for tournaments held throughout the region. Isla holds its own annual billfish tournament in mid-May, and there are dozens of privately run contests as well. During the rest of the year, you can fish for barracuda and tuna, as well as shad, sailfish, grouper, red snapper, and Spanish mackerel.

Lodging

The small hotel reigns here, but with more than 30 lodging places, Isla offers a surprisingly broad range of options—from charming beach-front properties to simpler, less expensive accommodations in the heart of town.

Snorkeling and Scuba Diving

Despite the widespread concern over loss of reef (some reef sections, particularly at El Garrafón National Park, are dead), the underwater spectacle here is still impressive for its abundance of fascinating sea life. In summer, fish are attracted to the mild temperatures and calm waters that prevail between 8 AM and 3 PM. The slightly cooler water in winter means less algae and better visibility.

EXPLORING ISLA MUJERES

To get your bearings, think of Isla Mujeres as an elongated fish, the head being the southeastern tip, the northwest prong the tail. The minute you step off the boat, you see how small Isla is. Directly in front of the ferry piers is the island's only town, known simply as El Pueblo. It extends the full width of Isla's northern "tail" and is sandwiched between sand and sea to the south, west, and northeast, with no high-rises to block the view.

The main road is Avenida Rueda Medina, which runs the length of the island; southeast of a village known as El Colonia, it eventually turns into Carretera El Garrafón. The smaller street names and addresses don't matter much here.

Inland from Rueda Medina, past the T-shirt and souvenir shops, is the island's true gathering spot—El Pueblo's main square. Bounded by Avenidas Morelos, Bravo, Guerrero, and Hidalgo, the *zócalo* (main square) is the ideal place to take in daily town life. Here locals congregate in front of the church while their children run around the playground or play basketball. On holidays and weekends the square is set up for dances, concerts, and fiestas. Areas around the square are closed to vehicles, with only pedestrian traffic allowed.

Numbers in the text correspond to numbers in the margin and on the Isla Mujeres map.

A Good Tour

The best way to explore the entire island is to take a taxi or rent either a moped or golf cart. You can walk to Isla's historic **Cemeterio** ① by going northwest from the ferry piers on Avenida López Mateos. Then head southeast (by car or other vehicle) along Avenida Rueda Medina past the piers to reach the Mexican naval base. It's off-limits to tourists—and the Mexican navy doesn't like anyone photographing the crew, base, or ships—but you can see the flag ceremonies from the road at sunrise and sunset. Continue southeast out of town; 2½ km (1½ mi) farther down the road is **Laguna Makax** ②, on the right.

Punta Norte

TO ISLA
CONTOY

Playa Norte

❶

Guerrero Hidalgo

El Cemeterio

Bravo

Piers　**Main Square**

Mexican Naval Base

TO
PUNTA SAM

TO
PUERTO JUÁREZ

Av. Rueda Medina

■ **Playa Gaviota**

Caribbean Sea

**Hotel Villa Rolandi
Gourmet & Beach Club**

❷　■ **Puerto Isla
Mujeres Resort &
Yacht Club**

Laguna Makax

Corredor Panorámico (Panoramic Hwy.)

Salina Grande

**Dolphin
Discovery**

Bahía de Mujeres

Cristalmar

Tortugranja ❹ ❸

Playa Paraíso **Hacienda
Mundaca**

**Playa
Lancheros**

**Playa
Indios**

**La Casa
de los Sueños**

**Hotel & Beach Club
Garrafón
de Castilla**

**El Garrafón
National Park** ❺

**Santuario Maya a la
Diosa Ixchel**

❻

Punta Sur

KEY

🚢 Ferry

0　　　　　　1 mile

0　　　　　1 km

At the southeast end of the lagoon, a dirt road to the left leads to the remains of the **Hacienda Mundaca** ③. About a block southeast of the hacienda, turn right off the main road at the sign that says SAC BAJO to a smaller, unmarked side road, which loops back northwest. Approximately ½ km (¼ mi) farther on the left is the entrance to the **Tortugranja** ④.

Return to Avenida Rueda Medina and continue southeast past Playa Lancheros to **El Garrafón National Park** ⑤. Slightly more than ½ km (¼ mi) farther along the same road, on the windward side of the tip of Isla Mujeres, sit the remains of a small Maya ruin dedicated to Ixchel, the **Santuario Maya a la Diosa Ixchel** ⑥. Although little of the ruin is left, the ocean and bay views from here are well worth seeing. Follow the paved eastern perimeter road northwest back into town. Known as the Corredor Panoraac:mico (Panoramic Highway), this is a beautiful, scenic drive with a few pull-off areas along the way, perfect for a secluded picnic. Swimming is not recommended along this coast because of the strong currents and rocky shore.

Sights to See

❶ **El Cemeterio** (Cemetery). Isla's unnamed cemetery, with its century-old gravestones, is on Avenida López Mateos, the road that runs parallel to Playa Norte. Filled with carved angels and flowers, the most beautiful of the decorated tombs are those in memory of children. Hidden among them is the tomb of the notorious Fermín Mundaca. This 19th-century slave trader—who's often billed more glamorously as a pirate—carved his own skull-and-crossbones tombstone with the ominous epitaph: AS YOU ARE, I ONCE WAS; AS I AM, SO SHALL YOU BE. Mundaca's grave is empty, however; his remains lie in Mérida, where he died. The monument is not easy to find—ask a local to point out the unidentified marker. ✉ *Av. López Mateos.*

❺ **El Garrafón National Park.** This national marine park has undergone a major commercialization with the addition of a three-floor facility with restaurants, bathrooms, and gift shops. The fancy buildings and walkways don't change the sad fact that much of the coral reef here has died—a result of too many snorkelers. Because the reef is dead, the fish must be bribed with food; sometimes they don't bite and there isn't much for snorkelers to see except for some clownfish and the occasional starfish. In addition, actual snorkeling time is limited, as is the number of snorkelers allowed at one time. The park has added kayaks and ocean playground equipment, in an effort to keep visitors entertained, but it is no longer the bargain it used to be. Bring a book if you intend to spend the day. (The Garrafón Beach Club, next door, is a much less expensive alternative and the snorkeling is equal to if not better than that in the park.) Marine-park tickets are available at any kiosk in Cancún and in Playa del Carmen; you can also get tickets at the park entrance. ✉ *Carretera El Garrafón, 2½ km (1½ mi) southeast of Playa Lancheros,* ☎ *9/883–3233 in Cancún; 9/873–2801 in Playa del Carmen,* WEB *www.garrafon.com.* 🎟 *$19.95.* ⊙ *Daily 8:30–6:30.*

❸ **Hacienda Mundaca.** A dirt drive and stone archway mark the entrance to the remains of the mansion that 19th-century slave trader–cum–pirate Fermín Mundaca de Marechaja built. When the British navy began cracking down on slavers, Mundaca settled on the island. He fell in love with a local beauty nicknamed La Trigueña (The Brunette). In order to woo her, Mundaca built a sprawling estate with verdant tropical gardens. Apparently unimpressed, La Trigueña married a young islander—and Mundaca went slowly mad waiting for her to change her mind. He finally died in a brothel in Mérida.

There is little to see of the actual hacienda; it has simply vanished. Locals say the government tore it down, or merely neglected its upkeep. All that remains are a small crumbling guardhouse, a rusted cannon, an arch, and a well. The most interesting things to see here are the ruined stone archway and triangular pediment, which is carved with the following inscription: *HUERTA DE LA HACIENDA DE VISTA ALEGRE MDC-CCLXXVI* (Orchard of the Happy View Hacienda, 1876). The gardens are well kept, lush, and colorful with tropical flora. ⊠ *East off Av. Rueda Medina (take main road southeast from town to "S" curve at the end of Laguna Makax and turn left onto dirt road)*, ☎ *no phone.* 🎫 *$1.* ☉ *Daily dawn–dusk.*

② **Laguna Makax.** Pirates are said to have anchored their ships in this lagoon as they lay in wait for the hapless vessels plying the Spanish Main (the geographical area in which Spanish treasure ships trafficked). These days the lagoon houses a local shipyard and is a safe harbor for boats during hurricane season. The lagoon is off of Avenida Rueda Medina about 2½ km (1½ mi) south of town, across the street from a Mexican naval base and some *salinas* (salt marshes).

⑥ **Santuario Maya a la Diosa Ixchel** (Sanctuary of the Goddess Ixchel). The sad vestiges of a Maya temple once dedicated to Ixchel are about 1 km (½ mi) southeast of El Garrafón National Park, at Isla's tip. Though Hurricane Gilbert walloped the ruin and succeeded in blowing most of it away in 1988, part of it has since been restored. A lovely walkway around the remains continues down to a natural arch underneath the ruin. The view from here, of the open ocean on one side and the Bahía Mujeres (Bay of Women) on the other, is spectacular. Adjacent is a **lighthouse.** The official word is that climbing to the top is no longer allowed, but a small tip and your powers of persuasion may convince the keeper to let you up to see the incredible view. The ruin is at the point where the road turns northeast into the Corredor Panorámico.

④ **Tortugranja** (Marina Turtle Farm). Run by an outfit called Eco Caribe, this facility is dedicated to the study and preservation of sea turtles. During hatching season, from May through September, upwards of 6,000 turtles hatch along the coast of Quintana Roo. Some are brought to the farm to be raised until they are large enough to survive at sea. Visitors can view hatchlings and young turtles of various species in outdoor tanks, go on a tour led by one of the biologists, and watch feedings. A small but well-designed museum explains the various stages of turtle life and different parts of the coral reef. ⊠ *Take Av. Rueda Medina south of town; about a block southeast of Hacienda Mundaca, take the right fork (the smaller road that loops back north); the entrance is about ½ km (¼ mi) farther, on the left.* ☎ *9/877–0595.* 🎫 *$3.* ☉ *Daily 9–5.*

NEED A BREAK?	Walk northwest from Tortugranja, the turtle farm, along the lovely beach, past the Cristalmar Hotel to reach **Hacienda Gomar** ($; ☎ 9/877–0541), a good Mexican restaurant with a buffet lunch and marimba music. A number of crafts stalls here sell local goods, and you can rest under a beach palapa. If you'd rather not eat inside, you can try the excellent barbecued grouper, snapper, or barracuda at the restaurants along Playa Lancheros, which is south of Tortugranja and has handicraft and souvenir shops, a beach bar, and small palapas for shade.

BEACHES

The superb **Playa Norte,** known for its congenial atmosphere, is easy to find: simply head north on any of the north–south streets in town until you hit it. The turquoise sea is as calm as a lake, and you can wade out for 40 yards in waist-deep water. According to Isleños, Hurricane Gilbert's only good deed was to widen this and other leeward-side beaches by blowing sand over from Cancún. You can have a drink or snack at one of several palapa bars; Buho's is popular with locals and tourists, who gather to chat, eat fresh seafood, drink cold beer, and watch the sun set. Stands along the beach rent out snorkeling gear, Jet Skis, floats, and sailboards.

The beaches between Laguna Makax and El Garrafón National Park, including **Playa Paraíso,** are good spots for having lunch or for shopping at the small stands that sell local handicrafts, souvenirs, and T-shirts. Some pet sea turtles and harmless *tiburones gatos* (nurse sharks) are housed in sea pens at **Playa Lancheros.** You can have your picture taken with one of the sharks. (These sharks are tamer than the *tintorera,* or blue sharks, that live in the open seas. They have seven rows of teeth and weigh up to 1,100 lbs.) **Playa Indios,** southeast of Laguna Makax, has a lovely beach with soft white sand, palm trees, and easy access to the water. However, it's also the staging point for the large and noisy Aletta Bay marine park, where day-trippers throng for snorkeling, water sports, and other planned activities.

DINING

As in the rest of Mexico, locals eat their main meal during siesta hours, between 1 and 4, and then have a light dinner in the evening. Unless otherwise stated, restaurants are open daily for lunch and dinner.

Generally, restaurants on the island are informal, though shirts and shoes are required in most indoor dining rooms. Some, but not all, outdoor terraces and palapas request that swimsuits and feet be covered.

CATEGORY	COST*
$$$$	over $30
$$$	$21–$30
$$	$10–$20
$	under $10

per person for a main course at dinner

$$–$$$$ ✕ **Casa Rolandi.** Part of the Rolandi family of restaurants, this Casa
★ Rolandi features the Swiss–northern Italian menu that won high marks at its Cancún location. The *carpaccio di tonno alla Giorgio* (thin slices of fresh tuna with extra-virgin olive oil and lime juice) is particularly good, as are the pastas—including lasagna and shrimp-filled black ravioli—which are prepared daily by the chef. The restaurant extends from the Hotel Villa Rolandi lobby to an open-air deck that juts out over the beach, so the water views are spectacular, particularly at sunset. Stained-glass accents behind the bar and along the windows are a nice touch, as are the crisp green and white linens. The waitstaff is warm, friendly, and discreet. ⊠ *Hotel Villa Rolandi Gourmet & Beach Club, Fracc. Laguna Mar Makax, Sm 7,* ☎ *9/877–0100. AE, MC, V.*

$–$$$ ✕ **Lo Lo Lorena.** The innovative menu at this restaurant, one of the is-
★ land's best, changes daily according to what's available. However, because of their popularity, a few of the dishes created by Lolo, the flamboyant chef–owner, have become permanent fixtures, including "Lover's Salad," with conch and ginger, and a fantastic tarte Tatin. Lolo also puts on an entertaining show in the open kitchen. Wooden shut-

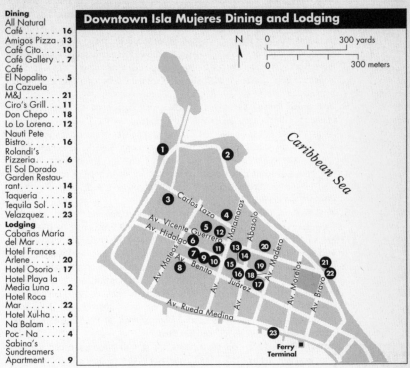

Downtown Isla Mujeres Dining and Lodging

ters, a wide porch, wicker furniture, and pastel colors give the old wooden house a lovely Caribbean flavor. ⊠ *Av. Guerrero 7,* ☎ *no phone. MC, V. No lunch.*

$–$$ ✗ **Ciro's Grill.** Fresh fish remains the focus at this old Isla favorite, which was renovated in 2000 and serves international, Caribbean, and Mexican cuisine. The look includes wrought-iron furniture and glass-topped tables, lots of leafy plants, a wide bar, and sliding doors that open onto the street. The menu has been expanded to include some excellent salads, desserts, and espresso. ⊠ *Av. Guerrero 14,* ☎ *9/877–0568. MC, V.*

$–$$ ✗ **Nauti Pete Bistro.** This sister restaurant of the adjacent All Natural Café opens in the evening to offer a menu of grilled meats and fish. The grilled tuna is especially fresh and done to perfection and served with wasabi on the side. During the season, Monday is U.S. football night, which attracts sports fans. ⊠ *Centro Hidalgo, Plaza Karlita,* ☎ *9/877–0720. MC, V. No lunch.*

$–$$ ✗ **Rolandi's Pizzeria.** Consistently good Italian food, such as lobster pizzas, calzones, and pastas, is the draw at this restaurant, part of a local chain. Grilled fresh fish and shrimp are highly recommended, as is the garlic bread—a puffed pita oozing butter and garlic. Red tables, yellow director's chairs, and green walls and window trim set an upbeat tone. In the heart of downtown, Rolandi is also a great place to stop for a drink and people-watch. ⊠ *Av. Hidalgo 110, between Avs. Francisco Madero and Abasolo,* ☎ *9/877–0430. AE, MC, V.*

$–$$ ✗ **Tequila Sol.** With its high ceilings, wood beams, and tile floors, this
★ restaurant is reminiscent of the old haciendas found throughout colonial Mexico. The excellent vegetarian and Mexican menu includes soy burgers and vegetarian fajitas, soups, and salads. Desserts, especially the chocolate cake and the flan, are very good, and the bar is well stocked. The staff is young, energetic, and eager to please. ⊠ *Avs. Hidalgo and Matamoros,* ☎ *no phone. MC, V.*

$ ✕ **All Natural Café.** This haven for vegetarians serves breakfast, lunch, and light dinners. The offerings include great combinations from the juice bar, such as the orange–carrot mix and the papaya–melon drink, along with fresh salads, soups, and veggie sandwiches served on baguettes. Owner Beatrix Ferasse is usually either here or next door, at Nauti Pete Bistro, which she also owns. ⊠ *Centro Hidalgo, Plaza Karlita,* ☎ *9/877–0720. MC, V.*

$ ✕ **Amigos Pizza.** The place for the pizza connoisseur, Amigos offers classic combinations with some interesting twists. Pick your favorite from 14 varieties, or opt for one of several fresh pasta dishes. There is also a simple but satisfying breakfast menu. The decor is very basic, with plastic tables and chairs and paper napkins, which helps to keep the prices among the lowest in town. The staff here is really charming. ⊠ *Av. Hidalgo between Avs. Matamoros and Abasolo,* ☎ *no phone. No credit cards.*

$ ✕ **Café Cito.** You can see sand and shell arrangements through the glass tops that cover the tables at this sunny café. Cito is one of the prettiest spots on the island, with a bright blue and white decor, photographs and simple watercolor paintings adorning the walls, and wind chimes dangling from the rafters. Breakfast choices include fresh waffles, fruit-filled crepes, and egg dishes, as well as great cappuccino and espresso. For dinner the chef whips up different daily specials. You can join the island's Harley Davidson Club here, or visit Sabrina next door for a tarot reading. ⊠ *Avs. Juárez and Matamoros,* ☎ *9/877–0438. Reservations not accepted. No credit cards.*

$ ✕ **Café Gallery.** Simple breakfasts are served amid sculptures, paintings, and murals by local Mexican artists in this beautiful colonial house. You can order freshly ground coffee (and cappuccino), yogurt with fruit, sweet pastries, and Mexican egg dishes such as *huevos rancheros* (eggs with salsa). Turtles live in the charming backyard, which has wall murals, flowering trees, and a small fountain; you can enjoy an early morning cup of caffeine while paying the pets a visit. ⊠ *Av. Juárez 26,* ☎ *no phone. Reservations not accepted. No credit cards. No lunch or dinner.*

$ ✕ **Café El Nopalito.** You can choose from homemade bread, granola, yogurt, and freshly squeezed tropical juices at this breakfast joint. There's no need to rush; you can sit for a while and chat. ⊠ *Av. Guerrero 17,* ☎ *no phone. Reservations not accepted. No credit cards. No dinner.*

$ ✕ **La Cazuela M&J.** At this oceanfront eatery next to the Roca Mar
★   Hotel, a fresh breeze and a spectacular Caribbean view are the backdrops for the terrific food. In addition to the freshly ground, dark Colombian coffee, breakfast offerings include fruit, crepes, and omelets. Or try "La Cazuela," the house specialty created by chef–owner Marco Fraga; it's somewhere between an omelet and a soufflé. Grilled chicken with homemade barbecue sauce and thick, juicy hamburgers are on the lunch menu. ⊠ *Calle Nicolas Bravo, Zona Maritima,* ☎ 𝔽𝔸𝕏 *9/877–0101. No credit cards. No dinner.*

$ ✕ **Don Chepo.** Mexican grill cuisine (tacos, fajitas, and steak) is offered in a lively atmosphere with good service. The Arracera is a fine cut of meat that's grilled and served with rice, salad, baked potato, warm tortillas, and beans. ⊠ *Avs. Hidalgo and Francisco Madero,* ☎ *no phone. MC, V.*

$ ✕ **El Sol Dorado Garden Restaurant.** Decorated with a sun motif, this funky restaurant serves great food morning, noon, and night. For breakfast consider coffee and hotcakes; for lunch, soup and salad; and for dinner, fresh-grilled fish or chicken. Out back is a delightful garden oasis. A pool table and a giant TV screen showing the latest blockbuster film are inside, so it's not surprising that this is a popular hangout for locals. ⊠ *Av. Abasolo between Avs. Guerrero and Hidalgo,* ☎ *no phone. MC, V.*

$ ✕ **Taquería.** For an inexpensive and delicious meal of Yucatán specialties including *sabutes* (fried corn tortillas smothered in chicken and salsa), *tortas* (sandwiches), *panuchos* (beans, chicken, and avocado over fried tortillas), and tamales, check out this small hole in the wall, open daily 10–10. The two sisters who do the cooking are a treat. They don't speak English but communicate with you using sign language and their version of Spanglish. ⊠ *Av. Juárez 1 block south of cemetery,* ☎ *no phone. No credit cards.*

$ ✕ **Velazquez.** This family-owned palapa-style restaurant on the beach
★ is open until dusk and serves the freshest seafood on the island. You haven't eaten Yucatecan until you've tried the regional specialty called *tikinchic*—fish marinated in a sour-orange sauce and achiote paste, wrapped in banana leaves, and cooked over an open flame. It's excellent here. Feasting on a fantastic fish meal while you sit outside and watch the boats go by is a true Isla experience. Watch your head going into the restaurant, as the ceiling is quite low. ⊠ *Av. Rueda Medina (2 blocks northwest of the ferry docks),* ☎ *no phone. No credit cards.*

LODGING

Isla has plenty of hotels. Generally the older, more modest places are in town, and the newer, more expensive resorts tend to front the beach around Punta Norte or on the peninsula near the lagoon. Most hotels have ceiling fans, and some have air-conditioning, but few have TVs or phones. Local travel agents can provide information about luxurious, self-contained time-share condominiums, which are another option.

CATEGORY	COST*
$$$$	over $125
$$$	$60–$125
$$	$25–$60
$	under $25

All prices are for a standard double room, excluding 12% tax.

$$$$ 🏨 **La Casa de los Sueños.** Tucked away at Isla's south end, this daz-
★ zling residence–turned– (no-smoking) bed-and-breakfast is honeymoon-perfect. A large interior courtyard leads to a sunken, open-air living room decorated in sunset colors. The living room extends into an open-air terrace that ends with a two-tier swimming pool on a cliff overlooking the ocean. There's also a glassed-in dining room, a well-stocked kitchen (simple salad lunches are available), and a staircase down to the private dock. All nine rooms are individually decorated, with artwork and wooden furniture, and have ocean-view balconies or terraces. The master bedroom has a whirlpool bath with a sunset view. Room rates include a full American breakfast; scuba lessons in the pool; and the use of bicycles, kayaks, and snorkeling equipment. Note that two Great Danes live in the house and like to mingle with the guests. ⊠ *Carretera El Garrafón, 77400,* ☎ *9/877–0651 or 800/ 551–2558,* 🖷 *9/877–0708. 9 rooms. Dining room, air-conditioning, fans, pool, beach, dock, snorkeling, boating, bicycles. AE, MC, V.*

$$$$ 🏨 **Hotel Villa Rolandi Gourmet & Beach Club.** This compact hotel is
★ as posh as any Cancún property. A private yacht delivers you to the island; a smart cocktail awaits in the hotel's elegant open-air lobby. All 20 suites are decorated in bright colors and have either two double beds or a single king-size bed. A small sitting area looks out on an oceanfront balcony with a heated whirlpool bath. In the bathroom, the showers have six adjustable heads, seats, and a window with water

views. Both the Casa Rolandi restaurant, which serves first-class cuisine, and the lovely garden pool overlook the Bahía Mujeres and lead down to an intimate beach. Room rates include Continental breakfast and lunch or dinner. Children under age 13 are discouraged from visiting. Smoking isn't allowed. ⊠ *Fracc. Laguna Mar Makax, Sm 7, Mz 75, 77400,* ☎ *9/877–0100,* 𝖥𝖠𝖷 *9/877–0700,* 𝖶𝖤𝖡 *www.rolandi.com. 20 suites. Restaurant, air-conditioning, pool, spa, gym, beach, dock, boating. AE, MC, V.*

$$$$ 🏨 **Puerto Isla Mujeres Resort & Yacht Club.** The best-kept secret on Isla overlooks the lagoon. Each of the five villas and 21 suites has a private terrace, living-room area, small refrigerator, private whirlpool bath, stereo, TV, and VCR; villas also include fully equipped kitchenettes. The grounds are spacious, with lots of room for wandering, and the pool contains a fountain and a swim-up bar off to the side. If you miss the ocean, a water taxi can shuttle you over to the property's deluxe beach club, which includes a pool and a restaurant. Families are warmly welcomed. The best part is that all this comfort comes at a relatively reasonable rate. ⊠ *Puerto de Abrigo, Laguna Makax, 77400,* ☎ *9/877–0093 or 800/960–4752,* 𝖥𝖠𝖷 *9/877–0093. 21 suites, 5 villas. Air-conditioning, refrigerators, kitchenettes (some), in-room VCRs, pool, hot tub, beach, dock, marina. AE, MC, V.*

$$$ 🏨 **Cristalmar.** On Isla's southeastern shore, with the lovely Laguna Makax behind and gorgeous Playa Paraíso in front, this resort offers serenity. Each of the spacious one- and two-bedroom suites is decorated with elegant wood furniture and tasteful artwork and has a fully equipped kitchenette, a living room, a dining room, and large double beds. All units face the water; balconies overlook the pool and palapa bar. You can snorkel, fish off the pier, swim, or just laze about. Scuba diving and deep-sea fishing expeditions can be arranged through the front desk. A taxi ride into town costs about $5. ⊠ *Fracc. Laguna Mar Makax 16, 77400,* ☎ *9/877–0398 or 888/571–3239,* 𝖥𝖠𝖷 *9/877–0401. 38 suites. Restaurant, bar, air-conditioning, kitchenettes, pool, beach, snorkeling, fishing. AE, MC, V.*

$$$ 🏨 **Hotel & Beach Club Garrafón de Castilla.** The snorkeling at the beach club of this small family-owned hotel next door to El Garrafón National Park is better than what you're likely to experience at the park. Plus, the beach here is bigger, with easy water access. The rooms have balconies that look out onto the water and double beds; some rooms have refrigerators. ⊠ *Carretera Punta Sur, Km 6, 77400,* ☎ *9/877–0107,* 𝖥𝖠𝖷 *9/877–0508. 14 rooms. Snack bar, air-conditioning, minibars, refrigerators (some), beach, dive shop, snorkeling, motorbikes. MC, V.*

$$$ 🏨 **Hotel Roca Mar.** The turquoise sea is the star here, as this is one of the
★   few downtown hotels overlooking the water. You can see, smell, and hear the ocean as soon as you step into your room. The private balcony, the wooden slats on the windows, and the simple furnishings—all are designed to be inconspicuous. Of course, the lovely courtyard, which is filled with plants, birds, and strategically placed benches, overlooks the ocean, too. ⊠ *Calle Nicolas Bravo, Zona Maritima, 77400,* ☎ 𝖥𝖠𝖷 *9/877–0101. 31 rooms. Restaurant, fans, pool, beach, snorkeling. AE, MC, V.*

$$$ 🏨 **Na Balam.** This intimate hotel on Playa Norte may satisfy all your
★   tropical-paradise fantasies. Each room in the main building has a palapa roof, eating area, large bathroom, and either a patio or balcony facing the ocean. Decorated with Mexican folk art or photographs, the rooms are simple yet elegant. Across the street are eight more spacious rooms, each with a balcony, sitting area, double bed, and palapa roof. There's also a swimming pool, garden, and meditation room. Breakfast at the restaurant is a delightful way to kick off the day. ⊠ *Calle Zazil-Ha 118, 77400,* ☎ *9/877–0279 or 800/552–4550,* 𝖥𝖠𝖷 *9/877–0446. 31 rooms. Restaurant, bar, air-conditioning, pool, beach. AE, MC, V.*

$$–$$$ 🏨 **Cabañas María del Mar.** This establishment offers an eclectic mix of rooms in three locations. Farthest from the beach (and therefore least expensive) are the simply furnished bungalows, with patios that face a garden and pool. Rooms in the Tower are decorated with Mexican folk art and have ocean-view balconies, refrigerators, and large beds. Across the street is the Castle; its rooms have hand-carved wood furnishings and Mexican tiles. Each Castle room also has a refrigerator and large terrace overlooking Playa Norte. Rates include a Continental breakfast. Buho's beach bar, with hammock seats, lively music, delicious fruit cocktails, and daily volleyball games, is a popular meeting spot for locals as well as visitors. ⊠ *Av. Carlos Lazos 1, 77400,* ☎ *9/ 877–0179 or 800/223–5695,* FAX *9/877–0213. 42 rooms, 14 bungalows. Restaurant, bar, air-conditioning, refrigerators (some), pool, motorbikes, travel services. MC, V.*

$$ 🏨 **Hotel Frances Arlene.** The budget prices belie the high standards of this small peach-color hotel. The Magaña family takes great care to maintain both the property and its ambience—signs everywhere remind you of the rules. Rooms center on a pleasant courtyard and are fitted with double beds, bamboo furniture, and refrigerators. Some have kitchenettes. The beach and downtown are a short stroll away. ⊠ *Av. Guerrero 7, 77400,* ☎ *9/877–0430,* FAX *9/877–0429. 11 rooms. Air-conditioning, fans, kitchenettes (some), refrigerators. AE, MC, V.*

$$ 🏨 **Hotel Playa la Media Luna** (Half-Moon Hotel). This charming and breezy three-story bed-and-breakfast is on Half-Moon Beach. All 18 guest rooms, done in soft pastel colors, have a refrigerator and a balcony or terrace that overlooks the ocean and pool. Thatch roofs and wooden walkways give the place a castaway feel. Breakfast is served in a sunny dining room. ⊠ *Sección Rotas, Punta Norte, 77400,* ☎ *9/ 877–0759 or 800/223–5695,* FAX *9/877–1124. 18 rooms. Dining room, refrigerators, pool, beach. AE, MC, V.*

$$ 🏨 **Playa Gaviota.** The real plus at this hilltop hotel sandwiched between
★ a garden and the ocean is the private beach with its barbecue, palapas, coconut trees, white sand, and gorgeous sunset views. Each of the 10 suites, decorated in basic blue and white, has a fully equipped kitchenette, two queen-size beds, a small eating area, and a large terrace facing the ocean. Three smaller, older (but still comfortable) cabins on the beach are for rent as well. The owners, a quiet Mexican family, live on site. ⊠ *Carretera El Garrafón, 77400,* ☎ FAX *9/877–0216. 10 suites, 3 cabins. Air-conditioning, fans, kitchenettes, beach. No credit cards.*

$$ 🏨 **Sabina's Sundreamers Apartments.** Each of the three studio apartments, built in 1999, offers a double bed, living and dining areas, a small but complete kitchenette, and a tiled bathroom. Mexican textiles and art provide the decoration. Weekly rentals are welcomed. Reservations can be made via the Internet. ⊠ *Avs. Juárez and Matamoros (beside Café Gallery), 77400,* ☎ *no phone,* WEB *www.sundreamers.com. 3 studios. Kitchenettes. No credit cards.*

$ 🏨 **Hotel Osorio.** This heart-of-town hotel is one of Isla's least expensive. Rooms are very clean and comfortable—with two double beds, a private bathroom, and ceiling fans—and open onto a courtyard. The family that owns and operates the hotel is quite cordial. ⊠ *Avs. Juárez and Francisco Madero, 77400,* ☎ *9/877–0056. 18 rooms. Fans. No credit cards.*

$ 🏨 **Hotel Xul-ha.** If you like being close to the action, this downtown hotel may be for you: It borders the latest nightlife hot spot, Plaza Isla Mujeres. Rooms are simple but very clean, with double beds, ceiling fans, and private bathrooms. The courtyard is clean, with some plants and benches. ⊠ *Av. Hidalgo 23, 77400,* ☎ *9/877–0075. 20 rooms. Fans. No credit cards.*

$ ⚉ **Poc-Na.** The island's co-ed youth hostel remains one of the best deals in El Pueblo. Poc-Na has hammocks and mattresses in a dormitory setting that sleeps eight. Proximity to Playa Norte is a bonus. ⊠ *Av. Matamoros 15, 77400,* ☎ *9/877–0090 or 9/877–0059. 8 beds. Dining room. No credit cards.*

NIGHTLIFE AND THE ARTS

The Arts

The island celebrates many religious holidays and festivals in El Pueblo's main square, usually with live entertainment on the outdoor stage. Carnival is in February and is spectacular fun. Other popular events include the springtime regattas and fishing tournaments. Founding Day, August 17, marks the island's official founding by the Mexican government. During the **Isla Mujeres International Music Festival,** held the second week in October, the island fills with music and dancers from around the world. The Isla Mujeres tourist office (☎ 9/877–0767) can provide further information about the festival.

Casa de la Cultura (⊠ Av. Guerrero, ☎ 9/877–0639), near the youth hostel, offers art, drama, yoga, and folkloric-dance classes year-round. It's open Monday through Saturday 9–1 and 4–8.

Nightlife

A pedestrian "Cancún corridor" set up along Plaza Isla Mujeres at Avenidas Hidalgo and Guerrero includes a number of bars and restaurants open until the wee hours. The liveliest (and loudest) are **Koko Nuts** (⊠ Plaza Isla Mujeres, Av. Hidalgo 85, ☎ 9/877–8787) and **Slices** (⊠ Plaza Isla Mujeres, Av. Hidalgo 82, ☎ no phone). **Chiles Loco** (⊠ Plaza Isla Mujeres, Av. Hidalgo 81, Local A-4, ☎ no phone), a holdover from quieter days, has a large bar and a huge television. **Buho's** (⊠ Cabañas María del Mar, Av. Carlos Lazo 1, ☎ 9/877–1479), the bar–restaurant at Cabañas María del Mar on Playa Norte, is a good choice for a relaxing drink in the evening.

OUTDOOR ACTIVITIES AND SPORTS

For water sports, beaches on the north and west sides are the calmest.

Fishing

If you're interested in participating in the **Red Cross Billfish Tournament,** held in the spring, contact Michael Creamer (☎ FAX 9/877–0443).

Captain Ricardo Gaitan (⊠ Av. Francisco Madero 16, ☎ FAX 9/877–0434) offers specialized fishing trips aboard his 29-ft vessel, starting at $600 a day. **Sea Hawk Divers** (⊠ Calle Carlos Lazo, Playa Norte, ☎ 9/877–0296) runs fishing trips—for barracuda, snapper, and smaller fish—that start at $150 for a half day. The **Sociedad Cooperativa Turistica** (☎ 9/877–0274) offers four hours of fishing close to shore for $100; eight hours farther out is $240.

Marinas

Puerto Isla Mujeres Resort & Yacht Club (⊠ Puerto de Abrigo, Laguna Makax, ☎ 9/877–0093), the only place along the coast to get your boat repaired, has a full-service marina for vessels up to 170 ft. Daily mooring costs are $1.50 for vessels up to 89 ft and $2 for vessels 90 ft and over. The marina offers a full-service fuel station, a 150-ton lift, customs assistance, 110/220 V single and three-phase hookups, crew services, 24-hour security, and laundry, interior cleaning, and boatyard services. If you need to sleep over on land, the luxury resort is steps away from the docks.

Marina y Club Yates (✉ Av. Rueda Medina, 2 blocks north of the ferry terminal, ☎ 9/877–0211) is a small marina off Isla's downtown, with room for 30 yachts up to 48 ft in length. It includes a full-service dock for gas and diesel fuel and a small store with a palapa-style restaurant.

Snorkeling and Scuba Diving

DIVE SITES

The famous coral reefs at **El Garrafón National Park** have suffered tremendously because of human negligence, boats dropping anchors (now outlawed), and the effects of Hurricane Gilbert. Most of the reef is dead, far from its past splendor, but there are still some sights to be seen farther out from shore. Some good snorkeling can be had near Playa Norte on the north end. In the waters near the lighthouse is a partially buried but still visible statue of the Virgin Mary.

Offshore, there's excellent diving and snorkeling at **Xlaches** (pronounced *ees*-lah-chayss) reef, due north on the way to Isla Contoy. One of Contoy's most alluring dives is the **Cave of the Sleeping Sharks,** east of the northern tip. The caves were discovered by an island fisherman known as Vulvula and extensively explored by Ramon Bravo, a local diver, cinematographer, and Mexico's foremost expert on sharks. *National Geographic* and the late Jacques Cousteau had also studied the curious phenomenon of the snoozing black tip, bull, and lemon sharks. The theories about why the sharks sleep here vary; they cover everything from the amount of salt in the water to the lack of carbon dioxide in the caves. It's a fascinating 150-ft dive for experienced divers only.

At the extreme southern end of the island on the leeward side lies **Los Manchones.** At 30 ft–40 ft deep and 3,300 ft off the southwestern coast, this coral reef is a good dive site. During the summer of 1994, an ecology group hoping to divert divers and snorkelers from El Garrafón commissioned the creation of a 1-ton, 9¾-ft bronze cross, which was sunk here. Named the Cruz de la Bahía (Cross of the Bay), it is a tribute to all the people who have died at sea. Together the cross and the reef make for a dramatic, fascinating dive. **Los Cuevones,** to the southwest near La Bandera, reaches a depth of 45 ft. On the windward side of the islet north of Mujeres is an unnamed site with two sunken galleons. Dive shops are able to direct you to this spot and others. Most area dive spots are also described in detail in *Dive Mexico,* a colorful magazine readily available in local shops.

DIVE SHOPS

Coral Scuba Dive Center (✉ Av. Matamoros 13-A, ☎ 9/877–0371) offers two tank dives for $39; shipwreck dives or photo dives for $59; and snorkel trips for $14. **Mundaca Divers** (✉ Av. Francisco Madero 10, ☎ 9/877–0607, FAX 9/877–0601) rents tanks starting at $45 along with snorkeling gear for $5 a day. **Sea Hawk Divers** (✉ Calle Carlos Lazo, Playa Norte, ☎ 9/877–0296) rents two tanks for $40; it also has dive gear and snorkeling equipment. Mundaca Divers and Sea Hawk Divers both offer dive trips to the reefs and the Cave of the Sleeping Sharks.

Water Parks

At **Aletta Bay** (✉ Playa Indios, ☎ 9/887–8619 or 9/887–8652), a marine park, you can swim with dolphins ($135) and sea lions ($85) in a fenced off area in the ocean (sessions last 30 minutes). Or you can choose a shorter session during which you can pet manta rays, nurse sharks, snakes and lizards, and birds. The $5 general admission lets you swim at the beach here and look at the animals. A buffet and snorkeling tours are extra. Reservations are recommended.

Dolphin Discovery (☎ 9/883–0777 or 9/883–0779) offers humans the chance to play with the delightful sea mammals in a small, supervised group in a pool. There are four swims daily, at 9, 11, 1, and 3. Each session consists of a 30-minute instruction video and 30 minutes in the water. The cost is $134 and includes the boat ride from Cancún and an all-you-can-eat Mexican buffet.

SHOPPING

Shopping on Isla Mujeres is a mixture of stores selling T-shirts, suntan lotion, beer, and groceries and those that sell Mexican crafts, including silver and jewelry, folk art, textiles, and clothes. Most shops accept credit cards. Hours are generally Monday through Saturday 10–1 and 4–7, although quite a few stores stay open through siesta hours (1–4).

Crafts

Many local artists display their works at the public **Artesanias Market** (⊠ Av. Matamoros and Calle Carlos Lazo, ☎ no phone), which offers plenty of bargains.

Casa del Arte Mexica (⊠ Av. Hidalgo 6, ☎ 9/877–0459) has a good selection of fine limestone carvings along with silver jewelry, batiks, wood carvings, leather goods, and hammocks.

Casa Isleno II (⊠ Av. Guerrero Nte. 3-A, ☎ FAX 9/877–0265) offers hand-painted T-shirts in beautiful colors as well as a collection of shells and crafts.

Grocery Stores

For fresh produce, the **Mercado Municipal** (municipal market; ⊠ Av. Guerrero Nte., near the post office, ☎ no phone), is your best bet. It's open daily until noon. **Panaderia La Reina** (⊠ Avs. Francisco Madero and Juárez, ☎ 9/877–0419), open Monday through Saturday starting at 7 AM, has terrific breads and baked sweets. **Super Betino** (⊠ Av. Morelos 3, in the plaza, ☎ 9/877–0127), Isla's main grocery store, is well stocked with all the basics.

Specialty Stores

Cosmic Cosas (⊠ Av. Matamoros 82, ☎ 9/877–0806) is the only English-language bookstore on the island. The friendly shop offers two-for-one book trades (no Harlequin romances), e-mail and computer services (scan your vacation photos and send them home via e-mail), and a message board. It also rents out a variety of board games—great for children on rainy days.

The **Martin Good Gallery** (⊠ Carretera El Garrafón, ☎ 9/877–0651) specializes in contemporary Mexican fine art paintings and sculpture. **Sueño Azul** (⊠ Av. Hidalgo Centro, ☎ no phone) has a selection of Venetian glass, imported from Italy.

Jewelry on Isla ranges from tasteful creations to junk. Bargains are to be found, but beware the street vendors—most of their wares, especially the amber, are fake. On the other hand, **Van Cleef & Arpels** (⊠ Avs. Juárez and Morelos, ☎ 9/877–0331) offers an incredible selection of rings, bracelets, necklaces, and earrings in 18K gold mounted with precious stones such as diamonds, Colombian emeralds, sapphires, rubies, and tanzanite. Many of the designs are innovative and the prices lower than in the United States. Across the street is the sister sterling-silver shop, which offers designer pieces at bargain prices.

SIDE TRIP TO ISLA CONTOY

Some 30 km (19 mi) north of Isla Mujeres, Isla Contoy (Isle of Birds) is a national wildlife park and bird sanctuary. Six and a half kilometers (4 miles) long and less than 1 km (about ½ mi) wide, the island is a protected area—the number of visitors is carefully regulated in order to safeguard the flora and fauna. Isla Contoy has become a favorite among birders, snorkelers, and nature lovers, who come to enjoy its unspoiled beauty.

Some 70 bird species—everything from gulls, pelicans, petrels, and cormorants to cranes, ducks, flamingos, herons, frigates, sea swallows, doves, quail, spoonbills, and hawks—fly this way in late fall, some of them to nest and breed. Although the number of species is diminishing—partly as a result of human traffic, partly from the effects of Hurricane Gilbert—Isla Contoy is still a rare treat for bird-watchers.

There is an abundance of sea life around the island as well. Snorkelers can see brilliant coral and fish. Manta rays, which average about 5 ft across, are visible in the shallow waters. Surrounding the island are large numbers of shrimp, mackerel, barracuda, flying fish, and trumpet fish. In December, lobsters pass through in great (though diminishing) numbers, on their southerly migration route.

Sand dunes inland on the east coast rise as high as 70 ft above sea level. Black rocks and coral reefs fringe the island's east coast, which drops off abruptly 15 ft into the sea. The west coast is fringed with sand, shrubs, and coconut palms. At the north and the south you find nothing but trees and small pools of water.

The island is officially open to visitors from 9 to 5:30; overnight visits are not allowed. Other than the birds and the dozen or so park rangers who make their home here, the island's only denizens are iguanas, lizards, turtles, hermit crabs, and boa constrictors.

Everyone landing on Isla Contoy must purchase a $5 authorization ticket; the price is usually included in the cost of a guided tour. Check with your tour operator to make sure that you will be landing on the island. Many of the larger companies simply cruise past. The best tours tend to be those that leave directly from Isla Mujeres; these operators know the area and therefore are more committed to protecting Isla Contoy (☞ Tours *in* Isla Mujeres A to Z, *below*). Tours that leave from Cancún can charge up to three times as much for the same tours that run from Isla Mujeres.

Once on shore, be sure to visit the outdoor museum, which has a small display of animals along with photographs of the island. Climb the nearby tower for a bird's-eye view. Remember to obey all the rules in order to protect the island: it's a privilege to be allowed here. Government officials may at some point stop all landings on Isla Contoy in order to protect its fragile environment.

ISLA MUJERES A TO Z

To research prices, get advice from other travelers, and book travel arrangements, visit www.fodors.com.

AIR TRAVEL

The island has a small landing strip for private planes and military aircraft, so the Cancún airport is really the only option.

Three companies can pick you up at the Cancún airport in an air-conditioned van and deliver you to the ferry docks at Puerto Juárez: AGI

Tours, Executive Services, and Best Day. Fares start at $12 one-way ($24 round-trip); reservations are recommended.

➤ AIRPORT TRANSFERS: **AGI Tours** (☎ 9/887–6967). **Best Day** (☎ 9/881–7037). **Executive Services** (☎ 9/887–0959).

BIKE AND MOPED TRAVEL

You can rent bicycles on Isla, but keep in mind that it's very hot here and the road conditions aren't great (especially those unexpected speed bumps). Don't ride at night; many roads don't have streetlights, so drivers have a hard time seeing you. David's Bikes for Rent and Rentadora El Zorro rent bicycles; rates start at about $3 an hour.

Rentals of mopeds, a favored mode of transportation on Isla, also are available. Most places charge $20–$25 a day, or $5–$10 per hour, depending on the moped make and year.

➤ RENTALS: **Ciro's Motorent** (⊠ Av. Guerrero Nte. 11, at Av. Matamoros, ☎ 9/877–0578). **David's Bikes for Rent** (⊠ Av. Rueda Medina 15, ☎ no phone). **P'pe's Rentadora** (⊠ Av. Hidalgo 19, ☎ 9/877–0019). **R Cárdenas** (⊠ Av. Guerrero 105, ☎ 9/877–0079). **Rentadora El Zorro** (⊠ Av. Guerrero 7, ☎ no phone).

BOAT AND FERRY TRAVEL

Speedboats and passenger ferries run between the main dock on Isla and Puerto Juárez on the mainland. Faster and more expensive shuttles to Isla's main dock leave from Cancún's Hotel Zone. Other departure points include Playa Linda, Plaza Caracol, and Playa Tortuga. Municipal ferries carry vehicles and passengers between Isla's dock and Cancún's Punta Sam.

The passenger ferries (*Sultana del Mar* and *Blanca Beatriz*) are the least expensive option. A one-way ticket is $1 and the trip takes at least 45 minutes. Delays and crowding aren't unknown, but often there is live music on board, which contributes to a partylike atmosphere.

The speedboats *Caribbean Lady* and *Miss Valentina* are air-conditioned cruisers with bar service. A one-way ticket costs $3.50 and the crossing takes about 20 minutes.

Passenger ferries and speedboats leave every half hour from Cancún and Isla Mujeres 5 AM–8 PM, and make a few more trips before 11 PM. Always check the times posted at the dock, as the schedule is subject to change depending on the season and weather conditions.

Shuttles from Cancún cost about $15 round-trip and take approximately 30 minutes, depending on weather conditions. Colon Tours has a shuttle that leaves Playa Linda at 9:30 AM and Isla at 4 PM. Asterix Water Taxi departs from Plaza Caracol at 9, 11, 1, and 3; return trips leave Isla at 10, noon, 2, and 5. A shuttle service called Isla leaves Playa Tortuga at 9, 11, 1, and 3:45 and Isla at 10, 12:30, 2:30, and 5. Call ahead, as schedules change according to demand.

You don't need a car to get around on Isla, but you can bring one over on a municipal ferry. The ride takes about 45 minutes and the fare is $1.25 per person and about $35 a vehicle. From Punta Sam, the ferry leaves at 8, 11, 2:45, 5:30, 6:45, and 8:15. Departures from Isla are at 6:30, 9:30, 12:45, 3, 4:15, 5:30, and 7:15. Again, check the schedule. Landlubbers' note: if you have a sensitive stomach, this ferry offers the smoothest ride when the sea is rough.

➤ BOAT AND FERRY INFORMATION: **Asterix Water Taxi** (☎ 9/886–4847). *Caribbean Lady* and *Miss Valentina* (☎ 9/877–0254 or 9/877–0253). **Colon Tours** (☎ 9/884–5333). **Ferry office** (☎ 9/877–0065). **Isla shuttle service** (☎ 9/883–3448).

BUS TRAVEL

Municipal buses run at 20- to 30-minute intervals daily between 6 AM and 10 PM, generally following the ferry schedule. The route goes from the Posada del Mar hotel on Avenida Rueda Medina out to Colonia Salinas on the windward side. Service is slow because the buses make frequent stops. Fares are about 25¢.

➤ BUS INFORMATION: **Municipal buses** (☎ 9/877–0529 or 9/877–4173).

CAR TRAVEL

There is little reason to bring a car to Isla Mujeres. Taxis are inexpensive and the island is small. In addition, driving can be slow going. Although the main road is paved, it has frequent speed bumps, and the remaining roads are cobblestone. The town core is a maze of one-way streets partially blocked off for pedestrians. At night, the lighting is poor.

E-MAIL

Café Internet and Cosmic Cosas offer Internet access starting at $3 an hour.

➤ SERVICES: **Café Internet** (⊠ Centro Hidalgo, Plaza Karlita, ☎ 9/877–0451). **Cosmic Cosas** (⊠ Av. Matamoros 82, ☎ 9/877–0806).

EMERGENCIES

The Centro de Salud offers 24-hour emergency service and accepts regular visits 8 AM–8 PM. Isla also has an excellent Red Cross Clinic, which is run by a British doctor. Payment is by donation (the clinic doesn't receive government funding and operates on a shoestring budget). Your hotel can also help you find an English-speaking doctor.

A couple of pharmacies are open late: Farmacia Isla Mujeres, 9 AM–10 PM Monday through Saturday and 9–3 on Sunday, and Farmacia La Gloria, daily 8 AM–11 PM, with 24-hour service available.

➤ CONTACTS: **Centro de Salud** (⊠ Av. Guerrero 5, on the plaza, ☎ 9/877–0217). **Police** (☎ 9/877–0082). **Port Captain** (☎ 9/877–0095). **Red Cross Clinic** (⊠ Colonia La Gloria, south side of the island, ☎ 9/877–0280).

➤ LATE-NIGHT PHARMACIES: **Farmacia La Gloria** (⊠ Carretera El Garrafón, Mz 67, Lote 5, ☎ 9/877–0885). **Farmacia Isla Mujeres** (⊠ Av. Juárez 8, ☎ 9/877–0178).

ENGLISH-LANGUAGE MEDIA

Islander is a small monthly publication (free) with maps, phone numbers, history about the island, and other useful information. You can pick up a copy at the tourist office or at your hotel.

LODGING

Some of the private homes on Isla are available as long- and short-term rentals. Mundaca Travel & Real Estate handles many of the rentals.

➤ LOCAL AGENTS: **Mundaca Travel & Real Estate** (☎ 9/877–0025 or 9/877–0026, FAX 9/877–0076).

MAIL AND SHIPPING

The post office is open weekdays 8–7 and Saturday 9–1. You can have mail for you sent to "Lista de Correos, Isla Mujeres, Quintana Roo, Mexico"; the post office will hold it for 10 days.

➤ POST OFFICE: ⊠ Av. Guerrero, ½ block from the market, ☎ 9/877–0085.

MONEY MATTERS

Bital, the only bank on the island, is open weekdays 8–7 and Saturday 9–noon. The ATM often runs out of cash, especially at the end of the day (be sure to save some money for the ferry ride back to the mainland). Sunday is especially bad, with long lines and little available cash.

Bital changes currency 10–noon Monday through Saturday. You can also exchange money at Cunex Money Exchange, which is open weekdays 8:30–7 and Saturday 9–2.

➤ BANKS: **Bital** (✉ Av. Rueda Medina 3, ☎ 9/877–0104 or 9/877–0005).
➤ EXCHANGE SERVICES: **Cunex Money Exchange** (✉ Av. Hidalgo at Av. Francisco Madero 12-A, ☎ 9/887–0421).

TAXIS

Taxis line up by the ferry dock around the clock. Fares run $1 to $2 from the ferry or downtown to the hotels on the north end, at Playa Norte. You can also hire a taxi for a private island tour at about $15 an hour.

➤ TAXI COMPANIES: **Sitio de Taxis** (Taxi Syndicates; ✉ Av. Rueda Medina, ☎ 9/877–0066).

TELEPHONES

Isla's area code is 987, but the 87 must be dialed even when making local calls. Keep in mind that some of the printed material on Isla doesn't reflect this and shows the old style: 987/1–23–45.

Isla has plenty of phones. Those that encourage you to "pick up and dial 0" charge ridiculously high prices. It's better to use the TELMEX phones that accept Ladatel phone cards. You can buy the cards from local stores in blocks equivalent to $3, $5, $10, and $20. Once connected, you can dial direct anywhere in the world.

To place a collect call, dial 090 for an international operator from any phone booth (no card is required) and ask for *para cobrar* (literally, "to pay").

TOURS

Cooperativa Lanchera runs four-hour trips to the submerged Virgin statue, the lighthouse, the turtles at Playa Lancheros, the coral reefs at Los Manchones, and El Garrafón, for about $25 including lunch. Cooperativa Isla Mujeres rents boats for a maximum of four hours and six people ($120). An island tour with lunch (minimum six people) costs $15 per person.

Sundreamers offers daytime and sunset tours around the island on its 52-ft catamaran. Prices start at $45 per person and include food and drinks.

Sociedad Cooperativa Isla Mujeres and La Isleña launch boats to Isla Contoy daily at 8:30 AM and return at 4 PM. Groups are a minimum of 6 and a maximum of 12 people, depending on the size of the boat. Captain Ricardo Gaitan, a local Isla Contoy expert, offers an excellent tour for large groups aboard his *Keen M.*

The trip to Isla Contoy takes about 45 minutes, depending on the weather and the boat; the cost is $30–$40. Sociedad Cooperativa Isla Mujeres tour operators provide a fruit breakfast on the boat and stop at Xlaches reef on the way to Isla Contoy for snorkeling (gear is included). The tour of Contoy's leeward side includes views from the water of Bird Beach and Puerto Viejo Lagoon. Along the way your crew trolls for the lunch it cooks on the beach—you may be in for anything from barracuda to snapper (beer and soda are also included). While the catch is being barbecued, you have time to explore the island, snorkel, check out the small museum and biological station, or just laze under a palapa.

➤ FEES AND SCHEDULES: **Captain Ricardo Gaitan** (✉ Av. Francisco Madero 16, ☎ FAX 9/877–0434). **Cooperativa Lanchera** (✉ waterfront near dock, ☎ no phone). **Cooperativa Isla Mujeres** (✉ Av. Rueda Medina, ☎ 9/877–0274). **La Isleña** (✉ corner of Avs. Morelos and Juárez, ½ block from pier, ☎ 9/877–0578). **Sociedad Cooperativa Isla Mujeres** (✉ pier, ☎ 9/877–0500). **Sundreamers** (✉ Mz 127, Lote 20, ☎ 9/894–3916, WEB www.sundreamers.com).

TRANSPORTATION AROUND ISLA MUJERES

Many places on Isla rent golf carts, a fun way to get around the island, especially when traveling with children. Ciro's Motorent has rates as low as $50 for 24 hours; it has more than 30 carts and accepts credit cards. El Sol and P'pe's Rentadora also rent carts. Most island motorists are quite accommodating, but be prepared to move to the side of the road to let vehicles pass you.

➤ RENTALS: **Ciro's Motorent** (✉ Av. Guerrero Nte. 11, at Av. Matamoros, ☎ 9/877–0578). **El Sol** (✉ Av. Francisco Madero 5, entrance off Av. Guerrero and Playa Norte, ☎ 9/877–0068). **P'pe's Rentadora** (✉ Av. Hidalgo 19, ☎ 9/877–0019).

TRAVEL AGENCIES

Mundaca Travel sells plane and bus tickets, offers Federal Express services, and arranges airport transfers, tours, and house rentals.

➤ LOCAL AGENCIES: **Mundaca Travel** (✉ Av. Hidalgo, ☎ 9/877–0025, 9/877–0026, or 888/501–4952, FAX 9/877–0076).

VISITOR INFORMATION

The Isla Mujeres tourist office is open weekdays 9–2 and 7–9 and has general information about Isla Contoy. Isla's official Web site, www.islamujeres.net, offers excellent information about the island.

➤ TOURIST INFORMATION: **Isla Mujeres tourist office** (✉ Plaza Isla Mujeres, Avs. Hidalgo and Matamoros, ☎ 9/877–0767).

3 COZUMEL

Mexico's largest cruise-ship port, Cozumel is at once commercial and laid back. Along with day-trippers who kick around town and then head to the beach, the island attracts those eager to explore its inland jungle and ruins. Sportfishing is a fine way to while away hours at sea, but the hands-down best things here lie under the waves; divers flock to Cozumel to wall-, drift-, and hole-dive along some of the world's most spectacular reefs.

Updated by
Shelagh
McNally

COZUMEL STRIKES A BALANCE between Cancún and Isla Mujeres. It has the former's sophistication combined with Isla's relaxed island atmosphere. Fast-food outlets, cable television, and English usage are widespread on Cozumel, aimed at pleasing North American tastes. While development continues, even creeping into the farthest corners, Cozumel is managing to leave some of its environment unspoiled and to protect what wildlife is left on the island. The recipe here for a good vacation includes white-sand beaches, excellent snorkeling and scuba diving, sailing and water sports, luxury resorts and modest hotels, fine dining and family eateries, great shops, and even a scattering of Maya ruins. It attracts a variety of people, but none more so than underwater enthusiasts who come for one of the world's best coral reefs. Despite the inevitable effects of docking cruise ships—shops and restaurants along the main drag practically drag customers in—the island's earthy charm and tranquillity are intact.

A 490-square-km (189-square-mi) island 19 km (12 mi) east of the Yucatán peninsula, Cozumel is mostly flat, with an interior covered by parched scrub, dense jungle, and marshy lagoons. White, sandy beaches with calm waters line the island's leeward (western) side, which is fringed by a spectacular reef system, while the windward (eastern) side, facing the Caribbean Sea, has powerful surf and rocky strands. A lot of Cozumel has been developed, but a good deal of the land and the shores has been set aside as national park; a few Maya ruins provide what limited sightseeing there is aside from the island's glorious natural attractions. San Miguel is the only town.

Cozumel's name comes from the Maya Ah-Cuzamil-Peten ("land of the swallows"). For the Maya, this was a sacred island as well as a key center of trade and navigation. Pilgrims from all over Mesoamerica came to honor Ixchel, the goddess of fertility, childbirth, the moon, and rainbows. One of the oldest goddesses, considered to be mother of all other gods, Ixchel was often depicted with swallows at her feet. Every Maya woman was required to visit her site at least once in a lifetime; the women made the perilous journey from the mainland to the island by canoe. Cozumel's main exports were salt and honey, both considered more valuable than gold at the time.

In 1518 Spanish explorer Juan de Grijalva arrived on Cozumel in search of slaves. His tales of treasures inspired Hernán Cortés, Mexico's most famous Spanish explorer, to visit the island the following year. There he met Geronimo de Aguilar and Gonzales Guerrera, Spanish men who had been shipwrecked on Cozumel for a number of years, living as slaves until they were accepted by the Maya. When Cortés and his company landed, Aguilar apparently jumped into the ocean and swam to the ship, while Guerrera refused to leave his Maya wife and children. Aguilar joined forces with Cortés, becoming a deadly foe to the local people; he helped set up a military base on Cozumel and used his knowledge of the Maya to defeat them. On the other hand, Guerrera died defending his adopted community and is considered a hero by the Maya. By 1570 most of the Maya islanders had been massacred or killed by disease, and by 1600 the island was abandoned.

During the 17th and 18th centuries pirates discovered that Cozumel made a perfect hideout. The notorious Jean Laffite and Henry Morgan favored the island's safe harbors and hid their treasures in the catacombs and tunnels dug by the Maya. These bandits laid siege to numerous cargo ships, many of which still lie in the briny depths close to the island. By 1843, Cozumel had once again been abandoned. Five years later, 20 families fleeing Mexico's brutal War of the Castes resettled the island. Many of their descendants still live on Cozumel.

Around the turn of the 20th century the island began to capitalize on its abundant supply of *zapote* (sapodilla) trees, which produce chicle, prized by the chewing-gum industry (think Chiclets). Shipping routes began to include Cozumel, whose deep harbors made it a perfect stop for large vessels. Forays into the jungle in search of chicle led to the discovery of ruins, and soon archaeologists began visiting the island. Some of the ruins still stand, but Cozumel's importance as a seaport and a chicle-producing region diminished with the arrival of the airplane and the invention of synthetic chewing gum.

For decades Cozumel was just another backwater where locals fished, hunted alligators and iguanas, and worked on coconut plantations to produce *copra*, the dried kernels from which coconut oil is extracted. Cozumeleños subsisted largely on the fruits of the sea, which remain staples of the economy. During World War II, the U.S. army built an airstrip and maintained a submarine base on the island. Unfortunately it also dismantled some of the larger Maya ruins, not realizing what was being destroyed. In the 1950s Cozumel eked out an existence as a health resort for wealthy Yucatecans. It was the famous underwater explorer Jacques Cousteau who helped make Cozumel the vacation destination that it is today. After his first visit, in 1961, word of the island's incredible reefs spread among scuba divers and viewers of Cousteau's popular television show. It's now one of the most popular dive locations in the world.

Pleasures and Pastimes

Beaches

Inviting, sandy beaches line the leeward side of the island. The most popular, Playa San Francisco, a 5-km (3-mi) expanse, has restaurants, a bar, and water-sports equipment for rent. Cozumel's windward side is pounded by the rough surf of the Caribbean. Its rocky coves and narrow beaches are fine for sun worshiping but are usually too rough for swimming.

Dining

Restaurants here serve a wide variety of cuisines ranging from Yucatecan and Mexican specialties to Italian, Cajun, French, and Mediterranean, and just about everything in between. The emphasis is on seafood: lobster, shrimp, king crab, grouper, and red snapper are among the highlights.

Fishing

The waters off Cozumel swarm with more than 230 species of fish, which makes this one of the world's best places for deep-sea fishing. During billfish migration season, from late April through June, swordfish, blue marlin, white marlin, and sailfish are plentiful and world-record catches aren't uncommon.

Deep-sea fishing for tuna, barracuda, wahoo, and kingfish is good year-round. Fishing enthusiasts also can opt for bottom fishing for grouper, yellowtail, and snapper on the shallow sand flats at the north end of the island. There you can drop lines for bonefish, tarpon, snook, grouper, and small sharks, too.

Lodging

Cozumel's hotels are located in three areas. Lavish resorts line the north and south beaches, inexpensive hotels are closer to town, and the true budget places are in San Miguel. There's no shortage of luxury accommodations, but the number of economical hotels has been dwindling.

Scuba Diving and Snorkeling

Because of the diversity of coral formations and the dramatic under-water peaks and valleys, divers consider Cozumel's Palancar Reef to be one of the top five in the world. With more than 30 charted reefs whose depths average 50–80 ft and water temperatures around 75°F–80°F during peak diving season (June through August, when hotel rates are coincidentally at their lowest), Cozumel is far and away *the* place to dive in Mexico. Sixty thousand divers come here each year to explore the underwater coral formations, caves, sponges, sea fans, and tropical fish.

Snorkeling falls just behind diving among the island's popular sports. There's good snorkeling in the morning off the piers at the Presidente Inter-Continental and La Ceiba hotels—because they feed the fish. The shallow reefs in Chankanaab Bay, Playa San Francisco, and the north-ern beach near Plaza Las Glorias also offer good views of brilliantly colored fingerlings, parrot fish, sergeant majors, angelfish, and squir-rel fish, along with elk coral, conch, sea fans, and sand dollars.

Shopping

Shopping is an even bigger industry for Cozumel than diving, thanks to the number of passengers who pour off cruise ships. (Cozumel is Mexico's largest cruise-ship port.) Thousands of tourists disembark at the three cruise-ship docks and swarm San Miguel every Wednesday. In response, Cozumel is undergoing a shopping-mall building boom with three more malls under way offering a huge range of stores. The prices are relatively high compared to those in, say, Mérida, but the variety of folk art ranges from downright shoddy curios to some fine silver jewelry, pottery, painted balsa-wood animals, blown glass, hand-crafted textiles, and *huipiles* (embroidered cotton dresses).

EXPLORING COZUMEL

Cozumel is 53 km (33 mi) long and 15 km (9 mi) wide and, aside from the road leading to Punta Molas, has excellent paved roads. Beware of flash flooding during the rainy season; the dirt roads can become difficult to navigate in minutes.

Aside from the 15% of the island that has been developed, Cozumel is made up of expanses of sandy or rocky beaches, quiet little coves, palm groves, lagoons and swamps, scrubby jungle, and a few low hills (the maximum elevation is 45 ft). Brilliantly feathered tropical birds, lizards, armadillos, coati, deer, and small foxes populate the undergrowth and mangroves. Several minor Maya ruins dot the eastern coast of the island. One of them, El Caracol, served as an ancient lighthouse. There are also a couple of minuscule ruins—El Mirador (The Balcony) and the El Trono (The Throne)—identified by roadside markers.

The town of San Miguel was given its name a century ago when work-ers digging near the current airport found a statue of St. Michael on September 29, which happens to be the saint's holy day. Thought to have been a gift to the locals from Juan de Grijalva, the first Spanish explorer to the island in 1518, the statue is now displayed in the church of San Miguel.

Cozumel's main road is Avenida Rafael E. Melgar, which runs paral-lel to the waterfront, down the western shore, and eventually changes to Carretera Chankanaab (also known as Carretera Sur). When it reaches the most southern point on the island it takes a turn toward the northeast and from that point on is referred to simply as the coastal road. Alongside Avenida Rafael E. Melgar in San Miguel is the 14-km (9-mi) walkway called the *malecón*, which is congested with shops and restaurants and can be impossible to navigate when the cruise ships are in. Avenida Benito Juárez is the other major road. It stretches east from the pier for 16 km (10 mi), dividing both the town and the island into north and south.

San Miguel is laid out in a typical Mexican grid fashion. *Avenidas* are roads that run north or south; they're numbered in increments of five (5, 10, 15, etc.). A road that starts out as an "avenida norte" turns into an "avenida sur" when it crosses Benito Juárez. *Calles* are streets that run east–west; those north of Benito Juárez have even numbers (Calle 2 Nte., Calle 4 Nte., etc.) while those south have odd numbers (Calle 1 Sur, Calle 3 Sur, etc.).

Plaza Central is the main square. Most often simply called *la plaza,* it's directly across from the docks—hard to miss. The square is the heart of San Miguel, where everyone congregates in the evening, especially on Sunday, when there's a free concert at 8. Shops and restaurants abound here. Heading inland (east) takes you away from the touristy zone and toward the residential sections.

The heaviest commercial district is concentrated between Calle 10 Norte and Calle 11 Sur as far up as Avenida Pedro Joaquin Coldwell. The airport road has little development until you reach the North Hotel Zone. South of town, development continues uninterrupted to a second cluster of hotels and shops that is adjacent to two international cruise-ship terminals; many resorts are in this area.

Numbers in the text correspond to numbers in the margin and on the Cozumel map.

A Good Tour

Taxis have become so costly on the island that it's worth renting some kind of vehicle to explore Cozumel. Be forewarned that most car-rental companies have a policy that voids your insurance when you leave the southern roads and journey north to Punta Molas. This dirt road is not maintained, so proceed with great caution (if at all), especially after rain.

Head south from **San Miguel** ① and in about 15 minutes you come to **Parque Chankanaab** ②. Continue past the park to reach the beaches: Playa Corona, Playa San Clemente, Playa San Francisco, and Playa Sol. If you stay on this road you eventually reach, on your left, the turnoff for the ruins of **El Cedral** ③. Look for the red arch alongside the road announcing the turnoff.

Back on the main coast road, continue south until you reach the turnoff for Playa del Palancar, where the famous reef lies offshore. Continue to the point where the road swings north—the most southern point of the island—and you come to the **Parque Punta Sur** ④ entrance. The park encompasses Laguna Colombia and Laguna Chunchacaab as well as an ancient Maya lighthouse, El Caracol, and the modern lighthouse, Faro de Celarain. You have to leave your car at the gate and use either the bicycles or public bus provided by the park.

At Punta Sur the coast road turns north. Not far from the Parque Punta Sur entrance are the minuscule ruins of **El Mirador** and **El Trono.** This road also passes one beach after another: Playa Paraíso, Punta Chiqueros, Playa de San Martín, and Punta Morena. At Punta Este, the coast road intersects with Avenida Benito Juárez, which crosses the is-

Cozumel

TO PUERTO MORELOS

Punta Molas

Punta Molas Faro ⑥

⑤ **Castillo Real**

Playa Bonita

Sea

Punta Norte

Isla de Pasión

⑦ **San Gervasio**

Playa Santa Pilar

Caribbean *Sea*

Playa San Juan

✈ **Airport**

TO PLAYA DEL CARMEN

Av. Benito Juárez

Playa Los Cocos

① **San Miguel**
La plaza

Av. Rafael Melgar

Punta Este

Punta Morena

Caribbean

■ **La Ceiba**

② **Parque Chankanaab**

Playa de San Martín

Playa Corona

Playa San Clemente

Punta Chiqueros

Playa San Francisco

El Trono

El Mirador

Playa Sol

③ **El Cedral**

Nachi Cocom

Playa Paraíso

Punta Francesca

Parque Punta Sur
④

Playa del Palancar

R E E F S

El Caracol

Laguna Colombia

Laguna Chunchacaab

Punta Celerain Faro

KEY
🚢 Ferry
🚢 Cruise Ship

0 ——————— 6 miles
0 ——————— 9 km

land to the opposite coast. You can take this road back into San Miguel or continue toward Punta Molas.

The road to Punta Molas is quite rough and only half of it is accessible by car—you must walk the rest of the way. The beaches on this part of the island are marvelously deserted: Ixpal Barco, Los Cocos, Hanan Reef, Ixlapak, and then Playa Bonita, with the small **Castillo Real** ⑤, another Maya site. Farther north are a number of other minor ruins, including a lighthouse, **Punta Molas Faro** ⑥, at the island's northern tip.

If you take Avenida Benito Juárez from Punta Este, you come to the turnoff (just past the army airfield) for the ruins of **San Gervasio** ⑦. Turn right and follow this well-maintained road for 7 km (4½ mi) to get to the ruins. To return to San Miguel, return to Avenida Benito Juárez and continue driving west.

Sights to See

 ⑤   **Castillo Real** (Royal Castle). A Maya site on the coast near the northern tip of the island, the *castillo* (castle) includes a lookout tower, the base of a pyramid, and a temple with two chambers capped by a false arch. The waters here harbor several shipwrecks, and it's a fine spot for snorkeling, because there are few visitors to disturb the fish. Note, however, that the surf can get quite strong, so pick a time when the sea is tranquil.

⑤   **El Cedral.** Once the hub of Maya life on Cozumel, this was the first site found by Spanish explorers in 1518. It was also the island's first official city, founded in 1847. These days it's a quaint farming community with small houses and gardens that show little evidence of its past glory. Conquistadors tore down much of the temple, and the U.S. Army Corps of Engineers destroyed the rest during World War II to make way for the island's first airport. All that remains of the ruins is a small structure with an arch; be sure to look inside to see the faint traces of paint and stucco. Alongside is a green-and-white cinder-block church, decorated inside with crosses shrouded in embroidered lace where, reportedly, the first Mass in Mexico was celebrated. Every May there's a fair here, with dancing, music, bullfights, and a cattle show, celebrating the area's agricultural roots. Hidden in the surrounding jungle are other small ruins, but you need a guide to find them. Check with the locals near the ruins who offer excellent tours on horseback. ⊠ *Turn at Km 17.5 off Carretera Sur or Av. Rafael E. Melgar, then drive 3 km (2 mi) inland to the site,* ☎ *no phone.* ⊠ *Free.* ☉ *Daily dawn–dusk.*

Isla de Pasión (Passion Island). In Abrigo Bay, east of Punta Norte, this tiny island is part of a state reserve. It's quite difficult to get to, but its beaches are extremely secluded. Fishing is permitted, but there are no facilities on the island, and since so few people come here, there are no scheduled tours. You have to find a local boat owner and bargain heavily if you want to visit.

☼   **Museo de la Isla de Cozumel** (Museum of the Island of Cozumel). The museum is housed on two floors of what was once the island's first luxury hotel. The first floor is dedicated to natural history, with exhibits about the origins of the island, its endangered species, its topography, and an explanation of coral-reef ecology. Upstairs, the history of Cozumel is illustrated with Maya artifacts, cannons and swords of the conquistadors, and maritime instruments. Another upstairs room features a pictorial display of Cozumel during the 20th century. Guided tours are available. ⊠ *Av. Rafael E. Melgar, between Calles 4 and 6 Nte.,* ☎ *9/872–1475.* ⊠ *$3.* ☉ *Daily 10–6.*

NEED A
BREAK?

On the terrace off the second floor of the Museo de la Isla de Cozumel, the **Restaurante del Museo** (☎ 9/872–0838) serves breakfast from 8 until 2. The typical Mexican fare is enhanced by a great waterfront view.

❷ Parque Chankanaab (Chankanaab Park). A 15-minute drive south of San Miguel, Chankanaab (the name means "small sea") is a lovely salt-water lagoon that the government has made into a national park with an archaeological park, botanical garden, dolphin aquarium, and wildlife sanctuary.

Scattered throughout the archaeological park are 60 reproductions of Olmec, Toltec, Aztec, and Maya stone carvings from well-known sites in Mexico. Guides lead interesting, informative tours, explaining the history of the most significant pieces. Also on site is a good example of a typical Maya house.

The botanical garden has more than 450 species of plants from the region. Enjoy a cool walk through pathways leading to the lagoon, home to 60-odd species of marine life, including fish, coral, turtles, and various crustaceans. Unfortunately, swimming is no longer allowed in the lagoon; the area's ecosystem has become quite fragile since the collapse of the underwater tunnels linking the lagoon to the sea.

But you can swim, scuba dive, or snorkel at the beach. There's plenty to see under the sea: a sunken ship, crusty old cannons and anchors, a Maya Chacmool (the revered rain god), and a beautiful sculpture of the Virgin del Mar (Virgin of the Sea). In addition, hordes of brilliant fish swim around the coral reef. To maintain the health of the reef ecosystem, park rules forbid the use of suntan lotion (the chemicals come off your body in the water and kill the fish and coral), the feeding of fish, and touching the coral reef.

Close to the beach are four dive shops, two restaurants, three gift shops, a snack stand, and a dressing room with lockers and showers. At the park's dolphin aquarium, visitors can swim with the fascinating marine mammals or watch them do their workouts. A small but worthwhile museum near the beach has photographs illustrating the history of the park, coral and shell exhibits, and some sculptures. There's also a sea-lion park, where children can enjoy watching the sea lions perform at one of their daily shows. Come early, as the park fills up fast, particularly on the days when cruise ships dock. ⌂ *Carretera Sur, Km 9,* ☎ *no phone.* ☒ *$7, free after 5 PM.* ☉ *Daily 7–6.*

❹ Parque Punta Sur. The 247-acre national preserve, at Cozumel's southernmost tip, is home to numerous birds and animals, including crocodiles, flamingos, foxes, egrets, and herons. Cars aren't allowed on the premises, so visitors must use park transportation: bicycles or public buses. From observation towers you can spot crocodiles and birds in **Laguna Colombia** or **Laguna Chunchacaab.** Or visit the ancient Maya lighthouse, **El Caracol,** constructed to whistle when the wind blows in a certain direction. At the southernmost point of the park (and the island) is the **Faro de Celarain** (Celarain Lighthouse), now a navigational museum outlining the history of seamanship in the area. The beaches here are deserted and wide, and there's great snorkeling offshore. Snorkeling equipment is available for rent, as are kayaks. The park also has an excellent restaurant, information center, small souvenir shop, and rest rooms. If you don't rent a vehicle to get here, a round-trip taxi ride from San Miguel costs close to $60. ⌂ *Southernmost point in Punta Sur Park and the coastal road,* ☎ *no phone.* ☒ *$10, free after 3 PM.* ☉ *Daily 7–4.*

⑥ Punta Molas Faro (Molas Point Lighthouse). At the northernmost point of Cozumel, the lighthouse is an excellent spot for sunbathing, birding, and camping. The jagged shoreline and the open sea offer magnificent views, making it well worth the time-consuming and somewhat difficult trip. Be prepared to walk some of the way. Area car-rental companies actively discourage visitors from driving here. Access is easier by boat, or you may prefer to take a guided tour.

⑦ San Gervasio. Standing in a lovely forest, these remarkable ruins make up the largest existing Maya and Toltec site on Cozumel. San Gervasio was once the island's capital and ceremonial center, dedicated to the fertility goddess Ixchel. The Classic- and Postclassic-style buildings were continuously occupied from AD 300 to AD 1500. Typical architectural features include limestone plazas and arches atop stepped platforms, as well as stelae and bas-reliefs. Be sure to see the "hands" temple, which has red hand imprints all over its altar. Plaques clearly identify each of the ruins in Maya, Spanish, and English. At the entrance there's a snack bar and some gift shops. If you want a rugged hike, take the 15-km (9-mi) dirt road that travels north to the coast and Castillo Real. ✉ *From San Miguel, take Av. Benito Juárez east to San Gervasio access road; turn left and follow road for 7 km (4½ mi).* ✇ *Access to road $1; ruins $3.50.* ☉ *Nov.–Sept., daily 8–5.*

❶ San Miguel. Although highly commercialized and packed with tourists, Cozumel's only town has retained some of the flavor of a Mexican village. Stroll along the malecón and take in the ocean breeze. The main square is where townspeople and visitors hang out, particularly on Sunday night, when musical groups join the assortment of food and souvenir vendors.

BEACHES

Cozumel's beaches vary from long, treeless, sandy stretches to isolated coves and rocky shores. Most development is on the leeward (western) side, where the coast is relatively sheltered by the proximity of the mainland 19 km (12 mi) to the west. Beach-club mania has gripped this side of the island, and a number of places have opened up; some even charge admission, even though beaches in Mexico are public property. The clubs offer the usual tourist fare: souvenir shops under a *palapa* (thatch roof), restaurants, kayaks, and cold beer. Reaching beaches on the windward (eastern) side is more difficult and requires transportation, but you'll be rewarded if you're looking for solitude.

Leeward Beaches

The best sand beaches lie along 5 km (3 mi) of the southern half of Cozumel's west side.

Playa Santa Pilar, which runs along the northern hotel strip and ends at Punta Norte, has a rocky shore with little sand. There's little privacy here, as the beach is surrounded with hotels that have been carving it up and blocking off sections for their guests—technically an illegal practice, as all beaches in Mexico are public property. **Playa San Juan,** south of Playa Santa Pilar, has a rocky shore with no easy access to the ocean. It's usually crowded with guests from the nearby hotels.

Next to Parque Chankanaab is **Playa Corona,** which shares access to the Yucab reef and offers the same brilliant marine fauna and wonderful flora as the park. Snorkeling equipment is available for rent, and the restaurant here serves conch and shrimp ceviche. The crowds that visit Chankanaab haven't yet discovered this tranquil neighbor. The next beach south of Playa Corona, **Playa San Clemente** has wide, sandy beaches and shallow waters, and it has managed to retain its laid-back feel.

South of Parque Chankanaab and Playa San Clemente is **Playa San Francisco,** an inviting 5-km (3-mi) stretch of sandy beach that's considered one of the longest and finest on Cozumel. It encompasses the beaches known as Playa Maya and Santa Rosa and usually is packed with cruise-ship passengers during high season. On Sunday locals flock here to eat fresh fish and hear live music. Its amenities include two outdoor restaurants, a bar, dressing rooms, gift shops, volleyball nets, beach chairs, and a variety of water-sports equipment for rent. Divers also use this beach as their jumping-off point for the San Francisco reef and the Santa Rosa wall. However, the abundance of turtle grass in the water makes this a less-than-ideal spot for swimming.

Playa Sol is in danger of becoming a serious tourist trap. The entrance prices are high and you must first pass through a maze of aggressive souvenir shops to get to the beach. This aside, the beach is beautiful and excellent for swimming or snorkeling. With lots of planned activities and loud music, this beach isn't exactly tranquil, but it's a great place to go for a party. Come early to avoid most of the crowds. The beach club **Mr. Sancho's** (☎ 9/872–1986) shares the same sands as Playa Sol and has better food than its neighbor, and it doesn't charge admission.

Nachi-Cocom (☎ 9/872–0844), south of Playa Sol, has a wide, uncluttered, and shallow beach, a freshwater pool, lounge chairs, a dive shop, a restaurant, and a beach bar. It gets around charging an admission by having a food-or-beer minimum of $10 per adult and $5 per child.

South of all the resorts lies the mostly ignored (and therefore serene) Punta Francesca, on the outskirts of **Playa del Palancar.** Offshore is the famous Palancar Reef. There's also a water-sports center and a bar–café. Playa del Palancar has kept its prices down in order to keep drawing divers, who are generally more bargain-minded than other visitors. The beach is more mellow than many of the other beaches.

Windward Beaches
The east coast of Cozumel presents a splendid succession of mostly deserted rocky coves and narrow, powdery beaches poised dramatically against the turquoise Caribbean. Swimming can be treacherous here if you go too far out—in some parts there's a deadly undertow that can sweep you out to sea in minutes. But these beaches are perfect for solitary sunbathing.

Note that Playa Bonita can refer to two different areas, depending on whom you talk to. This is what the locals call the beach at Punta Chiqueros, where there's a restaurant that also goes by the name Playa Bonita. However, officially the name refers to the beach near the Castillo Real ruins.

Playa Paraíso (also known as Playa Bosh) begins at El Mirador and is the southernmost of Cozumel's windward beaches. This windswept place is good for beachcombing or sunbathing; you can cool off with a cold beer at the restaurant–bar.

North of Playa Paraíso, **Punta Chiqueros** is a moon-shape cove sheltered from the sea by an offshore reef. Part of a longer stretch of beach that most locals, confusingly, call Playa Bonita, it has fine sand, clear water, and moderate waves. You can swim and camp here, watch the sun set and the moon rise, and eat fresh fish at a restaurant, also called Playa Bonita.

Not quite 5 km (3 mi) north of Punta Chiqueros begins a long stretch of beach where the Chen Río Reef is located. Turtles come to lay their eggs on the section known as **Playa de San Martín** (some people call it Chen Río, after the reef). During full moons in May and June, the beach is blocked by soldiers or ecologists whose goal is to prevent the poaching of the turtle eggs. Directly in front of the Chen Río Reef is a small bay with clear waters and a surf that isn't too strong, thanks to a rock formation protecting the bay. This is a particularly good spot for camping and swimming. You can dine here on excellent fresh fish, shrimp, and lobster dishes, at a restaurant called Chen Río. Nearly 1 km (½ mi) north of here, the island road becomes hilly, providing a panoramic view of the ocean.

Surfers and boogie-board lovers have adopted **Punta Morena,** north of Playa de San Martín, as their official hangout. The pounding surf makes for great waves, and the local restaurant serves typical surf food (think hamburgers, hot dogs, and french fries) and rents out primitive rooms for $10 a night.

The beach at **Punta Este** has been nicknamed Mezcalitos, after a much-loved restaurant here. (The Mezcalito Café offers seafood and beer and has a very pleasant staff.) The beach is a typical windward beach—great for beachcombing but unsuitable for swimming.

Where the paved road toward Punta Molas Faro ends and the dirt takes over starts a long stretch of deserted beaches, including **Playa Bonita,** which extends to Punta Molas at the island's northern tip. It's unspoiled and quite beautiful—perfect for sunbathing and communing with nature—and well worth the serious effort it takes to get up here.

DINING

Dining options on Cozumel reflect the nature of the place as a whole: breezy and relaxed with the occasional harmless pretensions. The downtown core has more than 80 restaurants, so you can choose among fast food, great regional dishes, and gourmet seafood. Many restaurants accept credit cards; café-type places generally don't. A dining tip: don't follow the suggestions of cab drivers, who are usually paid to recommend restaurants and don't discriminate.

Reservations and Dress

Casual dress and no reservations are the rule in most $ and $$ Cozumel restaurants. In $$$ and $$$$ restaurants you wouldn't be out of place if you dressed up, and reservations are advised.

CATEGORY	COST*
$$$$	over $30
$$$	$20–$30
$$	$10–$20
$	under $10

per person for a main course at dinner

$$$ ✕ **La Cabaña del Pescador Lobster House.** Walk the gangplank to this palapa restaurant with seashells and nets hanging from the walls. Yes, it's kitschy but worth it if you're looking for the freshest lobster on the island. There really isn't a menu—just crustaceans sold by weight (at market prices). You pay for the lobster, and the rest of your meal is included in the price. Another local favorite is La Cabaña's sister establishment, the less expensive El Guacamayo King Crab House, which is next door. ⊠ *Carretera San Juan, Km 4, across from Playa Azul Hotel,* ☎ *9/872–0795. AE, MC, V. No lunch.*

Cozumel Hotel Zones Dining and Lodging

Dining

Arrecife **8**

La Cabaña
del Pescador
Lobster House **3**

Chen Río
Restaurant **11**

Lodging

Casa del Mar **7**

Coral Princess
Hotel & Resort **1**

El Cozumeleño
Beach Resort **2**

Fiesta Americana
Cozumel Reef **9**

Iberostar **10**

Playa Azul Hotel **4**

Plaza Las Glorias **5**

Presidente
Inter–Continental
Cozumel **8**

Villablanca
Garden
Beach Hotel **6**

Punta Molas Faro

Punta Molas

Caribbean Sea

TO PUERTO MORELOS

Castillo Real

Playa Bonita

Punta Norte

Isla de Pasión

San Gervasio

❶ ❷
❸
❹

Playa San Juan

Airport

La plaza

SAN MIGUEL

TO PLAYA DEL CARMEN

Av. Benito Juárez

Punta Este

❺

Av. Rafael Melgar

❻
❼

Punta Morena

Playa de San Martín

❽
Parque Chankanaab
❾

⓫
Punta Chiqueros

Playa Corona

El Trono

Playa San Francisco

El Mirador

Playa Sol

El Cedral

⓾

Playa Paradiso

R E E F S

Playa de Palancar

Laguna Colombia

El Caracol

Punta Celerain Faro

KEY

Ferry

Cruise Ship

0   6 miles

0   9 km

San Miguel Dining and Lodging

$$-$$$ ✕ **Arrecife.** A well-trained staff and impeccably prepared dishes put this casually elegant hotel restaurant in a class by itself. Tall windows providing excellent views of the sea complement the stylish decor of potted palms, white wicker furniture, and pink walls. Live music adds to the romantic mood. Specialties include delicious lobster, shrimp, conch, and other local seafood. The rack of lamb and the homemade pasta dishes are also exceptional. ⊠ *Presidente Inter-Continental Cozumel, Carretera Chankanaab, Km 6.5,* ☎ *9/872–0322. AE, DC, MC, V. No lunch.*

$$-$$$ ✕ **Pepe's Grill.** Practically a landmark, Pepe's has a nautical air, complete with ship wheels and weather vanes covering the walls and model ships on display. The dining room is upstairs, where tall windows provide an exceptional view of the waterfront and sunsets. Steaks are the specialty here; chateaubriand, T-bone, rib eye, and prime rib are all done to perfection. This is a popular place with the cruise-ship crowds, so expect a long line. ⊠ *Av. Rafael E. Melgar Sur, at Calle Adolfo Rosada Salas,* ☎ *9/872–0213. Reservations not accepted. AE, MC, V. No lunch.*

$-$$$ ✕ **Pancho's Backyard.** The fresh margaritas here are famous on the island, and the menu offers much to please the gringo or gringa stomach, toning down the hotter elements without losing the authentic Mexican flavors. Good choices include *corazón de filete de chipotle* (beef tenderloin with chili) and the fish, which arrives on its own little grill. *Flan de café al rompope* (coffee flan laced with liqueur) is a nice ending to the meal. The building that houses Pancho's originally was a warehouse transformed into a luxury hotel. The hotel is long gone and the building now houses the classy Los Cinco Soles crafts store, in front, and Pancho's, in back. You can sit inside, amid the gorgeous Mexican decor, or outside, in the lush garden terrace with a water fountain. ⊠ *Av. Rafael E. Melgar 27, between Calles 8 and 10,* ☎ *9/872–2141. AE, MC, V.*

$–$$$ ✕ **La Veranda.** This charming wooden Caribbean house oozes ro-
★ mance and is the obvious choice for that special dinner—or for the wed-
ding reception that follows. Inside, there's comfortable rattan furniture,
soft lighting, and good music. Outside, a terrace looks into a lush trop-
ical garden that extends back to a small gazebo where you can sit and
enjoy the evening. Choices might include poblano chilies stuffed with
goat cheese, cilantro ravioli with jalapeño pesto, and fillet of fish mar-
inated in strawberry beer. The French onion soup and Caesar salad are
classics, and the flambé desserts are sensational. ✉ *Calle 4 Nte. 140,
between Avs. 5 and 10 Nte.,* ☎ *9/872–4132. AE, MC, V. No lunch.*

$$ ✕ **French Quarter.** This is the restaurant that introduced Louisiana-Cajun
cuisine to the island. Owner Mike Slaughter is here nightly making sure
that everyone is happy. The options include home-style gumbo and jam-
balaya as well as the more exotic, like glazed frogs' legs in a Cajun mari-
nade. On the grill are the finest cuts of Canadian Black Angus. You
can dine outside on the spacious terrace or inside with the colorful murals. The bar is comfortable and well stocked. ✉ *Av. 5-A Sur, one block
off the plaza,* ☎ *9/872–6321. AE, MC, V.*

$–$$ ✕ **Azul Cobalto Restaurant and Bar.** Paintings by local artists are
showcased at this restaurant, where the menu combines Chilean and
Mexican flavors. The squid Pil Pil (in garlic butter sauce) is delicious,
as are the pizzas, which are baked in a wood-burning oven. Save room
for dessert; the ice cream cake is fabulous. ✉ *Avs. 10-A and Benito
Juárez 181-B (in front of the plaza church),* ☎ *9/872–3318. No credit
cards. Closed Mon.*

$–$$ ✕ **Chen Río Restaurant.** The best fish on Cozumel is served here, on
★ the east side of the island at Playa de San Martín. The restaurant is
run by a Maya family whose sons go out in the morning to catch the
fish they serve for lunch. Relax under the coconut trees, watch the surf,
or go for a swim while you wait for your meal to arrive. The combo
plate—with shrimp, lobster, fish, rice, and vegetables—is a phenomenal bargain. ✉ *East-coast road, Km 28,* ☎ *no phone. No credit cards.*

$–$$ ✕ **La Cocay.** The name is Maya for "firefly," and, like its namesake,
★ this place is a bit magical. Atop a small hill, the restaurant offers some
of the most innovative and flavorful cuisine on the island. The chef
and manager create a menu every four to five weeks; dishes might include spiced-nut-and-tamarind-crusted chicken breast, pumpkin-stuffed
medialunas (half-moon pasta) with sage and Parmesan butter sauce,
and rack of lamb with a red-onion sauce. The decor is simple yet sophisticated, with wood tables, wrought-iron chairs, soft lighting, great
music, and an open-air kitchen that lets you watch the staff do its magic.
Desserts are fantastic, and the wine list has a nice selection. ✉ *Av. 17
Sur 1000, at Av. 25,* ☎ *9/872–5533. No credit cards. Closed Sun. and
Oct. No lunch.*

$–$$ ✕ **Cucina Italiana.** The homemade pastas at this charming restaurant
are exceptional. But that's not surprising; the owners, the Tarroni
family, brought their family recipes with them when they moved to
Cozumel from their village near Venice, Italy, in the early 1990s. The
kitchen also does its best to accommodate anyone on a special diet—
vegan and low-cholesterol menus are available. ✉ *Calle 2 Nte. and
Av. 10-A,* ☎ *9/872–5230. AE, MC, V.*

$–$$ ✕ **Guido's.** Top-quality pasta dishes and pizzas, including lasagna and
the "Four Seasons" pie (with ham, zucchini, mushrooms, and black
olives), are the draw here. Guido's also offers some good daily specials. Tables in the dining room facing the malecón tend to be noisy;
request one on the patio out back, where you can sit beneath a tree
and sip sangria. ✉ *Av. Rafael E. Melgar 23, between Calles 6 and 8
Nte.,* ☎ *9/872–0946. AE. Closed Sun.*

$–$$ ✕ **Prima.** On a breezy second-floor terrace, this is the best Italian
★   restaurant on the island. Everything here is fresh: the meat is flown in
daily from the United States, and the vegetables come from local gardens. The pastas are wonderful, salads exemplary, and the steaks juicy
and tender. Try the salad with blue cheese, and then move on to pasta
with pesto sauce, seafood ravioli, veal scallopini, or an Angus steak.
Coffee and desserts such as the key-lime pie are the perfect end to a
perfect meal. There can be lines during the busy season (even if you
have a reservation), but you can wait for your table downstairs in the
cigar–sports bar. ✉ *Calle Adolfo Rosado Salas 109-A,* ☎ *9/872–4242.
AE, MC, V. No lunch.*

$–$$ ✕ **Las Tortugas.** The motto at this simple eatery is "delicious seafood
at accessible prices," and Las Tortugas lives up to it in a big way. The
menu lists only the freshest fish, lobster, and conch caught by local fishermen. This means daily special changes according to what's available.
Fajitas and other traditional Mexican dishes also are available. This
is a great place to experience the hospitality of Cozumel. ✉ *Av. 10 Nte.
82,* ☎ *9/872–1242. MC, V.*

$ ✕ **Café Caribe & Backyard.** Coffee junkies and folks with a serious sweet
tooth flock to this sweet café for its mouthwatering selection of coffees (Cuban, Irish, espresso, cappuccino) and for its Belgian waffles,
yogurt, ice cream, freshly baked cakes, pies and muffins, and great sandwiches. The cheery interior is decorated with colorful art posters, and
there's an engaging courtyard out back. It's a perfect spot for both breakfast and after-dinner coffee and dessert. ✉ *Av. 10 Sur 215,* ☎ *9/872–
3621. No credit cards. Closed Sun.*

$ ✕ **Diamond Café.** Here's an affordable diamond. With its wrought-iron
chairs, artwork, and linens, this discreetly elegant café in back of the
main plaza serves up great deli food—sandwiches and salads along with
desserts. You can pick up a Diamond Maya cake to take home as a
souvenir; the coffee-liqueur cake is said to be based on an ancient recipe
found at the Ixchel ruins. (Advertising hype aside, the cake really is
good.) ✉ *Av. Rafael E. Melgar 131,* ☎ FAX *9/872–5782. No credit cards.
Closed Sun.*

$ ✕ **El Foco.** Here's a fun spot to grab a *cerveza* (beer) and a bite to eat.
This traditional Mexican joint is essentially a *taquería* (taco stand), offering soft tacos stuffed with pork, chorizo, cheese, or chilies. The graf-
fiti on the walls provides the entertainment. ✉ *Av. 5 Sur 13-B, between
Calles Adolfo Rosado Salas and 3 Sur,* ☎ *no phone. No credit cards.*

$ ✕ **Jeanie's Waffle House.** A great way to start the day, Jeanie's serves
light, fluffy waffles in more variations than you can imagine. Also on
the menu are eggs and omelets done the way you want, fresh juice, and
coffee. Daily dinner specials may include fish, tamales, or pasta dishes.
Jeanie's is open 6 AM–2 PM and 6 PM–10 PM. ✉ *Av. Rafael E. Melgar,
in the Vista del Mar Hotel,* ☎ *9/872–4145. No credit cards. No lunch.*

$ ✕ **Plaza Leza.** The best fajitas and ceviche in town are served in this
unpretentious Mexican sidewalk café. You can let the hours slip away
while enjoying the great food and watching the action in the square.
For more privacy, go indoors to the somewhat secluded, cozy inner patio
for everything from *poc chuc* (pork chops grilled Yucatecan style with
hot spices), enchiladas, and lime soup to chicken sandwiches and coconut ice cream. You can get breakfast here, too. ✉ *South side of the
main plaza,* ☎ *9/872–1041. AE, MC, V.*

$ ✕ **Rock 'n Java Caribbean Café.** Healthful is the key word here. The
★   extensive breakfast menu offers such delights as whole-wheat French
toast and cheese blintzes. For lunch or dinner, consider the vegetarian
tacos or lasagna, or choose from the selection of more than a dozen
salads. To balance things out there are scrumptious pies, cakes, and
pastries baked daily on the premises. Enjoy your healthy meal or your

sinful snack while sitting on the wrought-iron studio chairs and watching the waterfront out back. ☒ *Av. Rafael E. Melgar 602-6,* ☎ *9/872–4405. No credit cards. Closed Sun.*

$ ✕ **El Turix.** Off the beaten track, about 10 minutes by cab from down-
★ town, this simple place is worth the trip for a chance to experience true Yucatecan cuisine served by the amiable owners, Rafael and Maruca. Don't miss the *pollo pibíl* (chicken baked in banana leaves with pumpkin-chili sauce) or the *poc chuc* (pork marinated in a sour-orange sauce and pickled onions). There are also daily specials, and paella on request. ☒ *Av. 20 Sur, between Calles 17 and 19,* ☎ *9/872–5234. No credit cards. No lunch.*

LODGING

All of Cozumel's hotels are on the leeward (west) side of the island. Hotels north and south of San Miguel tend to be the larger, all-inclusive resorts, while less expensive places are in town. Because of the proximity of the reefs, divers and snorkelers tend to congregate at the southern properties, while sailors and anglers prefer the hotels to the north, where the beaches are better.

Cozumel has more than 3,200 hotel rooms and 85-plus private homes, condos, villas, and apartments to rent. Before booking you should call around or surf the Internet; you can find many bargains in the form of air, hotel, and dive packages, especially in the off-season (April to June and September to November). Make Christmas reservations at least three months ahead.

The majority of the resort hotels (north and south of town) are affiliated with international chains and have all the usual amenities; they usually rent water-sports equipment and can arrange excursions. The more costly properties generally have air-conditioning, no-smoking rooms, and on-site travel agencies and transportation rentals and furnish guest rooms with in-room hair dryers, safes, minibars, satellite TV, and telephones.

CATEGORY	COST*
$$$$	over $160
$$$	$90–$160
$$	$40–$90
$	under $40

Prices are for a high-season standard double room, including breakfast, tax (12%), and service charge.

North Hotel Zone

$$$$ ⊡ **Coral Princess Hotel & Resort.** Tasteful, elegant, and artistic, this is
★ one of the best hotels in the North Hotel Zone (Zona Hotelera Norte). The lobby, with its water fountain of leaping dolphins and sculptures of wrought iron and glass, resembles an art gallery. Rooms are decorated with Mexican furnishings and artwork. Princess Villas have two bedrooms, two bathrooms, a kitchen, a dining room, and private terrace; the Coral Villas have one bedroom with a combined kitchen–dining area and terrace. Except for 61 studios, all rooms overlook the ocean. There isn't much of a beach, but there's a wonderful spacious pool and huge deck leading down to the ocean. Inside there's a game room, convention salon, and a pretty celestial-theme bar perfect for a romantic drink before dinner at El Galeón restaurant (off the main lobby). ☒ *Zona Hotelera Norte, Km 2.5, 77600,* ☎ *9/872–3200 or 800/253–2702,* ℻ *9/872–2800,* ⓦⒺⒷ *www.coralprincess.com. 100 rooms, 37 villas, 2 penthouses. Restaurant, bar, air-conditioning, pool, volleyball, dive shop, dock, snorkeling, fishing, car rental. AE, MC, V.*

$$$ ⛱ **El Cozumeleño Beach Resort.** This all-inclusive resort is geared toward families (children under seven stay free and have their own pool), with lots of activities—especially on the wonderful beach. Rooms are large and fitted with contemporary pine furniture; all have ocean views and terraces. Included in the package: all meals and drinks, snorkel and scuba lessons, tours, miniature golf, tennis, kayaking, windsurfing, bike tours, a game room, and a daily children's camp. Other water activities, such as waterskiing or parasailing, can be arranged for an additional charge. The resort has two restaurants and one snack bar. ✉ *Zona Hotelera Norte, Playa Santa Pilar, Km 4.5, 77600,* ☎ *9/872–0050 or 800/742–4726,* FAX *9/872–0381,* WEB *www.elcozumeleno.com. 254 rooms. 2 restaurants, 2 bars, snack bar, 2 pools, hot tub, tennis court, basketball, health club, dive shop, boating, children's programs (ages 2–12), car rental. AE, MC, V.*

$$$ ⛱ **Playa Azul Hotel.** At this quiet, comfortable hotel, bright, airy rooms have either great ocean views or face beautiful tropical gardens. All have sliding doors leading to sun-filled terraces. Some of the rooms have couches that convert to beds, which is ideal for families. Along the beach, small palapas are set up with comfortable chairs. Snorkeling, scuba diving, and fishing trips depart daily from Playa Azul's own dock. The Palma Azul restaurant serves delicious meals centered on fresh fish. You can also eat at Mr. Sancho's beach club, at the south end of the island, and charge it to your room. ✉ *Carretera San Juan, Km 4, 77600,* ☎ *9/872–0199,* FAX *9/872–0110,* WEB *www.playa-azul.com/. 31 rooms. Restaurant, 2 bars, pool, massage, dive shop, dock, snorkeling, fishing, billiards, car rental. AE, MC, V.*

South Hotel Zone

$$$$ ⛱ **Presidente Inter-Continental Cozumel.** Luxury, comfort, efficiency,
★   and privacy are hallmarks of the Presidente. The stylish rooms are done in bright, contemporary colors with white cedar furnishings and private terraces; a majority of the rooms overlook the ocean, while garden rooms look out on the beautifully kept grounds. Trees, plants, and shrubs along the corridors contribute to the exotic, tropical feel of the hotel. The pool is modest, but the beach is the nicest on the island and has great snorkeling: clown fish, angelfish, and parrot fish all swim in the waters a few feet off the beach. There's also a professional dive and water-sports center, tennis courts, and a serene botanical garden. The Arrecife restaurant is highly recommended. ✉ *Carretera Chankanaab, Km 6.5, 77600,* ☎ *9/872–0322 or 800/327–0200,* FAX *9/872–1360,* WEB *www.interconti.com. 253 rooms. 2 restaurants, 3 bars, coffee shop, pool, hot tub, 2 tennis courts, gym, dive shop, motorbikes, shops, children's programs (ages 4–12), meeting rooms, car rental. AE, DC, MC, V.*

$$$ ⛱ **Fiesta Americana Cozumel Reef.** Hard to miss since it's painted a blinding orange, this property is ideally situated for snorkeling and scuba diving. Although the hotel building itself is across the road from the water, a pedestrian walkway provides easy access to the dive shop, dock, beach, pool, and restaurant. Standard rooms are large, with light-wood furnishings; all have oceanfront balconies. There's also a 56-room semicircular cluster of villas with patios and ocean views. Reasonable prices and a good location have made the Fiesta Americana one of the most popular hotels on the island. There are some great sailing packages as well. ✉ *Carretera Chankanaab, Km 7.5, 77600,* ☎ *9/872–2622 or 800/343–7821,* FAX *9/872–2666,* WEB *www.cozumel-hotels.net/fiesta-americana/. 172 rooms, 56 villas. 3 restaurants, 3 bars, 2 pools, 2 tennis courts, dive shop, dock, motorbikes, travel services, car rental. AE, MC, V.*

$$$ ⊞ **Iberostar.** This all-inclusive resort at the southernmost point of Cozumel has managed to keep the local flora and fauna intact, so that it has an exotic jungle setting. Rooms are small but pleasantly decorated with Mexican wrought iron and have either a king-size bed or two queen-size beds; all have terraces or patios. The one drawback: there isn't much privacy, since paths through the resort wind around the rooms. The resort has so many activities for the whole family to do that you may never make it to town (which is an expensive 20-minute cab ride away). ⊠ *Carretera Chankanaab, Km 17, 77600 (past El Cedral turnoff),* ☎ *9/872–9900,* FAX *9/872–9909. 292 rooms, 8 villas. 4 restaurants, 3 bars, 2 pools, hair salon, spa, 2 tennis courts, dive shop, dock, boating, theater, children's programs (ages 4–12), car rental. AE, MC, V.*

$$$ ⊞ **Plaza Las Glorias.** This large salmon-color hotel is five blocks south of downtown. A Mediterranean atmosphere prevails, with marble floors and wrought-iron details in the large, expansive lobby. There's a lobby bar that shows sporting events. The modern suites have private terraces and ocean views with roomy sitting areas and small refrigerators. The pool here is quite beautiful, and there's fantastic snorkeling just offshore where fish gather in the rocky crevices. Small docks and ladders provide easy access to the water. ⊠ *Carretera Chankanaab, Km 1.5, 77600,* ☎ *9/872–2000 or 800/342–AMIGO,* FAX *9/872–1937. 168 suites. 2 restaurants, 2 bars, pool, dive shop, shops. AE, MC, V.*

$$ ⊞ **Casa del Mar.** The cheerful rooms at this three-story hotel are decorated with Mexican artwork and yellow-tile headboards and nightstands; each has a small balcony with a view of either the pool or the ocean across the road. The bi-level cabañas, which sleep three or four, are a very good deal. The hotel has been set up to accommodate divers (rooms for equipment, lots of showers and towels). Close by are the Del Mar Dive Shop along with several boutiques, sports shops, bars, and restaurants. Thirteen kilometers (8 miles) south is the property's beach club, Nachi Cocom. ⊠ *Carretera Chankanaab, Km 4, 77600,* ☎ *9/872–1944 or 800/877–4383,* FAX *9/872–1855,* WEB *www.cozumel-hotels.net/casa_del_mar/. 98 rooms, 8 cabañas. 2 restaurants, 2 bars, pool, hot tub, dive shop, travel services, car rental. AE, MC, V.*

$$ ⊞ **Villablanca Garden Beach Hotel.** Beautiful architecture and a refined
★ atmosphere set this apart from other divers' hotels. Standard rooms have an open-air design, with a large double bed placed between two pillars and an archway. On the other side of the arch is a separate sitting area with doors opening onto the garden. Suites have refrigerators, sunken bathtubs, and private terraces. Everything is done in white, with flower arrangements providing the color. La Veranda, the hotel restaurant, is very accommodating and can prepare special dinner menus for groups or for those with dietary restrictions. Outside are a pool, tennis courts, and a huge garden. Excellent dive packages are available at bargain prices. The on-site compressor is also a bonus. ⊠ *Carretera Chankanaab, Km 3, 77600,* ☎ *9/872–07300,* FAX *9/872–0865,* WEB *www.villablanca.net. 25 rooms, 25 suites. Restaurant, refrigerators (some), pool, tennis court, dock. AE, MC, V.*

Downtown Hotels

$$$ ⊞ **Casa Mexicana.** The attention to detail and beautiful architecture (including a romantic windswept lobby and dramatic staircase) at this downtown hotel make it a standout. Spacious oceanfront rooms have spectacular views, are decorated in subtle blues and yellows, and have either a king-size or two double beds. A full breakfast is included in the price. Sister properties Hotel Bahía and Suites Colonial offer equally comfortable but less expensive suites with kitchenettes (the Bahía has

the ocean views while the Colonial is on the square). You can contact all three hotels using the central reservation number. ⊠ *Av. Rafael E. Melgar 457 Sur, between Calles 5 and 7, 77600,* ☎ *9/872–0209 or 877/ 228–6747,* FAX *9/872–1387,* WEB *www.casamexicanacozumel.com. 90 rooms. Pool, gym, business services. AE, MC, V.*

$$ ⊞ **Casa Martillo Condos.** These luxury condos come equipped with every-
★ thing you need for a comfortable stay. All units face the pool and have full kitchens, dining and living areas, sofa beds, and balconies or pa-tios. Second-floor condos are split-level, with the bedroom and bath-room upstairs. Other pluses include daily maid service, a laundry facility, local phone service, individual dive-gear storage, and shopping carts for visits to the local grocery store. It's three blocks from the beach and a five-minute cab ride to town. The staff is wonderful and pays a lot of attention to details while keeping the place spotless. If you share, these condos are a great bargain. ⊠ *Calle 19 Sur and Av. 15 Sur, 77600,* ☎ *9/872–2629 or 877/627–8455,* FAX *530/623–2671,* WEB *www.snowcrest.net/hammer/CasaMartillo.html. 6 apartments. Pool, laundry service. AE, MC, V.*

$$ ⊞ **Hotel Flamingo.** Since 1986, this colonial-style hotel has been a pop-ular destination for travelers from around the world. Three blocks from the ferry, it's a comfortable place to stay. Relax in the laid-back lobby or in the charming courtyard, or step up to the rooftop sundeck, where the Caribbean views are yours to enjoy. Rooms are large and decorated in bright colors; some have air-conditioning. Those at the front of the hotel have balconies overlooking the street and can be noisy. The hotel offers a program of intensive Spanish lessons and some great dive packages. ⊠ *Calle 6 Nte. 81 (near the Cozumel Museum), 77600,* ☎ *9/872–4760 or 800/806–1601,* WEB *www.hotelflamingo.com. 22 rooms. Air-conditioning (some), fans. AE, MC, V.*

$$ ⊞ **Tamarindo Bed & Breakfast.** The owners of this five-room charmer have created a place that combines the flavor of Mexico with the ele-gance of France. Rooms are gracefully decorated with individual touches. Breakfasts consist of fresh breads, fruits in season, homemade yogurt, and French pressed coffee. The staff arranges diving expedi-tions, and there's a rinse tank and gear-storage facility on the premises. ⊠ *Calle 4 Nte. 421, between Avs. 20 and 25, 77600,* ☎ FAX *9/872– 3614. 5 rooms. Fans, massage, bicycles, baby-sitting, laundry service. MC, V.*

$ ⊞ **Charrita's.** This charming bed-and-breakfast has a Western flavor and
★ is a great deal (particularly the huge Mexican breakfast). Its quiet lo-cation in a residential neighborhood seven blocks from the beach gives you a chance to experience a slice of Mexico you won't find at other hotels. Each of the five rooms is extremely comfortable, with individ-ual decorations and a private bath. Upstairs there's a terrace for sun-bathing or taking in sunsets. The private entrance means you can come and go when you like. If this place is full, ask to stay at Les Delphines, the delightful sister residence on Calle 15 Sur; it has four luxurious guest rooms set up for maximum privacy. ⊠ *Calle 21 Sur, between Felipe An-geles and Av. 40 Sur, 77600,* ☎ FAX *9/872–4760, charritas@yahoo.com. 5 rooms. Fans. No credit cards.*

$ ⊞ **Hotel Pepita.** One of Cozumel's first hotels, this bargain hotel of-fers basic, clean rooms and a well-laid-out courtyard with plants and places to sit. Discounts are given for longer stays. ⊠ *Av. 15 Sur 120, 77600,* ☎ *9/872–0098,* FAX *9/872–0201. 15 rooms. Fans, refrigerators. No credit cards.*

NIGHTLIFE AND THE ARTS

The Arts

The arts scene on Cozumel tends to focus on the local culture; every Thursday there's a folkloric dance performance at the **Fiesta Americana** (☎ 9/872–2622). The whole island explodes with music, costumes, dancing, parades, and parties for Carnival, which takes place just before the start of Lent. Visitors from around the world are encouraged to dress up and catch the fever.

Movies
Cine Cecillo Borge (⊠ Av. Benito Juárez, between Avs. 30 and 35, ☎ no phone) shows recent Hollywood movies, usually in English with Spanish subtitles. You can see the latest blockbusters (generally in English) at **Cine Cozumel** (⊠ Av. Rafael E. Melgar, between Calles 2 and 4 Nte., ☎ 9/872–0766). Both theaters show movies nightly, starting at 9.

Nightlife

Cozumel offers enough daytime activities to make you want to retire early, but that doesn't keep the island from hopping late into the night. A word to the wise: avoid the temptation to buy or use drugs here. Mexican drug laws are draconian and the jails positively medieval.

Bars
Cactus (⊠ Av. Rafael E. Melgar 145, ☎ 9/872–3045) has a disco, live music, and a bar that stays open until 5 AM. Serious bar hoppers like the wild, raucous, and at times obnoxious **Carlos 'n' Charlie's** (⊠ Av. Rafael E. Melgar 11, between Calles 2 and 4 Nte., ☎ 9/872–0191). Sports fiends can catch all the news on ESPN at **Sports Page Video Bar and Restaurant** (⊠ Av. 5 Nte. and Calle 2, ☎ 9/872–1199).

Discos
The oldest disco on the island, **Neptune Dance Club** (⊠ Av. Rafael E. Melgar at Av. 11, ☎ 9/872–1537) still lets you boogie into the night. **Viva Mexico** (⊠ Av. Rafael E. Melgar, ☎ 9/872–0799) has a DJ who spins dance music until the wee hours. There's also an extensive snack menu.

Live Music
For sophisticated jazz, smart cocktails, and great cigars, check out the **Havana Club** (⊠ Av. Rafael E. Melgar, between Calles 6 and 8, second floor, ☎ 9/872–6599). **Hog's Breath Saloon** (⊠ Av. Rafael E. Melgar, ☎ no phone) has live music—various kinds—every night. The food isn't the draw at **Joe's Lobster House** (⊠ Av. 10 Sur 229, between Calles Adolfo Rosada Salas and 3 Sur, ☎ 9/872–3275), but the reggae and salsa bring in the crowds nightly, from 10:30 until dawn. Sunday evenings 8–10, locals head for the *zócalo*, or *la plaza* (the plaza), to hear mariachis and island musicians playing tropical tunes.

OUTDOOR ACTIVITIES AND SPORTS

Most people come to Cozumel for the water sports—scuba diving, snorkeling, and fishing are particularly popular. Services and equipment rentals are available throughout the island, especially through major hotels and water-sports centers such as **Scuba Du** (⊠ Calle 3 Sur 33, between Avs. Rafael E. Melgar and 5 Sur, ☎ 9/872–1994).

Fishing

Regulations forbid commercial fishing, sportfishing, spear fishing, and collecting any marine life in certain areas around Cozumel. It's illegal to kill certain species, including billfish, so be prepared to return prize catches back to the sea. (Regular participants in the annual billfish tournament have seen some of the same fish caught over and over again.) U.S. Customs allows you to bring up to 30 pounds of fish back into the country.

For the past 22 years the annual **International Billfish Tournament** (⊠ A.P. 442, 77600, ☎ 800/253–2701, FAX 9/872–0999), held the last week in April or the first week in May, has drawn anglers from around the world to Cozumel.

Charters

You can charter high-speed fishing boats for $400 for a half day or $500 for a full day (maximum six people). **Albatros Deep Sea Fishing** (☎ 9/872–5619 or 888/333–4643) is a local outfit specializing in fishing trips. **Marathon Fishing & Leisure Charters** (☎ 9/872–1986) is popular with fishermen. Full-day rates for both places include the boat and crew, tackle and bait, and lunch with beer and soda. Your hotel can help you arrange daily charters—some hotels have special deals, with boats leaving from their own dock.

Go-Carts

Zooming around the **Cozumel Go-Karts** raceway (⊠ Carretera Chankanaab, Km 3.5, beside Casa del Mar, ☎ 9/872–1876) in souped-up carts is great fun. Children are heartily welcomed, as are groups. The more laps you buy, the cheaper it gets. Admission is $10 for 12 laps, $20 for 26 laps. The raceway is open daily from noon to midnight.

Miniature Golf

If you're not a fan of miniature golf, **Cozumel Mini–Golf** (⊠ Calle 1 Sur, No. 20, ☎ 9/872–6570) might just convert you. The jungle-theme course with its banana trees and birds has two fountains and a waterfall. You can order drinks via walkie-talkies and they'll be delivered as you try for that hole in one. Admission is $5; it's open Monday through Saturday 11–11, Sunday 5 PM–11.

Scuba Diving

The options for divers in Cozumel include deep dives, drift dives, shore dives, wall dives, and night dives, as well as theme dives focusing on ecology, archaeology, sunken ships, and photography. With so many shops to choose from (there are now more than 100), divers should look for high safety standards and documented credentials. The best places are those that offer small groups and individual attention. Avoid places that care only about volume. Next to your equipment, your dive master is the most important aspect of your dive, particularly if you're new to diving. More attention is far better than less.

Make sure your instructor has PADI certification (or FMAS, the Mexican equivalent) and is affiliated with a good recompression chamber. The **Cozumel Recompression Chamber** (⊠ San Miguel Clinic, Calle 6 between Avs. 5 and 10, ☎ 9/872–3070, 9/872–2387, or 9/872–1848) is a fully equipped recompression center. There's a reputable recompression chamber at the **Buceo Medico Mexicano** (⊠ Calle 9 Sur 21-

B, ☎ 9/872–2387). These chambers, which aim for a 35-minute response time from reef to chamber, treat decompression sickness, commonly known as "the bends," which occurs when you surface too quickly and nitrogen is absorbed into the bloodstream. Recompression chambers are also used to treat nitrogen narcosis, collapsed lungs, and overexposure to the cold. Most of the dive shops in town offer complete dive-accident coverage for just $1 per day. Also consider getting DAN (Divers Alert Network) insurance, which covers dive accidents.

Diving requires that you be reasonably fit. Be sure to listen to your instructor and don't attempt anything that you're not comfortable doing. The "resort" course has become a popular way to introduce people to diving. But don't let them fool you into thinking you're ready for deep dives in the open sea after a two-hour lesson. It's best to take a few more lessons to be comfortable and safe. When diving, stay at least 3 ft above the reef, not just because the coral can sting or cut you but also because coral is easily damaged and grows very slowly: it has taken 2,000 years for it to reach its present size.

The Cozumel Reef has been turned into a National Marine Park, and you must pay a fee of $2 per diver-snorkeler per day to visit the reef. Wear your assigned identifying bracelet at all times to avoid paying a fine. Proceeds go toward protecting the reef.

Dive Shops and Tour Operators

Most dive shops can provide you with all the incidentals you'll need, as well as with guides and transportation. You can choose from a variety of two-tank boat trips and specialty dives ranging from $45 to $60; two-hour resort courses cost about $50–$60, and 1½-hour night dives, $30–$35. Basic certification courses, such as PADI's Discover Scuba or Naui's introductory course, are available for about $350, while advanced certification courses cost as much as $700. Equipment rental is relatively inexpensive, ranging from $6 for tanks or a lamp to about $8–$10 for a regulator and BC vest; underwater-camera rentals can cost as much as $35, video-camera rentals run about $75, and professionally shot and edited videos of your own dive are priced at about $160.

Because dive shops tend to be competitive, it's well worth your while to shop around. Many hotels have their own on-site operations, and there are many in town. **ANOAAT** (Aquatic Sports Operators Association; ☎ 9/872–5955) has listings of affiliated dive operations. Before signing on, ask some experienced divers about the place, check credentials, and look over the boats and equipment.

Aqua Safari (⊠ Av. Rafael E. Melgar 429, between Calles 5 and 7 Sur, ☎ 9/872–0101).

Black Shark (⊠ Av. 5 Sur, between Calles Adolfo Rosado Salas and 3 Sur, ☎ 9/872–0396).

Blue Bubble (⊠ Av. 5 Sur at Calle 3, ☎ 9/872–1865), for PADI instruction.

Chino's Scuba (⊠ Calle Adolfo Rosado Salas 16-A, ☎ 9/872–5836).

Cozumel Equalizers Scuba Centre (⊠ Calle Adolfo Rosado Salas 72, ☎ FAX 9/872–3511).

Dive Cozumel (⊠ Calle Adolfo Rosado Salas 72, at Av. 5 Sur, ☎ 9/872–4567).

Eagle Ray Dive School (⊠ Avs. Chichén and Pamuul, ☎ 9/872–5735).

Emerald Dolphin Dive Services (⊠ Calle 19 Sur 1134, ☎ FAX 9/872–3270).

Flash Adventures (⊠ Av. 5 Nte. between Calles 5 and 7, ☎ 9/872–0570).

Gran Azul (⊠ Av. 25a No. 1081, ☎ FAX 9/872–3223).

Michelle's Dive Shop (✉ Av. 5 Sur 201, at Calle Adolfo Rosado Salas, ☎ 9/872–0947).
Papa Hog's Scuba Emporium (✉ Carretera Chankanaab, Km 3, ☎ 9/872–1651).

Reef Dives

Cozumel's reefs stretch for 32 km (20 mi), beginning at the international pier and continuing on to Punta Celarain at the southernmost tip of the island. The following is a rundown of Cozumel's main dive destinations.

CHANKANAAB REEF

This inviting reef lies just south of Parque Chankanaab, about 350 yards offshore. Here large underground caves are filled with striped grunt, snapper, sergeant majors, and butterfly fish. At 55 ft is another large coral formation that's often filled with crabs, lobster, barrel sponges, and angelfish. Drift a bit farther south to see the Balones de Chankanaab, balloon-shape coral at 70 ft. It's an excellent place for beginners.

COLOMBIA REEF

Several miles off Palancar, the reef reaches 82–98 ft and is best suited for experienced divers who want to take some deep dives. Its underwater structures are as varied as those of Palancar Reef, with large canyons and ravines to explore. Clustered near the overhangs are large groupers, jacks, eagle rays, and even an occasional sea turtle.

MARACAIBO REEF

Considered the most difficult of all the Cozumel reefs, Maracaibo is a thrilling dive—you don't even see the ledge of the reef until you go 121 ft below the surface. At the southern end of the island, this reef lends itself to drift dives because of its length. Although there are shallow areas, only advanced divers who can cope with the current should attempt Maracaibo. Dive shops don't stop here on their regular trips, so you must make advance reservations.

PALANCAR REEF

The most famous of all the reefs on Cozumel, located 2 km (1 mi) offshore, Palancar is actually a series of varying coral formations with about 40 dive locations. It's filled with winding canyons, deep ravines, narrow crevices and archways, tunnels, and caves. Black and red coral and huge elephant-ear and barrel sponges are among the attractions at the bottom. A favorite of divers is the section called Horseshoe, where a series of coral heads form a natural horseshoe shape at the top of the drop-off. Visibility here ranges from 150 ft to 250 ft, making it one of the most sensational dives in the Caribbean.

PARAÍSO REEF

About 330 ft offshore, running parallel to the international cruise-ship pier, this reef averages 30–50 ft. It's a perfect spot to dive before you head for deeper drop-offs such as La Ceiba and Villa Blanca. There are impressive formations of star and brain coral as well as sea fans, sponges, sea eels, and yellow rays. It's wonderful for night diving.

PASEO EL CEDRAL

Also known as Cedar Pass, this seldom-dived flat reef, just northeast of Palancar Reef, has gardenlike valleys full of fish, with angelfish, lobster, and thick-lipped grouper. At depths ranging 35–55 ft, you can also spot sea turtles, moray eels, and eagle rays.

PLANE WRECK

During a 1977 Mexican film shoot, this 40-passenger Convair airplane was sunk about 300 ft away from the La Ceiba pier. Because of its reassuring proximity to the shore and shallow depths—only 9–30 ft—

it's a favorite training ground for neophyte divers. Enormous coral structures and colorful sponges surround the wreck.

SAN FRANCISCO REEF
Considered Cozumel's shallowest wall dive (35–50 ft), this 1-km (½-mi) reef runs parallel to San Francisco Beach and has many varieties of reef fish. It requires the use of a dive boat.

SANTA ROSA WALL
A site for experienced divers, just north of Palancar, Santa Rosa is renowned for deep dives and drift dives; at 50 ft there's an abrupt yet sensational drop-off to enormous coral overhangs. The strong current drags you along the tunnels and caves where there are huge sponges, angelfish, groupers, and eagle rays—maybe even a shark.

TORMENTOS REEF
The abundance of sea fans, sponges, sea cucumbers, arrow crabs, green eels, groupers, and other marine life—against a terrifically colorful backdrop—makes this a perfect spot for underwater photography. This variegated reef has a maximum depth of around 70 ft.

YUCAB REEF
South of Punta Tormentos Reef, this relatively shallow reef is close to shore, making it an ideal spot for beginners. About 400 ft long and 55 ft deep, it's teeming with queen angelfish and sea whip swimming around the large coral heads. The one drawback is the strong current, which can reach 2 or 3 knots.

Snorkeling

Snorkeling equipment is available at the Presidente Inter-Continental and La Ceiba (⊠ Costera Sur, Km. 4.5, ☎ 9/872–0844) hotels as well as at Chankanaab Bay, Playa San Francisco, and Playa Soland directly off the beach near the Fiesta Americana Cozumel Reef and Playa Corona for less than $10 a day.

Tour Operators
One option is to contact the dive shops to see if you can tag along when they go out to a suitable snorkeling reef. Official snorkeling tours run from $25 to $50, depending on the duration, and take in the shallow reefs off Palancar, Colombia, and Yucab. **Fiesta Cozumel** (⊠ Calle 11 Sur 598, between Avs. 25 and 30, ☎ 9/872–0725, FAX 9/872–1389) runs snorkeling tours from the 45-ft catamarans *El Zorro* and *Fury.* Rates begin at about $50 per day and include equipment, a guide, soft drinks and beer, and a box lunch. Sunset cruises aboard *El Zorro* are also available; they include unlimited drinks and live entertainment and cost about $35.

SHOPPING

As in other Mexican resort areas, Cozumel's shops accept dollars as readily as pesos, and many goods are priced in dollars. You'll get a better price everywhere on Cozumel if you pay with cash or traveler's checks, since there's a hefty surcharge on credit cards that you'll be asked to pay. MasterCard and Visa are the two most popular cards, followed by American Express. The many warnings you'll receive about buying from street vendors is good advice—the quality of their merchandise leaves much to be desired, although this may not be apparent until it's too late.

There are three cruise-ship docks (one in the center of town). Most cruise ships land on Wednesday, overcrowding the streets with tourists on a timetable. Expect the shops, restaurants, and streets to be extremely crowded and hard to maneuver between 10 AM until 2 PM. Cruise-ship tourists are given priority, since their time is limited. Come back later when things are calmer for leisurely dining and shopping. Traditionally, stores are open from 9 to 1 (except Sunday) and 5 to 9, but a number of them, especially those nearest the pier, tend to stay open all day and on weekends, particularly during high season. Most of the shops are closed Sunday morning.

Don't pay much attention to written or verbal offers of "20% discounts, today only" or "only for cruise-ship passengers"—they're nothing but bait to get you inside. Similarly, many of the larger stores advertise "duty-free" wares, but these are of greater interest to Mexicans from the mainland than to North Americans, since the prices tend to be higher than retail prices in the United States.

A last word of caution: don't buy black coral—it's an endangered species and really overpriced on the island. Plus, you might not be allowed to bring it to the United States and other countries.

Department Stores

Relatively small and more like U.S. variety stores, Cozumel's department stores nevertheless carry a relatively wide array of goods, from the useful to the frivolous. **Luxury Avenue (Ultrafemme)** (⊠ Av. Rafael E. Melgar 341, ☎ 9/872–1217) sells high-end goods including watches and perfume. **Pama** (⊠ Av. Rafael E. Melgar Sur 9, ☎ 9/872–0090), near the pier, carries imported luxury items. **Prococo** (⊠ Av. Rafael E. Melgar Nte. 99, ☎ 9/872–1875 or 9/872–1964) offers a good selection of liquor, jewelry, and gift items. **Viva Mexico** (⊠ Av. Rafael E. Melgar at Calle Adolfo Rosada Salas, ☎ 9/872–0791) sells souvenirs and handicrafts from all over Mexico.

Shopping Districts, Streets, and Malls

Cozumel's main shopping area is **downtown** on the waterfront along Avenida Rafael E. Melgar, and on some of the side streets around the plaza (there are more than 150 shops in this area alone). There's a **crafts market** (⊠ Calle 1 Sur, behind the plaza) in town, which sells a respectable assortment of Mexican wares. In addition, small clusters of shops can be found at **Plaza del Sol** (on the east side of the main plaza), **Villa Mar** (on the north side of the main plaza), and **Plaza Confetti** (on the south side of the main plaza). A huge shopping center with more than 95 shops and 53 fast-food restaurants was, at press time, under construction at Plaza Langosta, across from the dock, at Calle 7 Sur. As a general rule, the newer, trendier shops line the waterfront, while the area around Avenida 5a houses the better crafts shops. South of the city, past Casa del Mar, is **Plaza Maya,** a collection of shops selling low-end souvenirs at high-end prices. The crafts market **Puerto Maya,** where the cruise ships dock, has some crafts at good prices, but watch out for tipsy tourists coming off the boats.

For fresh produce try the **town market** (⊠ Calle Adolfo Rosada Salas, between Avs. 20 and 25 Sur, ☎ no phone), open Monday through Saturday 8–5. The main grocery store, **Chedraui** (⊠ Carretera Chankanaab, Km 1.5, and Calle 15 Sur, ☎ 9/872–3655), is open daily 8 AM–10 PM.

Specialty Stores

Clothing

Several trendy sportswear stores line Avenida Rafael E. Melgar between Calles 2 and 6. **Bikinis do Brasil** (⊠ Calle 1 Sur, between Avs. 10 and 15, ☎ 9/872–0260) features a collection of Brazilian swimwear and sundresses. **Poco Loco** (⊠ Av. Rafael E. Melgar 18 and Av. Benito Juárez 2-A, ☎ 9/872–5499) sells casual wear and beach bags.

Jewelry

Jewelry on Cozumel is pricey, but it tends to be of higher quality than what you'll find in many other Yucatán towns. **Diamond Creations** (✉ Av. Rafael E. Melgar Sur 131, ☎ 9/872–5330) lets you custom-design a piece of jewelry from its collection of loose diamonds, emeralds, rubies, sapphires, or tanzanite. You may also want to check out its other branches, Just for Men and Tanzanite International, two blocks north. You'll find silver, gold, and coral jewelry—bracelets and earrings especially—at **Joyería Palancar** (✉ Av. Rafael E. Melgar Nte. 15, ☎ 9/872–1468). **Nautilus** (✉ Plaza Vista del Mar, ☎ no phone) has 14-karat-gold jewelry shaped like sharks, marlins, and manta rays. Quality gemstones and striking designs are the strong points at **Rachat & Romero** (✉ Av. Rafael E. Melgar 101, ☎ 9/872–0571). Innovative designs and top-quality stones can be found at **Van Cleef & Arpels** (✉ Av. Rafael E. Melgar Nte., across from the ferry, ☎ 9/872–6540).

Mexican Crafts

Bugambilias (✉ Av. 10 Sur, between Calles Adolfo Rosado Salas and 1 Sur, ☎ 9/872–6282) sells handmade Mexican linens. **Los Cinco Soles** (✉ Av. Rafael E. Melgar Nte. 27, ☎ 9/872–0132) is the best bet for one-stop shopping for quality items. The nearly block-long store stocks an excellent variety of well-priced, well-displayed items, including blue-rim glassware, brass and tin animals from Jalisco, tablecloths and place mats, cotton gauze and embroidered clothing, onyx, T-shirts, papier-mâché fruit, reproduction Maya art, Mexican fashions, silver jewelry, soapstone earrings and beads, handmade furniture, and other Mexican wares. **Mayan Feather** (✉ Av. 5 and Calle 2 Nte., ☎ no phone) has original paintings on feathers from birds of the area. Prices are reasonable, and many of the pictures are quite beautiful. **Talavera** (✉ Av. 5 Sur 349, ☎ 9/872–0171) carries beautiful ceramics from all over Mexico, including tiles from the Yucatán, masks from Guerrero, brightly painted wooden animals from Oaxaca, and carved chests from Guadalajara. **Unicornio** (✉ Av. 5 Sur 1, ☎ 9/872–0171) specializes in Mexican folk art, including ceramic notions and etched wooden trays, but you'll have to sift through a lot of souvenir junk to find the good-quality items.

COZUMEL A TO Z

To research prices, get advice from other travelers, and book travel arrangements, visit www.fodors.com.

AIR TRAVEL

CARRIERS

Continental flies nonstop from Houston to Cozumel; Mexicana has nonstop service from Miami and San Francisco. Mexicana subsidiaries Aerocaribe and Aerocozumel fly between Cozumel and Cancún and other destinations in Mexico, including Chichén Itzá, Chetumal, Mérida, and Playa del Carmen.

➤ AIRLINES AND CONTACTS: Aerocaribe (☎ 9/872–0503). Aerocozumel (☎ 9/872–0928). Continental (☎ 9/872–0487). Mexicana (☎ 9/872–0157).

AIRPORTS

The Cozumel airport is 3 km (2 mi) north of San Miguel.
➤ AIRPORT INFORMATION: Cozumel airport (☎ 9/872–0928).

AIRPORT TRANSFER

Because of an agreement between the taxi drivers' and bus drivers' unions, there is taxi service *to* the airport but not *from* the airport. The *colectivo,* a van that seats up to eight, takes arriving passengers to their hotels; the fare is about $7. If you want to avoid waiting for the van to fill or for other passengers to be dropped off, you can hire an *especial*—an individual van. A trip via an individual van to one of the hotel zones costs about $15; a trip to the city runs about $10. Taxis to the airport cost between $8 to $25 from the hotel zones and approximately $5 from downtown.

BOAT AND FERRY TRAVEL
Passenger-only ferries to Playa del Carmen leave Cozumel's main pier (☎ no phone) approximately every hour on the hour from 6 AM to 11 PM (no ferries at noon, 2, 8, and 10 PM). They leave Playa del Carmen's dock also about every hour on the hour, from 4 AM to 10 PM (no service at 5 and 11 AM, 1, 7, and 9 PM). The trip takes 45 minutes. Call to verify the times. Bad weather often prompts cancellations.

There is a car ferry from Puerto Morelos, but it's not recommended. The trip takes three to four hours, the ferry is infrequent, the departure times aren't convenient, and the fare is about $70 for small cars (more for larger vehicles) and $6 per passenger.
➤ BOAT AND FERRY INFORMATION: **Playa del Carmen dock** (☎ 9/872–1508).

BUS TRAVEL
Because of a union agreement with taxi drivers, public buses cannot operate in the North and South Hotel zones; local bus service runs mainly within the town of San Miguel, although there is a route from town to the airport. Service is irregular but inexpensive.

CAR RENTAL
A rental car is a great way to get around the island, particularly as taxi prices are high here. A vehicle with four-wheel drive (check to make sure that it hasn't been disconnected) is a must if you want to get to the more secluded beaches and ruins.

All the large hotels have rental offices, and most of the major car-rental companies have a location at the airport. Rental rates start at about $40 a day. Insurance doesn't cover trips off the main roads. Many of the smaller companies carry only standard transmission cars, so request an automatic in advance.
➤ MAJOR AGENCIES: **Avis** (☎ 9/872–0099 airport). **Hertz** (☎ 9/872–3888 airport).
➤ LOCAL AGENCIES: **Aguila Rentals** (✉ Calle 11 No. 101, ☎ 9/872–0729). **Cocodrilos Car Rental** (✉ Av. Rafael E. Melgar 601, ☎ 9/872–5030). **Rentadora Islena** (✉ Calle 7 No. 49, ☎ 9/872–0788).

CAR TRAVEL
A car is a great way to see the island. For getting to the out-of-the-way beaches and off-the-beaten-path ruins, you need a four-wheel-drive vehicle. There are two gas stations on Cozumel: one at the corner of Avenida Benito Juárez and Avenida 30 on the way to San Gervasio, the other at Avenidas Pedro Joaquin Coldwell and Benito Juárez. Both are open daily 7 AM–midnight.

CRUISE TRAVEL
At least a dozen cruise lines call at Cozumel and/or Playa del Carmen, including, from Fort Lauderdale, Celebrity Cruises, Cunard Line, and Princess Cruises; from Miami, Carnival Cruise Lines, Costa Cruise Lines, Norwegian Cruise Line, Premier Cruises, and Royal Caribbean; from New Orleans, Commodore Cruise Line; and from Tampa, Holland America Line.

➤ CRUISE LINES: Carnival Cruise Lines (☎ 800/327–9501). Celebrity Cruises (☎ 800/437–3111). Commodore Cruise Line (☎ 800/327–5617). Costa Cruise Lines (☎ 800/327–2537). Cunard Line (☎ 800/221–4770). Holland America Line (☎ 800/426–0327). Norwegian Cruise Line (☎ 800/327–7030). Premier Cruises (☎ 800/222–1003). Princess Cruises (☎ 800/568–3262). Royal Caribbean (☎ 800/327–6700).

E-MAIL
Internet access on Cozumel is expensive. Diamond Internet and Calling Station have the most reasonable rates; they charge $3 for 30 minutes of computer usage, including Internet access.
➤ SERVICES: Calling Station (✉ Av. Rafael E. Melgar 27, at Calle 3 Sur, ☎ 9/872–7868). Diamond Internet (✉ Av. 10 Nte. 200, between Calles 4 and 6 Nte., ☎ 9/872–1153).

EMERGENCIES
Both the Centro Medico de Cozumel (Cozumel Medical Center) and the Medical Specialties Center offer 24-hour air-ambulance service and a 24-hour pharmacy. The Centro de Salud clinic offers round-the-clock emergency care.

The Farmacia Dori is open daily 7 AM–midnight; Farmacia Joaquin is open Monday through Saturday 8 AM–10 PM and Sunday 9–1 and 5–9. Farmacias Canto, open 24 hours, delivers to hotels.
➤ CONTACTS: Air Ambulance (☎ 9/872–4070). Centro Medico de Cozumel (Cozumel Medical Center; ✉ 1A Sur 101, corner of Av. 50, ☎ 9/872–3545 or 9/872–5370). Centro de Salud (✉ Av. 20 Sur at Calle 11, ☎ 9/872–0140). The Chiropractic Center (✉ Av. 5 Sur 24-A, between Calles 3 and 5, ☎ 9/872–5099). Medical Specialties Center (✉ Av. 20 Nte. 425, ☎ 9/872–1419 or 9/872–2919). Police (✉ Anexo del Palacio Municipal, ☎ 9/872–0092). Recompression Chamber (✉ Calle 5 Sur 21-B, between Avs. Rafael E. Melgar and 5 Sur, ☎ 9/872–2387). Red Cross (✉ Calle Adolfo Rosada Salas at Av. 20 Sur, ☎ 9/872–1058).
➤ LATE-NIGHT PHARMACIES: Farmacias Canto (☎ 9/872–5377). Farmacia Dori (✉ Calle Adolfo Rosada Salas, between Avs. 15 and 20 Sur, ☎ 9/872–0559). Farmacia Joaquin (✉ north side of the plaza, ☎ 9/872–2520).

ENGLISH-LANGUAGE MEDIA
The tourist office and most shops and hotels around town offer the *Blue Guide to Cozumel* and *Cozumel, People & Places*. These free publications contain good information and maps of the island and downtown.

LODGING
The Cozumel Island Hotel Association has 15 member properties, and it can give you information about them and about attractions on the island. It doesn't take reservations, however.
➤ CONTACTS: Cozumel Island Hotel Association (✉ Calle 2 Nte. 15-A, ☎ 9/872–3132, FAX 9/872–2809).

MAIL AND SHIPPING
The local post office (*correos*), six blocks south of la plaza, is open weekdays 8–8, Saturday 9–5, and Sunday 9–1. Holders of American Express cards can receive mail at Fiesta Cozumel Holidays/American Express, which is open weekdays 8–1 and 5–8, Saturday 8–5.
➤ SERVICES: Fiesta Cozumel Holidays/American Express (✉ Calle 11 Sur 598, between Avs. 25 and 30, ☎ 9/872–0725). Post office (✉ Calle 7 Sur at Av. Rafael E. Melgar, ☎ 9/872–0106).

MONEY MATTERS

Most of the banks are in the main square and are open weekdays 9–1:30. Many change currency, but often only until noon.

➤ BANKS: **Banamex** (✉ Av. 5 Nte., at the plaza, ☎ 9/872–3411). **Bancomer** (✉ Av. 5 Nte., at the plaza, ☎ 9/872–0550). **Banco Serfín** (✉ Calle 1 Sur, between Avs. 5 and 10 Sur, ☎ 9/872–0930). **Bancrecer** (✉ Calle 1 Sur, between Avs. 5 and 10, ☎ 9/872–4750). **Bital** (✉ Av. Rafael E. Melgar 11, ☎ 9/872–0142).

CURRENCY EXCHANGE

After banking hours, you can exchange money at Promotora Cambiaria del Centro, open from Monday through Saturday 8 AM–9 PM.

➤ EXCHANGE SERVICES: **Promotora Cambiaria del Centro** (✉ Av. 5 Sur between Calles 1 Sur and Adolfo Rosada Salas, ☎ no phone).

MOPED TRAVEL

Mopeds are popular here, but also extremely dangerous because of heavy traffic, potholes, and hidden stop signs; accidents happen all too frequently. Mexican law requires all riders to wear helmets (it's a $25 fine if you don't). If you do decide to rent a moped, drive slowly, check for oncoming traffic, and don't ride when it's raining or if you've had any alcoholic beverages. Mopeds rent for about $25 per day; insurance is included. RC Scooter Rentals seems to have the newest machines, and it drops them off at hotels.

➤ MOPED RENTALS: **Auto Rent** (✉ Carretera Costera Sur, ☎ 9/872–0844 ext. 712). **RC Scooter Rentals** (✉ Av. 30 Nte. 700, between Calles 7 and 11 Sur, ☎ 9/872–5009). **Rentadora Cozumel** (✉ Calle Adolfo Rosada Salas 3-B, ☎ 9/872–1503; ✉ Av. 10 Sur at Calle 1, ☎ 9/872–1120). **Rentadora Marlin** (✉ Av. Adolfo López Mateos, ☎ 9/872–1586).

TELEPHONES

In order to accommodate a growing number of telephone lines, the last two digits of the 987 area code (87) have been added as a prefix to local phone numbers. Some of the printed material on Cozumel does not reflect this change.

The least-expensive way to make an international call is to buy a Ladatel phone card (sold in blocks of $3, $5, $10, and $20) and use the TELMEX public phones. The TELMEX phones can be hard to find, as they are being replaced with private services' blue and red phones that urge you to "pick up and dial zero" and have very high rates. However, you can make local calls from these phones using peso coins. Local calls start at the equivalent of about 10¢. An alternative to the phone card is the *caseta de larga distancia*—the long-distance telephone office. There's an office on Calle 1, on the south side of the plaza; it's open 8–1 and 4–9. These offices have specially designed booths where you take your call after the number has been dialed by a clerk.

More expensive than the TELMEX phones but a handier option is the Calling Station, at Avenida Rafael E. Melgar 27 and Calle 3 Sur. It also offers video and cell-phone rentals, currency exchange, Internet access, and dry cleaning and is open 8 AM–11 PM daily during high season.

TOURS

ATV AND JEEP TOURS

You can travel to the northern part of the island as part of Wild Tours' all-terrain-vehicle excursions. Rates start at $63 for a single passenger, or $93 for a driver and one passenger. Rates for jeep trips offered by Tarzan Tours start at $75 a person. Both tours include a light lunch, drinks, a visit to one of the northern Maya ruins, and a beach stop. Whether you take an ATV or a jeep, the ride through the jungle is exhilarating and the scenery incredible. Tickets are available through any local travel agent.

▶ FEES AND SCHEDULES: **Tarzan Tours** (☎ 9/872–0788). **Wild Tours** (☎ 9/872–5876).

BOAT AND SUBMARINE TOURS

Fiesta Cozumel Holidays offers three-hour trips aboard the *Principe*, a glass-bottom boat, or *Nautilus IV*, a vessel that goes partially underwater. Tours cost $26 each, including soft drinks and beer. Atlantis Submarines runs 1½-hour submarine rides that explore the Chankanaab Reef and surrounding area; tickets for the tours are $74 for adults, $38 for children.

▶ FEES AND SCHEDULES: **Atlantis Submarines** (✉ Carretera Chankanaab, Km 4, across from Hotel Casa del Mar, ☎ 9/872–5671). **Fiesta Cozumel Holidays/American Express** (✉ Calle 11 Sur 598, between Avs. 25 and 30, ☎ 9/872–0725).

HORSEBACK TOURS

Aventuras Naturales offers four-hour guided horseback tours. They start at $45 and visit Maya ruins and the beach. Rancho Buenavista offers four-hour horseback rides through the jungle starting at $65 per person. Tours run by Rancho Palmitas, near the turn off from Carretera Chankanaab (Carretera Sur) to El Cedral village, take you through the jungle to the Maya ruins; they start at $35 a person. The small Rancho San Manuel has seven horses and offers jungle tours for $20 an hour.

▶ FEES AND SCHEDULES: **Aventuras Naturales** (✉ Carretera Sur, 1 km, or ½ mi, past the international pier, ☎ 9/872–1628). **Rancho Buenavista** (☎ 9/872–1537). **Rancho Palmitas** (✉ Carretera Chankanaab, Km 16.5, ☎ no phone). **Rancho San Manuel** (✉ Playa Paraíso, Av. Rafael E. Melgar, Km 3.5, ☎ no phone).

ORIENTATION

Tours of the island's sights, including the San Gervasio ruins, El Cedral, Parque Chankanaab, and the Museo de la Isla de Cozumel, cost about $45 a person and can be arranged through travel agencies. Fiesta Cozumel Holidays, which has representatives in most major hotels, and Caribe Tours sell a number of similar tours. Another option is to take a private tour of the island via taxi, which costs about $50 to $70 for the day, depending on which parts of the island you visit.

▶ FEES AND SCHEDULES: **Caribe Tours** (✉ Av. Rafael E. Melgar at Calle 5 Sur, ☎ 9/872–3100). **Fiesta Cozumel Holidays/American Express** (main office: ✉ Calle 11 Sur 598, between Avs. 25 and 30, ☎ 9/872–0725).

TAXIS

You can hail taxis on the street, and cabs wait at all the major hotels. The fixed rates (at press time but subject to change) run about $1.50 within town; $5–$8 between town and either hotel zone; $10 from most hotels to the airport; and about $20–$40 from the northern hotels or town to Parque Chankanaab or Playa San Francisco. The cost from the cruise-ship terminal to San Miguel is about $6. Prices quoted by the drivers should be in pesos. Tipping isn't necessary, as most drivers own their vehicles.

Despite the established taxi fares, many of the younger and quite aggressive cab drivers have begun charging double or even triple these rates. If you have to take a taxi, be firm on a price before getting into the car. If the driver refuses to give you a quote, get out of the cab immediately, as this means he is likely to overcharge when you reach your destination. Familiarize yourself with the established rates but be prepared to argue with some drivers. Taxi drivers have also been known to tell passengers that certain restaurants are closed or that certain hotels don't exist, in an effort to have you pick their alternative—from which they get a commission. If you feel you have been overcharged, misled, or mistreated in any way, contact the Sitio de Taxis (Taxi Syndicate; ☎ 9/872–0041) and report the cab driver (you need the cab number to be able to do this). Drivers are fined heavily (up to a three-day work suspension) for overcharging.

TRANSPORTATION AROUND COZUMEL

Taxi fares on Cozumel run very high. If you plan to visit any of the sites, you are likely to save yourself some hassles and a lot of money by renting a car or a scooter instead of using a taxi to get around. The local buses aren't a good option because they don't go to any of the tourist sights and operate only within the town's perimeter.

TRAVEL AGENCIES

A number of local travel agencies offer tours. Fiesta Cozumel Holidays and Turismo Aviomar are represented in the lobbies of several hotels.
➤ LOCAL AGENTS: **Caribe Tours** (✉ Av. Rafael E. Melgar at Calle 5 Sur, ☎ 9/872–3100). **Fiesta Cozumel Holidays/American Express** (✉ Calle 11 Sur 598, between Avs. 25 and 30, ☎ 9/872–0725). **IMC** (✉ Calle 2 Nte. 101–8, ☎ 9/872–1535). **Turismo Aviomar** (✉ Av. 5 Nte. 8, between Calles 2 and 4, ☎ 9/872–0588).

VISITOR INFORMATION

The island's official Web site is www.islacozumel.com.mx. The state tourism office is open weekdays 9–2:30. The Cozumel Island Hotel Association offers information on affiliated hotels and tour operators.
➤ TOURIST INFORMATION: **Cozumel Island Hotel Association** (✉ Calle 2 Nte. 15-A, ☎ 9/872–3132, FAX 9/872–2809). **SECTUR** (Secretario de Turismo, or State Tourism Office; ✉ upstairs at Plaza del Sol, at the east end of the main square, ☎ FAX 9/872–0972).

4 THE CARIBBEAN COAST

Although the eastern shore of the Yucatán from Cancún to Chetumal is becoming more developed, the so-called Riviera Maya still has some secluded beaches. Get your fill of the social scene and Euro beach culture in Playa del Carmen, and then head to more isolated spots like the mangrove-filled Sian Ka'an Biosphere Reserve and the tranquil Xcalak Peninsula. Visit the Maya ruins of Tulum and rub elbows with iguanas and cruise-ship passengers, or examine ancient civilizations in solitude at the Río Bec sites of Dzibanché and Kinichná.

Updated by
Shelagh
McNally

ABOVE ALL ELSE, beaches are what define the east coast of the Yucatán peninsula—soft, blinding white strands of sand embracing clear turquoise waters; shorelines that curve into calm lagoons; waves that crash against cliffs; mangrove swamps with minuscule islands where only the birds hold sway alongside freshwater cenotes (sinkholes). Paralleling the coast, a magnificent coral reef teems with kaleidoscopic marine life swimming lazily among the shipwrecks and relics left by pirates. Landscapes change from savanna to wetland to scrubby limestone terrain to jungle, the flora and fauna varying with each setting. All this makes Quintana Roo's Caribbean coast a marvelous place for lovers of the outdoors.

The destinations on the coast are varied. While Puerto Morelos still has the relaxed atmosphere of a Mexican fishing village, Playa del Carmen is filled with resorts as glitzy and hectic as those in Cancún and Cozumel. The beaches here, from Punta Tanchacté to Tulum, are beloved by scuba divers, snorkelers, birders, and beachcombers. Rustic but comfortable fishing and scuba-diving lodges on the secluded Boca Paila and Xcalak peninsulas have a well-deserved reputation for excellent bonefishing and superb diving on virgin reefs. Unfortunately, the coast has been under siege from developers, who continue to build sprawling all-inclusive resorts, and the environment is starting to suffer.

Against this backdrop is Maya culture. While the modern Maya live in the cities and villages along the coast, their history can be seen at the ruins. At Tulum, dramatic ruins sit on a bluff overlooking the Caribbean, welcoming the sunrise each morning. Cobá, a short distance inland, has towering jungle-shrouded pyramids, testaments to its importance as a leading center of commerce in the ancient Maya world. Farther south, digs at Kohunlich have unearthed temples, palaces, and pyramids in the distinct Río Bec architectural style. They have been beautifully restored but are still largely unvisited. At the Belizean border is the capital of Quintana Roo—Chetumal. With its bright wooden houses and sultry sea air, it feels more Central American than Mexican.

During your trek along the coast, you are likely to encounter expats from around the world who are running lodges and restaurants where you'd least expect to find them. Chat with them for a bit and find out how they succumbed to the spell of the Caribbean coast.

Pleasures and Pastimes

Beaches
Caribbean coast beaches—many blessed with white sand and clear, calm waters and fringed by dense jungle foliage—are so varied that they attract everyone from amateur archaeologists to professional divers and devoted sun worshipers.

Dining
Restaurants here vary from the simple beachside affairs with outdoor tables and *palapas* (thatch roofs) to more elaborate establishments. Decor ranges from quirky to sophisticated. Casual attire is usually acceptable, and reservations generally are optional. In addition to their relaxed ambience, restaurants here offer some bargains, especially when it comes to seafood. Fresh local fish, including grouper, dorado, and sea bass, is tasty and inexpensive. On the other hand, shrimp, lobster, oysters, and other shellfish are often flown in frozen from the gulf or Pacific coast, which makes them more expensive. Tourism and an expatriate

presence mean that a variety of flavorful foods is available in some surprising places, such as Bacalar and Puerto Morelos. Playa del Carmen and Puerto Aventuras have more-urbane restaurants, as well as fast-food places serving pizza, burgers, and pasta.

CATEGORY	COST*
$$$$	over $30
$$$	$21–$30
$$	$10–$20
$	under $10

*per person for a main course at dinner

Fishing

Along with diving and snorkeling, fishing is one of the most popular activities along the coast. If you want to go fly-fishing, you can rent boats from locals who have beachside stalls. Charter captains at coastal marinas can take you out for deep-sea catches such as marlin, bonito, and sailfish. The Boca Paila Peninsula is great for a week of serious fishing.

Lodging

From Puerto Morelos down to Tulum, you can find the whole range of accommodations options: campsites, strictly functional palapas, and bungalows to decent mid-range hotels and luxury resorts and condominiums. However, the coast has become one of the most expensive areas in Mexico and Central America. Many of the luxury properties are centered on Playa del Carmen, Akumal, and Puerto Aventuras.

Tulum has a number of ecological hotels that are luxurious for their tranquillity and close proximity to nature. South of Tulum accommodations are scarce, and the more-remote hotels tend to be either very primitive or very expensive. Chetumal has a respectable number of quality lodging options, as well as a few holdouts that appear to have been last renovated during the War of the Castes. The latter category—popular with backpackers—reflects the town's origins as a pit stop for traders en route to or from Central America.

Of the all-inclusive resorts along the Riviera Maya, some are better than others. Many are in remote areas with little to do; to get to the sights, or to get some decent food, you may find yourself at the mercy of the hotel shuttle service (if there is one) or waiting for long stretches of time for the bus or spending large sums of money for taxis. The rule seems to be that the larger the hotel, the more bland the food. To avoid *turista* (traveler's diarrhea), be especially wary of the all-inclusive buffet that has been sitting around for hours.

Hotel rates drop as much as 25% in the low season (September to approximately mid-December). In the high season, it's virtually impossible to find hotels in the $ price range, especially in Playa del Carmen, unless you opt to camp out. Some hotels include breakfast in their rates. Hotel addresses listed below are the street addresses. Mailing addresses are not generally used, and hotels do not rely on the mail for reservations, as service is slow or nonexistent. You are much safer making your reservation over the phone or via fax or e-mail.

CATEGORY	COST*
$$$$	over $100
$$$	$70–$100
$$	$30–$70
$	under $30

*All prices are for a standard double room in the high season (Dec.–Apr.), excluding service and the 12% tax.

Maya Ruins

This corner of the Yucatán has some fantastic archaeological treasures—Maya cities built when local people controlled the trade routes along the Caribbean. Tulum, the last city to be built, Cobá, an important trade center, and Kohunlich, a political center with majestic stucco masks, are all breathtaking. Mysterious temples with hidden chambers, stelae carved with images of deities, and the sounds of wildlife hidden in the jungles intermingle at these sites. If you plan to visit any of the ruins, don't forget to bring bug repellent.

Nature

The wildlife on the Caribbean coast is unsurpassed in Mexico, except perhaps in Baja California. The reefs, lagoons, cenotes, and caves along the Caribbean and down the Río Hondo (Hondo River, along the border between Mexico, Belize, and Guatemala) that have been left untouched by development are filled with alligators, giant turtles, sharks, and tropical fish. The forests are home to wild pigs, foxes, turkeys, iguanas, lizards, and snakes that can be spotted in the clearings. Jaguars, monkeys, white-tail deer, armadillos, tapir, wild boars, peccaries, ocelots, raccoons, and badgers all inhabit the tropical jungle's most isolated retreats. Birders come to stare into the jungle and the seaside marshes for glimpses of parrots, toucans, terns, herons, and ibis. Casual onlookers easily stumble across yellow, blue, and scarlet butterflies; singing cicadas and orioles; sparkling dragonflies; kitelike frigates; and night owls nesting in the trees.

At dusk, colorless crabs scuttle sideways toward the coconut groves over pale white limestone sand while tiny persistent mosquitoes and gnats bore through the smallest rips in window screens, tents, and mosquito nets. The seasons are marked here by the wildlife: northern songbirds return in winter, newborn jellyfish invade beaches in spring, clouds of butterflies are born in the early summer heat, and sea turtles crowd the beaches in the middle to late summer to lay thousands of eggs. It all unfolds before your eyes.

Scuba Diving and Snorkeling

Scuba divers and snorkelers flock to Quintana Roo for its transparent turquoise-and-emerald waters strewn with rose, black, and red coral reefs and sunken pirate ships. Schools of black, gray, and gold angelfish; luminous green-and-purple parrot fish; earth-color manta rays; and scores of other jewel-tone tropical species seem oblivious to the curious humans and their underwater cameras. The visibility in these waters reaches 100 ft, so you can actually see the marine life and topography without getting wet. Akumal and Puerto Morelos have particularly good diving. If you want to get away from all nondiving distractions, except fishing, head for Banco Chinchorro.

A series of cenotes lies just off the highway between Playa del Carmen and Tulum. They're favorites with divers, snorkelers, and swimmers. Highway signs make them easy to find.

Exploring the Caribbean Coast

The coast is divided into two major areas: Punta Tanchacté to Tulum, which has the most sites and places to lodge, and south of Tulum to Chetumal, where civilization thins out quite a bit and you can find the most alluringly beautiful and remote beaches, coves, inlets, lagoons, and tropical landscapes. The Río Bec Route starts west of Chetumal and continues into Campeche.

Numbers in the text correspond to numbers in the margin and on the Mexico's Caribbean Coast map.

Great Itineraries

Three to five days gives you enough time to visit the area from Punta Tanchacté to Tulum. With seven days you can cover the entire coast; even longer visits allow you to see every attraction and village. Playa del Carmen is a convenient base—it's closest to the major ruins of Tulum and Cobá, and it has the best bus, taxi, and rental-car services outside Cancún. You need a car to venture south of Tulum, preferably a Jeep or other vehicle that can efficiently negotiate ruts and puddles the size of small Maya settlements.

IF YOU HAVE 3 DAYS

Get a room in ⌖ **Playa del Carmen** ⑤ and start out by visiting **Akumal** ⑩ for diving or deep-sea fishing, snorkeling, or swimming. Later in the day cycle on a rented mountain bike or drive to the tiny lagoon of Yalkú, which was around during the time of the Maya traders. On Day 2, head out to the cenote at **Xel-Ha** ⑫, where you can snorkel, swim, sunbathe, and see some more-modest ruins. In the afternoon visit the prehistoric underground caves at Aktun-Chen. On Day 3 head for **Tulum** ⑭ to take in the cliff-side Castillo temple. Afterward, climb down to the small adjacent beach for a dip in the ocean. In the afternoon head over to Tulum's hotel area, where you can enjoy a long walk along the marvelous coastline and sample a lunch of fresh fish.

IF YOU HAVE 5 DAYS

Again, station yourself in ⌖ **Playa del Carmen** ⑤. Begin your travels at **Xcaret** ⑥, a Disneylike ecological theme park where you can swim with dolphins, snorkel in a cenote, and watch a flashy folkloric performance at night. Spend the morning of Day 2 at **Tulum** ⑭; you can then spend the afternoon cooling off at **Xel-Ha** ⑫ or at one of the numerous cenotes along Highway 307. On Day 3, explore the beaches at **Paamul** ⑦ and **Xpu-há** ⑨ and continue on to **Akumal** ⑩ and Yalkú. Spend Day 4 at the Maya site **Cobá** ⑮ and on Day 5, take a tour of **Sian Ka'an Biosphere Reserve** ⑯.

IF YOU HAVE 7 DAYS

Follow the five-day itinerary above; on Day 6 drive to the enormous **Laguna de Bacalar** to marvel at its transparent layers of turquoise, green, and blue waters—figure about three hours to drive straight through. Visit the colonial San Felipe Fort in the village of **Bacalar** ㉑ and spend the night in ⌖ **Chetumal** ㉒, visiting the Museo de la Cultura Maya. On Day 7, head to **Kohunlich** ㉓, known for its huge stucco masks of ancient Maya rulers and the surrounding jungle's ruins. Head into the nearby farmlands to visit the majestic pyramids of **Dzibanché** ㉔ and **Kinichná;** then drive back up the coast to ⌖ **Playa del Carmen** ⑤, stopping at the **Cenote Azul,** the largest sinkhole in Mexico, and at **Muy-il** ⑰, with its small Maya temple and remote lagoon.

When to Tour the Caribbean Coast

High season or not, if you are driving, start early in the day to beat the tour buses; most come from nearby Cancún and Playa del Carmen, Mexico's most popular resorts. Be sure to get to your overnight stop before dark.

PUNTA TANCHACTÉ TO TULUM

The Caribbean coast in Mexico is in the state of Quintana Roo (keen-*tah*-nah *roh*-oh), bordered on the northwest by the state of Yucatán, on the west by Campeche, and on the south by Belize. Quintana Roo didn't exist until Mexican politicians decided to develop the area for tourism. It was officially recognized in 1974—the same year the first two hotels popped up in Cancún, where development was first focused.

Mexico's Caribbean Coast

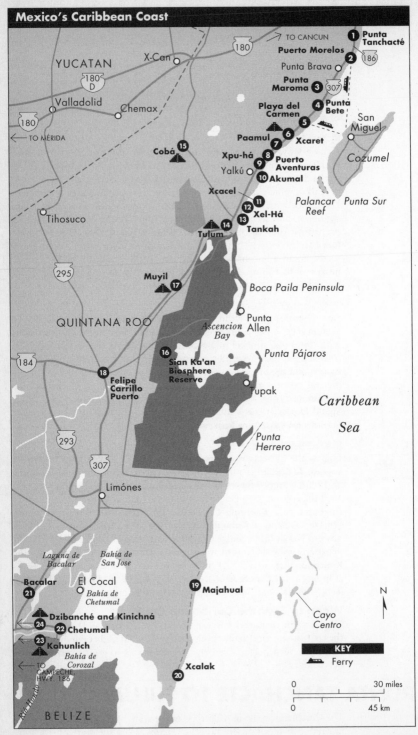

TO CANCUN

1 **Punta Tanchacté**

Puerto Morelos

180

YUCATAN

180 D

X-Can

Valladolid

Chemax

180

← TO MÉRIDA

Punta Brava

2 186

Punta Maroma **3** 307

4 **Punta Bete**

Playa del Carmen **5**

San Miguel

Paamul **7** **6**

Xcaret

Cobá **15**

Xpu-há **8**

9 **Puerto Aventuras**

Yalkú

10 **Akumal**

Cozumel

Xcacel

11

12

13 **Xel-Há**

Palancar Reef

Punta Sur

14 **Tankah**

Tulum

Tihosuco

295

Muyil **17**

Boca Paila Peninsula

QUINTANA ROO

Ascencion Bay

Punta Allen

184

16

Punta Pájaros

Sian Ka'an Biosphere Reserve

18 **Felipe Carrillo Puerto**

Tupak

Caribbean

Sea

293

Punta Herrero

307

Limónes

Laguna de Bacalar

Bahía de San Jose

Bacalar El Cocal

21 *Bahía de Chetumal*

19 **Majahual**

Cayo Centro

N

Dzibanché and Kinichná

24 **22** **Chetumal**

23 **Kahunlich**

Bahía de Corozal

← TO CAMPECHE, HWY. 186

Xcalak

20

KEY

🚢 Ferry

0   30 miles

0   45 km

BELIZE

It takes patience to discover the coast's treasures. Beaches and towns are not easily visible from the main highway—the road from Cancún to Tulum is 1–2 km (½–1 mi) from the coast. Thus there is little to see but dense vegetation, lots of billboards, a couple of roadside markets, and signs marking entrances to the businesses, ruins, resorts, beaches, and campgrounds hidden off the road.

The old PRI (Institutional Revolutionary Party) Mexican government sold vast tracts of land and beaches to various corporations and they have built huge resorts. The frenzy of building has affected the wildlife and coral reefs along the coast—as well as the beachside Maya communities, which have had to relocate to the jungle. Beach access has been limited to others, too, as the highway from Playa del Carmen to Tulum is lined with what seems like a giant barbed-wire fence punctuated with security gates. Many David-and-Goliath battles are taking place along the coast as environmentalists fight to preserve what land and wildlife are left against the onslaught of progress and keep the beaches open for everyone to enjoy. Fortunately, thanks to the federal government's foresight, 1.3 million acres of coastline and jungle have been set aside as the Sian Ka'an Biosphere Reserve. Whatever may happen along the coast, this protected area gives the wildlife, and the travelers who seek the Yucatán of old, someplace to go.

Apart from the decidedly U.S. influence—thanks to Cancún—in northern Quintana Roo, the music, food, and cultural traditions of the Caribbean coast are Yucatecan. Although the beach resorts' "international" restaurants and modern shopping malls flourish within 16 km (10 mi) of small Maya settlements, the culture remains intact.

Aside from Playa del Carmen and Puerto Aventuras, there isn't much in the way of nightlife on the coast unless you happen upon some entertainment in a fancy hotel bar. Nor is shopping sophisticated along the coast. There is little in the way of high-quality crafts here, except in Playa del Carmen and its vicinity, where the number of good folkart and crafts shops has been increasing.

Punta Tanchacté

❶ *27½ km (17 mi) south of Cancún on Hwy. 307.*

The Riviera Maya experience starts here, with small hotels on long stretches of beach caressed by the turquoise waters. It's quieter in Punta Tanchacté than in Cancún, and you can walk for miles with only the birds for company.

Lodging

$$$$ 🏨 **Escape Paraiso Maya Hotel.** Each room at this tasteful all-inclusive hotel on a secluded stretch of beach has a private ocean view. The grounds are lush and laced with palapa-covered walkways. Rooms have either two twins beds or one double and are decorated with natural fabrics, Maya designs, and art in fresh colors. The pools are on the small side but still pleasant, as is the outdoor Jacuzzi. Activities such as volleyball, snorkeling, diving, and evening shows are offered, and the food is excellent. Still, everything is low key. A free shuttle transports guests to nearby Puerto Morelos, Cancún, or Playa del Carmen. ⊠ *Cancún–Puerto Morelos Hwy./Hwy. 307, Km 27.5,* ☎ 𝔽𝔸𝕏 *9/872–8088. 60 rooms. Restaurant, bar, air-conditioning, 2 pools, dive shop, snorkeling, dance club, theater. MC, V.*

$$–$$$ 🏨 **Sand Castle.** This beautifully designed private property has a Mediterranean flavor. A spectacular atrium with a high, arched ceiling and pillars overlooks the beach. You can rent the whole house (great for families), one floor, or one studio. The first-floor villa has a full-size kitchen, a living room, two bedrooms, and 2½ exceptionally large bathrooms with tubs and a small patio facing the ocean. The upstairs studios have private baths, small kitchenettes, large sundecks, and a balcony atrium. Out back is a swimming pool, hot tub, garden, and small basketball court. The Sand Castle also has hammocks, a gift shop, and a massage area. The entire house can sleep 10 people, so if you share, this is a great bargain. ⊠ *Cancún–Puerto Morelos Hwy./Hwy. 307, Km 27.5,* ☎ *9/872–8094,* FAX *9/872–8093. 1 villa, 2 studios. Air-conditioning, fans, pool, beach, snorkeling. MC, V.*

Outdoor Activities and Sports

WATER SPORTS

Snorkeling Adventure (☎ 9/880–6559) offers great all-day snorkeling trips. This personable operation is on the Punta Tanchacté beach, with a palapa bar, hammocks, and a volleyball net. The trip includes three snorkel excursions to two different reefs, all you can drink (beer and tequila included), and a buffet lunch. It will even pick you up in Cancún.

Puerto Morelos

❷ *8 km (5 mi) south of Punta Tanchacté on Hwy. 307, 36 km (22 mi) south of Cancún.*

For years, Puerto Morelos was known as the small, relaxed coastal town where the car ferry left for Cozumel. This lack of regard actually helped it to avoid the tidal wave of development that had engulfed other communities. However, the construction of two massive all-inclusive resorts (640 rooms in total) may spoil the fishing-village atmosphere. Still, more and more people are discovering that Morelos, exactly halfway between Cancún and Playa del Carmen, makes a great base for exploring the region.

In ancient times this was a point of departure for Maya women making pilgrimages by canoe to Cozumel, the sacred isle of the fertility goddess, Ixchel. Remnants of Maya ruins exist along the coast here, but nothing has been restored. Foreigners increasingly have been buying up the land in town to build Mediterranean-style houses and condos, so most of the native population now lives across the highway in what is called the *cruzceros* (crossroads). Unfortunately, the building boom isn't translating into inexpensive rooms—long-term accommodation is impossible to find, and there are few budget options.

The town itself is small, with a central plaza surrounded by shops and restaurants; its trademark is a leaning lighthouse. Puerto Morelos's greatest appeal lies out at sea: the superb coral reef only 1,800 ft offshore, which provides excellent grounds for snorkeling and scuba diving. Dive sites include an intact Spanish galleon with coral-crusted cannons and the Cave of the Sleeping Sharks (of documentary-movie fame), 8 km (5 mi) east of the town. The proximity of the reef creates an exceptionally calm and safe beach, though it isn't as pretty as others, as it isn't cleared of seaweed on a regular basis. Still, you can walk for miles here and see only a few people, who invariably will say hello. In addition, the mangroves in back of town are home to 36 species of birds, making it a great place for birders.

Aside from a few decent restaurants, there is no nightlife in Puerto Morelos—which has prompted locals to affectionately name it "Muerto Morelos" (Dead Morelos). But there is a strong community of environmentalists and artists here, and thanks to them the coral reef has been declared a national marine park. This status should provide some protection against the encroaching commercial development and help Morelos retain its fragile ecosystem and charming milieu.

Dining and Lodging

$$ ✕ **Che Carlito's.** Some of the best food in town is at this lovely restau-
★ rant run by Carlito and his family, in the Casita del Mar. Choices in-
clude delicious empanadas, chicken fajitas, fresh salads, pastas, and
incredible steaks that rival anything you would get at the larger steak
houses in Cancún (and for half the price). The restaurant has an out-
door terrace with a palapa bar that leads down to the beach; it's a pleas-
ant stop for breakfast, lunch, or dinner. ⊠ *Casita del Mar, Calle
Heriberto Frias 6,* ☎ *9/871–0522. No credit cards.*

$$ ✕ **Twin Delphines Taquería & Restaurant.** The local Mexican chef who
runs this open-air restaurant creates delicious dinners, such as mari-
nated shark with sauteed vegetables. The menu changes according to
the season and what's available. You can have an ice-cold beer and watch
the moon rise as you wait for your dinner. When the weather is bad,
this place is closed. ⊠ *Twin Delphines Aquarium, Av. Rafael Melgar,*
☎ *no phone. No credit cards.*

$ ✕ **Johnny Cairo's.** A former Ritz-Carlton chef brought many of his fa-
vorite recipes to this colorful rendezvous with colonial Mexican furniture and art. The chicken wings and fish with mango sauce are good
choices, but as the menu changes daily, you can expect some surprises.
On Sunday there's all-you-can-eat barbecue for $10 per person. Ask
for a table on the large terrace, which overlooks the ocean, or enjoy
the palapa bar on the beach, which is particularly lively during the hotel's
monthly full-moon party. ⊠ *Hacienda Morelos, Av. Rafael Melgar,* ☎
9/871–0449. No credit cards.

$$$$ 🏨 **Ceiba del Mar Hotel & Spa.** For peace and quiet, this all-inclusive
beachside hotel may be the ticket. It's in a residential part of town,
so there are few outside facilities around and there's absolutely no
nightlife. Rooms are clustered in eight buildings, each with three
floors, and all have ocean-view terraces. The contemporary Mexican
decor uses a lot of wrought iron and bamboo. The spa offers massage (shiatsu, too) and aromatherapy. The reef is 20 minutes away,
great for snorkelers and divers, but the beach has a lot of turtle grass.
⊠ *Av. Niños Heroes s/n,* ☎ *9/871–0533 or 800/235–5892,* FAX *9/871–
0458,* WEB *www.ceibadelmar.com. 120 rooms, 6 suites. 2 restaurants,
bar, air-conditioning, pool, tennis court, spa, beach, dive shop, travel
services, car rental. AE, MC, V.*

$$$ 🏨 **Casita del Mar.** Renovated in 2001, the hotel has an incredible
beach, lovely pool, and a great restaurant—Che Carlito. Rooms are
average size, painted in muted Mexican colors of burnt sienna, taupe,
and yellow with either king-size beds or two twin beds. The bathrooms
are exceptionally clean and well done. Ask for the ocean-facing suites;
they have a fantastic beach view and are perfect for watching the sun-
rise. The beach, cleaned daily, has lounge chairs, palapas, kayaks, and
an on-site snorkeling–fishing shop. ⊠ *Calle Heriberto Frias 6, 4 blocks
north of town,* ☎ FAX *9/871–0301,* WEB *www.caribbeanmag.com/nho-
tels/Casita/. 17 rooms. Restaurant, bar, air-conditioning, pool, beach.
No credit cards.*

$$ 🏨 **Casa Caribe.** This small, pretty hotel sits a few blocks from the town
★ center and five minutes from the beach. The breezy rooms have re-
frigerators, king-size beds, and roomy tile baths. Terraces have hammocks and views of the ocean or the mangroves. A large kitchen
leading to a huge terrace is available for guests' use. The grounds include a walled courtyard and a fragrant tropical garden. Children
under 10 stay free. ⊠ *Av. Javier Rojo Gomez and Ejercito Mexicano
(3 blocks north of town),* ☎ *9/871–0049; 763/441–7630 in the U.S.,*
WEB *www.us-webmasters.com/Casa-Caribe/. 6 rooms. Refrigerators, fans.
No credit cards.*

$$ ⌂ **Hotel Ojo de Agua.** Travelers looking for friendly lodging in a peaceful atmosphere on the beach are likely to be pleased by this family-run hotel. Half of the guest rooms have kitchenettes, and all rooms are decorated in cheerful colors with ceiling fans and views of the sea and courtyard gardens. An open-air restaurant serves good regional Mexican dishes along with American food such as hamburgers and fries. The beach is one of the best around, with great snorkeling directly out front, including *ojo de agua,* an underwater cenote shaped like an eye. The dive shop rents out snorkeling equipment and arranges scuba-diving expeditions. ✉ *Av. Javier Rojo Gomez and Lazaro Cardenas, 2 blocks north of town,* ☎ *9/871–0027,* FAX *9/871–0202,* WEB *www.ojo-de-agua.com. 36 rooms. Restaurant, air-conditioning (some), fans, kitchenettes (some), pool, beach, dive shop, snorkeling. MC, V.*

$ ⌂ **Hotel Inglaterra.** The pluses at the Inglaterra, the only budget hotel in town, are that it's clean, secure, and close to the beach. In addition, it offers free tea or coffee, has a large, sunny upstairs deck, and the price is right particularly if you don't choose the breakfast option. However, the staff can be cranky and there isn't much atmosphere here. The hotel is sparse, with basic rooms: one double, one single bed, a functional bathroom, ceiling fans, and absolutely no view (or air) from the windows. ✉ *Av. Niños Héroes 29,* ☎ FAX *9/871–0418. 17 rooms. Fans. No credit cards.*

Outdoor Activities and Sports

WATER SPORTS

Enrique at **Almost Heaven Adventures** (☎ 9/871–0230), in the main square by the currency exchange, can set up snorkeling and fishing trips. **Brecko's** (✉ Casita del Mar, Calle Heriberto Frias 6, ☎ 9/871–0301) offers snorkeling and deep-sea fishing in a 25-ft boat. Owner Shade Haseman also takes people out on sailing excursions aboard his Hobie Cat. Snorkeling trips start at $15–$20 and fishing trips at $200. On a day trip with **H.E.A.D. South** (High Energy Adventure Day; ☎ 9/871–0483, headsouthmx@yahoo.com), Billy Alexander takes you out to snorkel at the beaches littered with treasure from Spanish shipwrecks or to explore nearby cenotes. Trips start at $65. **Sub-Aqua Explorers** (☎ 9/871–0018) can set up scuba-diving excursions, as can divemaster **David Sanchez** (☎ 9/871–0006).

Shopping

Alma Libre Libros (✉ Av. Tulum, on the main plaza, ☎ 9/871–0264) is the only English-language bookstore on the coast, with more than 20,000 books in stock. You can trade in your books for 25% of their cover prices and replenish your holiday reading. It's open October through April, Tuesday through Saturday, 9–noon and 6–9.

The **Collectivo de Artisans de Puerto Morelos** (Puerto Morelos Artists' Cooperative; ✉ Avs. Javier Rojo Gomez and Isla Mujeres, ☎ no phone) is a series of palapa-style buildings where local artisans display their jewelry, hand-embroidered clothes, hammocks, and other items that make good souvenirs. You might find some real bargains here. It's open daily from 8 AM until dusk.

Rosario & Marco's Art Shoppe (✉ Av. Javier Rojo Gomez 14, ☎ no phone), close to the ferry docks, is run by the eponymous couple, from their living room. They paint regional scenes such as markets, colonial homes, and flora and fauna as well as portraits. Marco also creates replicas of Spanish galleons.

En Route   The biologists running the **Croco-Cun** (✉ Hwy. 307, Km 30, ☎ 9/884–4782) crocodile farm and miniature zoo just north of Puerto Morelos have collected specimens of many of the reptiles and some of the mammals indigenous to the area. They offer immensely informative tours—you may even get to handle a baby crocodile or feed the deer. Be sure to wave hello to the 500-pound crocodile secure in his deep pit. The farm is open daily 8:30–5:30; admission is $5.

South of Puerto Morelos, the 150-acre **Dr. Alfredo Barrera Marín Botanical Garden** (✉ Hwy. 307, Km 36, ☎ no phone) is one of the largest tropical gardens in Mexico. Named for a local botanist, it exhibits the plants and flowers of the peninsula labeled in English, Spanish, and Latin. There's also a tree nursery, a remarkable orchid and epiphyte garden, a reproduction of a *chiclero* (gum collector), an authentic Maya house, and an archaeological site. A nature walk goes directly through the mangroves for some great bird-watching (bring that bug spray). A tree-house lookout offers a spectacular view—but the climb is not for those afraid of heights. The garden is open daily 9–5, and admission is $4.

Punta Brava

7 km (4½ mi) south of Puerto Morelos on Hwy. 307.

Punta Brava is also known as South Beach in Puerto Morelos. It's a long, winding beach strewn with seashells. On windy days, its shallow waters are whipped up into waves large enough for bodysurfing.

Lodging

$$$$ 🏨 **El Dorado Royale.** This luxurious adults-only, all-inclusive spa resort is surrounded by 500 acres of tropical jungle and 1½ mi of unspoiled beach. It offers junior suites with Mexican furnishings, small sitting rooms, king-size beds, indoor hot tubs, and ocean-facing terraces. The casitas have domed roofs with mahogany beams, white walls, king-size beds, and oceanfront palapa terraces. The food is exceptional, with an à la carte menu in all four restaurants. Enjoy the pool or treatments at the state-of-the-art spa while gazing out at the ocean. (Use of the spa facilities costs extra; packages are available.) The real standout here is the staff, which, despite the posh surroundings, is friendly, warm, and down to earth. ✉ *Hwy. 307, Km 25, Kantenah Bay,* ☎ *9/ 884–8341 or 800/290–6679,* 𝖥𝖠𝖷 *9/884–8342,* 🕸 *www.eldorado-resort.com. 200 rooms, 70 suites. Restaurant, bar, air-conditioning, pool, spa, beach, snorkeling. AE, MC, V.*

Punta Maroma

❸ *2 km (1 mi) south of Punta Brava on Hwy. 307.*

Nestled in a bay where the winds don't reach the waters, this gorgeous beach remains calm even on blustery days. To the north you can see the land curve out to another beach, **Playa del Secreto;** to the south the curve that leads eventually to Punta Bete is visible.

Dining and Lodging

$$$$ ✕🏨 **Maroma.** This place captures the essence of a romantic tropical
★ oasis with an ambience that is at once stylish, alluring, and relaxed. Peacocks wander through the jungle walkways; birds fly in from the perfect beach; flowers scent the air. Everything has been designed to delight the senses. Rooms, decorated with whimsical artifacts and original artwork, have king-size beds draped in mosquito nets and small sitting areas. A full breakfast (included in the room rate) is served every morning on each room's private terrace, with either an ocean or garden view. On the grounds are a library, a theater, and a spa with a Mayan sauna. The Maroma restaurant (reservations required) is a gourmet affair offering delights such as lobster bisque and honeyed rack of lamb.

Staff members are polished yet offer heartfelt hospitality. Not surprisingly, this adults-only hotel is a favorite place for weddings and honeymoons. ✉ *Hwy. 307, Km 51,* ☎ *9/872–8200,* 🆀 *9/872–8220,* 🆆 *www.maromahotel.com. 31 rooms, 3 suites, 2 villas. Restaurant, bar, grill, pool, massage, spa, steam room, horseback riding, beach, snorkeling, windsurfing, theater, library. AE, MC, V.*

Punta Bete

❹ *13 km (8 mi) south of Punta Maroma on Hwy. 307, then about 2 km (1 mi) off the main road.*

The one concession to "progress" here has been a slight improvement in the road. Take this bumpy 2½-km (1½-mi) ride through the jungle to arrive at a 6½-km-long (4-mi-long) isolated beach dotted with bargain bungalow-style hotels and thatch-roof restaurants. A few more-comfortable accommodations are available if you want to spare yourself some grit in your personal belongings.

Lodging

$$$$
★ 🏨 **Kai Luum II.** This much-loved vacation spot is the lazy man's answer to camping out. Right on the beach, Kai Luum offers "tentalapas"—large canvas tents under palapa roofs with ocean-view porches and hammocks—for adults only (over age 16). Inside are double beds with fluffy pillows and bedside tables. The tentalapas are private, but bathrooms and showers are shared. The outdoor restaurant, serving Yucatecan specialties, is under a giant palapa roof lit by oil lamps (there is no electricity here). The atmosphere has fostered lasting friendships; many of the guests are repeat visitors. ✉ *Hwy. 307, Km 62, beyond Posada del Capitán Lafitte (reservations: Turquoise Reef Group, Box 2664, Evergreen, CO 80439),* ☎ *9/850–4826 or 800/538–6802,* 🆀 *303/674–8735, in the U.S.,* 🆆 *www.mexicoholiday.com. 29 tents. Restaurant, bar, beach, snorkeling. AE, MC, V.*

$$$$ 🏨 **Posada del Capitán Lafitte.** This remains a really sweet all-inclusive resort aimed at families, with clusters of three-unit cabañas as well as some duplexes. Opt for the newer cabañas on the north end of the beach, which are furnished Mexican-style. Here the beach is an invitingly long stretch of tranquillity. You can enjoy the view from the main dining room. The resort is known for its warm atmosphere, and activities such as snorkeling trips and horseback riding are encouraged here. The on-site dive shop offers PADI certification courses for guests and nonguests alike. All reservations must be prepaid, and rates include breakfast and dinner. ✉ *Hwy. 307, Km 62 (reservations: Turquoise Reef Group, Box 2664, Evergreen, CO 80439,* 🆀 *303/674–8735),* ☎🆀 *9/873–0212 or* ☎ *800/ 538–6802,* 🆆 *www.mexicoholiday.com. 62 rooms. Restaurant, bar, pool, beach, dive shop, airport shuttle, car rental. AE, MC, V.*

$$ 🏨 **Cocos Cabañas.** Enjoy tranquillity and seclusion at these cozy palapa bungalows set back 30 yards from the beach. The cabañas are colorful and bright, and have a queen- or king-size bed, bath, hammocks, and a terrace that leads to a tropical garden. Enjoy breakfast, lunch, or dinner at the Grill Bar, which serves fresh fish and Italian food. ✉ *Playa Xcalacoco (follow signs and take dirt road off Hwy. 307, Km 42, for about 3 km [2 mi]),* ☎ *9/874–7056,* 🆀 *9/887–9964. 5 cabañas. Restaurant, beach. No credit cards.*

$ 🏨 **Cabañas Xcalacoco.** Roughing it on the beach is romantic in one of these seven white cabañas. All have double beds, hammocks, and small porches, but there's no electricity—kerosene lamps light the nights. There are also camping facilities with showers and a place to park recreational vehicles, which by no means interfere with cabaña views. ✉ *Playa Xcalacoco (follow signs and take dirt road off Hwy.*

307, Km 42, for about 3 km [2 mi]), ☎ no phone. 7 cabañas. Beach, camping. No credit cards.

Playa del Carmen

❺ *10 km (6 mi) south of Punta Bete, 68 km (42 mi) south of Cancún.*

Once upon a time, Playa del Carmen was a fishing village with a ravishing, deserted beach. The villagers fished and raised coconut palms to produce copra, and foreigners were infrequent visitors. These days it's one of the fastest-growing cities in Mexico, with a population of more than 30,000, and it's as exciting and fast-paced as Cancún. The beach is still delightful—alabaster-white sand, turquoise-blue waters—it's just not deserted.

The most consistent sound you hear throughout Playa del Carmen is that of jackhammers. For the past few years Playa's construction boom has transformed the city every few months. Hotels, restaurants, and shops are multiplying faster than you can say "Kukulcán," and many new businesses are branches of Cancún establishments whose owners have taken up permanent residence in Playa or commute daily between the two. Some of the changes have been for the better. Avenida 5, the first street parallel to the beach, has been turned into a pedestrian walkway with quaint cafés and street art and entertainment. Unfortunately, these changes have made driving to the beachfront hotels difficult, unless you know exactly where you're going, and parking has become a nightmare.

Avenida Juárez, running east–west from the highway to the beach, is the main commercial zone for the Riviera Maya corridor. Here, locals go about their everyday business, visiting the food shops, pharmacies, auto-parts and hardware stores, and banks that line the curbs. People traveling the coast by car usually stop here to stock up on supplies—it's the last bank and department store until Chetumal and the last gas station until Tulum. A bus station marks the end of Avenida Juárez.

The ferry pier, where boats arrive from and depart for Cozumel (on the hour), is another bustling part of town. Take a stroll north from the pier along the beach to find the serious sun worshipers. On the south side of the pier is the edge of the sprawling Playacar complex. The development is a labyrinth of residential homes and all-inclusive resorts bordered by an 18-hole championship golf course. The excellent 32,550-acre **Xaman Ha Aviary** (⊠ Paseo Xaman-Ha, Playacar, ☎ no phone), in the middle of the Playacar development, is home to more than 30 species of native birds. It's open daily 9–5, and admission is about 80¢.

Playa del Carmen is no longer the budget haven it once was, as prices, particularly in hotels, have been rising steadily. It's one of the most expensive stops along the coast. Things change fast here, and while peace and quiet may no longer describe the town, Playa does make a fun introduction to the Caribbean coast.

Dining and Lodging

Playa has hundreds of hotels, and more are opening. Playa's most luxurious rooms are at the 880-acre Playacar development. The most expensive hotels in town line the beach; the more modest rooms are farther north. Competition among the smaller hotels is fierce, so most ask for a deposit (usually the price of one night) before taking your reservation. As for the dining scene, mediocrity reigns supreme, though most restaurants have great decor.

$$ ✕ **Palapa Hemingway.** The theme of this palapa restaurant is Cuba and its revolution; the menu highlights seafood. The grilled shrimp, fish, and steaks are good choices, but so are the fresh salads, pastas, and chicken dishes. ⊠ *Av. 5 between Avs. 12 and 14,* ☎ *9/873–0004. MC, V.*

$–$$ ✕ **Johnny Cairo's.** This cosmopolitan restaurant's innovative cuisine is served in a relaxed, casual setting with Caribbean overtones. Enjoy your meal tucked away under the palapa roof or watch all the action from the terrace. Consider hickory-smoked duck with a red-onion marmalade as a starter and the shrimp "steak" with a tamarind glaze as a main course. ⊠ *Calle 5,* ☎ *9/873–0111. MC, V. No lunch.*

$–$$ ✕ **La Parrilla.** The excellent Mexican fare is the draw at this boisterous (especially when the mariachis start playing), touristy restaurant. The smell of the sizzling *parrilla mixta* (a grilled, marinated mixture of lobster, shrimp, chicken, and steak) can make it difficult to resist grabbing one of the few available tables. It offers live music, friendly service, and strong margaritas until well after the witching hour. ⊠ *Av. 5 at Calle 8,* ☎ *9/873–0687. AE, MC, V. No lunch.*

$–$$ ✕ **Zas.** The Canadian couple that runs this stylish restaurant has brought the best of Toronto's cuisine and combined it with Mexican flavors. Owner–chef Carla is in the kitchen daily, creating dishes such as chicken stuffed with sun-dried tomatoes. The breakfast menu includes delicious pancakes and omelets. A sister restaurant, Media Luna, on Avenida 5 at Calle 8 (no phone), offers a great vegetarian menu in a cozy place decorated with Mexican and Guatemalan accents. ⊠ *Av. 5 at Calles 12 and 14,* ☎ *no phone. No credit cards.*

$ ✕ **Café Sasta.** This sweet little café offers a variety of fantastic coffee drinks (cappuccino, espresso, mocha blends), teas, light sandwiches, and excellent baked goods. The staff is very pleasant—something that is becoming rare in Playa. ⊠ *Avs. 5 and Constituyentes,* ☎ *9/873–3030. No credit cards.*

$ ✕ **Hot.** Open at 6 AM, this is the place to stop for breakfast. The egg dishes are very good, especially the chili–cheese omelet, as are the baked goods and the hot coffee. Salads and sandwiches are lunch options. ⊠ *Calle 10 between Avs. 5 and 10,* ☎ *9/876–4370. No credit cards.*

$ ✕ **Little Saint.** The decor, music, and menu give this bistro a cosmopolitan air. Dishes such as goat-cheese salad are elegant, simple, and delicious. For lunch try the fragrant meat loaf. Breakfast fare includes omelets and fresh juices. ⊠ *Calle 2 between Avs. 5 and 10,* ☎ *no phone. No credit cards.*

$ ✕ **Sabor.** The prices have gone up and beer and wine are now on the menu, but the savory salads, sandwiches, and baked goods are still tasty, and the location is great. Seats at breakfast and lunch are hard to find. ⊠ *Av. 5, between Calles 3 and 4,* ☎ *no phone. No credit cards.*

$ ✕ **Lo Sfizio.** If you can handle the slightly chaotic and at times indifferent service, this is the place to get great Italian food. Try the carpaccio, gnocchi with four cheeses, ravioli with tomato sauce, or the pizzas. Everything is fresh and authentic. ⊠ *Calle 4 between Avs. 10 and 15,* ☎ *no phone. No credit cards.*

$ ✕ **Yaxche.** This is the best restaurant along the Riviera Maya. The owner
★   shows his love of the Maya culture and cuisine; decorations include hand-carved stelae from famous ruins along with ceiling and wall murals of Maya gods and kings. The real knockout is the food; dishes such as *halach winic* (chicken in a spicy four-pepper sauce) and *tikinchic* (fish in a sour orange–onion sauce with achiote) bring Maya cuisine to gourmet levels. Finish off your meal with a Maya Kiss (Kahlúa and Xtabentun, a local liqueur flavored with anise and honey). Book a reservation for the backyard patio if you want to have your meal amid the

fountain, plants, and Maya art. ⊠ *Calle 8 at Avs. 5 and 10,* ☎ *9/873–2502. AE, MC, V.*

$ ✕ **Zulu Lounge.** Despite the odd combination of African decor, Thai food, techno music, and pool tables, this funky restaurant keeps visitors coming back for its good food and laid-back service. Classic Thai dishes such as spring rolls and *pad thai* (a noodle dish) are available, but those with bold palates should consider trying the curries. ⊠ *Av. 5 near Calle 8,* ☎ *9/873–0056. MC, V. No lunch.*

PLAYACAR RESORT

$$$$ ⚄ **Iberostar Tucan and Quetzal.** This unique, luxurious, all-inclusive resort has two personalities. The Quetzal side is decorated with Mexican colonial art and furniture, while the Tucan has reproductions of famous stelae and carvings from Maya ruins. The hotel has worked hard at preserving the natural surroundings, and among the resident animals are flamingos, ducks, hens, turtles, fish, toucans—even a family of monkeys. Spacious rooms are decorated in cheerful Caribbean colors and have ocean or jungle views. The restaurants serve decent Mexican and international fare. Also on the premises are a fully equipped water-sports center and a health club. Playa del Carmen is a 20-minute walk or a $4 cab ride north. ⊠ *Fracc. Playacar,* ☎ *9/873–0200 or 888/923–2722,* FAX *9/873–0424,* WEB *www.iberostar.com. 700 rooms. 3 restaurants, 2 bars, 4 pools, air-conditioning, spa, 2 tennis courts, basketball, health club, dive shop, nightclub, children's program (ages 4–12). AE, MC, V.*

$$$$ ⚄ **Royal Hideaway.** Sitting on a breathtaking stretch of beach, this 13-
★ acre, ultraluxurious adults-only resort offers exceptional amenities and superior service. The two- and three-story villas are a fusion of Spanish–Mexican colonial architecture set on grounds with winding rivers, waterfalls, and fountains. Each villa has its own concierge to take care of your needs. Deluxe rooms have two queen beds, sitting areas, and ocean-view terraces done in royal blue, cream, and yellow. Duplex suites have elegant dining and living rooms as well. Furnishings throughout the hotel, particularly the lobby area, are a medley of the best art and artifacts from around the world. Meals at the five restaurants are à la carte. This is also one of the few resorts that are wheelchair accessible. ⊠ *Fracc. Playacar, Lote 6,* ☎ *9/873–4500 or 877/284–0935,* FAX *9/873–4506,* WEB *www.allegroresorts.com. 192 rooms, 8 suites. 5 restaurants, 3 bars, air-conditioning, in-room data ports, 2 pools, spa, 2 tennis courts, health club, travel services. AE, MC, V.*

HOTELS IN TOWN

$$$$ ⚄ **Baal Nah Kah.** True to its name, which means "home hidden among
★ the gum trees" in Maya, this small hotel is quite homey. Guests have the use of a large kitchen, common sitting room, and barbecue pit. The five bedrooms and one studio are on different levels, affording complete privacy. Two rooms have spacious balconies with a panoramic view of the ocean; all have tile baths, fans, double or king-size beds, and Mexican decor. A small café next door serves breakfast, snacks, and light meals. The beach is a block away. ⊠ *Calle 12 near Av. 5,* ☎ *9/873–0110,* FAX *9/873–0050,* WEB *www.cancunsouth.com/baalnahkah. 5 rooms, 1 apartment. Fans. No credit cards.*

$$$$ ⚄ **Shangri-La Caribe.** Here's a sign of how much Playa has grown: Shangri-La used to be on the outskirts of town, but now it's considered part of northern downtown. Still, it has kept its magic and remains a tranquil beachside resort with attractive whitewashed bungalows. Comfortable beds, tile floors, baths, and balconies or patios with hammocks decorate the rooms. A large circular palapa where you can have light American or Mexican fare is a gathering spot for guests. ⊠ *Calle 38 between Av. 5 and Zona Playa (reservations: Turquoise Reef Group,*

Box 2664, Evergreen, CO 80439), ☎ *9/873–0611 or 800/538–6802,* FAX *9/873–0500,* WEB *www.mexicoholiday.com. 70 bungalows. Restaurant, bar, coffee shop, fans, pool, beach, dive shop, snorkeling, fishing, car rental. AE, MC, V.*

$$$ ⊞ **Hotel Molcas.** Steps from the ferry docks, this colonial-style hotel has been in business since the early 1980s and it has aged gracefully. The rooms have air-conditioning and are graced with dark-wood furniture; they face the pool, the sea, or the street. The second-floor pool area is quite glamorous, with white tables, umbrellas, and uniformed waiters. Although it's in the heart of all the bustle, the hotel is well insulated from the noise and is rather serene. ⊠ *Av. 5 at Calle 1 Sur,* ☎ *9/873–0070,* FAX *9/873–0138,* WEB *www.molcas.com. 25 rooms. Restaurant, bar, air-conditioning, pool. AE, MC, V.*

$$$ ⊞ **Mosquito Blue.** This beautiful hotel has become a landmark in Playa
★ for its artistic design and architecture. The rooms and lobby, with their lovely mahogany furniture, Indonesian decor, and soft lighting, are at once casual, exotic, and elegant. King-size beds, great views, and kitchenettes round out the rooms. A cloistered courtyard has a garden, pool, and open-air bar. A dive shop is on site, the beach a five-minute walk away. Note that children under age 16 are not allowed. ⊠ *Calle 12 between Avs. 5 and 10,* ☎ FAX *9/873–1335,* WEB *www.mosquitoblue.com. 16 rooms, 8 suites. Restaurant, 2 bars, air-conditioning (some), fans (some), kitchenettes, 2 pools, massage, gym, dive shop. AE, MC, V.*

$$$ ⊞ **El Tukan Condotel Villas and Beach Club.** The look is exclusive and expensive, but the rates aren't as high as you might expect. Rooms and suites are well separated from one another and offer private terraces, tiny kitchenettes, and attractive accents such as burnished tile floors and painted wood furniture. The large jungle garden has a pool and a natural cenote; the tranquil spot is quite popular with guests, many of whom are European. Included in the room rate is a buffet breakfast at the Tucan Maya restaurant across the street, which also offers lunch and dinner à la carte. ⊠ *Av. 5, between Calles 14 and 16,* ☎ *9/873–0417,* FAX *9/ 873–0668. 56 rooms, 39 suites. Bar, grocery, air-conditioning, kitchenettes, pool, beach, bicycles. MC, V.*

$$ ⊞ **Delfín.** One of the older hotels in town, the Delfín retains the old Playa laid-back charm. In the heart of Playa, although not on the beach, the hotel is a good choice for its bright, airy rooms cooled by sea breezes and decorated with colorful mosaics. Rooms also have fans or air-conditioning, safes, refrigerators, and wonderful ocean views. Everything you need or want is within close walking distance. The management is exceptionally helpful. ⊠ *Av. 5 at Calle 6,* ☎ FAX *9/873–0176,* WEB *www.hoteldelfin.com. 14 rooms. Air-conditioning (some), fans (some), refrigerators. MC, V (5% fee for credit cards).*

$$ ⊞ **Hotel Casa Tucan.** The owners have worked hard at creating a cozy community a short distance from the main drag. The peaceful gardens here are home to a small menagerie of rabbits, ducks, birds, and turtles, and the hotel has a variety of clean and cheerful rooms geared to different budgets. The property also includes a restaurant, a game room with billiards, a meditation palapa, a TV bar, a language school, and a specially designed dive pool that is used by the on-site dive center. Families are welcome here. ⊠ *Calle 4 between Avs. 10 and 15,* ☎ *9/873–0283. 20 rooms. Restaurant, bar, pool, dive shop, billiards, recreation room. MC, V.*

$$ ⊞ **Maya Brick.** The best thing about this hotel is that it's in the middle of Avenida 5 and—because it is set back from the street and is surrounded by a tropical garden—surprisingly quiet. Rooms are small but clean, with a double bed and private bath, and open onto the garden and small pool. The staff is a bit cool, however. ⊠ *Av. 5 between Calles*

8 and 10, ☎ *9/873–0011,* FAX *9/873–2041. 29 rooms. Restaurant, airconditioning, fans, pool. MC, V.*

$$ 🏨 **Paraiso Azul's (Casa de Gopala).** For years this small hotel, formerly known as Casa de Gopala, has been a favorite destination for travelers seeking clean, comfortable, and reasonably priced accommodations. Once you pass through the wooden doors, you enter a private jungle that is cool and tranquil. Rooms are spacious, bright, and airy, with large windows, two double beds, and Mexican accents. Guests can use the pool at the Hotel Casa Tucan. This is a great place to experience the laid-back rhythm of the old Playa. ✉ *Calle 2 between Avs. 10 and 15,* ☎ FAX *9/873–0054. 16 rooms. Fans. No credit cards.*

$$ 🏨 **Posada Mariposa.** One of the best hotels in Playa, the Mariposa is
★ in the quiet north section of town. Not only does it have impeccable style, it's also comfortable and well priced. Rooms center on a tropical garden filled with plants, flowers, trees, and a small fountain. All have ocean views, luxurious bathrooms with bidets, and shared patios, and are furnished with queen-size beds and wall murals each with a different theme. Suites have full kitchens. Sunset on the rooftop is quite spectacular and the beach is five minutes away down a private road. ✉ *Av. 5 No. 314, between Calles 24 and 26,* ☎ *9/876–4117 or 800/416–2747,* FAX *9/873–1054,* WEB *www.hotelmariposa.com. 16 rooms, 8 suites. Airconditioning, fans. No credit cards.*

$ 🏨 **Posada Freud.** On the main strip behind the Media Luna restaurant (where guests get a discount) is this quirky little hotel with a European flavor. Each room is decorated differently, with Mexican textiles and wall murals. The bigger rooms have refrigerators and coffee makers. The inner courtyard and garden do a remarkable job of keeping out the Avenida 5 noise. ✉ *Av. 5 between Calles 8 and 10,* ☎ FAX *9/ 873–0601. 12 rooms. Fans, refrigerators (some). No credit cards.*

$ 🏨 **La Ruinas Camp Grounds.** The cheapest place in Playa is near the beach, and it's also the only authorized campground in town. Cabañas (with baths), palapas, tent spaces, and RV spaces are the lodging options here. ✉ *Calle 2 and Av. 5 Nte.,* ☎ FAX *9/873–0405. 5 cabañas. Camping. No credit cards.*

Nightlife and the Arts

Most of Playa closes down around 11 PM, but a growing number of bars and discos stay open until the wee hours of the morning. Unfortunately, Playa's drug culture sometimes surfaces in the clubs. Resist the temptation to indulge, not only because it can land you in jail but because you may get robbed during drug transactions.

The **Blue Parrot** (✉ Calle 12 at Av. 1, ☎ 9/873–0083) has live music every night until midnight; the bar sometimes stays open until 3 AM. **Capitán Tutix** (✉ Calle 4 Nte., ☎ no phone) is a beach bar designed to resemble a ship. Good drink prices and music keep the crowd of locals and visitors dancing until dawn. To party off the beach check out **Requiem** (✉ Calle 6 between Avs. 5 and 10, ☎ 9/973–3189), a dance club that plays the latest in techno and house music.

Outdoor Activities and Sports

DIVING

Playa del Carmen's scuba scene has grown considerably in the past few years. Most dive shops offer similar services, but the quality of the equipment and dive instructors varies; it's best to shop around. The **Abyss** (☎ 9/873–2164) offers training courses in addition to dive trips. The oldest shop in town, **Tank-Ha Dive Shop** (☎ FAX 9/873–5037), has PADI-certified teachers and runs diving and snorkeling trips to the reefs and caverns. **Yucatek Divers** (☎ 9/873–0283) specializes in cenote dives, diving packages, and works with divers who have disabilities.

GOLF

The golf course in Playa is an 18-hole, par-72 championship course designed by Robert Von Hagge. Greens fees range from $110 to $165 with a special twilight rate. Information is available from the **Casa Club de Golf** (☎ 9/873–0624).

HORSEBACK RIDING

Rancho Dos Amigos (☎ 9/883–1138) offers horseback expeditions on the beach and in the jungle. The two-hour trips start at $35 and include food, drinks, and bilingual guides. Two-hour trips run by **Rancho Loma Bonita** (☎ 9/887–5465) start at $45.

MOUNTAIN BIKING

You can rent bicycles from **Universal Rent** (⊠ Av. 10 between Calles 12 and 14, ☎ 9/879–3358). **Alemaya Motorent** (⊠ Hotel Eclipse, Av. 5 between Calles 12 and 14, ☎ 9/873–0629) rents bikes out of Hotel Eclipse. The best (and safest) bike path is through Playacar.

SKYDIVING

Thrill seekers can take the plunge high above Playa in a tandem sky dive (you're hooked up to the instructor the whole time). **SkyDive** (⊠ Plaza Marina 32, Playacar, ☎ 9/873–0192) even videotapes your trip so you have proof that you did it.

Shopping

Avenida 5 between Calles 4 and 10 is the best place to shop along the coast. Unique shops and boutiques sell folk art and textiles from around Mexico, and clothing stores carry original designs created from hand-painted Indonesian batiks. Shops usually are open from about 10 in the morning to 9 or 10 at night.

Amber Museum Shop (⊠ Av. 5 between Calles 4 and 6, ☎ FAX 9/873–0446) has elegantly crafted amber jewelry by a local designer who imports the amber from Chiapas; there is also a small jewelry-making workshop for children. **La Calaca** (⊠ Av. 5 between Calles 6 and 8 or Av. 5 and Calle 4, ☎ 9/873–0177 for both) has an eclectic collection of wooden masks and other carvings. The playful devils and angels are of note. **Telart** (⊠ Av. Juárez 10, ☎ 9/873–0066) carries textiles from all over Mexico.

Xcaret

⚓ ☝ ❻   *11 km (6½ mi) south of Playa del Carmen, 72 km (45 mi) south of Cancún.*

South of Playa del Carmen is where Disney meets the Maya. Xcaret, once a sacred Maya city and port, is a 250-acre ecological theme park on a gorgeous stretch of coastline. You can't escape it, as it's the most heavily advertised park on the coast, with its own buses, magazines, and stores. Billed as "nature's sacred paradise," it's expensive, contrived, and crowded. If you're a Walt Disney World fan, you're likely to love it.

Highlights of the park include an aviary, a butterfly pavilion, botanical gardens, riding stables, a tropical aquarium with a sea-turtle nursery, an artificially created beach for snorkeling and swimming, a dive center with myriad sporting activities, a replica of a Maya village, a small zoo, some Maya ruins, and an underground river ride where you snorkel through a series of caves. There is even a Dolphinarium, where you can attend a dolphin workshop and swim with the dolphins for $80 a person (book early; only 36 people a day are allowed).

Evenings, there are folkloric extravaganzas that begin with a reenact-ment of the Maya ball game and end with a performance by the famed Voladores de Papantla (Fliers of Papantla) from Veracruz. Plan to spend both the day and plenty of money. The $49 (per adult) entrance fee covers only access to the grounds and the exhibits; all other expenses, from lockers to snorkel and swim gear to horseback riding, are extra. You can buy tickets from any travel agency or major hotel along the coast. ☎ 9/880–6618, *in Cancún.* ✉ *Mon.–Sat. $49 (including show); Sun. $30 (no show).* ✆ *Apr.–Oct., daily 8:30 AM–10 PM; Nov.–Mar., daily 8:30 AM–9 PM.*

Paamul

➐ *10 km (6 mi) south of Xcaret.*

Beachcombers and snorkelers are fond of Paamul, a crescent-shape la-goon with clear, placid waters sheltered by a coral reef at the lagoon's mouth. Shells, sand dollars, and even glass beads—some from the sunken pirate ship at Akumal—wash onto the sandy parts of the beach. In June and July you can see one of Paamul's chief attractions: sea-tur-tle hatchlings on the beach.

Lodging

$$ ☷ **Cabañas Paamul.** On a perfect white-sand beach, this small hostelry is the place for seclusion and comfort. Seven bungalows painted white and peach face the sea. All have two double beds, ceiling fans, hot-water showers, and hammocks. A large palapa houses the restaurant. The prop-erty includes 140 full-service hookups (gas, water, and drainage) for motor homes and tents and a full-service dive shop. Many of the guests have stayed here before, which contributes to the sense of community. ✉ *Hwy. 307, Km 85,* ☎ *9/875–1051. 7 bungalows. Restaurant, bar, fans, beach, dive shop, camping. No credit cards.*

Puerto Aventuras

➑ *5 km (3 mi) south of Paamul.*

While the rest of the coast has been caught up in development fever, Puerto Aventuras has been quietly doing its own thing. Consequently it's emerged as one of the nicest places to vacation, particularly for fam-ilies. It's not the place to experience Yucatecan culture, but this planned community gives you an opportunity to get away from it all without really leaving it all behind. The 900-acre self-contained resort is built around its 95-ship marina. It also offers a beach club, an 18-hole golf course, restaurants, shops, a great dive center, tennis courts, doctors, a school, and an excellent museum. The **Museo CEDAM** displays arti-facts—coins, sewing needles, nautical devices, clay dishes—recovered from sunken ships by members of the Mexican Underwater Explorers Club (CEDAM). Hours are irregular and the entrance fee is by dona-tion. Even if you don't stay at the complex, the museum is worth a visit.

Dining and Lodging

$–$$$ ✗ **Café Olé International.** Serving three meals a day, this café is the laid-back hub of Aventuras. The food is fresh and delicious and the menu is varied. Chicken satay and coconut shrimp are two good lunch or dinner choices. At night musicians from around the world play until the wee hours—this is one of the few places along the coast to offer nightlife. ✉ *Across from the Omni Puerto Aventuras hotel,* ☎ *9/873–5125. MC, V.*

$$$$ ☷ **Cameleon Marival Puerto Aventuras.** The design of this all-inclu-sive resort in the Aventuras complex was intended to create a village atmosphere, and the effect is one of intimacy and comfort—despite the

Cameleon's large size. Rooms are bright and sunny, in yellow and blue, with wrought-iron furniture, tile floors, king-size beds, and small sitting areas that lead to private ocean-view balconies. Two pools look onto a perfect beach, and there's a water-sports center. Golfing, sailing, and bicycling are major activities here. ⊠ *North of marina,* ☎ *9/875–1020,* WEB *www.cameleonmarival.com. 324 rooms. 4 restaurants, 3 bars, 3 pools, 18-hole golf course, gym, beach, boating, dive shop. AE, MC, V.*

$$$$ 🖭 **Omni Puerto Aventuras.** Low key and elegant, this all-inclusive resort is a good place for some serious pampering. Each room has a king-size bed, sitting area, ocean-view balconies or terraces, and a hot tub. The calm beach is steps away, and the pool seems to flow right into the sea. A complimentary Continental breakfast and newspaper arrive at your room every morning by way of a secret cubbyhole to avoid disturbing your slumber. You are within walking distance of a golf course and marina. ⊠ *Carretera Chetumal–Puerto Juárez (on beach near marina),* ☎ *9/873–5101,* FAX *9/873–5102,* WEB *www.omnihotels.com. 30 rooms. 2 restaurants, bar, 2 pools, 2 tennis courts, gym, beach, dive shop. AE, MC, V.*

Outdoor Activities and Sports

DIVING

Aquanuts (⊠ Center Complex, by marina, ☎ FAX 9/873–5280) is a full-service dive shop that specializes in cave and cenote diving and offers certification courses.

En Route The Maya-owned and -operated eco-park called **Cenotes Kantún Chi** has a series of cenotes and underground caverns that are great for snorkeling and diving. The site includes some small Maya ruins and a botanical garden. The place is not at all slick, so it offers a nice break from the more commercial attractions along the coast. ⊠ *Hwy. 307, 3 km (2 mi) south of Puerto Aventuras,* ☎ FAX *9/873–0021.* 🎟 *$2.* ☺ *Daily 8:30–5.*

Xpu-há

❾ *3 km (2 mi) south of Puerto Aventuras.*

This used to be a tranquil little beach until developers snatched it up and turned it into an overpriced "eco-park," which subsequently closed. At press time, the beach had been restored to its former tranquillity, but probably not for long: one resort has been finished and two more-secluded places are to be built.

Lodging

$$$ 🖭 **Copacabana.** This lavish, all-inclusive resort is working hard to do it right. It was designed around the surrounding jungle, cenotes, and beach, to leave them virtually untouched. The lobby reflects the junglelike atmosphere with bamboo furniture and a central waterfall underneath a giant palapa roof. The rooms are spacious and tranquil and have beautiful wood furniture, king-size beds, and private terraces that look out into the jungle. Three large pools, separated from the outdoor hot tubs by an island of palm trees, look out onto the spectacular beach, and there's a water-sports center. The food is exceptional and served à la carte. ⊠ *Carretera Chetumal/Hwy. 307, Km 264.5,* ☎ *9/875–1800 or 866/321–6880,* FAX *9/875–1818,* WEB *www.hotelco-pacabana.com. 224 rooms. 4 restaurants, 4 bars, air-conditioning, 3 pools, spa, gym, beach, dance club, recreation rooms, baby-sitting, travel services. MC, V.*

$$ 🖭 **Hotel Villas del Caribe.** Leon, the laid-back manager, makes sure you are well looked after at this throwback to simpler days. The rooms are

basic, with double beds, simple furniture, and hot water—all you need for sleeping on the beach. You can have great, inexpensive food (especially the fish) at Café del Mar morning, noon, and night. ✉ *Hwy. 307, Xpu-há X-4 (look for sun sign),* ☎ *9/873–2194. 14 rooms. Restaurant, bar, beach. No credit cards.*

Akumal

⑩ *37 km (23 mi) south of Playa del Carmen, 102 km (63 mi) south of Cancún.*

The Maya name means "place of the turtle," and for hundreds of years this beach has been a nesting ground for turtles. The place first attracted international attention in 1926, when explorers discovered the *Mantanceros,* a Spanish galleon that sank in 1741. In 1958, Pablo Bush Romero, a wealthy businessman who loved diving these pristine waters, created the first resort, which became the headquarters for the club he formed—the Mexican Underwater Explorers Club (CEDAM). Akumal soon became a gathering spot for wealthy underwater adventurers who flew in on private planes and searched the waters for sunken treasures, some of which you can see at the Museo CEDAM in Puerto Aventuras.

These days Akumal, where little Spanish is heard and the 4th of July is a bigger holiday than Mexican Independence Day, is probably the most Americanized community on the coast. Hotels and private homes and condos line the streets, which can become very crowded. Akumal doesn't have a center but consists of three distinct areas: Half Moon Bay, with some pretty beaches, the best snorkeling around, and the greatest concentration of rentals; Akumal Proper, a large resort with a market, grocery stores, laundry facilities, a pharmacy, and, farther up across the highway, the original Maya community; and Akumal Aventuras, to the south, with more condos and homes. The large community of ex-patriots and repeat visitors is really the heart and soul of Akumal. They are responsible for starting up some important ecological movements along the Quintana Roo coast, such as recycling, animal rescue, and reef protection. Be sure to visit the **Ecological Center,** on the main road.

Akumal is famous for its underwater scenery. The reef, which is about 425 ft offshore, shelters the bay and its exceptional coral formations and sunken galleon; the sandy bottom allows snorkelers to wade out at the rocky north end, where they can view the diverse underwater topography. Fishing for giant marlin, bonito, and sailfish is also popular.

Area dive shops sponsor resort courses and certification courses, and luxury hotels and condominiums have year-round packages that cover airfare, accommodations, and diving. Hotel rooms are at a premium during the high season, mid-December through April, for which reservations should be made well in advance.

Devoted snorkelers may want to walk to **Yalkú,** a couple of miles north of Akumal along an unmarked dirt road. A series of small lagoons which gradually reach the ocean, Yalkú is home to schools of parrot fish in superbly clear water with visibility to 160 ft. It's now an "eco-park," which means it has a toilet, a small parking lot, and an entrance fee of about $6.

Dining and Lodging

$-$$ ✕ **La Lunita.** The breakfast and dinner menus change daily at this converted condo in Half Moon Bay, but the quality doesn't; the food is consistently great, with service to match. Choices include ceviche and grilled or fried chicken and fish. The atmosphere is friendly and inclusive, so you're likely to pick up some tips on local events. ⊠ *Hacienda de la Tortuga (enter through Club Akumal Caribe and turn left, or north, at the dirt road to Half Moon Bay),* ☎ *9/875–9070. AE, MC, V. No lunch.*

$ ✕ **Restaurante Oscar y Lalo.** A few kilometers outside of Akumal, at Bahías de Punta Soliman, is this wonderful restaurant run by a local Maya couple. The seafood is excellent and the pizza divine. If you're inspired to sleep on the beach, campgrounds and RV hookups are available. ⊠ *Hwy. 307 north of Akumal (look for faded white sign),* ☎ *no phone. No credit cards.*

$ ✕ **Turtle Bay Café & Bakery.** This funky café offers delicious (and healthful) breakfasts and lunches. The real specialties are great smoothies and fresh baked goods. It has a pretty garden to sit and drink coffee in, and its location by the ecological center makes it the closest thing to a downtown Akumal has. ⊠ *Plaza Ukana I, Local 15 (beginning of Half Moon Bay road),* ☎ *no phone. No credit cards. No dinner.*

$$$$ ⊡ **Club Oasis Akumal.** One of the all-inclusive pioneers, this hotel remains intimate, sophisticated, and understated. The atmosphere is enhanced by the gorgeous mahogany railings, doors, furniture, and floors amid the tropical plants and flowers. Rooms are spacious, with nice terraces, king-size beds, and sitting areas. The bathrooms are exceptional: sunken tile showers with Moorish arches and windows with beach views. The food is good, and the beach has been preserved, so it is still a beacon for all water-sports activities. ⊠ *South of Akumal off Hwy. 307,* ☎ *9/875–7300,* fax *9/875–7302,* web *www.oasishotels.com.mx. 182 rooms. Restaurant, 2 bars, 4 pools, tennis court, beach, dive shop, bicycles, travel services, car rental. AE, MC, V.*

$$$ ⊡ **Club Akumal Caribe & Villas Maya.** On the edge of the cove, this
★ beachfront resort offers congenial accommodations and staff. Rooms in the hotel have rattan furniture; large, comfortable beds; lovely tile work; and harbor views. The quaint but rustic bungalows are surrounded by a tropical garden and have great kitchens and bathrooms. More-secluded options are the one-, two-, and three-bedroom condominiums called the Villas Flamingo, on Half Moon Bay, with their own beach and pools (definite bargains). Diving, fishing, and other water sports are all within walking distance. The restaurant, Lol Ha, is a nice beachside spot that offers tasty fare. ⊠ *Hwy. 307, Km 104,* ☎ *9/875–9012; 800/351–1622; 800/343–1440 in Canada,* web *www.hotelakumal-caribe.com. 21 rooms, 40 bungalows, 4 villas, 5 condos. 3 restaurants, bar, air-conditioning, pool, beach, 2 dive shops, children's program (ages 5–14). AE, MC, V.*

$$ ⊡ **Vista Del Mar.** Each room has an ocean view, king-size bed, small refrigerator, and brightly colored decor with Guatemalan–Mexican accents. Next door are more-expensive condos with Spanish colonial decor. The spacious one-, two-, and three-bedroom units have full kitchens, living and dining rooms, and oceanfront balconies. They are a great bargain off-season. ⊠ *South end of Half Moon Bay,* ☎ *9/875–9060 or 800/925–6325 ext. 15,* web *www.akumalinfo.com. 17 rooms, 6 condos. Restaurant, air-conditioning, kitchenettes (some), refrigerators, pool, beach. AE, MC, V.*

Outdoor Activities and Sports

SCUBA DIVING

Akumal Dive Center (⊠ about 10 mins north of Club Akumal Caribe, ☎ 9/875–9025) is the oldest and most experienced dive operation, offering reef or cenote diving, fishing, and snorkeling.

En Route   **Aktun-Chen** is Maya for "the cave with cenote inside." These amazing underground caves, estimated to be about 5 million years old, are the largest in the area. You walk through the underground passages, past stalactites and stalagmites, until you reach the underground cenote with its various shades of deep green. You don't want to miss this one. ⊠ *Hwy. 307 between Akumal and Xel-Ha, Km 107,* ☎ *9/884–0444,* WEB *www.aktunchen.com.* ⊡ *$7.* ☉ *Daily 8:30–4.*

Xcacel

⑪ *7 km (4½ mi) south of Akumal.*

Xcacel is a symbol of what has gone wrong along the coast. It's one of the few remaining nesting grounds for the endangered Atlantic green and loggerhead turtles. For years it was a federally protected zone, until it was sold—illegally—in 1998 to a Spanish conglomerate. The group immediately tried to push through an elaborate development plan that would have destroyed the nesting grounds. This prompted Greenpeace, in cooperation with biologists, scientists, and other locals, to begin an international campaign to save the turtles, and the battle continues. In the meantime, you can visit the turtle center or offer to volunteer. The Friends of Xcacel Web site (www.turtles.org/xcacel.htm) has more information.

Xel-Ha

⑫ *3 km (2 mi) south of Laguna de Xcacel.*

Brought to you by the people who manage Xcaret, Xel-Ha (pronounced shel-*hah*) is a natural aquarium made from coves, inlets, and lagoons cut out of the limestone shoreline. The name means "where the water is born," and the river here forms a natural spring that flows out to meet the saltwater, creating a perfect habitat for tropical marine life. Scattered throughout the park are small Maya ruins, including **Na Balaam,** known for a yellow jaguar painted on one of its walls. Low wooden bridges over the lagoons allow for leisurely walks around the park, and there are spots to rest or swim. While there seem to be fewer and fewer fish each year, and the mixture of fresh- and saltwater can cloud visibility, there is still enough here to impress novice snorkelers.

The place gets overwhelmingly crowded, so come early, before the tour buses. The grounds are well equipped with bathrooms, restaurants, and a shop. Please note that sunscreen isn't allowed, because it kills the fish. Try a long T-shirt instead. ☎ *987/54070 or 987/54071.* ⊡ *$15.* ☉ *Daily 8–8.*

If you're sick of tour buses, head across the road to the compact, little-visited **Xel-Ha Archaeological Site.** Its squat structures are thought to have been inhabited from the Late Preclassic until the Late Postclassic period. The most interesting sights are on the north end of the ruins, where remains of a Maya *sacbé* (road) and mural paintings in the **Jaguar House** sit near a tranquil, deep cenote. ☎ *No phone.* ⊡ *$1.50, free Sun.* ☉ *Daily 8–5.*

Tankah

⑬ *9½ km (6 mi) south of Xel-Ha on the dirt road off Hwy. 307.*

Between Xel-Ha and Tulum, Tankah is maintaining its own as a quiet beach with not too much development. A number of very small hotels offer rooms and cabañas at reasonable prices.

Dining and Lodging

$ ✕ **Casa Cenote.** Location is everything. This restaurant stands beside a large fresh- and saltwater cenote full of tropical fish. You can go for a quick snorkeling trip and then rest in the shade while you wait for your meal. It's simple beach food, nothing complicated—burgers, chicken, fish, beer, and margaritas. Casa Cenote is still the only place to eat on the beach. ⊠ *Turn left at the end of the dirt road from Hwy. 307 into Tankah (look for Casa Cenote sign),* ☎ *no phone. Reservations not accepted. No credit cards.*

$$$ 🏨 **Tankah Inn.** A friendly East Texas family runs this guest house on a windswept, deserted stretch of beach. There is great diving off the shore, so the inn is geared toward and popular with divers. Rooms are large and bright, with just enough accessories to make it comfortable, but not luxurious. The views from the main room and upstairs restaurant–living room are spectacular. The kitchen here is casual, turning out great meals on request or letting the guests cook. ⊠ *Bahía Tankah 16,* ☎ *987/42188, tankahdiveinn@lycos.com. 5 rooms. Restaurant, beach, dive shop. No credit cards.*

Tulum

🔺 **⑭** *2 km (1 mi) south of Tankah, 130 km (81 mi) south of Cancún.*

One of the Caribbean coast's biggest attractions, Tulum is the Yucatán Peninsula's most visited Maya ruin, attracting more than 2 million people annually. Unfortunately, this means you have to share the site with roughly half of the tourist population of Quintana Roo on any given day, even if you arrive early. Though most of the architecture here is of unremarkable Postclassic (AD 900–1541) style, the amount of attention that Tulum receives is not entirely undeserved. Its location by the blue-green waters of the Caribbean is indeed breathtaking.

The Tulum parking lot, just off the highway, has separate areas for cars ($1) and buses. There's an enormous cement slab building filled with burger joints and tacky shops selling junky souvenirs manned by aggressive salespeople. An electric shuttle car hustles visitors from the parking lot to the temples ($1 each way); otherwise it's a ½-km (¼-mi) walk. Another small open market selling souvenirs is at the shuttle stop.

At the entrance to the ruins you can hire a guide, but keep in mind that some of their information is more entertaining than historically accurate. (Disregard that stuff about virgin sacrifices atop the altars.) Because you are not allowed to climb or enter the fragile structures—only three really merit close inspection anyway—you can take in the ruins in two hours. You might, however, want to allow extra time for a swim or a stroll on the beach, where ancient Maya beached their canoes.

Tulum is the only Maya city known to have been inhabited when the conquistadors arrived in 1518. Its pre-Columbian name, Zama, from the word *zamul* (dawn), suggests "city of the dawn"; Tulum means "wall." When the Spaniards arrived, Juan de Grijalva and his men, who spotted Zama from their ships, were so intimidated by the enormity of its vivid 25-ft-high blue, white, and red walls that they were reluctant to land. What they had seen was four towns so close to one another that they appeared to be one continuous metropolis.

Tulum has long held special significance for the Maya. A key city in the League of Mayapán (AD 987–1194), it was never conquered by the Spaniards, although it was abandoned about 75 years after the Conquest. For 300 years thereafter, it symbolized the defiance of an otherwise subjugated people; it was one of the last outposts of the Maya during their insurrection against Mexican rule in the War of the Castes, which began in 1846. Uprisings continued intermittently until 1935, when the Maya ceded Tulum to the government.

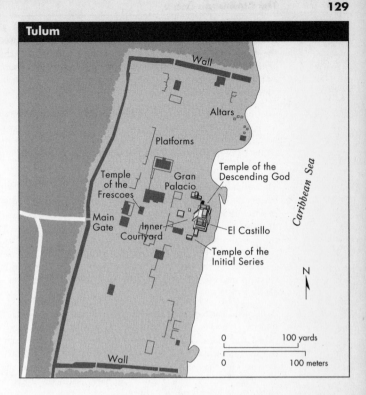

Tulum

The Postclassic architecture at Tulum reflects strong Toltec influences, the result of the encroaching empire of central Mexico. Although artistic refinements found elsewhere in the Maya world are missing here, the site is well preserved. Frederick Catherwood sketched its magnificent ruins during his 1842 explorations with John L. Stephens. Those sketches eventually illustrated a book by Stephens, *Incidents of Travel in Central America, Chiapas and Yucatan,* which became the archaeological bible of its time.

You enter the archaeological site through a low limestone gateway in a crumbling wall. Low-lying structures dot the site's 60-acre grassy field, wrapped on three sides by a 3,600-ft-long wall. The first significant structure is the two-story **Temple of the Frescoes,** to the left of the entryway. The temple's vault roof and corbel arch are examples of classic Maya architecture. Faint traces of blue-green frescoes outlined in black on the inner and outer walls refer to ancient Maya beliefs (the clearest frescoes are hidden from sight now that you can't walk into the temple). Reminiscent of the Mixtec style, the frescoes depict the three worlds of the Maya and their major deities and are decorated with stellar and serpentine patterns, rosettes, and ears of maize and other offerings to the gods. One scene portrays the rain god seated on a four-legged animal—probably a reference to the Spaniards on their horses.

The largest and most famous building, the **Castillo** (castle), looms at the edge of a 40-ft limestone cliff just past the Temple of the Frescoes. Atop the castle, at the end of a broad stairway, sits a temple with stucco ornamentation on the outside and traces of fine frescoes inside the two chambers. (The stairway has been roped off, so the top temple is inaccessible.) The front wall of the Castillo has faint carvings of the Descending God and columns depicting the plumed serpent god, Kukulcán, who was introduced to the Maya by the Toltecs. The regal structure overlooks the rest of Tulum and an expanse of dense jungle to the west; the blue Caribbean blocks access from the east. Footpaths are etched at the sides of the Castillo wherever it's possible to catch a snapshot of the ruins against the sea. Researchers think the Castillo may have functioned as a watchtower to monitor enemy approaches by sea.

To the left of the Castillo is the **Temple of the Descending God**—so called for the carving of a winged god plummeting to earth over the doorway. The same deity is seen in stucco masks in the corners and is thought either to be Ab Muzen Cab, the bee god, or to be associated with the planet Venus, guardian of the coast and of commerce.

The other buildings at the site typically have flat roofs resting on wood beams and columns with few distinguishing features. Buildings were laid out along straight streets running the length of the site with a slight dip, or culvert, between two gentle slopes. The tiny cove to the left of the Castillo and Temple of the Descending God is a good spot for a cooling swim, but there are no changing rooms. A few small altars sit atop a hill at the north side of the cove and have a good view of the Castillo and the sea. ☎ *$8, free Sun.; use of video camera extra.* ☉ *Daily 8–5.*

At the old turnoff on Highway 307 to the ruins, which is called the *crucero* (it no longer provides access), are two small hotels, two restaurants, and a Pemex gas station. A few feet south is the current entrance to the ruins, clearly marked with overhead signs. Still farther south is a turnoff for the road leading to the coast and eventually the Sian Ka'an preserve. The majority of hotels, cabañas, campgrounds, beaches, and restaurants are along this route.

Back on the highway about 4 km (2½ mi) south of the ruins is the present-day village of Tulum. As Tulum's importance as a commercial center increases, markets, restaurants, shops, services, and auto-repair shops continue to spring up along the road. Growth has not been kind to the pueblo, however, and it has become rather unsightly, with a wide four-lane highway running down the middle. Despite this blight, its restaurants offer good food, especially vegetarian dishes.

Dining and Lodging

Tulum's official Web page for hotels and cabañas is www.hotelstulum.com.

$$$$ ✕▦ **Las Ranitas.** Here is a perfect example of the self-sustaining ho-
★ tels springing up in Tulum that don't sacrifice comfort, style, and elegance to be ecologically correct. Las Ranitas (The Froggies) uses wind-generated electricity, solar energy, and recycled water, but what you really notice is how chic the rooms are. Each is decorated with gorgeous tile and fabric from Oaxaca. Terraces overlook the gardens and ocean, and jungle walkways lead down to the breathtaking beach. The pool, tennis court, and terrace are spectacular as well. But the real pièce de résistance is the French chef, who creates incredible food that matches the hotel's magic (in the $$ price range). ✉ *Carretera Tulum–Boca Paila (last hotel before Sian Ka'an Biosphere Reserve),* ☎ FAX *9/877–8554,* WEB *www.lasranitas.com. 14 rooms. Restaurant, pool, tennis court, beach. No credit cards.*

$ ✕▦ **Don Armando Cabañas.** Come here to get primitive. Accommodations are your basic Maya hut made out of cut wood with screened windows, cement floors, double beds, and hammock. The beach location makes it all worthwhile. You won't find anything cheaper in the area. ✉ *Carretera Tulum–Boca Paila, Km 0.47,* ☎ *9/871–2417. 46 rooms. Beach. No credit cards.*

$$$ ⊡ **Cabañas La Conchita.** This bed-and-breakfast has simple cabañas done in all natural woods. Exposed beams and wooden windows and floors add to the charming, rustic feel. The bathrooms have plenty of hot water and are comfortable. All cabañas are on the water's edge hidden in a lovely inlet. The tropical breakfast is the perfect compliment to roughing it mildly on the beach. ⊠ *Carretera Tulum–Boca Paila, Km 4.5,* ☎ *9/871–2092. Restaurant, bar, beach. No credit cards.*

$$ ⊡ **Cabañas Tulum.** Idyllically set in a coconut grove on the beach, this property offers palapa bungalows with comfortable double beds and hot water. The rooms are basic and clean, with two large double beds, overhead fans, and private bathrooms. There is also a good indoor–outdoor restaurant with a large menu. ⊠ *Carretera Tulum–Boca Paila, Km 7,* ☎ *9/871–2009. 32 cabañas. Restaurant, bar, fans, beach, recreation room. No credit cards.*

COBÁ TO CHETUMAL

The coastal area south of Tulum is more purely Maya than the tourist stretch between Cancún and Tulum. Here, seaside fishing collectives and close-knit communities carry on ancient traditions while the close proximity to Belize lends a Caribbean flavor, particularly in Chetumal, where you'll hear both Spanish and the local Caribbean patois.

Cobá

🔺 ⑮ *49 km (30 mi) northwest of Tulum, 167 km (104 mi) southwest of Cancún.*

Cobá, Maya for "water stirred by the wind," flourished from AD 800 to AD 1100, with a population of as many as 55,000. Now it stands in solitude, with the jungle having taken many of its buildings. Cobá exudes a certain stillness, the silence broken by the occasional shriek of a spider monkey or the call of a bird. Processions of huge army ants cross the footpaths as the sun slips through openings between the tall hardwood trees, ferns, and giant palms.

Situated on five lakes between coastal watchtowers and inland cities, Cobá exercised economic control over the region through a network of at least 16 *sacbéob* (white stone roads), one of which measures 100 km (62 mi) and is the longest in the Maya world. The city once covered 70 square km (27 square mi), making it a noteworthy sister state to Tikal in northern Guatemala, with which it had close cultural and commercial ties. It is noted for its massive temple–pyramids, one of which is 138 ft tall, the largest and highest in northern Yucatán.

Archaeologists estimate that some 6,500 structures are present in the Cobá area, but only 5% have been uncovered, and it will take decades before the work is completed. Discovered by Teobert Maler in 1891, Cobá was subsequently explored in 1926 by the Carnegie Institute but not excavated until 1972. At present there is no restoration work under way.

The main groupings of ruins are separated by several miles of dense tropical vegetation, so the best way to get a sense of the immensity of the city is to scale one of the pyramids. It's easy to get lost here, so stay on the main road and don't be tempted by the narrow paths that lead into the jungle unless you have a qualified guide with you.

The first major cluster of structures, off the main path to your right as you enter the ruins, is the **Cobá Group,** whose pyramids are built around a sunken patio. At the near end of the group, facing a large plaza, you'll see the 79-ft-high Iglesia (church), where some Maya people still place offerings and light candles in hopes of improving their harvests.

Farther along the main path to your left is the **Chumuc Mul Group,** little of which has been excavated. The principal pyramid here is covered with the remains of vibrantly painted stucco motifs (*chumuc mul* means "stucco pyramid").

A kilometer (½ mile) past this site is the **Nohoch Mul Group** (Large Hill Group), the highlight of which is the pyramid of the same name, the tallest at Cobá. The pyramid, which has 120 steps—equivalent to 12 stories—shares a plaza with **Temple 10.** The Descending God (also seen at Tulum) is depicted on a facade of the temple atop Nohoch Mul, from which the view is excellent. The temple seems to have been erected much later than the pyramid itself. It was from the base of this pyramid that the longest sacbé started. It extended all the way to Yaxuná, 20 km (12 mi) southwest of Chichén Itzá. Because of their great width (up to 33 ft), there is considerable speculation about the function of the sacbéob. The Maya had no beasts of burden, so they carried all cargo on their own backs. Thus the roads may have been designed to allow people to walk abreast in processions, suggesting that they played a role in religion as well as in trade. The unrestored **Crossroad Pyramid,** opposite Nohoch Mul, was where three sacbéob met.

Beyond the Nohoch Mul Group is the **Castillo,** with nine chambers that are reached by a stairway. To the south are the remains of a ball court, including the stone ring through which the ball was hurled. From the main route follow the sign to **Las Pinturas Group,** named for the still-discernible polychrome friezes on the inner and outer walls of its large, patioed pyramid. An enormous stela here depicts a man standing with his feet on two prone captives. Take the minor path for 1 km (½ mi) to the **Macanxoc Group,** not far from the lake of the same name. The main pyramid at Macanxoc is accessible by a stairway. The portal of the temple at its summit is divided by a column; there is also a molded lintel and the remains of a stucco painting. Many of the stelae here are intricately carved with dates and other symbols of the history of Cobá.

If you're keen to see more buildings, venture farther to the small **Kukulcán Group,** one of the larger satellites of Cobá, 5½ km (3½ mi) south of the Cobá group. Only five structures remain, and they are among the more puzzling ruins in the Maya world; their design and use have yet to be explained by archaeologists. The three-story temple is particularly intriguing because it is the only Maya structure in which the top story does not rest on filled-in lower stories.

Cobá is a 35-minute drive northwest of Tulum along a well-marked and well-paved road that leads straight through the jungle. A number of freshwater cenotes along the way are worth stopping at for a swim. Don't even think of swimming at any of the lakes around Cobá—unless you want to become dinner for a member of the area's large and hungry crocodile population. Maps and books about the ruins are sold at the makeshift restaurants and shops that line the parking lot. None of the maps are particularly accurate. Several men with guide licenses congregate by the entrance and offer their services. Bring plenty of bug repellent and water. You can buy sodas and snacks at the entrance. You can rent a bicycle at Cobá. It's a bumpy ride but still a fun way to check out the ruins.

You can comfortably make your way around Cobá in a half day, but spending the night in town is highly advised as doing so will allow you to visit the ruins in solitude when they open at 8 AM. Even on a day trip, consider taking time out for lunch to escape the intense heat and mosquito-heavy humidity of the ruins. Buses depart from Cobá for Playa del Carmen and Tulum at least twice daily. Taxis to Tulum are still reasonable (about $12). ✉ *$1.75, free Sun.; use of video camera $4.* ☉ *Daily 8–5.*

Lodging

$$$ 🏨 **Villa Arqueológica Cobá.** A 10-minute walk from the ruins, this Club Med property overlooks one of the region's vast lakes. There is a slightly Mediterranean feel to the place, which has high arches, white stucco, and red paint. But this is a hit-and-miss operation: *sometimes* the rooms are clean and comfortable, and *sometimes* the food is well prepared. Other times, the rooms are hot and seem vaguely moldy and the food is bad. The staff is not forthcoming, so you must be quite firm to get decent service. Still, this is the only hotel in the area that offers any kind of amenities. ✉ *Lagoon road, west of the ruins,* ☎ *5254–7077 for reservations,* 𝖥𝖠𝖷 *5255–3164,* 𝖶𝖤𝖡 *www.clubmed.com. 40 rooms, 3 suites. Restaurant, bar, air-conditioning, pool, tennis court, library. AE, MC, V.*

$ 🏨 **El Bocadito.** The warmth of the family who owns and operates this hotel makes up for the lack of luxury here. Each of the extremely basic rooms has two double beds, a ceiling fan, toilet, and, if you are lucky, hot water. The ruins are a 10-minute walk away. Rooms here fill up quickly—if you're thinking of spending the night, stop here before visiting the ruins. The restaurant next door serves simple but tasty meals. ✉ *On road to ruins,* ☎ *987/42087. 10 rooms. AE, V.*

Sian Ka'an Biosphere Reserve

⓰ *15 km (9 mi) south of Tulum to the Punta Allen turnoff, located within Sian Ka'an; 137 km (85 mi) south of Cancún.*

Sian Ka'an ("where the sky is born") was first settled by the Maya in the 5th century AD. In 1986 the Mexican government established the 1.3-million-acre **Sian Ka'an Biosphere Reserve** as an internationally protected area. The next year, it was named a World Heritage Site by the United Nations Educational, Scientific, and Cultural Organization (UNESCO). In 1996 the reserve was extended by 200,000 acres.

Sian Ka'an participates in the UNESCO program "Man and the Biosphere," whose mandate is to maintain and preserve the ecological diversity in biologically rich areas while educating the locals to do likewise. Such reserves are particularly important in developing countries, where encroaching on dwindling resources is the only way large segments of the population know how to survive.

Under the program the land is divided for various purposes, including research, preservation, and economic activities in conjunction with conservation. Assisted by scientists, the local population in Sian Ka'an makes a living through fishing, lobster harvesting, and small farming and receives support from low-impact tourism, biological research, and sustainable development programs.

The Sian Ka'an reserve constitutes 10% of the land in Quintana Roo and covers 100 km (62 mi) of coast. Freshwater and coastal lagoons, mangrove swamps, watery cays, savannas, tropical forests, a barrier reef, hundreds of species of local and migratory birds, fish, other animals and plants, and fewer than 1,000 local residents (primarily Maya) share this area. There are approximately 27 ruins (none excavated) linked by a unique canal system—one of the few of its kind in the Maya world in Mexico. This is one of the last undeveloped stretches of coastline in North America.

Many species of the once-flourishing wildlife have fallen into the endangered category, but the waters here still teem with rooster fish, bonefish, mojarra, snapper, shad, permit, sea bass, and crocodiles. Fishing the flats for wily bonefish is especially popular, and the peninsula's few lodges also run deep-sea fishing trips. The beaches are wide and white, and although many of the palms have succumbed to the yellowing palm disease imported from Florida, the vegetation is growing back.

In order to see the sites you must take a guided tour offered by one of the private, nonprofit organizations, such as **Amigos de Sian Ka'an** (✉ Crepúsculo 18, at Amanecer, Sm 44, Mza 13, Cancún, Quintana Roo 77506, ☎ 9/848–1618, 9/848–2136, or 9/880–6024, ℻ 9/887–3080). The four-hour boat tour includes bird-watching, a visit to the Maya ruins of Xlapak (where you can jump into one of the channels and float downstream), and a tour of the mangroves. Tour groups depart from Cabañas Ana y José in Tulum every Wednesday and Saturday morning; the fee includes a bilingual guide and binoculars.

To explore on your own, follow the road past Boca Paila to the secluded 35-km (22-mi) coastal strip of land that is part of the reserve. You'll be limited to swimming, snorkeling, and camping on the beaches, as there are no trails into the surrounding jungle. The narrow, extremely rough dirt road down the peninsula is filled with monstrous potholes and after a rainfall is completely impassable. Don't attempt it unless you have four-wheel drive. Most fishing lodges along the way close for the rainy season in August and September, and accommodations are hard to come by. The road ends at Punta Allen, a fishing village whose main catch is spiny lobster, which was becoming scarce until ecologists taught the local fishing cooperative how to build and lay special traps to conserve the species. There are several small, expensive guest houses. If you haven't booked ahead, start out early in the morning so you can get back to civilization before dark.

Lodging

$$$$ 🏨 **Boca Paila Fishing Lodge.** Home of the "grand slam" (fishing lingo
★   for catching three different kinds of fish at once), this charming lodge sits amid the Sian Ka'an Biosphere Reserve. Nine spacious cottages offer comfortable accommodations with two double beds, couches, large bathrooms, and separate screened-in sitting areas. Catering principally to anglers, the lodge provides boats and guides for fly-fishing and bonefishing; guests can bring their own tackle or rent some at the lodge. Meals, included in the room rate, are excellent, ranging from fresh fish to Maya specialties. The beach is exceptionally lovely and tranquil. There is a separate transfer charge if you want to be picked up at the Cancún airport. A one-month advance reservation with 50% payment is recommended in the high season; bookings may be for shorter than a week during the low season. ✉ *Boca Paila Peninsula (reservations: Frontiers, Box 959, Wexford, PA 15090,* ☎ *724/935–1577 or 800/245–1950). 9 cottages. Restaurant, bar. No credit cards unless arranged with Frontiers.*

$$$$ 🏨 **Casa Blanca Lodge.** Punta Pájaros, to which this remote fishing re-
★   sort provides unique access, is reputed to be one of the best places in the world for light-tackle saltwater fishing. The American-managed, all-inclusive lodge—100 ft from the ocean—is set on a rocky outcrop covered with palm trees. Bonefish swarm in the mangrove swamps, flats, and shallow waters. The lodge's 10 large, modern guest rooms, painted white with turquoise trim, have slatted windows and tile and mahogany bathrooms and provide a pleasant tropical respite at dusk. An open-air thatch-roof bar and a large living and dining area welcome anglers with drinks, fresh fish dishes, fruit, and vegetables at the start

and end of the day. Rates are highest March through June, lowest January through March. During the high season, Saturday-to-Saturday stays and a 50% prepayment are required, but you may stay fewer days during the low season. Rates include a charter flight from Cancún to the lodge, all meals, a boat, and a guide. To book, contact either Frontiers or Outdoor Travel, both in the United States. ✉ *Punta Pájaros (reservations: Frontiers, Box 959, Wexford, PA 15090,* 📞 *724/935–1577 or 800/245–1950 for Frontiers; 713/526–3739 or 800/533–7299 for Outdoor Travel). 10 rooms. Restaurant, bar, fishing. MC, V.*

Muyil

🔺 ⑰ *24 km (15 mi) south of Tulum on Hwy. 307.*

This photogenic archaeological site is definitely underrated. Once known as Chunyaxché, it is now called by its ancient name, Muyil. Dating from the Late Preclassic era (300 BC–AD 200), it was connected by road to the sea and served as a port between Cobá and the Maya centers in Belize and Guatemala. A 15-ft-wide sacbé, built during the Late Postclassic period (AD 1200–1541), extended from the city to the mangrove swamp; today the remains of the sacbé get flooded during the rainy season.

Structures were erected at 400-ft intervals along the white limestone road, almost all of them facing west. At the beginning of the 20th century, the ancient stones were used to build a chicle (gum) plantation, which was managed by one of the leaders of the War of the Castes. The most notable site at Muyil today is the remains of the 56-ft **Castillo temple-pyramid**—one of the tallest on the Quintana Roo coast—at the center of a large patio. During excavations of the Castillo, jade figurines representing the moon goddess Chichén were found. Recent excavations at Muyil have uncovered some smaller structures, but these excavations were halted by the death of the archaeologist in charge.

The ruins stand near the edge of a deep-blue lagoon and are surrounded by nearly impenetrable jungle—bring bug repellent. You can drive down a dirt road on the side of the ruins to swim or fish in the lagoon. The bird-watching is also exceptional here. ✉ *$1.70, free Sun.* 🕐 *Daily 8–5.*

Felipe Carrillo Puerto

⑱ *99 km (61 mi) south of Tulum.*

Formerly known as Chan Santa Cruz, Felipe Carrillo Puerto is named after the man who became governor of Yucatán in 1920. He was hailed as a local hero after instituting a series of reforms to help the impoverished *campesinos* (farmers or peasants). Assassinated by the alleged henchman of the presidential candidate of an opposing party in 1923, he remained a popular figure long after his death.

The town was a political, military, and religious asylum during the 1846 War of the Castes; rebels fled here after being defeated at Mérida. It was also in this town that the famous cult of the Talking Cross took hold. The Talking Cross was a sacred symbol of the Maya; it was believed that a holy voice emanated from it, offering guidance and instruction. In this case the cross appeared emblazoned on the trunk of a cedar tree, and the voice urged the Indians to keep fighting. (The voice was actually an Indian priest and ventriloquist, Manual Nahuat, prompted by the Maya rebel José Maria Barrera.) Symbolic crosses were subsequently placed in neighboring villages, including Tulum, inspiring the Maya. They continued fighting until 1915, when the Mexican army finally gave up. The Cruzob Indians ruled Quintana Roo as an independent state, much to the embarrassment of the Mexican government, until 1935, when the Cruzob handed Tulum over and agreed to Mexican rule.

Felipe Carrillo remains very much a Maya city, with even a few old-timers who cling to the belief that one day the Maya will once again rule the region. It exists primarily as the hub of three highways, and the only vestige of the momentous events of the 19th century is the small, uncompleted temple—on the edge of town in an inconspicuous, poorly marked park—begun by the Indians in the 1860s and now a monument to the War of the Castes. The church where the Talking Cross was originally housed also stands. Several humble hotels, some good restaurants, and a gas station may be incentives for stopping here on your southbound trek.

Dining and Lodging

$ ╳🏨 **El Faisán y El Venado.** The area doesn't have much lodging, but here you can choose between rooms with air-conditioning or ceiling fans. Some also come with color TV and a refrigerator. The restaurant does a brisk business with the locals because it is centrally located and has good Yucatecan specialties such as *poc chuc* (pork marinated in sour-orange sauce), *bistec a la yucateca* (Yucatecan-style steak), and *pollo pibíl* (chicken baked in banana leaves). Everything is basic but clean and comfortable. ⊠ *Av. Benito Juárez 781,* ☎ *9/834–0702 hotel; 9/834–0043 restaurant. 21 rooms. Restaurant, air-conditioning (some), fans, refrigerators (some). No credit cards.*

Majahual

🔟 *71 km (44 mi) southeast of Felipe Carrillo Puerto on Hwy. 307 to the Majahual exit south of Limones; turn left and continue 56 km (35 mi).*

The road to Majahual is long, but once here you have a chance to see one of the last authentic fishing villages on the coast. It's very laid-back, with simple, inexpensive accommodations and lots of small restaurants serving fresh fish. Activities include lounging, fishing, snorkeling, and diving. With the airport already built but lying abandoned in a northern field, and a new cruise dock and shopping plaza in the works, this village is slated to become the next Cozumel. Come and enjoy it while it remains a simple and quaint village—a dying breed along this coast.

Lodging

$$$ 🏨 **Maya Ha Resort.** This modern resort rising disconcertingly out of the jungle is a glimpse of things to come in Majahual. The property resembles a modern-day Maya village—the architecture is based on the Maya sites of Chichén-Itzá and Kabah. In the restaurant–pool area is a giant pyramid decorated with reproductions of stelae found at famous ruins; it offers a spectacular view. The 16 suites nestled in the jungle have double beds, refrigerators, air-conditioning, and color TV. There's a state-of-the-art dive shop on the premises, and the resort offers special dive packages that include meals and drinks. ⊠ *Follow dirt road from Majahual village about 10 km (6 mi),* ☎ 📠 *983/10–065,* ☎ *800/346–6116,* 🌐 *www.mayaharesort.com. 16 suites. Restaurant, bar, refrigerators, pool, dive shop, boating. AE, MC, V.*

$ 🏨 **Las Cabañas del Doctor.** Each of these basic but quaint cabañas along the beach has a double bed; bathrooms are shared. There's electricity until 10 at night and fishing just outside the door. ⊠ *Av. Majahual 6, between Calles 2 and 4 Sur,* ☎ 📠 *983/22102. 7 cabañas. Restaurant, beach. No credit cards.*

Xcalak

㉒ *Hwy. 307 to the Majahual exit south of Limones; turn left, go 56 km (35 mi) to the checkpoint, and turn south (left) onto the new highway for 60 km (37 mi).*

It's quite a journey to get to Xcalak, but it's worth the effort. This peninsula is a combination of savannas, marsh, streams, and lagoons dotted with islands that act as a refuge for local wildlife. It's lush with tropical flowers, birds, and butterflies and has fabulously deserted beaches. Xcalak is on the tip of the peninsula that divides Chetumal Bay from the Caribbean. There are no tourist amenities and the hotels along the peninsula cater mostly to rugged types who come to bird-watch on **Bird Island** or to dive at **Banco Chinchorro,** a 42-km (26-mi) coral atoll and national park some two hours northeast by boat.

Dining and Lodging

$$$$ ✕ ▥ **Costa de Cocos.** For the ultimate in privacy and gorgeous scenery,
★ you can't beat Costa de Cocos, 2 km (1 mi) from Xcalak. It's so relaxed here that after a few days you're likely to feel like the owners and your fellow guests are family. Twelve cleverly crafted cabañas with double beds and private bathrooms offer 24-hour wind-powered electricity. The proprietor, Dave Randall, is immensely knowledgeable about the peninsula and the reef offshore and can help you plan special fly-fishing trips along the coast, sea-kayak outings, or bird-watching excursions to Bird Island. The full-service dive shop offers NAUI certification courses (more comprehensive than PADI) and great diving to the famed Chinchorro Banks and to San Pedro, Belize. For those who don't want to go far, there is excellent snorkeling just off the dock. All meals are included in the room rate. For those staying elsewhere, the Costa de Cocos restaurant offers a four-course meal for $9. Make your room reservations well in advance. ✉ *Xcalak Peninsula, follow Hwy. 307 to sign for Mahuahual, turn right at road to Xcalak,* ☎ *983/10–110,* ᵂᴱᴮ *www.costadecocos.com. 14 cabañas. Restaurant, beach, dive shop, dock, boating. No credit cards.*

$$$ ▥ **Villa Caracol.** The property offers cute little beachfront bungalows, ocean-view cabañas, or veranda rooms, all decorated with dried-flower arrangements, single beds, and flowered curtains. All are bright and clean with terrific water pressure and nice bathrooms. You can snorkel off the dock, and fishing trips can be arranged. The owners used to run a restaurant in Kansas, and they cook up some wonderful meals for guests. ✉ *Xcalak Peninsula, 54 km (33 mi) south of Majahual, 5 km (3 mi) past Costa de Cocos,* ☎ ℻ *983/81–872. 2 rooms, 2 cabañas, 2 bungalows. Restaurant, beach, dock. No credit cards.*

$$ ▥ **Sin Duda.** Margo and Robert offer five luscious rooms and three stylish studio apartments in their home, on a lovely, wild stretch of beach. Each room is different—smaller rooms come with single or double beds, trundle beds, plenty of closet space, and night lights. Guests share a fully equipped kitchen and a dining and balcony area. For more privacy you can opt for Studio 6, which is a self-contained studio in a separate building, or Suites 7 or 8, with their own kitchens and living rooms. All units have been decorated with collectibles such as Mexican pottery and furniture created by Robert. The house is solar-powered, and the couple have dubbed their style "frugal elegance." But they have done such a nice job that you really forget about the "frugal" part. ✉ *Xcalak Peninsula, 54 km (33 mi) south of Majahual, 15 km (10 mi) past Costa de Cocos (reservations: 1515 Belvedere St. N, Tucson, AZ 85712),* ☎ ℻ *983/10–006 or* ☎ *888/881–4774,* ᵂᴱᴮ *www.sindudavillas.com. 5 rooms, 3 studios. Beach, snorkeling. No credit cards.*

Bacalar

㉑ *112 km (69 mi) south of Felipe Carrillo Puerto, 320 km (198 mi) south of Cancún, 40 km (25 mi) northwest of Chetumal.*

Founded in AD 435, Bacalar is one of the oldest settlements in Quintana Roo. Of some historical interest is the **Fuerte de San Felipe** (San Felipe Fort), an 18th-century stone fort built by the Spaniards, using stones from the nearby Maya pyramids, as a haven against marauding pirates and Indians. It was later reclaimed by the Maya for use during the War of the Castes. The monolithic structure is right on the plaza and overlooks the lake. These days it houses government offices and a museum with exhibits on local history (ask for someone to bring a key if museum doors are locked). ☎ *No phone.* ✉ *$1.* ☼ *Tues.–Sun. 10–6.*

The spectacularly vast **Laguna de Bacalar,** also known as the Lake of the Seven Colors, is the second-largest lake in Mexico (56 km [35 mi] long) and is frequented by scuba divers and other lovers of water sports. Seawater and freshwater mix in the lake, intensifying the aquamarine hues, and the water contrasts starkly with the green jungle. Drive along the lake's southern shores to enter the affluent section of the town of Bacalar, with elegant waterfront homes. Also in the vicinity are a few hotels and campgrounds.

Just beyond Bacalar is the largest sinkhole in Mexico, **Cenote Azul,** 607 ft in diameter, with clear blue waters that afford unusual visibility even at 200 ft below the surface. With lush vegetation all around and underwater caves, the cenote (open daily 8–8) attracts divers who specialize in this somewhat tricky type of dive. At **Restaurant Cenote Azul** you can linger over fresh fish and a beer while gazing out over the deep blue waters or enjoy a swim off its docks.

Lodging

$$$ 🏨 **Puerta del Cielo.** Outside Bacalar and before the final military
★ checkpoint, this brightly colored and eclectically designed hotel has the feel of a summer lodge. The small cabins are staggered on a hill overlooking the lagoon. A garden path leads down to a lovely dock–restaurant area where you can swim or use the canoes. The rooms are simple, clean, and comfortably equipped with overhead fans, and the staff is hospitable. ⊠ *Hwy. 307, Km 40,* ☎ ℻ *9/837–0413 reservations. 12 cabins. Restaurant, bar, fans, kitchenettes, pool. No credit cards.*

$$$ 🏨 **Rancho Encantado.** On the shores of Laguna Bacalar, 30 minutes north of Chetumal, the Rancho comprises 12 Maya-theme *casitas* (cottages), each with Oaxacan furnishings, a patio and hammock, a refrigerator, a sitting area, and a bathroom. Breakfast and dinner are included in the room rate (no red meat is served). You can swim and snorkel off the private dock leading into the lagoon, and excellent tours to the ruins in southern Yucatán, Campeche, and Belize are available. The place also holds a variety of New Age seminars and conferences. The major drawback—especially for light sleepers—is the close proximity of Highway 307; you can hear trucks zooming by most of the night unless you are in a room close to the lagoon. ⊠ *South on Hwy. 307, look for sign (reservations: Box 1256, Taos, NM 87571, ℻ 505/751–0972 in the U.S.),* ☎ *9/831–0037 or 800/505–MAYA. 12 casitas. Restaurant, bar, refrigerators, hot tub, massage, travel services. No credit cards.*

Chetumal

㉒ *58 km (36 mi) south of Bacalar, 382 km (237 mi) south of Cancún.*

Chetumal is the final-stop town on Mexico's southern Caribbean shore. Originally called Payo Obis, it was founded by the Mexican government in 1898 in a partially successful attempt to gain control of the lucrative trade of precious hardwoods, arms, and ammunition and as a military base against the rebellious Indians. The city, which overlooks the Bay of Chetumal at the mouth of the Río Hondo, was devastated by a hurricane in 1955 and rebuilt as the capital of Quintana Roo and the state's major port. Though Chetumal remains the state capital, it attracts few visitors other than those en route to Central America or those traveling to the city on government business.

At times, Chetumal feels more Caribbean than Mexican; this is not surprising, given its proximity to Belize. The mixed population includes some black Caribbeans and Middle Eastern immigrants, resulting in an eclectic blend of music (reggae, salsa, calypso) and cuisines (Yucatecan, Mexican, and Lebanese). Although Chetumal's provisions are modest, the town has a number of parks along a pleasant, extended waterfront—the Bay of Chetumal surrounds the city on three sides. There is an excellent museum and a gorgeous university.

Paseo Bahía is the main thoroughfare and runs along the water for several miles. A walkway runs parallel to this road and is a popular gathering spot at night. If you follow the road it turns into the Chetumal–Calderitas highway and after 16 km (10½ mi) leads to the ruins of **Oxtankah.** Archaeologist believe this may be the city where the Chaktemal Kingdom was started by Gonzalo Guerrero, father of the Mestizo race (later known as Mexicans). It's open daily 8–5; admission is $1.70, except Sunday, when it's free.

Downtown Chetumal has been spruced up to attract tourists. Mid-range hotels and tourist-friendly restaurants have been popping up along Boulevard Bahía and on nearby Avenida Héroes. Tours are run to the fascinating nearby ruins of Kohunlich, Dzibanché, and Kinichná, a trio dubbed the "Valley of the Masks."

The sure standout in Chetumal is the **Museo de la Cultura Maya,** a sophisticated, interactive museum dedicated to the complex world of the Maya. Various exhibits explain Maya social classes, politics, and customs; Maya architecture; their use of plants for medicinal and domestic purposes; and the Maya calendar. The most impressive display is the three-story Sacred Ceiba Tree. The Maya use this symbol to explain the relationship between the cosmos and earth. The first floor represents the roots of the tree where the Maya underworld, Xibalba, reigns. The middle floor is the tree trunk known as Earth, or Middle World, home to humans and all their trappings. The top floor is the leaves and branches, the 13 heavens of the cosmic Otherworld. It's a fascinating introduction to the Maya world. ✉ *Av. Héroes and Calle Mahatma Gandhi,* ☎ 9/832–6838. 💳 *$3.* ⊙ *Tues.–Thurs. 9–7, Fri. and Sat. 9–8, Sun. 9–2.*

Dining and Lodging

Restaurants come and go quickly in Chetumal, but you can always find simple neighborhood eateries offering Mexican specialties such as tacos, enchiladas, and various chicken dishes.

$ ✕ **Expresso Cafe.** At this bright, modern café, you get an appealing view of the huge, placid Bay of Chetumal. Choose from more than 15 kinds of coffee as well as fresh salads, sandwiches, and chicken dishes. ✉ *Blvd. Bahía 12,* ☎ 9/832–2654. *No credit cards.*

$ ✕ **Sergio's Pizzas.** The pizzeria became so popular that the owners converted the small frame house into a bigger place and expanded the menu. Locals rave about the grilled steaks, barbecued chicken (made with Sergio's own sauce), and garlic shrimp, along with smoked-oyster and seafood pizzas. (Pasta is not the thing to order here.) ⊠ *Av. Alvaro Obregón 182, at Av. 5 de Mayo,* ☎ *9/832–0882. MC, V.*

$$$ 🖭 **Holiday Inn Puerta Maya.** This may be a small Holiday Inn, but it's working hard to provide luxury accommodations in Chetumal. The lobby resembles a nicely decorated living room with rattan furniture. Room also have rattan furniture, as well as soft sunset colors and small terraces. A tropical garden with Maya sculptures surrounds the moderate-size pool. The hotel location, directly across from the museum, is a bonus. ⊠ *Av. Héroes 171, Col. Centro,* ☎ *9/832–1100,* FAX *9/832–1676. 108 rooms, 7 suites. Restaurant, bar, air-conditioning, no-smoking rooms, pool, travel services. MC, V.*

$$ 🖭 **Los Cocos.** The lush, jungle-theme decor of this hotel's outdoor restaurant and lobby ends when you enter the rooms. However, the rooms are comfortable, with powerful air-conditioning, in-room phones, and TVs, and there is a pleasant garden area with a large swimming pool. The waterfront is within easy walking distance; the restaurant is popular with both locals and travelers. ⊠ *Av. Héroes 134, at Calle Chapultepec,* ☎ *9/832–0544,* FAX *9/832–0920. 80 rooms. Restaurant, bar, air-conditioning, pool. AE, MC, V.*

$$ 🖭 **Hotel Marlon.** This clean, comfortable hotel decorated in pastel colors is one of the best deals in town. It offers plenty of hot water, air-conditioning, fans, a nice outdoor pool, a great little restaurant, and a small but sweet piano bar. The staff exemplifies traditional Mexican hospitality. ⊠ *Av. Juárez 87,* ☎ *9/832–9411 or 9/832–9522,* ☎ FAX *9/832–6555. 36 rooms. Restaurant, piano bar, air-conditioning, fans, pool, meeting room, travel services, car rental. AE, MC, V.*

THE RÍO BEC ROUTE

The area known as the Río Bec Route enjoyed little attention for years, but the Mexican government has opened it up by building a highway, preserving previously excavated sites, and uncovering more ruins. Visiting here has no less of a decidedly pioneer feel, however, because of the rustic conditions and continuing discoveries taking place.

Río Bec is one of the principle Maya architectural styles, recognizable by the stone roof combs that stand atop temples like latticework. Río Bec doorways were often carved like open mouths, and steep pyramids often have narrow staircases leading up to a cone-shape top. The Río Bec Route continues beyond Quintana Roo's **Valley of the Masks** into Campeche. Xpujil, the first major site in Campeche, is 115 km (72 mi) west of Chetumal.

Hotels and restaurants in the area are scarce, so it's best to make Chetumal your base for exploring.

Kohunlich

🏕 ㉓ *42 km (26 mi) west of Chetumal on Rte. 186, 75 km (47 mi) east of Xpujil.*

Kohunlich is renowned for the giant stucco masks on its principal pyramid, the **Edificio de los Mascarones** (Mask Building). It also has one of the oldest ball courts in Quintana Roo, and the remains of a great drainage system at the **Plaza de las Estelas** (Plaza of the Stelae). The masks—about 6 ft tall—are set vertically into the wide staircases; first thought to represent the Maya sun god, they are now considered to be composites of the actual rulers of Kohunlich. Archaeologists have determined that Kohunlich was built and occupied during the Early and Late Classic periods and believe there are at least 500 mounds on the site waiting to be explored. Excavations have turned up 29 individual and multiple burial sites inside a residence building called **Temple de Los Viente-Siete Escalones** (Temple of the Twenty-Seven Steps). This site does not have a great deal of tourist traffic, so there is thriving flora and fauna. ☎ *No phone.* 🎫 *$2.* 🕐 *Daily 8–5.*

Lodging

$$$$ 🏨 **Explorean Kohunlich.** Amid the remains of the Kohunlich ceremonial grounds, this all-inclusive ecological resort is the solution if you want some adventure without giving up many amenities. Daily excursions include trips to the nearby ruins, lagoons, and forests for kayaking, rock climbing, hiking, and other activities. You return in the evening to your luxurious quarters, which are dressed in natural textiles, wood, and rattan. Soft earth tones are enhanced with the gentle, natural lighting. Showers open onto a small backyard garden, and the private terraces look out at the jungle. The outdoor pool and hot tub are on a hill, from which the ruins can be seen off in the distance. ✉ *Chetumal–Escarega Hwy., Km 5.65 (same road as the ruins),* ☎ *5201–8350 or 877/397–5672,* WEB *www.theexplorean.com. 38 suites. Restaurant, bar, pool, bicycles, boating. Credit cards by previous arrangement.*

Dzibanché and Kinichná

🔺 ㉔ *1 km (½ mi) east of turnoff for Kohunlich on Rte. 186; follow signs for 24 km (15 mi) north to fork for Dzibanché (1½ km [1 mi] from fork) and Kinichná (3 km [2 mi] from fork).*

Sister cities Dzibanché and Kinichná are thought to have been the most powerful alliance ruling southern Quintana Roo during the Maya Classic period (AD 300–AD 900). The fertile farmlands surrounding the ruins are still being used today as they were hundreds of years ago, and the winding drive deep into the fields makes you feel like you're coming upon something undiscovered. Indeed, the area's ruins have not yet been fully restored. On your way back from these two sites, look for a large hill on the right side of the road. The stone structures protruding from the hill suggest that it contains another enormous temple, buried under layers of vegetation.

Despite the absence of visitors, these ruins have been well restored and are very accessible. At Dzibanché ("place where they write on wood"), several carved wooden lintels have been discovered; the most perfectly preserved sample can be found in a supporting arch at the **Plaza of Xibalba.** Also at the plaza is the **Temple of the Owl,** where a recessed tomb was found atop the temple, the second discovery of its kind in Mexico (the first was at Palenque in Chiapas). Also in the tomb were magnificent clay vessels painted with white owls—messengers of the underworld gods. Several other plazas are surround by temples, palaces, and pyramids, all in the telltale Río Bec style. The carved stone steps at **Edificio 13** and **Edificio 2** still bear traces of stone masks. The famed lintel of **Temple IV,** with eight glyphs dating to AD 618, is housed in the Museo de la Cultura Maya in Chetumal. ☎ *No phone.* 🎫 *$1.* 🕐 *Daily 8–5.*

After you see Dzibanché, make your way back to the fork in the road and head to **Kinichná** ("house of the sun"). The site consists of a two-level pyramidal mound split into Acropolis B and Acropolis C, apparently dedicated to the sun god. Two mounds at the foot of the pyramid suggest that the temple was a ceremonial site. Here a giant Olmec-style jade figure was found. At its summit, Kinichná affords one of the finest views of any archaeological site in the area. ☎ *No phone.* 🎫 *$1.* 🕐 *Daily 8–5.*

THE CARIBBEAN COAST A TO Z

To research prices, get advice from other travelers, and book travel arrangements, visit www.fodors.com.

AIR TRAVEL

Almost everyone who arrives by air into this region flies into Cancún. In Chetumal, however, there is an airport on the southwestern edge of town, along Avenida Alvaro Obregón where it turns into Route 186. In Playa del Carmen, there's an air strip across from Plaza Antigua.

➤ AIRPORT INFORMATION: **Chetumal airport** (✉ Rte. 186, Chetumal, ☎ no phone).

BOAT AND FERRY TRAVEL

Passenger-only ferries and two large speedboats depart from the dock at Playa del Carmen for the 45-minute trip to the main pier in Cozumel. They leave approximately every hour on the hour 5 AM–11 PM, with no ferries at noon, 2, 8, or 10. Return service to Playa runs every hour on the hour 4 AM–10 PM, with no ferries at 5, 11 AM, 1, 7, or 9 PM. Call ahead to verify the schedule as it changes often.

➤ BOAT AND FERRY INFORMATION: **Playa del Carmen passenger ferry** (☎ 9/872–1508, 9/872–0588, or 9/872–0477).

BUS TRAVEL

The bus station in Chetumal (Avenida Salvador Novo 179) is served by ADO, Caribe Express, and other lines. Buses run regularly from Chetumal to Cancún, Villahermosa, Mexico City, Mérida, Campeche City, and Veracruz, as well as Guatemala and Belize.

Playa del Carmen has two bus stops. Buses arriving from south of Playa and continuing north to Cancún drop people off at the terminal on the highway. All other buses leave from downtown. All the major bus lines run express, first-class, and second-class buses to major destination points. Service to Cancún is every 10–20 minutes and buses to Chetumal leave twice daily. It's always best to check the times at the main bus terminal (Avenida Juárez at Avenida 5). The scheduled times change frequently.

➤ BUS INFORMATION: **ADO** (☎ 9/832–9877). **Caribe Express** (☎ 9/832–7889).

CAR RENTAL

Most first-class hotels in Puerto Aventuras, Akumal, and Chetumal also rent cars. In Puerto Morelos you are better off renting from Cancún, as there aren't many bargains in town. In Playa del Carmen, it's best to stick with the bigger rental agencies: Hertz, Budget, and Thrifty. If you want air-conditioning or automatic transmission, reserve your car at least one day in advance.

➤ MAJOR AGENCIES: **Budget** (✉ Continental Plaza, Playa del Carmen, ☎ 9/873–0100). **Hertz** (✉ Plaza Marina, Local 40, Playa del Carmen, ☎ 9/873–0702). **Thrifty** (✉ Calle 8 between Avs. 5 and 10, Playa del Carmen, ☎ 9/873–0119).

CAR TRAVEL

The entire coast from Punta Sam near Cancún to the main border crossing to Belize at Chetumal is traversable on Highway 307. This straight road is entirely paved and has been widened into four lanes south to Xcaret. Drive with caution—there are lots of speed demons on this highway. Puerto Morelos, Playa del Carmen, and Tulum have one gas station. Be sure to fill up in Felipe Carrillo Puerto, because there are no gas stations until Chetumal.

Highway 307, also known as Route 186, parallels the coastline for the 382 km (237 mi) between Cancún and Chetumal. Although buses do travel regularly along the coast and are suitable for day trips, a rental car or four-wheel-drive vehicle allows you to explore more thoroughly and creatively.

Good roads that run into Highway 307 from the west are Route 180 (from Mérida and Valladolid), Route 295 (from Valladolid), Route 184 (from central Yucatán), and Route 186 (from Villahermosa and, via Route 261, from Mérida and Campeche). There is an entrance to the *autopista* toll highway between Cancún and Mérida off Highway 307 just south of Cancún. Approximate driving times are as follows: Cancún to Felipe Carrillo Puerto, 4 hours; Cancún to Mérida, 4½ hours (3½ hours on the new *autopista* toll road, $27); Carrillo Puerto to Chetumal, 2 hours; Carrillo Puerto to Mérida, about 4½ hours; Chetumal to Campeche, 6½ hours.

The road from Cancún to Xcaret is a well-lit, four-lane highway with traffic lights, but it is often filled with seemingly crazed drivers commuting between Cancún and Playa del Carmen. Defensive driving is a must. Past Xcaret, the road converts to a two-lane coastal highway with reflectors but no lights. Nonetheless, most drivers continue to travel at breakneck speeds until Tulum. Past Tulum, things slow down and the road is in good shape, although it's deserted at night and exceptionally dark. Follow proper road etiquette—vehicles in front of you that have their left turn signal on are saying "pass me," not "I'm going to turn."

If you drive south of Tulum, keep an eye out for military and immigration checkpoints. Have your passport handy, be friendly and cooperative, and don't carry any items, such as firearms or drugs, that might land you in jail.

ECOTOURISM

You can visit the ruins of Cobá and the Maya village of Pac-Chen, located deep in the jungle, with Alltournative Expeditions. The group offers a variety of other ecotours as well.

ATV Explorer offers two-hour rides through the jungle on all-terrain vehicles; explore caves, see ruins, and snorkel in a cenote. Tours start at $38.50.
➤ CONTACTS: **Alltournative Expeditions** (⊠ Av. 10 No. 1, Plaza Antigua, Playa del Carmen, ☎ 9/873–2036, WEB alltournative.com). **ATV Explorer** (⊠ Hwy. 307, 1 km [½ mi] north of Xcaret, ☎ 9/873–1626).

E-MAIL

Many of the more remote places on the Caribbean coast rely on e-mail and the Internet as their major form of communication. In Playa del Carmen, Internet service is cheap and readily available. The best places charge $3 per half hour and include Cyberia Internet Café and Atomic Internet Café. In Tulum, try the Internet Club.
➤ SERVICES: **Atomic Internet Café** (⊠ Av. 5 at Calle 8, Playa del Carmen). **Cyberia Internet Café** (⊠ Calle 4 at Av. 15, Playa del Carmen). **Internet Club** (⊠ Av. Ote. 89, Tulum).

EMERGENCIES

In Puerto Morelos, there are two drugstores in town on either side of the gas station on Highway 307.

In Playa del Carmen, there's a pharmacy at the Plaza Marina shopping mall; several others are on Avenida 5 between Calles 4 and 8. There are two pharmacies on Avenida Juárez between Avenidas 20 and 25.

➤ CHETUMAL: **Chetumal Hospital General** (✉ Av. Andres Quintana Roo, ☎ 9/832–1932). **Farmacia Social Mechaca** (✉ Av. Independencia 134-C, ☎ 9/832–0044). **Police** (✉ Av. Insurgentes and Av. Belice, ☎ 9/832–1500). **Red Cross** (✉ Av. Héroes 279, ☎ 9/832–0571).

➤ PLAYA DEL CARMEN: **Centro de Salud** (✉ Av. Juárez at Av. 15, ☎ 9/872–1230 ext. 147). **Police** (✉ Av. Juárez between Avs. 15 and 20, ☎ 9/873–0291). **Red Cross** (✉ Av. Juárez at Av. 25, ☎ 9/873–1233).

LODGING

The Internet is a great tool for finding rentals. Akumal has a good Web presence, and with a bit of surfing you can find some bargains. For information about Akumal condo rentals try www.akumal-villas.com or www.lascasitas.com.

Puerto Aventuras has a large community of condo owners who rent out their properties. Caribbean Realty has price lists and availability information.

Mary Lowers of Mayansites Bookings can help you arrange house and apartment rentals in other areas along the coast.

➤ CONTACTS: **Caribbean Realty** (Sally Wood Evans at ✉ Centro Comercial Marina, Puerto Aventuras, ☎ 9/873–5098, ℻ 9/873–5158, WEB www.caribbean-realty.com). **Mayansites Bookings** (☎ 877/620–8715, WEB www.mayansites.com).

MAIL AND SHIPPING

The Chetumal post office is open weekdays 8–7, Saturday 8–noon. The Playa del Carmen post office is open weekdays 8–7.

➤ POST OFFICES: **Chetumal** (✉ Calle Plutarco Elias 2, ☎ 9/832–2578). **Playa del Carmen** (✉ Av. Juárez, next to the police station, ☎ 9/873–0300).

MONEY MATTERS

Local banks in Playa del Carmen include Bital, Bancomer, Banamex, Inverlat, and Bancrecer. In Chetumal, Bital and Bancomer offer banking services, including currency exchange.

➤ BANKS: **Banamex** (✉ Av. Juárez between Avs. 20 and 25, Playa del Carmen, ☎ 9/873–0825). **Bancomer** (✉ Av. Juárez between Calles 25 and 30, Playa del Carmen, ☎ 9/873–0356; ✉ Av. Alvaro Obregón 222, at Av. Juárez, Chetumal, ☎ 9/832–5300). **Bancrecer** (✉ Av. 5 by the bus station, Playa del Carmen, ☎ 9/873–1561). **Bital** (✉ Av. Juárez between Avs. 10 and 15, Playa del Carmen, ☎ 9/873–0272; ✉ Av. 30 between Avs. 4 and 6, Playa del Carmen, ☎ 9/873–0238; ✉ Av. Héroes 37, Chetumal, ☎ 9/832–2776). **Scotiabank Inverlat** (✉ Av. 5 between Av. Juárez and Av. 2, Playa del Carmen, ☎ 9/873–1488).

TELEPHONES

In Chetumal the government-run telephone office, TELMEX, is at Avenida Juárez and Calle Lázaro Cárdenas. For long-distance and international calls, you might also try the booths on Avenida Héroes: one is on the corner of Ignacio Zaragoza, and the other is just opposite Avenida Efraín Aguilar, next to the tourist information booth.

There are TELMEX phones all over Playa del Carmen; several long-distance calling stations are on Avenida 5 as well as in front of the post office on Avenida Juárez and at the corner of Avenidas Juárez and 5.

Note that telephone numbers are being changed throughout Mexico; the process is expected to take several years. In many Caribbean coast towns, changes have already been made, with the last two digits of the former area code added as a prefix to local phone numbers.

TOURS

Although some guided tours are available in this area, the roads are quite good for the most part, so renting a car is an efficient and enjoyable alternative. Most of the sights you see along this stretch are natural, and you can hire a guide at the ruins. If you would like someone else to do the planning and driving for you, contact Maya Sites Travel Services, which offers inexpensive tours and the chance to create your own travel itinerary.

AIR TOURS

From Playa del Carmen, AeroFerinco has daily flights to Cancún, Chetumal, Belize, Tikal, Veracruz, and Villahermosa.

MAYA RUINS

Based in Playa del Carmen, Tierra Maya Tours runs trips to the ruins of Chichén Itzá, Uxmal, Palenque, and Tikal. It can also help you with transfers, tickets, and hotel reservations. Many first-class hotels in Playa del Carmen and Puerto Aventuras can arrange day tours to Tulum, Chichén Itzá, and Cobá.

In Chetumal, Turistica Maya de Quintana Roo offers tours to Kohunlich, Dzibanché, the Laguna de Bacalar, and Fuerte de San Felipe.
➤ TOUR-OPERATOR RECOMMENDATIONS: **AeroFerinco** (☎ 9/873–0636, WEB www.aeroferinco.com). **Maya Sites Travel Services** (☎ 719/256–5186 or 877/620–8715, WEB www.mayasites.com). **Tierra Maya Tours** (✉ Av. 5 at Calle 6, Playa del Carmen, ☎ 9/873–1385, FAX 9/873–1386). **Turistica Maya de Quintana Roo** (✉ Av. Héroes 165-A, Chetumal, ☎ 9/832–0555, FAX 9/832–9711).

TRANSPORTATION AROUND THE CARIBBEAN COAST

You can hire taxis in Cancún to go as far as Playa del Carmen, Tulum, or Akumal, but the price is steep unless you have many passengers. Fares run about $65 or more to Playa alone; between Playa and Tulum or Akumal, expect to pay at least another $25. It's much cheaper from Playa to Cancún, with taxi fare running about $30; negotiate before you hop into the cab. Getting a taxi along Highway 307 can take a while. Ask your hotel to call one for you.

TRAVEL AGENCIES

There are more major travel agencies and tour operators along the coast than ever, and first-class hotels in Playa del Carmen, Puerto Aventuras, and Akumal usually have their own in-house travel services.
➤ LOCAL AGENT REFERRALS: **Alltournative Expeditions** (✉ Av. 10 No. 1, Plaza Antigua, Playa del Carmen, ☎ 9/873–2036). **IMC** (✉ Plaza Antigua, Playa del Carmen, ☎ 9/873–1439, FAX 9/873–1439, WEB www.imcplay.com). **Turistica Maya de Quintana Roo** (✉ Holiday Inn Puerta Maya, Chetumal, ☎ 9/832–0555 or 9/832–2058, FAX 9/832–9711).

VISITOR INFORMATION

The Tourist Information Booth in Chetumal is open weekdays 8:30–2:30 and 6–9. In Playa del Carmen it's open Monday through Saturday, 8 AM–9 PM.
➤ TOURIST INFORMATION: **Chetumal** (✉ Av. Héroes opposite Av. Efraín Aguilar, ☎ 9/832–3663). **Playa del Carmen** (✉ Av. Juárez by the police station, ☎ 9/873–2804).

5 MÉRIDA AND THE STATE OF YUCATÁN

Ancient Maya ruins—the spectacular Chichén Itzá and Uxmal foremost among more than a dozen sites—have long been the main appeal of the State of Yucatán. But the less-traveled city of Mérida, with its superb restaurants, markets, cultural offerings, and its unique mix of Spanish and French architectural styles, is also well worth exploring. The peninsula's north coast is the kind of often-ignored place that allows you to discover your own Mexico, along with flocks of flamingos at the Celestún and Río Lagartos estuaries.

Updated by
Patricia Alisau

C ULTURALLY, the Yucatán is one of the richest parts of Mexico. It is the heart of a fascinating juxtaposition of two powerful civilizations—that of the Maya and that of transplanted Europeans. Vestiges of the past are evident in this land of oval thatch-roof huts and stately old mission churches, and in its people—particularly the women who still dress in traditional garb. Mysterious "lost cities" lie hidden in the forests. Small fishing villages dot beaches that are so far unjaded by the tourist industry. In the midst of this exotic landscape stands the elegant city of Mérida, for centuries the main stronghold of Spanish colonialism in the land of the Maya.

There is a marvelous eccentricity about Mérida. Fully urban, with maddeningly slow-moving traffic, it has a self-sufficient, self-contented air that would suggest a small town more than a state capital. Gaily pretentious turn-of-the-20th-century buildings have an Iberian-Moorish ornate flair, but most of the architecture is low-lying, and although the city sprawls, it is hardly imposing. Grandiose colonial facades adorned with iron grillwork, carved wooden doors, and archways conceal marble tiles and lush gardens that hark back to the city's heyday as the wealthiest capital in Mexico.

Mérida is a city of obvious contrasts, from its opulent facades to its residents, who—although increasingly aware and proud of Maya accomplishments—a century ago looked to Europe for their cultural identity. The Maya Indian presence is unmistakable: people are short, with square faces and almond eyes; women wear *huipiles* (hand-embroidered, tuniclike white dresses), and craftspeople and vendors from the outlying villages come to town in their huaraches (woven leather sandals). The Maya—long portrayed (falsely) as docile and peace-loving—for centuries provided the Spaniards and the mainland Mexicans with one of their greatest challenges. So many centuries after the Spanish conquest, Yucatán remains one of the last great strongholds of Mexico's indigenous population. Indeed, to this day the Maya in more-remote or isolated villages speak no Spanish, or just enough to get by.

Yucatán tried to secede from the rest of Mexico in the 1840s and, as late as the 1920s and 1930s, rebellious pockets of Maya communities held out against the *dzulobs* (outsiders). Yucatecans speak of themselves as *peninsulares* first, Mexicans second. Don't be surprised to see locals wearing T-shirts that say, "Republic of Yucatán." It could well have been this independent attitude that induced Governor Salvador Alvarado, in 1915, to convene the first feminist congress in the country (and Latin America as well) here, with the idea of liberating women "from being social wards and from the traditions that have suppressed them for years." This congress, which Alvarado described as "brilliant," was so successful that it was followed by the second congress in Mexico City in 1921, when women asked for the right to vote. They were finally granted that right in 1953.

Maya civilization—one of the world's great ancient cultures—thrived for about 1,500 years. The Maya were in a state of decline when the conquistadors arrived in AD 1527; the invaders burned defiant Maya warriors at the stake and drowned and hanged local women. Huge agricultural estates brought riches to the Spaniards, and Mérida soon became a strategic administrative and military foothold, the gateway to Cuba and to Spain. Francisco de Montejo's conquest of Yucatán took three gruesome wars, a total of 24 years. "Nowhere in all America was resistance to Spanish conquest more obstinate or more nearly successful," wrote the historian Henry Parkes. By the 18th century, huge maize and cattle plantations flourished throughout the peninsula, and the wealthy *hacendados* (plantation owners), left largely to their own devices by the viceroys in faraway Mexico City, accumulated fortunes under a semi-feudal system. The social structure—based on Indian peonage—barely changed as the economic base shifted to the export of dyewood; henequen, or sisal, a natural fiber used to make rope; and chicle, or gum arabic, a chewing-gum staple.

Insurrection came during the War of the Castes in the mid-1800s, when the enslaved indigenous people rose up with religious fervor and massacred thousands of whites. The United States, Cuba, and Mexico City finally came to the aid of the ruling elite, and between 1846 and 1850 the Indian population of Yucatán was effectively halved. Those Maya who did not escape into the remote jungles of neighboring Quintana Roo or get sold into slavery in Cuba found themselves worse off than before under the dictatorship of Porfirio Díaz, who had brought Yaqui prisoners from northern Mexico to the peninsula as forced labor under the rapacious grip of the hacendados. Díaz's legacy is evident in the pretentious French-style mansions that stretch along Mérida's Paseo Montejo.

Yucatán was then and still is a largely agricultural state, although the economic importance of tourism and the *maquiladoras* (assembly plants or factories, usually foreign-owned) has grown since the federal government cut subsidies to the henequen industry in 1990. These factories cut and assemble goods for such U.S. brand names as Gap and Liz Claiborne. More than 65 maquiladoras employ over 25,000 workers (up from 6,200 in 1995) around Mérida, and additional plants are expected to open.

With more than 500,000 inhabitants, the capital accounts for over a third of the state's population, but everyone else lives in villages, maintaining conservative traditions and lifestyles. Apart from the goods produced by the maquiladoras specifically for overseas markets, the state also exports honey, textiles, henequen, orange-juice concentrate, fresh fish, hammocks, and wood products.

Physically, too, Yucatán differs from the rest of the country. Its geography and wildlife have more in common with Florida and Cuba—with which it was probably once connected—than with the central Mexican plateau and mountains. A mostly flat limestone slab possessing almost no bodies of water, it is rife with cenotes (sinkholes) both above the ground and below, caves with stalactites, small hills, and intense (but short and dry) jungle. Wild ginger and spider lilies grow in profusion, and vast flamingo colonies nest at swampy estuaries on the northern and western coasts, where undeveloped sandy beaches extend some 370 km (230 mi). Deer, turkeys, boars, ocelots, tapirs, and armadillos once flourished in this semitropical climate (the average temperature is 82°F, or 28°C)—they now survive in a few protected areas.

But it is, of course, the celebrated Maya ruins, Chichén Itzá and Uxmal above all, that bring most people to the State of Yucatán. Indeed, the Puuc hills south of Mérida have more archaeological sites per square mile than any other place in the hemisphere. Most of the roads in this region are paved and two-lane, and the government is accelerating the pace at which it is fixing up the rest. Local travel agencies are adept at running tours.

Pleasures and Pastimes

Beaches

Although Yucatán's few-and-far-between beach resorts are no match for those of Cancún and the Caribbean coast, the north coast of the peninsula has long stretches of wide, soft white-sand beaches shared mainly by local children and fishermen—and the occasional sunbather. Progreso, where Mérida residents go to beat the heat, is unpretentious and affordable, and on summer weekends it can be as lively as any place on the Mexican Caribbean. Empty beaches stretch for about 64 km (40 mi) to the east, punctuated by small fishing villages that are catching the eye of developers as tourism takes off. Other popular beaches are in Celestún, Sisal, and Telchac Puerto, although their numbers are boosted more by bird-watchers and nature lovers than by sun worshipers.

Bird-Watching

More than 300 bird species are abundant in the Yucatán, both along the coast and inland. The most famous are the flamingos, which can be seen in the natural parks at Celestún and Río Lagartos at any time of year. The largest flocks of both flamingos and birding enthusiasts can be found during the spring months, when thousands of the birds—90% of the entire flamingo population of the Western Hemisphere—come to Río Lagartos to nest.

Dining

Dining out is a pleasure in Mérida. The city's 50-odd restaurants dish out a superb variety of cuisines—primarily Yucatecan, of course, but also Lebanese, Italian, French, Chinese, and Mexican—at very reasonable prices. And tony cafés have been sprouting up in atmospheric colonial edifices that lend a European air to casual dining. Generally, reservations are advised for $$$ restaurants, but only in high season. Casual but neat dress is acceptable at all Mérida restaurants. Avoid wearing shorts in the more-expensive places.

Beach towns north of Mérida such as Progreso, Sisal, and Telchac Puerto, as well as Río Lagartos to the east and Celestún to the west, serve fresh-caught seafood, although the dishes are prepared quite simply. A real gourmet dish is the blue crab at Celestún. However, you can't go wrong with most restaurants, whether they are thatch-roof affairs along the beach or in-town eateries.

In Pisté, the village nearest to Chichén Itzá, the food is only fair and in general overpriced. It's better to try one of the *palapa* (thatch-roof) cafés along the main road or the small markets and produce stands, which can provide the makings for a modest picnic.

If you enjoy eating with local people, stop at one of the many *loncherías* (diners) in the small towns and downtown districts of cities for *panuchos* (small, thick tortillas stuffed with beans and topped with shredded meat or fish), empanadas (turnovers filled with meat, fish, potatoes, or, occasionally, beans), tacos, or *salbutes* (fried tortillas smothered with diced turkey, pickled onion, and sliced avocado). However, take care with the habañero chilies, which can have smoke coming out of your ears if not used in moderation.

All restaurants are open for breakfast, lunch, and dinner unless otherwise noted.

CATEGORY	COST*
$$$$	over $15
$$$	$11–$15
$$	$6–$10
$	under $6

per person for a main course at dinner

Fishing

Those interested in sportfishing for such catch as grouper, red snapper, and sea bass, among others, are likely to get their fill in Yucalpetén, west of Progreso. Río Lagartos also has good fishing in its murky waters. In the Parque Natural del Flamenco Mexicano in Celestún, you have your choice of river or gulf fishing.

Lodging

The state of Yucatán has 7,000 hotel rooms, about a third the number of rooms in Cancún. Accommodations outside Mérida fit the low-key, simple pace of the region. Internationally affiliated properties are the exception rather than the rule. Instead, charmingly idiosyncratic old mansions or former haciendas such as the Hacienda Katanchel, restored and opened as a hotel in 1996, work as a base from which to explore the countryside. Eco Paraíso in Celestún and Reef Club outside Progreso, opened in the late 1990s, have diversified the offerings somewhat. In addition, surging tourism in the region is prompting hotels outside Mérida to renovate and expand.

Mérida has a refreshingly broad range of choices, among them top-end chain establishments, classic older hotels housed in charming colonial or turn-of-the-20th-century mansions, and basic lodgings geared toward budget travelers less concerned with creature comforts. As in the rest of Mexico, the facade rarely reveals the character of the hotel behind it, so check out the interior before turning away.

Location is very important: if you plan to spend most of your time enjoying Mérida, stay in the vicinity of the main square or along Calle 60. If you're a light sleeper, however, you may be better off staying in one of the places along or near Paseo Montejo, about a 30-minute stroll from the *zócalo* (main square)—or choose a room with double-pane windows to cut out traffic noise. In general the public spaces in Mérida's hotels are prettier than the sleeping rooms. Most hotels have air-conditioning, and even budget hotels have been installing air-conditioning in at least a few rooms, to keep up with the competition.

CATEGORY	COST*
$$$$	over $90
$$$	$60–$90
$$	$25–$60
$	under $25

*All prices are for a standard double room, excluding service and the 17% tax.

Ruins

Ancient Maya ruins from the Classic period, about AD 200–AD 900, are Yucatán's greatest claim to fame and world acclaim. The Maya city of Chichén Itzá, midway between Cancún and Mérida, was the first Yucatán ruin to be excavated and extensively restored for public viewing, in the late 1930s. Its main pyramid is one of the most familiar images of Mexico. Uxmal, south of Mérida, is almost as spectacular. Since the early 1990s, a combination of government interest in these ruins as a matter of national pride and Mexico's participation in the Mundo Maya program with four Central American nations has been fueling a restoration boom. (In addition, increased government funding has spurred a surge in excavations during the past few years.) The archaeological sites along the Ruta Puuc (Puuc Route) south of Uxmal, though not large, are among the most beautiful in Mexico, and more-recently discovered sites such as Aké and Ek Balam invite adventuresome travelers to explore where few people have set foot in the past few centuries.

The dates for many major events that took place here are only good estimates (unless precise dates have been found in Maya writings). Unfortunately, many of these historical records were lost with the near total destruction of the Maya codices (or books) by the obsessive Bishop Diego de Landa in the 16th century.

But Maya temples are not the only ruins that tug at the imagination in Yucatán. Grandiose Spanish colonial churches, built—often on the same site—with stones scavenged from ancient pyramids, dominate Maya villages throughout the state. The opulence of a more recent era can be seen at haciendas where wealthy plantation owners grew henequen. Originally, there were 500 haciendas. Some plantations still operate on a small scale, and some of the lavish mansions have been turned into museums or allowed to crumble, but a few are being restored as lodging establishments.

Shopping

Although Yucatecan artisans don't produce that many high-quality crafts, what items they do create are among the finest in the country. For the most part, Mérida is the best place in Yucatán to buy local handicrafts at reasonable prices. The main products include *hamacas* (hammocks), *guayaberas* (shirts for men that are worn outside the trousers), huaraches, huipiles, baskets, *jipis* (Panama hats, made from guano palm, that can be rolled up), leather goods, gold- and silver-filigree jewelry, masks, painted gourds, and piñatas.

Hammocks are one of the most popular craft items sold here. They are available in cotton, nylon, and silk, as well as in the very rough and scratchy henequen fiber. Silk is the most expensive material and lasts longest, but it is harder to find. Nylon hammocks dry quickly and may be best for humid or wet climates. Cotton is comfortable, but the colors fade fastest. Double-threaded hammocks are sturdier and stretch less than single-threaded ones, a difference that can be identified by studying the density of the weave. Hammocks come in different sizes: *sencillo,* for one person (a rather tight fit); *doble,* very comfortable for one but crowded for two; *matrimonial* (also called "king-size"), which decently accommodates two; and *familiares* or *matrimoniales especiales,* which can theoretically sleep an entire family. For a good-quality matrimonial nylon or cotton hammock, expect to pay about $25, about $65 for one in silk. Sencillos go for $10–$15. Unless you are an expert, it's best to buy a hammock at one of the specialty shops in Mérida, many of which let you climb in to try the size.

Exploring the State of Yucatán

Mérida is the hub of Yucatán and the best base for exploring the rest of the state. From there, highways radiate in every direction. To the east, along Route 180 to Cancún, are the famous Chichén Itzá ruins and the low-key colonial city of Valladolid. Heading south on Route 261, you come to Uxmal and the Ruta Puuc, a series of the most outstanding small ruins in Yucatán. Route 261 north from Mérida takes you to the seaport and beach resort of Progreso. To the west, separate secondary highways go to Celestún and Sisal, two fishing villages with white-sand beaches, the former on the edge of the Parque Natural Celestún wildlife preserve.

Most roads in the state are narrow, paved two-lane affairs that pass through small towns and villages. There are also two toll roads in operation—one from Mérida to Cancún and the other from Mérida to Campeche City. Rarely is traffic heavy on them, and they are in good shape, usually devoid of potholes and unexpected bumps. But do watch out for unattended children and stray dogs, cows, and horses. Highway 176, which runs parallel to the north coast from Mérida, was widened to four lanes in 2000, improving access to a series of small inland towns.

Numbers in the text correspond to numbers in the margin and on the State of Yucatán and Mérida maps.

Great Itineraries

IF YOU HAVE 3 DAYS

Spend two days in ▦ **Mérida** ①–⑯, savoring the city's unique character as you make your way among the historic churches and mansions and enjoy the parks and restaurants. On Day 3, drive or take a tour to one of Yucatán's most famous Maya ruins—either **Chichén Itzá** ⑳ or **Uxmal** ㉔. Each is within about two hours of Mérida, making for an ideal day trip.

IF YOU HAVE 7 DAYS

First explore the sights of **Mérida** ①–⑯, and then take two separate overnight excursions from the city. Spend the night at one of the archaeological hotels near ▦ **Uxmal** ㉔, and the next day explore the Ruta Puuc, the series of lost cities south of Uxmal that includes **Kabah** ㉕, **Sayil** ㉖, and **Labná** ㉗, as well as the fascinating **Loltún Caves** ㉘, returning to Mérida through **Ticul** ㉙. On the second excursion, to ▦ **Chichén Itzá** ⑳, allow as much as a full day en route to explore some of the more recently discovered ruins along the way, such as **Aké** ⑰. You can also stop at present-day Maya villages along the way, such as ▦ **Izamal** ⑱. After visiting Chichén Itzá, you may wish to beat the afternoon heat by exploring the **Cave of Balancanchén** ㉑ or swimming in one of the cool subterranean cenotes nearby. You might also head north from **Valladolid** ㉒ to see the flamingo nesting grounds at **Parque Natural Río Lagartos** ㊷.

IF YOU HAVE 10 DAYS

In addition to visiting the sights noted above, you may also want to add one or more beach days to your itinerary. An obvious choice is **Progreso** ㉟, with a stop en route from **Mérida** ①–⑯ to see the ruins of **Dzibilchaltún** ㉞, and perhaps side trips to explore smaller, more traditional north-coast beach towns such as **Yucalpetén** ㊱, **Telchac Puerto** ㊳, and **Dzilám de Bravo** ㊵. If you prefer a secluded fishing village, try either **Celestún** ㉜ or **Sisal** ㉝. Guided boat trips are available from Celestún into **Parque Natural del Flamenco Mexicano**, a tropical wetlands teeming with birds and sea life.

When to Tour Mérida and the Yucatán

Sunday is special in Yucatán. Mérida blocks off traffic in the downtown area as what seems to be the entire population of the city mingles in the zócalo and other parks and plazas for entertainment and food. Sidewalk cafés along this route are perfect vantage points from which to watch the passing parade of people as well as the folk dancers and singers. Sunday is also the day when admission to museums and archaeological sites is free, an important consideration given that entrance fees at the various ruins have been on the rise. This is also something to keep in mind if you plan to explore the Ruta Puuc, where you can visit seven Maya sites, each of which charges a separate admission on other days of the week.

Thousands of people, from international sightseers to Maya shamans, swarm to Chichén Itzá for the vernal equinox (the first day of spring), when the afternoon light creates a shadow that looks like a snake moving slowly down the stairway of the main pyramid. The phenomenon also occurs on the autumnal equinox, but the rainy weather typical at that time of year tends to discourage visitors.

Another good time to come is November 1, Mexico's traditional Day of the Dead, which, in Mérida, is called by its Maya name, Hanal Pixan, or "food for departed souls." On the eve of this celebration, the fam-

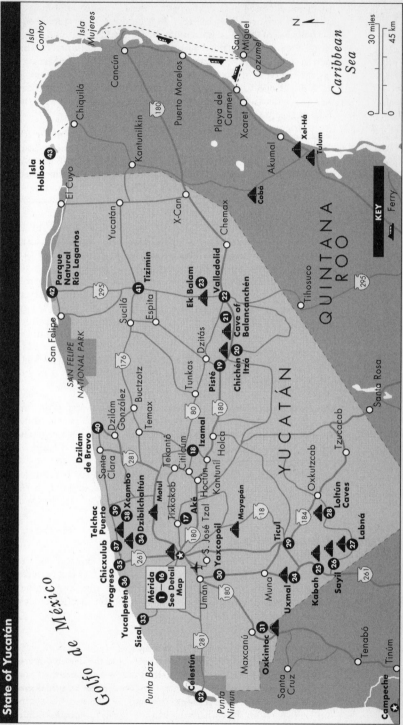

State of Yucatán

Golfo de México

Caribbean Sea

QUINTANA ROO

YUCATÁN

SAN FELIPE NATIONAL PARK

Parque Natural Río Lagartos

Isla Contoy

Isla Mujeres

Cancún

San Miguel

Cozumel

Chiquilá

Puerto Morelos

Playa del Carmen

Xcaret

Xel-Há

Tulum

Akumal

Cobá

Kantunilkin

Isla Holbox

El Cuyo

Yucatán

X-Can

Chemax

Tihosuco

Santa Rosa

Santa Cruz

Tenabó

Tinúm

Campeche

Punta Baz

Punta Nimun

Celestún

Sisal

Yucalpetén

Progreso

Chicxulub Puerto

Telchac Puerto

Dzilám de Bravo

San Felipe

Tizimín

Espita

Sucilá

Valladolid

Ek Balam

Cave of Balamcanché

Chichén Itzá

Pisté

Dzitás

Tunkas

Izamal

Holca

Kantunil

Hoctún

Citilcum

Tekantó

Motul

Tixkokob

Aké

S. José Tzal

Yaxcopoil

Mérida

Umán

Maxcanú

Oxkintoc

Uxmal

Muna

Ticul

Oxkutzcab

Izucab

Loltún Caves

Labná

Sayil

Kabah

Mayapán

Dzilám González

Temax

Buctzotz

Santa Clara

Xcambo

Dzibilchaltún

San José Tzal

30 miles / 45 km

KEY — Ferry

Route numbers visible: 180, 295, 176, 281, 261, 184, 80, 18

Numbered markers: 1-16, 17, 18, 19, 20, 21, 22, 23, 24, 25, 26, 27, 28, 29, 30, 31, 32, 33, 34, 35, 36, 37, 38, 39, 40, 41, 42, 43 ily of the deceased puts the favorite foods of the dead out on a small altar at home or at the cemetery. Mérida dresses up its main square with dozens of "huts" representing different villages around the state. Inside are small altars filled with the time-honored offerings to the departed souls of children and adults. If you happen to be in Mérida during the last week of October or the first two weeks of November, don't miss the Otoño Cultural, or Autumn Cultural Festival. Free or inexpensive classical-music concerts, dance performances, and art exhibits take place almost nightly at the Teatro Peón Contreras.

High season here generally corresponds to high season in the rest of Mexico: Christmastime, Easter week, and the months of July and August. Rainfall is heaviest between June and October, bringing with it an uncomfortable humidity. The coolest months are November through January; April and May are usually the hottest.

MÉRIDA

Travelers to Mérida are a loyal bunch, content to return again and again to favorite restaurants, neighborhoods, and museums. The city's traffic, complete with diesel fumes and noise, is frustrating, particularly after a peaceful stay on the coast or at one of the archaeological sites, but the city's merits far outweigh its flaws. Mérida is the cultural and intellectual center of the peninsula, with museums, schools, and attractions that can greatly enhance your insights into the history and character of Yucatán. Indeed, the quality and number of its offerings make it one of Mexico's leading cultural centers. Consider making it one of the first stops in your travels, and make sure your visit includes a Sunday, when traffic is light and the city seems to revert to a more gracious era.

Most streets in Mérida are numbered, not named, and most run one way. North–south streets have even numbers, which ascend from east to west; east–west streets have odd numbers, which ascend from north to south. Street addresses are confusing because they don't progress in even increments by blocks; for example, the 600s may occupy two or even 10 blocks. A particular location is therefore usually identified by indicating the street number and the nearest cross street, as in "Calle 64 at Calle 61," or "Calle 64 between 61 and 63," which is written "Calle 64 x 61 y 63."

Zócalo and Surroundings

The zócalo, the oldest part of town, has been dubbed the Centro Histórico (Historic Center) by city officials. The city has been restoring all the colonial buildings in the area to their original splendor, and it's not uncommon to see work proceeding on facades on several streets at once.

A Good Walk

Start at the **zócalo** ①: see the **Casa de Montejo** ② (now a Banamex bank), on the south side; the **Palacio Municipal** ③ and the **Centro Cultural de Mérida Olimpo** ④, on the west side; the **Palacio del Gobierno** ⑤, on the northeast corner, and, catercorner, the **Catedral de San Ildefonso** ⑥; and the **Museo de Arte Contemporáneo** ⑦ on the east side. Step out on Calle 60 from the cathedral and walk north to **Parque Hidalgo** ⑧ and the **Iglesia de la Tercera Orden de Jesús** ⑨, which is across Calle 59. Continue north along Calle 60 for a short block to the **Teatro Peón Contreras** ⑩, which lies on the east side of the street; the entrance to the **Universidad Autónoma de Yucatán** ⑪ is on the west side of Calle 60 at Calle 57. A block farther north on the west side of Calle 60 is the **Parque de Santa Lucía** ⑫. From the park, walk north four blocks and turn right on Calle 47 for two blocks to **Paseo Montejo** ⑬. Once on this street, continue north for two long blocks to the **Palacio Cantón** ⑭. From here look either for a *calesa* (horse-drawn carriage) or cabs parked outside the museum to take you back past the zócalo to the **Mercado de Artesanías "García Rejón"** ⑮ and the **Mercado Municipal** ⑯—or walk if you're up to it.

Sights to See

❷ **Casa de Montejo.** This stately palace sits on the south side of the plaza, on Calle 63. Francisco de Montejo—father and son—conquered the peninsula and founded Mérida in 1542; they built their "casa" 10 years later. The property remained with the family until the late 1970s, when it was restored by banker Agustín Legorreta and converted to a bank. Built in the French style during Mérida's heyday as the world's henequen capital, it now represents the city's finest—and oldest—example of colonial Plateresque architecture, which typically features elaborate ornamentation. It also incorporates a great deal of *porfiriato*, architectural details characteristic of the reign of dictator Porfirio Díaz that mimicked 19th-century French style in such traits as mansard roofs, gilded mirrors, and the use of marble. A bas-relief on the doorway—which is all that remains of the original house—depicts Francisco de Montejo the younger, his wife, and daughter as well as Spanish soldiers standing on the heads of the vanquished Maya. Even if you have no banking to do, step into the building weekdays between 9 and 5 to glimpse the leafy inner patio.

❻ **Catedral de San Ildefonso** (St. Ildefonse Cathedral). Begun in 1561, this is the oldest cathedral in Mexico and the second-oldest on the North American mainland. It sits on the east side of the plaza. It took several hundred Maya laborers, working with stones from the pyramids of the ravaged Maya city, 36 years to complete it. Designed in the somber Renaissance style by an architect who had worked on the Escorial in Madrid, its facade is stark and unadorned, with gunnery slits instead of windows, and faintly Moorish spires. Inside, the black **Cristo de las Ampollas** (Christ of the Blisters) occupies a side altar to the left of the main one. The statue is a replica of the original, which was destroyed during the Revolution (this was also when most of the gold that typically burnished Mexican cathedrals was carried off). According to one of many legends, the Christ figure burned all night yet appeared the next morning unscathed—except that it was covered with the blisters for which it is named. The crucifix above the side altar is reputedly the second largest in the world. ✉ *Calle 60 at Calle 61,* ☎ *no phone.* ⊙ *Daily 7–11:30 and 4:30–8.*

❹ **Centro Cultural de Mérida Olimpo** (Mérida Olimpo Cultural Center). Referred to as just Olimpo, this is the best venue for free cultural events in the city. The beautiful, porticoed cultural center was built adjacent to City Hall in late 1999, occupying what used to be a parking lot. The marble interior is a showcase for top international art exhibits, classical music concerts, conferences, and theater and dance presentations. Next door, a movie house renovated to its 1950s look features film festivals, classics by such directors as Buñuel, Fellini, and Kazan, plus a Sunday family-movie series. The complex also includes a Librería Dante bookstore and El Via café. ✉ *Calle 62 between Calles 61 and 63,* ☎ *9/928–2020.* 🎟 *Free.* ⊙ *Tues.–Sun. 10–10.*

Ermita de Santa Isabel (Hermitage of St. Isabel). At the far south of the city stands the hermitage (circa 1748), part of a Jesuit monastery also known as the Hermitage of the Good Trip, which was restored in 1966. A resting place in colonial days for travelers heading to Campeche,

and the most peaceful place in the city, the restored chapel is an en-
chanting spot to visit at sunset (when it is open) and perhaps a good
destination for a ride in a calesa. Next door is a huge garden with many
botanical species, a waterfall, and footpaths bordered with bricks and
colored stones. ⊠ *Calles 66 and 77,* ☎ *no phone.* 🎫 *Free.* ☉ *Church
hrs are irregular; garden daily 9–5.*

⑨ Iglesia de la Tercera Orden de Jesús (Church of the Third Order of
Jesus or Church of the Jesuits). To the north of Parque Hidalgo is one
of Mérida's oldest buildings and the first Jesuit church in the Yucatán.
The church was built in 1618 of limestone from a Maya temple that
had stood on the site, and faint outlines of ancient carvings are still
visible on the stonework of the west wall. Although it is a favorite place
for society weddings because of its antiquity, the church interior is not
very ornate.

The former convent rooms in the rear of the building now host the small
Pinoteca Juan Gamboa Guzmán (State Repository of Paintings). The
first room is dedicated to temporary exhibits; the second displays striking bronze sculptures of the Yucatán's indigenous people by its most
celebrated 20th-century sculptor, Enrique Gottdiener. On the second
floor are about 20 forgettable oil paintings—mostly of past governors
and a few saints. ⊠ *Calle 59 between Calles 58 and 60,* ☎ *9/924–7912.*
🎫 *$1, free Sun.* ☉ *Tues.–Sat. 8–8, Sun. 8–2.*

⑮ Mercado de Artesanías "García Rejón" (García Rejón Crafts Market).
Shops somewhat sterile in appearance and selling dry goods, straw hats,
and hammocks occupy several long rows in this covered marketplace.
Local handicrafts and souvenirs are sold. ⊠ *Calle 60 at Calle 65,* ☎
no phone. ☉ *Weekdays 9–6, Sat. 9–4, Sun. 9–1.*

★ ⑯ **Mercado Municipal** (Municipal or Public Market). At this pungent, labyrinthine market, sellers of chilies, herbs, trinkets, and fruit occupy almost every patch of ground. In the early morning hours, the place is jammed with housewives and restaurateurs who come to pick the freshest of the fresh to serve that day. On the second floor of the main building is the **Bazar de Artesanías Municipales** (Municipal Handicrafts Bazaar), the principal handicrafts market, where you can buy pottery, embroidered clothes, men's guayabera dress shirts, hammocks, and straw bags. Jewelry (gold or gold-dipped filigree earrings) is sold on the first floor below the Bazar de Artesanías. ⊠ *Calle 65 between Calles 56 and 58,* ☎ *no phone.* ⊘ *Mon.–Sat. 8–7, Sun. 8–3.*

❼ **Museo de Arte Contemporáneo** (Museum of Contemporary Art). Originally designed as an art school but used until 1915 as a seminary, this enormous two-story building is full of light, just perfect for an art museum. It showcases the works of Yucatecan artists such as Gabriel Ramírez Aznar and Fernando García Ponce and has excellent international art exhibits in the second-floor galleries. These make up for the halfhearted reproductions of some of the world's masterpieces in the World History of Art room. There's also a bookstore (closed Sunday). ⊠ *Pasaje de la Revolución 1907, between Calles 58 and 60 (on main square),* ☎ *9/928–3258 or 9/928–3236.* ▨ *$2, free Sun.* ⊘ *Wed.–Mon. 10–5:30.*

Museo de Artes Populares (Museum of Folk Art). If you love Mexican crafts, trek several blocks east of the main square to this museum, housed in a fine old mansion. The ground floor is devoted to Yucatecan arts and crafts, such as weaving, straw baskets, filigree jewelry, carved wood, and beautifully carved conch shells, as well as exhibits on huipil products and the like. The second floor focuses on the popular arts of the rest of Mexico. ⊠ *Calle 59 No. 441, at Calle 50,* ☎ *no phone.* ▨ *Free.* ⊘ *Tues.–Sat. 9–8, Sun. 8–2.*

⑭ **Palacio Cantón.** The most compelling of the mansions on ☞ **Paseo Montejo,** the pale-peach palacio presently houses the air-conditioned **Museo de Antropología e Historia** (Museum of Anthropology and History). Designed by Enrique Deserti, who also did the blueprints for the Teatro Peón Contreras, the building has grandiose airs that seem more characteristic of a mausoleum than a home, but in fact it was built for a general between 1909 and 1911. There is marble everywhere, likewise Doric and Ionic columns and other Italianate Beaux Arts flourishes. From 1958 to 1967 the mansion served as the residence of the state governor. In 1977 it became a museum dedicated to the culture and history of the Maya. Although it's not as impressive as its counterparts in other Mexican cities, it can serve as an introduction to ancient Maya culture before you visit nearby Maya sites. Exhibits explain the Maya practice of dental mutilation and incrustation. A case of "sick bones" shows how the Maya suffered from osteoarthritis, nutritional maladies, and congenital syphilis. The museum also has conch shells, stones, and quetzal feathers that were used for trading. There is a bookstore on the premises; it's not open on Sunday. ⊠ *Calle 43 and Paseo Montejo,* ☎ *9/923–0557.* ▨ *$2, free Sun.* ⊘ *Tues.–Sat. 8–8, Sun. 8–2.*

❺ **Palacio del Gobierno** (State House). Occupying the northeast corner of the main square is this structure, built in 1885 on the site of the Casa Real (Royal House). The upper floor of the State House contains Fernando Castro Pacheco's vivid murals of the bloody history of the conquest of the Yucatán, painted in 1978. On the main balcony (visible from outside on the plaza) stands a reproduction of the **Bell of Dolores Hidalgo,** on which Mexican independence rang out on September 16, 1810, in the town of Dolores Hidalgo in Guanajuato. Every

September 16, the state governor tolls the bell to commemorate the occasion. ⊠ *Calle 61 between Calles 60 and 62.* ☎ *Free.* ◷ *Daily 8 AM or 9 AM–9 PM.*

③ Palacio Municipal (City Hall). The west side of the main square is occupied by this 17th-century building, which is painted pale yellow and trimmed with white arcades, balustrades, and the national coat of arms. Originally erected on the ruins of the last surviving Maya structure, it was rebuilt in 1735 and then completely reconstructed along colonial lines in 1928. It remains the headquarters of the local government. ⊠ *Calle 62 between Calles 61 and 63.* ◷ *Daily 9–8.*

⑫ Parque de Santa Lucía. The rather plain park at Calles 60 and 55 draws crowds to its Thursday-night performances by local musicians and folk dancers; shows start at 9. The small church opposite the park dates from 1575 and was built as a place of worship for the African and Caribbean slaves who lived here. The churchyard functioned as the cemetery until 1821.

⑧ Parque Hidalgo. A half block north of the main plaza, at Calles 60 and 59, is this small, cozy park, officially known as Cepeda Peraza. Renovated mansions turned hotels and sidewalk cafés line the south side of the park, which comes alive at night with marimba bands and street vendors.

ⓒ Parque Zoologico El Centenario. Mérida's great children's attraction, this is a large, somewhat tacky amusement complex consisting of playgrounds; rides (including ponies and a small train); a roller-skating rink; snack bars; and cages with more than 300 marvelous native monkeys, birds, reptiles, and other animals. It also has picnic areas, pleasant wooded paths, and a small lake where you can rent rowboats. The French Renaissance–style arch (1921) commemorates the 100th anniversary of Mexican independence. ⊠ *Av. Itzaes between Calles 59 and 65 (entrances on Calles 59 and 65),* ☎ *no phone.* ☎ *Free.* ◷ *Daily 8–5.*

⑬ Paseo Montejo. North of downtown, this 10-block-long street exemplifies the Parisian airs the city took on in the late 19th century, when wealthy plantation owners were building opulent, impressive mansions. The broad boulevard, lined with tamarinds and laurels, is sometimes wistfully referred to as Mérida's Champs-Elysées. Inside the mansions the owners typically displayed imported Carrara marble and antiques, opting for the decorative and social standards of New Orleans, Cuba, and Paris over styles that were popular in Mexico City. (At the time there was more traffic by sea via the Gulf of Mexico and the Caribbean than there was overland across the lawless interior.) Although some of the once stunning mansions have fallen into disrepair, they are being restored by a citywide beautification program bolstered by private investment. Upscale shops and restaurants have been sprouting up on the paseo.

⑩ Teatro Peón Contreras. This 1908 Italianate theater was built along the lines of the grand turn-of-the-20th-century European theaters and opera houses. In the early 1980s the marble staircase and the dome and frescoes were restored. Today, in addition to performing arts, the theater also houses temporary art exhibits and the main **Centro de Información Turística**, which is to the right of the lobby. The information center distributes maps and brochures and can provide details about local attractions. A café serving cappuccino and other coffees, plus light snacks and some meals, spills out to a patio from inside the theater to the right of the information center. ⊠ *Calle 60 between Calles 57 and 59,* ☎ *9/923–7354; 9/924–9290 tourist-information center.* ◷ *Theater daily 7 AM–1 AM; tourist-information center weekdays 8 AM–9 PM, weekends 8–8.*

⑪ **Universidad Autónoma de Yucatán.** The arabesque university plays a major role in the city's cultural and intellectual life. The folkloric ballet performs on the patio of the main building Friday at 9 PM ($9). A Jesuit college built in 1618 previously occupied the site; the present building, which dates from 1711, has crenellated Moorish ramparts and archways. Bulletin boards just inside the entrance announce upcoming cultural events. ⊠ *Calle 60 between Calles 57 and 59,* ☎ *9/924–8000 or 9/924–7260.*

❶ **Zócalo** (main square). The Meridanos also traditionally call this the Plaza Principal and Plaza de la Independencia, and it's a good spot from which to begin any tour of the city. Ancient, geometrically pruned laurel trees and *confidenciales* (S-shape benches designed for tête-à-têtes) invite lingering. The plaza was laid out in 1542 on the ruins of T'hó, the Maya city demolished to make way for Mérida, and is still the focal point around which the most important public buildings cluster. Lampposts, which keep the park beautifully illuminated at night, and a bank of public telephones were added in 2000, and the streets surrounding the park were repaved with attractive textured cement tiles. Eventually the work will cover all the streets in the Historic Center. ⊠ *Bordered by Calles 60, 62, 61, and 63.*

Dining and Lodging

$–$$ ✕ **Alberto's Continental Patio.** The romantic setting merits the kudos this restaurant has received, but the quality of the food isn't as good as it once was. The 1727 building is adorned with (later) mosaic floors from Cuba, the two dining rooms are fitted with dark-wood trim and stone sculpture, and tables are set with candles in glass lanterns. An inner patio surrounded by rubber trees is ideal for starlit dining. Order Lebanese food and your plate is heaped with servings of shish kebab, fried *kibi* (meatballs of ground beef, wheat germ, and spices), cabbage rolls, hummus, eggplant dip, and tabbouleh, accompanied by pita bread, almond pie, and Turkish coffee. The menu includes Mexican dishes and has meatless options for vegetarians. Consider skipping the wine, as it's considerably overpriced. ⊠ *Calle 64 No. 482, at Calle 57,* ☎ *9/928–5367. AE, MC, V.*

$–$$ ✕ **La Bella Epoca.** For a special dinner, nothing matches the elegance
★ and style of this second-story dining room, the former ballroom of an old mansion that has been restored beyond its original grandeur. Crystal chandeliers sparkle over tiny balcony tables overlooking Parque Hidalgo. You seem to pay for the ambience here, and the shills outside trying to entice customers inside take the image down a peg or two, but the food is still tops. An ambitious but almost unreadable handwritten menu includes French, Mexican, Middle Eastern, Yucatecan, vegetarian, and unusual Maya dishes. Consider the *sikil-pak* (a dip with ground pumpkin seeds, charbroiled tomatoes, and onions) or the succulent *pollo pibíl* (chicken baked in banana leaves). Arrive for dinner before 8 PM to claim one of the balcony tables overlooking the street. ⊠ *Hotel del Parque, Calle 60 between Calles 57 and 59,* ☎ *9/928– 1928. AE, MC, V.*

$–$$ ✕ **Habichuela.** The food and service at this quietly elegant spot are ex-
★ cellent. Custom-made hardwood furniture, marble floors, and lots of leaded-glass accents contribute to its clubby feel. Local businessmen hold power lunches here; at night, it's filled with families and couples. For starters, try the seafood crepes or salmon pâté. Main dishes feature meat, fish, and fowl prepared with flair; choices include butterflied shrimp with ginger, tamarind, or fruit sauce, and chicken Veronica stuffed with Serrano ham and bananas with sweet gravy on the side. The chocolate-mousse cake is the star of the dessert menu. The chef

welcomes special requests. ⊠ *Calle 1 No. 416, Col. México Oriente (about 20 mins by car from main square),* ☎ *9/926–3626. AE, MC, V. No dinner Sun.*

$ ✕ **Alameda.** You really get a good deal for your money here (the most expensive main dish is about $4). Middle Eastern and vegetarian specialties share the menu with standard Yucatecan fare at this nondescript side-street restaurant that Meridanos rave about. Businessmen linger over grilled beef shish kebab, pita bread, and coffee; some old couples have been coming in once a week for years. Everything is served without side dishes—if you want beans or potatoes with your eggs, you must ask for them. Meat-free dishes include tabbouleh and spongy, lemon-flavor spinach turnovers. Alameda is open only until 7:30 PM. ⊠ *Calle 58 No. 474 (across from Posada Toledo),* ☎ *9/928–3635. No credit cards. No dinner.*

$ ✕ **Los Almendros.** This Mérida classic takes credit for the invention of the regional specialty called *poc chuc* (slices of pork marinated in sour-orange juice and spices), although some dispute the claim. The food can be greasy, and local spices, such as achiote, can overwhelm the main ingredients. Still, Los Almendros is a good introduction to the variety of Yucatecan cuisine. The menu includes *cochinita pibíl* (pork baked in banana leaves), panuchos, pork sausage, *papadzules* (corn tortillas with chopped, hard-cooked egg and pumpkin-seed sauce), and *pollo ticuleño* (boneless, breaded chicken in tomato sauce filled with fried beans, peas, red peppers, ham, and cheese). Sangria—with or without alcohol—washes it all down. The English-language menu has pictures and descriptions of main dishes. There is live music from Monday through Saturday 2–5 and 7:30–11 and a regional show Friday at 8. ⊠ *Calle 50 No. 493 (between Calles 57 and 59),* ☎ *9/923–8135 or 9/928–5459. AE, MC, V.*

$ ✕ **Amaro.** Statesman Andres Quintana Roo was born in 1787 in this historic home, which takes on a romantic glow at night with candlelit tables in the open patio beneath a big tree. The focus here used to be vegetarian, so the menu is heavy on health drinks, made mostly with local vegetables, fruit, and herbs. If you're missing your favorite comfort foods, you can order a side of mashed potatoes or french fries, or a salad made with fresh local veggies washed with purified water. Recommended dishes include eggplant curry and soup made with *chaya,* a local vegetable that looks like spinach. Some of the staff can have a snooty attitude. ⊠ *Calle 59 No. 507 (between Calles 60 and 62),* ☎ *9/928–2451. No credit cards. Closed Sun. in Apr.–Nov.*

$ ✕ **Anfitrion.** The classic Lebanese-Yucatecan cuisine at this unpretentious local favorite screams "fresh." For starters, there's mounds of soft pita bread, chili-spiked olive oil for dipping (use sparingly), wonderful Lebanese dry yogurt, and hummus. There's a daily luncheon dish that might be breaded pork dressed in fresh tomato sauce with chopped ham, peas, and cheese, or a succulent tripe casserole with bacon, chickpeas, and ham (very Yucatecan). Daily specials cost $5 and come with rice, beans, coffee, and dessert. *Dulce de papaya* (cooked papaya flavored with a subtle fig essence) and *caballero pobre* (literally "poor gentleman"—old bread in a light raisin-and-cinnamon syrup) are typical desserts. ⊠ *Calle 62 No. 272 at Calle 27 (4 blocks from the Fiesta Americana hotel),* ☎ *9/925–6190. MC, V. Closed Tues. No dinner.*

$ ✕ **Café La Havana.** Old-fashioned ceiling fans and elegant wicker furniture contribute to the Old Havana nostalgia at this overwhelmingly popular café—an outpost of a famous coffee house in Mexico City that Fidel Castro supposedly frequented. The aroma of fresh-ground coffee fills the air at this casual 24-hour place, where you can comfortably linger, chat with friends, or hammer out a business deal. Sixteen javas are offered, including Irish, frappé, espresso, and Arab. The menu has light snacks such as lime soup, as well as some entrées, including spaghetti, fajitas, and breaded shrimp. The café is a few blocks north of the main square. ⊠ *Corner of Calles 59 and 62,* ☎ *9/928–6502. No credit cards.*

$ ✕ **La Casona.** This pretty mansion turned restaurant near Parque Santa Ana has an inner patio, arcade, and swirling ceiling fans. A bar features live romantic music on weekends. The accent is Yucatecan, with poc chuc, pollo pibíl, and *huachinango* (red snapper baked in banana leaves) among the recommended dishes. There are some Italian offerings, including homemade ravioli, manicotti, and linguine, as well. Vegetables or pasta accompany most orders. ⊠ *Calle 60 No. 434, between Calles 47 and 49,* ☎ *9/923–9996. MC, V. Closed Sun.*

$ ✕ **Dante's.** Lovers and families crowd this modern, bustling coffeehouse on the second floor of one of Mérida's largest bookshops. The house specialty is crepes, 18 varieties with either sweet or savory fillings; light entrées such as tacos and pizzas also are served. You can order cappuccino and specialty coffees as well as beer and wine. A small theater in back of the bookstore puts on evening comic sketches and live music from time to time, and puppet shows on Sunday. ⊠ *Prolongación Paseo Montejo 138-B (about 3 long blocks from the Holiday Inn and Fiesta Americana hotels),* ☎ *9/927–7441. MC, V.*

$ ✕ **Express.** This plain place has managed to keep a faithful following among dignified Meridano men in guayaberas who spend hours bonding in the Madrid café–style ambience. Paintings of Old Spain and Old Mérida, ceiling fans, and old-fashioned globe lights reinforce the mood. The menu is nothing fancy: broiled garlic chicken, shrimp, red snapper, and sandwiches. The name notwithstanding, service can be slow. ⊠ *Calle 60 No. 502, at Calle 59,* ☎ *9/928–1691. No credit cards.*

$ ✕ **Hong Kong.** If you tire of regional food, head for this sparkling eatery off Paseo Montejo for some of Mexico's most authentic Chinese food. The wontons and egg rolls are served hot and crispy. There's a preponderance of chicken and shrimp dishes, and only a few for vegetarians. During weekend lunch (when only the $9 buffet is served) the place is jammed with Meridanos—and the sound of clinking silverware and the sight of running waiters is in no way conducive to lingering. The easiest way to get here is by taxi, as it's a long walk down Paseo Montejo, even from the hotels on the street. ⊠ *Calle 31 No. 133, between Calles 22 and 24,* ☎ *9/926–1441 or 9/926–7439. AE, MC, V.*

$ ✕ **Pizza Bella.** Under an arcade in the main square, this restaurant serves espresso, cappuccino, and Mexican and American breakfasts as well as pizza. Checkered tablecloths atop wooden tables and an eclectic collection of wall decorations, from maps to beer advertisements, add atmosphere to an otherwise standard pizza joint. ⊠ *Calle 61 No. 500, Dept. E-2,* ☎ *9/923–6401. No credit cards.*

$ ✕ **Via Olimpo.** You can linger over a coffee and a good book (from the adjoining bookshop) at this main-square café, or spend an afternoon people-watching. On Sunday, this is a coveted spot from which to view the music and dance performances on the square. A student minstrel group sings Wednesday through Saturday underneath the old-fashioned high ceilings of the colonial dining room while clients feast on light dishes, including poc chuc, papadzules, smoked-turkey sandwiches, or hamburgers and french fries. Crepe dishes are a favorite, as is the $6.50 breakfast buffet. Businessmen and the local intelligentsia keep the place, open 7:30 AM to midnight, hopping. Wine and spirits are also served. ⊠ *Calle 62 between Calles 63 and 61,* ☎ *9/923–5843. AE, MC, V.*

$$$$ ✕🏠 **Hacienda Katanchel.** This romantic, rambling 17th-century
★ henequen hacienda on 740 acres was brought back to its original splendor by Anibal Gonzalez and his wife Monica Hernandez. The guest

suites are housed in spacious, freestanding pavilions built along a winding garden walkway. They have direct-dial telephones and are outfitted with overhead fans, hammocks, huge tile bathrooms, plunge pools, and double beds that look like pieces of modern sculpture. Everything at this member of the Small Luxury Hotels of the World has been carefully restored, even the 19th-century red Marseille tile roofs. The former Casa de Máquina (Processing Plant) is now a gorgeous restaurant that serves contemporary Yucatecan cuisine. The menu makes liberal use of the hacienda's organically grown fruits and vegetables; offerings include cream of beet soup, chicken in *pipian* (pumpkin seed) and pistachio sauce, and desserts such as vanilla ice cream with sweet and tangy sour-orange sauce. The wine list contains superb foreign and domestic vintages. Room rates include early-morning coffee or tea and biscuits, placed outside your door. Massages using herbs and floral essences bring pampering to a new level. Small jets, prop planes, and private cars are available for excursions at extra cost, and those who want to tie the knot can do so at the wedding chapel. ⊠ *25 km (15 mi) east of Mérida on Hwy. 180 (toward Cancún),* ☎ *9/923–4020 or 800/223–6510,* FAX *888/882–9470,* WEB *www.hacienda-katanchel.com. 39 suites. Restaurant, bar, air-conditioning, pool, massage, chapel, travel services, car rental, free parking. AE, MC, V.*

$$$$ ✕🏨 **Hacienda Teya.** The draw at this beautiful henequen-era hacienda
★ 8 mi from the city is the fabulous regional food; reservations for Sunday lunch or dinner are essential. After a typical lunch of cochinita pibíl or baked chicken, you can stroll in the orchard or surrounding gardens, or swim in the huge rectangular pool. There are six rooms for rent here, all nicely furnished with handmade rustic furniture, a TV, and a whirlpool bath; the rates include Continental breakfast. ⊠ *13 km (8 mi) east of Mérida on Hwy. 180,* ☎ *9/968–0800 or 9/968–5000,* FAX *9/968–5001. 6 rooms. Restaurant, bar, air-conditioning, pool, free parking. AE, MC, V.*

$$$$ 🏨 **El Conquistador.** Views of the city from El Conquistador's rooftop solarium and pool area (accessed by an ancient elevator) are superlative, the dining room is renowned for its daily breakfast buffet, and the staff is helpful. Still, the prices at this hotel, which caters to German tour groups, are relatively high considering that the amenities here aren't as extensive as at some of the other area hotels. The contemporary-style rooms have been modernized and include satellite TV; half have tile floors, the others carpeting. ⊠ *Paseo Montejo No. 458, 97000,* ☎ *9/926–2155 or 9/926–9199,* FAX *9/926–8829. 157 rooms, 4 suites. Restaurant, 2 bars, coffee shop, air-conditioning, room service, pool, travel services, free parking. AE, DC, MC, V.*

$$$$ 🏨 **Fiesta Americana Mérida.** This posh hotel and shopping/business
★ center caters to business travelers, conventions, and high-end travelers, but it also brings in locals who come to see and be seen. Its lovely pink facade mirrors the architecture of Paseo Montejo mansions on an epic scale. The colonial echoes carry into the spacious upper lobby with its massive columns, gleaming marble and brass work, and 300-ft-high stained-glass atrium. Floral prints, painted-wood furnishings, and slightly larger-than-life proportions maintain the theme of bygone elegance in the guest rooms, but the units have all the modern conveniences, including remote-control TVs concealed in armoires and three phones. There are 12 concierges, and guests on the business floor have access to the Fiesta Room for morning breakfast and newspapers or afternoon appetizers. ⊠ *Av. Colón No. 451, at Paseo Montejo, 97000,* ☎ *9/942–1111 or 800/343–7821,* FAX *9/942–1122,* WEB *www.fiestaamericana.com. 323 rooms, 27 suites. 2 restaurants, 2 bars, air-conditioning, in-room data ports, minibars, no-smoking rooms, room service, health club, 2 tennis courts, shops, concierge floor, business services, travel services, car rental, free parking. AE, MC, V.*

$$$$ ⌂ **Holiday Inn.** Room rates for this attractive hotel are reasonable for this part of town; the Holiday Inn is a half block from Paseo Montejo, near the swank Hyatt and Fiesta Americana hotels. The staff—from bellboys to waiters—exhibits good old-fashioned Mexican warmth and courtesy. There's a *fiesta* Mexicana on the patio Tuesday and Saturday. This is probably the most light-filled hotel in Mérida, with floor-to-ceiling windows throughout the lobby area and tiled dining room that are set off with bright yellows and pinks. Rooms and suites face an open courtyard and have floral-print bedspreads, a small table, comfy arm chairs, minibars, marble bathrooms, and color TVs with U.S. channels. ✉ *Av. Colón No. 468, at Calle 60, 97000,* ☎ *9/925–6877 or 800/465–4329,* FAX *9/925–7755,* WEB *www.basshotels.com. 209 rooms, 5 suites. 2 restaurants, bar, air-conditioning, minibars, no-smoking rooms, room service, pool, tennis court, travel services, car rental, free parking. AE, DC, MC, V.*

$$$$ ⌂ **Hyatt Regency Mérida.** When the 18-story Hyatt opened in 1994, it was the first of the deluxe hotels on Paseo Montejo and brought a new level of service to Mérida. The rooms are regally decorated with russet-hue bed quilts and rugs set off by modern blond-wood furniture and cream-color walls. Satellite TV and minibars have been attractively integrated into each unit. Amenities rare in the area but found here include a top-notch business center and the city's only tapas bar, not to mention bathtubs and hair dryers. The beautiful marble lobby comes alive with piano music at night and guests frequenting the popular Peregrina restaurant. ✉ *Av. Colón No. 344, at Calle 60, 97000,* ☎ *9/942–0202, 9/942–1234, or 800/233–1234,* FAX *9/925–7002,* WEB *www.hyatt.com. 296 rooms, 4 suites. 2 restaurants, bar, lobby lounge, air-conditioning, minibars, no-smoking rooms, room service, pool, 2 tennis courts, business services, travel services, car rental, free parking. AE, DC, MC, V.*

$$$ ⌂ **Casa del Balam.** This very pleasant hotel on well-heeled Calle 60
★ was built more than 60 years ago as the home of the Barbachano family, pioneers of Yucatán tourism. Today the hotel—owned and managed by Carmen Barbachano—has a lovely courtyard ornamented with a fountain, arcades, ironwork, and a black-and-white tile floor. Rocking chairs in the hallways impart a colonial feeling, as do the mahogany trimmings and cedar doorways. The rooms are capacious and well maintained, with painted sinks, wrought-iron accessories, and refrigerator–minibars. All rooms have hair dryers and double-pane windows. Cocktails and light meals are served in the lobby courtyard; meals are served in the restaurant. Guests have access to a golf and tennis club about 15 minutes (by car) from the hotel. ✉ *Calle 60 No. 488 (Box 988), 97000,* ☎ *9/924–8844, 9/924–2150, or 800/624–8451,* FAX *9/924–5011,* WEB *www.mayaland.com. 51 rooms, 3 suites. Restaurant, 2 bars, air-conditioning, minibars, no-smoking rooms, room service, pool, travel services, car rental, free parking. AE, DC, MC, V.*

$$$ ⌂ **Casa Mexilio.** Four block from the main square is this choice bed-
★ and-breakfast, run by partners Jorge and Roger. It has wonderfully eclectic decor—Middle Eastern wall hangings, French tapestries, colorful tile floors, tile sinks, and folk-art furniture. The exquisitely decorated rooms, each a private oasis in itself, along with the lush gardens and hidden terraces make it a romantic and serene escape. (The honeymooners' favorite is the Palomar Room.) Casa Mexilio lacks the amenities of the larger hotels—only five rooms have air-conditioning—but a stay here is more casual, like in a private home. A rooftop bistro offers creative cooking. ✉ *Calle 68 No. 495 (between Calles 57 and 59), 97000,* ☎ FAX *9/928–2505. Reservations in the U.S.:* ☎ *800/538–6802 or 303/674–9615,* FAX *303/674–8735,* WEB *www.mexicoholiday.com. 8 rooms. Restaurant, breakfast room, air-conditioning (some), pool. MC, V.*

$$$ 🏨 **Mérida Misión Park Inn Plaza.** Part of the city's landscape for decades—as the Hotel Mérida in an earlier incarnation—the Misión has two major assets: an excellent location in the heart of downtown and a genuine colonial ambience, with chandeliers, wood beams, archways, patios, and fountains in public areas, along with a pool and a bar with romantic music nightly. Rooms in the modern 11-story annex don't have as much character, but the ones on the upper floors have good city views. The rooms have wicker furniture, cable TV, hair dryers, minibars, and closet safes. Forty-five rooms in the old colonial section are set around a pretty courtyard, which gives them much more appeal. ✉ *Calle 60 No. 491, 97000,* ☎ *9/923–9500 or 888/224–8837,* FAX *9/923–7665. 137 rooms, 8 suites. Restaurant, bar, snack bar, air-conditioning, minibars, no-smoking rooms, room service, pool, travel services, car rental, free parking. AE, DC, MC, V.*

$$ 🏨 **Casa San Juan.** This B&B is housed in a beautifully restored colonial mansion that was built by a Portuguese family in the 1860s. Designated a historical monument by the government, the house has many original components, such as high ceilings decorated with Belgian railroad ties—a fashion of the time—tile floors, a stone fountain, and 10-ft-tall mahogany doors. Three patios and a sitting room surround a lush interior garden. Most guest rooms are extra large, with double beds, firm mattresses, and ceiling and floor fans; five have air-conditioning. Affable host Pablo da Costa, a former hotelier from Cuba, is one of the most knowledgeable people in Mérida; he can give you tips on visiting the city—in English, Spanish, German, Hebrew, or French. He can also arrange deals on reliable car rentals, guided tours to the Maya ruins, and bird-watching excursions. Room rates here include the tax. ✉ *Calle 62 No. 545-A (between Calles 69 and 71), 97000,* ☎ *9/986–2937,* FAX *305/559–3564 in the U.S.,* WEB *www.casasanjuan.com. 10 rooms. Breakfast room, air-conditioning (some), fans, travel services, parking (fee). MC, V (when booked from the U.S).*

$$ 🏨 **Dolores Alba.** A comfortable, friendly standby at the low end of the $$ range, the Dolores Alba is owned by the Sanchez family, which also owns the Dolores Alba in Pisté, near Chichén Itzá. The basic rooms, most with both air-conditioning and a fan, frame a courtyard with a small pool. You can keep drinks cold in a refrigerator in the attractive lobby, where guests gather to play the guitar or use the communal backgammon game. All three meals are available in the restaurant. ✉ *Calle 63 No. 464 (between Calles 52 and 54), 97000,* ☎ *9/928–5650,* FAX *9/928–3163,* WEB *www.doloresalba.com. 40 rooms. Restaurant, fans, pool, free parking. No credit cards.*

$$ 🏨 **Gran Hotel.** Cozily situated on Parque Hidalgo, this legendary 1901 hotel is the oldest in the city, and it has an aura of history. It's also one of the best hotel bargains around. The three-story neoclassical building is losing some of its charm; in particular, the Art Nouveau courtyard lobby hasn't looked the same since the owners replaced its antiques with plain white wooden tables and chairs. The guest rooms are filled with cedar antique furniture, and their high ceilings provide a sense of spaciousness. Some rooms have small double beds, so check before you accept. Half the rooms have balconies (request one of these if you don't mind noise from the park); most of the others have no windows at all. The rooms on the second floor in the back are the quietest. Fidel Castro chose one of these when he stayed here; Porfirio Díaz stayed in one of the sumptuous corner suites, which have small living and dining areas. ✉ *Calle 60 No. 496, 97000,* ☎ *9/923–6963 or 9/924–7632,* FAX *9/924–7622,* WEB *www.mayanroutes.com/hotels/merida/ghfactsheet.html. 25 rooms, 7 suites. Restaurant, bar, pizzeria, air-conditioning, fans, room service, travel services, free parking. MC, V.*

$$ ⌂ **Hotel el Español.** This three-story hotel is ideal if you want to be across the street from the Mérida bus stations and have your comforts, too. It's pretty, clean, has good service, and is rather reasonable considering what it offers. Decorated in tasteful rose and white tones right down to the floor tiles, it has a small, seven-table restaurant; an atrium with lots of hanging greenery; faux wrought-iron trimmings; and a pleasant receptionist. Rooms are outfitted with double beds, cable TV, air-conditioning, overhead fans, big closets, and bathrooms. ⊠ *Calle 69 No. 543-C, at Calle 70, 97000,* ☎ *9/923–2854,* FAX *9/923–4319. 27 rooms, 1 suite. Restaurant, bar, air-conditioning, fans, room service, free parking. AE, MC, V.*

$$ ⌂ **María del Carmen.** This modern Best Western hotel with a striking, salmon-color tile entrance caters to business travelers, bus groups, and those traveling by car who desire secured parking. The main square, the market, and other major sights are within easy walking distance. Rooms are modern and have ornate Chinese lamps and lacquered furniture. ⊠ *Calle 63 No. 550 (between Calles 68 and 70), 97000,* ☎ *9/923–9133 or 800/528–1234,* FAX *9/923–9290,* WEB *www.bestwestern.com. 80 rooms, 4 suites. Restaurant, bar, air-conditioning, room service, pool, meeting room, travel services, free parking. AE, MC, V.*

$$ ⌂ **Posada Toledo.** The beautiful old colonial house evokes its former elegance with high ceilings, floors of exquisite Moorish pattern tile, and old-fashioned carved furniture. The room where breakfast is served is particularly fine, with stained-glass door frames. Antiques clutter the halls, along with faded portraits of 19th-century family life, so that you feel more like a personal guest of the establishment than another nameless hotel client. However, guest-room quality varies much more than the rates do, so be sure to inspect your room before checking in. No. 5 is an elegant two-room suite that originally was the mansion's master bedroom. The posada's popularity is becoming a drawback; as in many hotels in converted mansions, noise reverberates through the halls. If you're a light sleeper, ask for a room away from the courtyard. ⊠ *Calle 58 No. 487, at Calle 57, 97000,* ☎ *9/923–1690,* FAX *9/ 923–2256. 20 rooms, 2 suites. Breakfast room, air-conditioning, fans, free parking. MC, V.*

$$ ⌂ **Residencial.** Location is the major draw at this classy bright-pink hotel. It sits on Calle 59, the main entrance to town, and has a gated parking lot. The hotel is a replica of a 19th-century French mansion and the French colonial decor is most evident in the small dining room with its silken drapes, linen cloths, and high-back chairs. The food is fine for breakfast but choose to eat the rest of your meals elsewhere. Rooms have powerful showers, comfortable beds, cable TV, and mirrored doors on the spacious closets. The small swimming pool in the central courtyard is pleasant for encountering fellow guests, but it's far from private. ⊠ *Calle 59 No. 589, at Calle 76, 97000,* ☎ *9/924– 3899 or 9/924–3099,* FAX *9/924–0266,* WEB *hotelresidencial.com.mx. 64 rooms, 2 suites. Restaurant, bar, air-conditioning, room service, pool, free parking. AE, MC, V.*

$ ⌂ **Trinidad Galería.** Eccentricity holds sway at this impossibly original, slightly ramshackle, nearly unidentifiable little hotel. In its previous lives it has been a hacienda, a car-rental shop, and a furniture store, but in the late 1980s owner Manolo Rivero made it into what he calls "a post-contemporary museum hotel." An adjacent art gallery has four yearly expositions of young talent, to which all hotel guests receive formal invitations. The large, chaotic lobby is filled with art, plants, a fountain, and yellow wicker furniture. Making your way through the maze that is the rest of the hotel, you encounter painted wooden angels, curved columns, and all sorts of installation-style art. Rooms are small and equally odd; rates are higher for the two that have air-conditioning ($$).

✉ *Calle 60 No. 456, at Calle 51, 97000,* ☎ *9/923–2463,* FAX *9/924–2319. 33 rooms, 2 suites. Café, air-conditioning (some), pool, free parking. No credit cards.*

Nightlife and the Arts

Mérida has an unusually active and diverse cultural life, including free government-sponsored music and dance performances most nights, as well as sidewalk art shows in local parks. On Saturday check out the **Noche Mexicana,** a free, outdoor spectacle of music, dance, and regional handicrafts that draws more locals than tourists. It happens 8 PM–11 PM at the foot of Paseo Montejo at Calle 47. On Sunday, when six blocks around the zócalo are closed off to traffic, you can hear live music at Plaza Santa Lucía and Parque Hidalgo (usually at 11 AM); mariachis, marimbas, folkloric dance, and other treats at the main plaza (1 PM).

For more information on these and other performances, consult the tourist office, the local newspapers, or the billboards and posters at the **Teatro Peón Contreras,** on Calle 60 at Calle 57, or the **Universidad Autónoma de Yucatán** or **Café Pop,** both on Calle 57 between Calles 60 and 62.

Bars

Dancing sometimes erupts spontaneously at **La Planta Alta** (✉ Paseo Montejo 444, at Calle 56–A, ☎ 9/927–9847), open daily from 5:30 PM until about 1 AM, but most people are content to converse (i.e. shout), listen to music, sip drinks, and watch large-screen music videos. **Pancho's** (✉ Calle 59 No. 509, between Calles 60 and 62, ☎ 9/923–0942), open daily 6 PM– 2 AM, is lively in a toss-down-the-shots sort of way.

Dancing

A number of restaurants have live music and dancing. **Ay Caray** (✉ Calle 60 No. 482, between Calles 55 and 57, ☎ 9/924–2323) is a lively video bar with salsa music, rock shows, and song impersonators until 1 AM, after which there's two hours of dancing. It's open 9 PM–3 AM. **Pancho's** (✉ Calle 59 No. 509, between Calles 60 and 62, ☎ 9/923–0942) attracts locals and foreigners for a mix of live salsa and Western music. **Vatzia** (✉ Fiesta Americana Mérida, Av. Colón No. 451, at Paseo Montejo, ☎ 9/942–1111) is a disco with different theme nights: Friday features 1970s and '80s music; Saturday is ladies' night.

Film

Downtown movie theaters include **Cine Fantasio** (✉ Calle 59 No. 492, at Calle 60, ☎ 9/923–5431), **Cine Internacional** (✉ Plaza Internacional, Calle 58 between Calle 59 and Callejón del Congreso, ☎ 9/923–0250), and **Cine Colón** (✉ Av. Reforma No. 363-A, at Av. Colón, ☎ 9/925–4500). They mostly show English action films with Spanish subtitles.

Folkloric Shows

Paseo Montejo hotels such as the Fiesta Americana, Hyatt Regency, and Holiday Inn stage dinner shows with folkloric dances; check with concierges for schedules. The **Folkloric Ballet of the University of Yucatán** presents a combination of music, dance, and theater, every Friday at 9 PM at the Universidad Autónoma de Yucatán (✉ Calle 57 between 60 and 62, ☎ 9/924–7260); tickets are $2. This includes the "University Serenade," with music, folkloric dance, and poetry. (There are no shows from August 1 to September 22 and during the last two weeks of December.) **Tianos** (✉ Calle 60 No. 461, between Calles 51 and 53, ☎ 9/923–7118) hosts a colorful show of regional dancing nightly at 8 PM (with dinner only). The service is slow and the mock sacrifice of a bare-midriffed damsel hokey, but the show is still fun.

Outdoor Activities and Sports

Baseball

Baseball is played with enthusiasm February through July at the **Kukulcán Sports Center** (⊠ Calle 14 No. 17, ☎ 9/924–0306), next to the Santa Clara brewery. You can buy baseball tickets through the local **Lion's Club** (☎ 9/925–3809 or 9/925–3409), or at the stadium box office.

Bullfights

Bullfights are held sporadically December through May and during holiday periods at the **Plaza de Toros** (⊠ Paseo de la Reforma near Calle 25, Col. Garcia Gineres, ☎ 9/925–7996). Contact your hotel travel desk or one of the tourist information centers for scheduling information and tickets; seats in the sun go for $5 to $20 and seats in the shade for $8 to $50, depending on the fame of the bullfighter.

Golf

The 18-hole championship golf course at **Club de Golf La Ceiba** (⊠ Carretera Mérida–Progreso, Km 14.5, ☎ 9/922–0053 or 9/922–054) is open to the public. It is about 16 km (10 mi) north of Mérida on the road to Progreso; greens fees are about $42; it's closed Monday.

Tennis

The one tennis court at **Holiday Inn** (⊠ Av. Colón No. 498, at Calle 60, ☎ 9/925–6877) is lighted at night. The **Hyatt Regency Mérida** (⊠ Calle 60 No. 344, at Av. Colón, ☎ 9/942–0202) has two lighted outdoor courts. At the **Fiesta Americana Mérida** (⊠ Av. Colón No. 451, at Paseo Montejo, ☎ 9/920–2194), guests have access to two lighted outdoor courts.

Shopping

A Shopping Tour

Mérida is the best place on the Yucatán to shop, and making a round of the shops is worthwhile for local color even if you don't buy a thing. Start in the market district, catercorner from the post office. You can pick up some sun protection for your head at **El Becaleño** (⊠ Calle 65 No. 483, between Calles 56 and 58, ☎ 9/985–0581), which produces Yucatán's fine Panama-style hats, often referred to as jipis. Then, hat-on-head, continue west to the huge **Mercado Municipal Lucas de Galvez,** turning right just past the post office onto Calle 56. Nip into the market under the EL PUERTO DE VERACRUZ sign; you can find lots of typical jewelry in this area. There isn't as much filigree being made as there once was, but the designs here are interesting and the quality is mostly good (usually 8-to-10-karat gold or gold-dipped).

Look for the stairway; the second floor has hammocks, guayaberas, and huipiles, cotton dresses, and blouses—some eyelet, others richly embroidered or decorated with silk ribbons. Leave the market the way you entered, then plunge back in directly under the MERCADO MUNICIPAL LUCAS DE GALVEZ sign. Ask around for *los huaraches*; dozens of stalls sell the fabulous native leather footwear, some with tire-tread bottoms. Many of these shoe and sandal styles have been used for hundreds of years. They are sturdy and, once you break them in, quite comfortable.

Return to Calle 65, turn right, and walk the length of the block between Calles 56 and 54. Here is piñata heaven: every imaginable shape and color, as well as the candy that goes inside.

By now you are likely to want to escape the frenzy of the marketplace for the relative calm of the central district. Turn left (north) on Calle 54 and walk three blocks to Calle 59. Go left again and walk 3½ blocks.

At **Ajúa!** (✉ Calle 59 between Calles 60 and 62, ☎ 9/928–6132) you can sample—and purchase—the Yucatán's famous Xtabentún (anise and honey liqueur), as well as tequila and mescal. Across the street on the same block, **Guayaberas Jack** (✉ Calle 59 No. 507 between Calles 57 and 59, ☎ 9/928–6002) has an excellent selection of guayaberas and typical women's cotton *filipinas* (house dresses) and blouses. Continue up the block and turn left onto Calle 62. The best selection of hammocks in Mérida is at **El Aguacate** (✉ Calle 62 No. 492, ☎ 9/923–1838). Now you can cool your hot heels under the arcade: walk south to the square and turn left to buy some refreshing sherbet from **Dulcería n Sorbetería Colón,** next door to the Nicte-Ha restaurant.

Malls

Mérida has several shopping malls, but the largest is **Gran Plaza** (✉ Calle 50 Diagonal 460, Fracc. Gonzalo Guerrero, ☎ 9/944–7657), with more than 90 shops. It's just outside town, on the highway to Progreso (called Carretera a Progreso beyond the Mérida city limits). **Pasaje Picheta** is a very pleasant, though tiny, mall on the north side of the zócalo, next to the Nicte-Ha restaurant. It has a travel agency, art gallery, Internet facility, newspaper stands, a music/CD store, some nice souvenir shops, and a food court.

Markets

The second floor of the **Mercado Municipal** (✉ between Calles 65 and 67 and Calles 54 and 56) has crafts, food, flowers, and live birds, among other items. Touts often approach tourists by this market. They expect a tip, and won't necessarily guide you to the best deals. You're better off visiting some specialty stores first to learn about the quality and types of hammocks, hats, and other crafts; then you'll have an idea of what you're buying—and what it's worth—if you want to bargain in the market.

If you are interested strictly in handicrafts, visit the government-run **Casa de Artesanías** (✉ Calle 63 No. 503, between Calles 64 and 66, ☎ 9/923–5392). It sells folk art from throughout Mexico, including hand-painted wooden mythical animals from Oaxaca, handmade beeswax candles and leather bags from Mérida, and hand-embroidered vests, shawls, blouses, and place mats from Chiapas. Look for good-quality hammocks here, too. The quality and variety of merchandise is always improving. There's also a showcase full of hard-to-find traditional filigree jewelry in silver, gold, and gold-dipped versions. The **Bazar García Rejón** (✉ Calle 65 at Calle 62) has rather sterile rows of indoor stalls with leather items, palm hats, and handmade guitars, among other things. Still, it's worth a look. The streets north of the main square, especially **Calle 60,** are lined with crafts and jewelry stores.

Sunday brings an array of wares into Mérida. Starting at 9 AM on Sunday, the **Bazar de Artesanías** (Handicrafts Bazaar; ✉ in front of the Palacio Municipal, across from the main square) is filled with huipiles, hats, and costume jewelry. The **Bazar de Artes Populares** (Popular Art Bazaar; ✉ Parque Santa Lucía, corner of Calles 60 and 55), which starts at 9 AM on Sunday, sometimes has work by local artists. It also offers huipiles, hats, and costume jewelry.

Specialty Stores

BOOKS

Librería Dante (✉ Calle 59 at Calle 68, ☎ 9/923–9060; ✉ Parque Hidalgo, ☎ 9/943–2319; ✉ Calle 17 No. 138-B, at Prolongación Paseo Montejo, Col. Itzimná, ☎ 9/927–7676; ✉ Calle 62 and 61, ☎ 9/928–2611) has several branches around Mérida, all of which carry a small selection of English-language books and a Mexico City daily newspaper.

All locations are open Monday through Saturday 8 AM–9:30 PM and Sunday 10–6.

CLOTHING

Miniaturas (⊠ Calle 59 between Calles 60 and 62, ☎ no phone) sells interesting miniatures of all kinds and types; you can find small versions of everything from wooden soldiers to doll houses to glass animals to the collages of Mexican painter Frido Kahlo. **Mexicanísimo** (⊠ Calle 60 No. 496, at Calle 61, on Parque Hidalgo, ☎ 9/923–8132) sells expensive designer cotton clothing inspired by regional dress.

You might not wear a guayabera to a business meeting as some men in Mexico do, but the shirts are cool, comfortable, and attractive; for a good selection, try **Camisería Canul** (⊠ Calle 62 No. 484, between Calles 57 and 59, ☎ 9/923–0158). Pick up a jipi at **El Becaleño** (⊠ Calle 65 No. 483, between Calles 56 and 58, ☎ 9/985–0581); the famous hats are made at Becal in Campeche by the González family.

GALLERIES

The **Galería Ateneo Peninsular** (⊠ Calle 60 between Calle 61 and Pasaje Revolución, ☎ 9/925–7952 or 9/925–8253) sponsors shows by international artists. The **Galería Casa Colón** (⊠ Av. Colón 507, ☎ 9/925–7952 or 9/925–8253) highlights modern-day Mexican painters in the setting of a colonial home. The **Galería Manolo Rivero** (⊠ Hotel Galería Trinidad, Calle 60 at Calle 61, ☎ 9/923–2463), run by the owner of the Hotel Galería Trinidad, shows paintings by contemporary local artists by appointment. Contemporary paintings and photographs are shown in the lobby of the **Teatro Peón Contreras** (⊠ Calle 60 between Calles 59 and 57, ☎ 9/923–7354).

HAMMOCKS

The best place in town for hammocks is **El Aguacate** (⊠ Calle 58 No. 604, at Calle 73, ☎ 9/928–6429; ⊠ Calle 62 between Calles 61 and 59, ☎ no phone), a family-run outfit with a wide variety of sizes and designs and two locations. **Tejidos y Cordeles Nacionales** (⊠ Calle 56 No. 516-B, between Calles 65 and 63, ☎ 9/928–5561), the oldest hammock store in Mérida, is a family-run, no-frills shop. **El Hamaquero** (⊠ Calle 58 No. 572, between Calles 62 and 71, ☎ 9/923–2117) has knowledgeable personnel who let you try out the hammocks before you buy.

JEWELRY

La Canasta (⊠ Calle 60 No. 500, at Calle 61, ☎ 9/928–1978) has a good selection of filigree jewelry, both sterling silver and gold-dipped. It also has lots of cotton blouses for women, and local liqueurs. **La Perla Maya** (⊠ Calle 60 Nos. 485–487, between Calles 59 and 61, ☎ 9/928–5886) sells old-fashioned, silver Yucatecan filigree earrings and pins, although the selection isn't as good as it once was. **Tane** (⊠ Hyatt Regency Hotel, Calle 60 No. 344, at Av. Colón, ☎ 9/942–0202) is an outlet for exquisite (and expensive) silver earrings, necklaces, and bracelets, some that incorporate ancient Maya designs.

CHICHÉN ITZÁ AND VALLADOLID

Although you can get to Chichén Itzá (120 km [74 mi] east of Mérida) along the shorter Route 180, it's far more scenic to follow Route 80 until it ends at Tekantó, then head south to Citilcúm, east to Dzitás, and south again to Pisté. These roads have no signs but are the only paved roads going in these directions. Among the several villages you pass along Route 80 is Tixkokob, a Maya community famous for its hammock weavers. A short detour southeast from Tixkokob are the ruins of Aké.

Aké

⚒ ⓱ *35 km (22 mi) southeast of Mérida, 5 km (3 mi) southeast of Tixkokob.*

This tiny site, opened to the public at the end of 1996, is a convenient stop along the Mérida–Izamal course, on Route 80. The bizarre sight of the remains of a hacienda built next to a Maya temple is the most striking feature here. In fact, the site is named after the Hacienda of San Lorenzo Aké; both the hacienda and the local church are constructed of stones taken from the Maya temple. Estimates put occupation of the site around 200 BC to AD 900. A wall surrounding the city along with several temples and roads—one of which measured 33 km (20 mi) long and leads directly to Izamal—have been discovered so far, indicating this was an important city in its day. All that's excavated is a pyramid with rows of columns (35 total) at the top, very reminiscent of the Toltec columns at Tula, outside Mexico City. You can climb to the top of the ruins to see farmers cultivating the surrounding fields. You need a vehicle with high ground clearance (such as a Jeep) to navigate the rutted dirt road that leads to the ruins. ▣ *$1.20.* ☉ *Daily 9–5.*

Izamal

⓲ *68 km (42 mi) southeast of Mérida.*

One of the best examples of a Spanish colonial town in the Yucatán, Izamal is nicknamed Ciudad Amarillo (Yellow City) because its buildings are painted earth-tone yellow by city ordinance. In the center of town stands the enormous 16th-century **Convento de San Antonio de Padua** (Monastery of St. Anthony de Padua), perched on—and built from—the remains of a Maya pyramid devoted to Itzamná, god of the heavens. The monastery's church, which Pope John Paul II visited in 1993, has a gigantic atrium, a colonnaded facade (supposedly second only to that of the Vatican in size), frescoes of saints (discovered in 1996), and rows of 75 yellow arches. The Virgin of the Immaculate Conception, to whom the church is dedicated, is the patron saint of the Yucatán. A statue of the Virgin was brought here from Guatemala in 1562 by the fanatic bishop Landa. Miracles are ascribed to her, and a yearly pilgrimage takes place in her honor.

Pony traps surround the town's large main square, which fronts the cathedral. There are far worse ways to spend an afternoon than to trot around this pleasant town and then lounge in the square enjoying the local action.

Kinich Kakmó, a pyramid that's all that remains of the royal Maya city that flourished here hundreds of years ago, is a few blocks from the Monastery of St. Anthony de Padua. It's under excavation, but it's worth walking over for a look.

On Sunday a special air-conditioned car attached to the regular train makes a round-trip excursion between Mérida and Izamal. The fare ($23) includes lunch, a folkloric show, and a city tour in a horse-drawn carriage. Tickets can be purchased through any travel agent. The train leaves the Mérida train station (☎ 9/926–1722 or 9/926–2057), on Calle 55 at Calle 48, Sunday at 8:15 AM and returns at 5 PM.

Coming to Izamal on Route 80 from Mérida, cut south at Tekantó and east again at Citilcúm (the road has no number, and there are few signs).

Pisté

⓳ *116 km (72 mi) southeast of Mérida.*

The town of Pisté serves mainly as a base camp for travelers to Chichén Itzá. Hotels, campgrounds, restaurants, and handicrafts shops tend to be less expensive here than south of the ruins. At the west end of town is a Pemex gas station, but the town's only bank has closed. On the outskirts of Pisté and a short walk from Chichén Itzá is **Pueblo Maya,** a pseudo-Maya village with a shopping and dining center for tour groups. The restaurant serves a bountiful buffet at lunch ($12).

Across from the Dolores Alba hotel, in town, is the **Parque Ik Kil** (Place of the Winds). The park is built around a lovely cenote where you can swim between 8 AM and 6 PM for $3. The park includes the Restaurant el Jardín, which serves Mexican and international fare, a swimming pool, bungalows inspired by Maya dwellings, and a row of shops where artisans demonstrate their crafts. ✉ *Carretera Libre Pisté–Cancún, Km 112,* ☎ *no phone.*

Dining and Lodging

$$ ✕🖬 **Pirámide Inn Resort.** All the rooms in this two-story, American-owned '50s-style motel are clean and comfortable, with tile floors, air-conditioning, and large square desks, but no phones or TVs. The garden contains a small Maya pyramid and an enormous rectangular swimming pool, and the restaurant is one of the best in Pisté. Some good vegetarian dishes are available, in addition to regional cuisine. ✉ *Calle 15A No. 30, Carretera Mérida–Puerto Juárez, Km 117, 97751,* ☎ *9/851–0115,* FAX *9/851–0114,* WEB *www.piramideinn.com. 35 rooms. Restaurant, air-conditioning, pool, free parking. MC, V.*

$$ 🖬 **Dolores Alba.** The best low-budget choice near the ruins is this family-run hotel, a longtime favorite in the area south of Pisté. Twelve rooms were added in 2000 and existing rooms got a face-lift, with colonial-style furniture, tile bathroom floors, and air-conditioning. Hammocks hang by one of the two pools, and breakfast and dinner are served family-style in the main building. Free transportation to Chichén Itzá is provided, and there is a covered, guarded parking lot. ✉ *Carretera Mérida–Cancún, Km 122, 3 km (2 mi) south of Chichén Itzá,* ☎ *9/ 928–5650,* FAX *9/928–3163,* WEB *www.doloresalba.com. 40 rooms. Restaurant, air-conditioning, 2 pools, free parking. AE.*

Chichén Itzá

🔺 ⓴ *About 1 km (½ mi) east of Pisté.*

One of the four most magnificent Maya ruins—along with Palenque in Chiapas in Mexico, Tikal in Guatemala, and Cobá in Honduras—Chichén Itzá was the most important city in Yucatán from the 10th through the 12th centuries. Its architectural mélange covers pre-Columbian Mesoamerican history and shows the influence of several different Maya groups.

Because epigraphers have been able to read 85% of the Chichén inscriptions, the site's history has become clearer to archaeologists. At one time it was believed that Chichén Itzá was dominated by the Toltecs from present-day central Mexico; now historians believe that was not the case. Chichén *was* altered by each successive wave of inhabitants, and archaeologists are able to date the arrival of these waves by the changes in the architecture and information contained in inscriptions. That said, they have yet to explain the long gaps of time when the buildings seem to have been uninhabited. The site is believed to have been first settled in AD 432, abandoned for an unknown period of time, then rediscovered in 868 by the Maya-speaking Itzás, who came from the southern Maya region of the Petén rain forest around Tikal (in what is now northern Guatemala). The latest data point to the city's being refounded by not only the Itzás but also by two other foreign groups—one from the Valley of Mexico (present-day Mex-

Chichén Itzá

Cenote Sagrado (Sacred Well)

N

Ball Court

TO MÉRIDA

Tzompantli

Temple of the Jaguar

Main Plaza

Venus Platform

Temple of the Warriors

Tourist Module

Platform of the Eagle and Jaguars

El Castillo

Ball Court

West Colonnade
Group of the Thousand Columns

Ball Court

Tomb of the High Priest

Ball Court

Steam Bath

House of the Deer

House of the Corn Grinders

The Market

Cenote Xtoloc

180

El Caracol (Observatory)

Casa de las Monjas (Nunnery)

Temple of the Carved Panels

TO OLD CHICHÉN ITZÁ

0   200 yards

0   200 meters

ico City) and another from Ek Balam. The trio formed a ruling triumvirate.

Chichén Itzá means "the mouth of the well of the Itzás." The Itzás may have also abandoned the site, but they were the dominant group until 1224, when the site appears to have been abandoned for all time. Francisco de Montejo established a short-lived colony here in the course of his conquest of Yucatán in the mid-1500s. At the turn of the 20th century, U.S. Consul General Edward Thompson, an engineer by training with a sharp eye for finding hidden pyramids, purchased Chichén Itzá and carried out some of the earliest excavations at the site, basing himself at a hacienda on the grounds (now the Hacienda Chichén) and carting most of the treasures away to the Peabody Museum at Harvard University. Years later, when the Mexican government realized what he had in his possession, it made him return the goodies.

The enormity and gracefulness of this site are unforgettable. Chichén Itzá incarnates much of the fascinating and bloody history of the Maya, from the steep temple stairways down which sacrificial victims may have been hurled to the relentlessly ornate beauty of the smaller structures. The site's audacity and vitality are almost palpable. Chichén Itzá encompasses approximately 6 square km (2½ square mi), though only 30 to 40 structures and buildings of the several hundred at the site have been fully explored. These buildings include the largest ball court in Mesoamerica; a sacrificial well once filled with precious offerings (it was dredged by Mexican diver Pablo Bush Romero, and many of its treasures are now at Harvard); and a round building—one of the only ones in the Maya lands—that was possibly the most elegant and sophisticated of the Maya observatories. Other features of the site include stone sculptures of Kukulcán (the Maya name for Quetzalcóatl, the plumed serpent god), reclining Chacmools (intermediaries or messengers between gods and humans), steam baths for ritual purification, ruined murals, astronomical symbols, and broad *sacbéob*, sometimes referred to as sacbé (literally "white roads" used for ceremonial purposes and as trade arteries), leading to other ancient centers.

Chichén Itzá is divided into two parts, called Old and New, although architectural motifs from the Classic period are found in both sections. A more convenient distinction is topographical, since there are two major complexes of buildings separated by a dirt path. The martial, imperial architecture of the Itzás and the more cerebral architecture and astronomical expertise of the earlier Maya are married in the 98-ft-tall pyramid called **El Castillo** (the Castle), which dominates the site and rises above all the other buildings.

Atop the Castillo is a temple dedicated to Kukulcán, the legendary Toltec priest–king from Tula in the Valley of Mexico who was held to be an incarnation of the mystical plumed serpent. According to ancient lore, Quetzalcóatl (or Kukulcán) went into exile, disappearing to the east but promising to return one day. The Aztecs, who adopted the cult of Quetzalcóatl after the Toltecs, later mistook the Spaniard Hernán Cortés for this god, transforming the prophecy into a nightmarish reality.

Four stairways, each facing a different cardinal point, provided access to the temple; two are used today. If you're afraid of heights, hold on to the rusty chain running down the center. Each access way consists of 91 very steep and narrow steps, which, when you count the temple platform itself, makes a total of 365 (one for each day of the Mayas' extraordinarily accurate solar calendar). Fifty-two panels on the sides stand for the years of a sacred cycle, while the 18 terraces symbolize the months of the year. An open-jawed plumed serpent rests on the balustrade of each stairway, and serpents reappear at the top of the temple as sculptured columns. This is one of the rare examples in the Maya world of a temple with four stairways, which represents the symbolic partitioning of the world into four parts, according to mythic lore.

At the spring and fall equinoxes, the afternoon light strikes one of these balustrades in such a way as to form a shadow representation of Kukulcán undulating out of his temple and down the pyramid to bless the fertile earth. Back then as now, this phenomenon is viewed from the broad plaza on the northern side of the pyramid, a space reserved for ritual ceremonies by the Maya. Tens of thousands of people travel to Chichén Itzá for the equinoxes, particularly in the spring, when there is little likelihood of rain. Hotel reservations for the event should be made well in advance; a year ahead is not unreasonable.

In 1937 archaeologists discovered a more ancient temple inside El Castillo. A humid, slippery stairway leads up to an altar that once held two statues: a Chacmool and a bejeweled red tiger. The tiger, which had jade-encrusted discs embedded into its body and a turquoise disc laid on top of it, probably as an offering, is now in the National Anthropology Museum (Museo Nacional de Antropología) in Mexico City. The inner temple is open to the public for only a few hours in the morning and again in the afternoon. Claustrophobes should think twice before entering: the stairs are narrow, dark, and winding, and there is often a line of tourists going both ways, making the trip somewhat frightening.

Each evening there's a sound-and-light show that highlights the architectural details in El Castillo and other buildings with a clarity the eye doesn't see in daylight. The accompanying narration is drawn rather loosely from the works of Bishop Landa and from the few surviving Maya texts, including the Books of Chilam Balam and Popul

Vuh. Some of the data are incorrect, showing a lack of respect for historical detail. Landa initially burned all the Maya manuscripts he collected but later, overcome with remorse and admiration for the Maya, wrote their history. Regardless of the flaws of the show, the narration and setting seem particularly powerful on nights of a full moon.

The temple rests on a massive trapezoidal square, on the west side of which is Chichén Itzá's largest **ball court,** one of seven on the site. Its two parallel walls are each 272 ft long, with two stone rings on each side, and 99 ft apart. The game played here was something like soccer (no hands were used), but it had a strictly religious significance. Bas-relief carvings at the court depict a player being decapitated, the blood spurting from his neck fertilizing the earth. Other bas-reliefs show two teams of opposing players pitted against each other during the ball game. Originally it was thought one team represented the invader Toltecs, but evidence points out the fact that the wardrobe design of the "Toltecs" has very Maya elements and that there never was a ball game between the two. The acoustics are so good that someone standing at one end of the court can in theory clearly hear the whispers of another person at the other end.

Between the ball court and El Castillo stands a **Tzompantli,** or stone platform, carved with rows of human skulls. In ancient times it was covered with stakes on which the heads of enemies were impaled. This motif was known in the Maya region, and a similar platform was found in Tenochtitlán, the onetime Aztec capital now known as Mexico City.

The predilection for human sacrifice was once believed to have been unknown to the Maya, but research has verified that they indulged in their own forms of the ritual for hundreds of years. Legend has it that the **Sacred Well,** a cenote 65 yards in diameter that sits 1 km (½ mi) north of El Castillo at the end of a sacbé, was used for human sacrifices; another cenote at the site supplied drinking water. Skeletons of about 50 people were found in the first well. The sacrificial victims, many of them children of both sexes, were drugged before being dropped into the well. It is said that if any of the victims survived until noon, they were fished out of the well in the hopes that they would recount the psychic visions they had experienced. Hunac Ceel, the notorious ruler of Mayapán in the 1250s, hurled himself into its depths to prove his divinity, and survived.

Many archaeologists believe that nonhuman sacrifices were carried out by local chiefs hundreds of years after Chichén Itzá was abandoned. Thousands of artifacts made of gold, jade, and other precious materials, most of them not of local provenance, have been recovered from the brackish depths of the cenote. Long on display at Harvard's Peabody Museum, many of the finds were returned to the Mexican government. Trees and shrubs have washed into the well over the centuries, and their remains have prevented divers from getting to the bottom; because the cenote is fed by a network of underground rivers, it cannot be drained. More treasure undoubtedly remains. The well's excavation (by Pablo Bush Romero) launched the field of underwater archaeology later honed by the late Jacques Cousteau.

Returning to the causeway, you see on your left the **Group of the Thousand Columns** with the famous **Temple of the Warriors,** a masterful example of the Itzá influence at Chichén Itzá. The temple was used as a meeting place for the high lords of the council that ruled Chichén Itzá. The temple-top sculpture of the reclining Chacmool—its head turned to the side, the offertory dish carved into its middle—is probably the most photographed symbol of the Maya. This temple also resembles

Pyramid B at Tula (sans Chacmool), the Toltecs' homeland, north of Mexico City. The resemblance is what originally led scholars to believe that there was a Toltec connection to the site. However, the carvings of the lords found here are equivalent to carvings discovered at Copán in Honduras.

Masonry walls carved with feathered serpents and frescoes of eagles and jaguars consuming human hearts are among the unmistakably Itzá details. Note the impressive feathered serpent columns with their jaws open. They symbolize the ancient War Serpents of the Itzá, mythical creatures that were thought to serve as vehicles for communicating with the underworld. Using columns and wood beams instead of the Maya arches and walls to divide space enabled the Maya architects to expand the interior and exterior spaces dramatically. These spaces were also used for ritual dancing and processions associated with the council meetings. Murals of everyday village life and scenes of war can be viewed here, and an artistic representation of the defeat of one of the Itzás' Maya enemies can be found on the interior murals of the **Temple of the Jaguar,** west of the Temple of the Warriors at the Ball Court.

To get to the less visited cluster of structures at **New Chichén Itzá**—often confused with Old Chichén Itzá—take the main path south from the Temple of the Jaguar past El Castillo and turn right onto a small path opposite the ball court on your left. Archaeologists have been restoring several buildings in this area, including the Tomb of the High Priest, where several tombs with skeletons and jade offerings were found, and the northern part of the site, which was used for military training and barracks for the army. Some smaller abodes not yet reconstructed are believed to have been guest houses or sleeping quarters for nobles who lived in the center of the city. The work of the Maya epigraphers is helping to identify the function of each of the structures. As work continues, certain ruins will be roped off and closed to visitors.

The most impressive structure within this area is the astronomical observatory called El Caracol. The name, meaning "snail," refers to the spiral staircase at the building's core. Built in several stages, El Caracol is one of the few round buildings constructed by the Maya. Judging by the tiny windows oriented toward the four cardinal points, and the structure's alignment with the planet Venus, it was used for observing the heavens. But it probably also served a religious function.

After leaving El Caracol, continue south several hundred yards to the beautiful La Casa de las Monjas (The Nunnery) and its annex, which have long panels carved with flowers and animals, latticework, hieroglyph-covered lintels, and Chaac masks (as does the nunnery at Uxmal). It was the Spaniards who gave the structure this sobriquet; no one knows how the Maya used it.

At so-called **Old Chichén Itzá,** south of the remains of Thompson's hacienda, "pure Maya" style—a combination of Puuc and Chenes styles, with playful latticework, Chaac masks, and gargoylelike serpents on the cornices—dominates. (This style also crops up at Uxmal, Kabah, Labná, and Sayil.) Highlights include the Date Group, so named because of its complete series of hieroglyphic dates; the House of the Phalli; and the Temple of the Three Lintels. Maya guides will lead you down the path by an old narrow-gauge railroad track to even more ruins, barely unearthed, if you ask. A fairly good restaurant and a great ice cream stand are in the entrance building, as is a gift shop where you can purchase film, bus tickets, postcards, and books. A small museum includes information on the migration patterns of the ancient Maya inhabitants and some small sculptures recovered from the site.

$8.50 (includes museum), free Sun.; sound-and-light show $4 in Span-ish (English speakers have to rent translating earphones for another $4); parking $2; use of video camera $7. ☉ Daily 8–5; sound-and-light show Apr.–Oct., daily at 8 PM, Nov.–Mar., daily at 7 PM.

Lodging

$$$$ 🏨 **Mayaland.** The hotel closest to the ruins, this charming 1920s lodg-
★ ing belongs to the Barbachano family, whose name is practically synonymous with tourism in Yucatán. In addition to a main hotel building,
a wing and several bungalows are set in a large garden on the 100-
acre site. You can actually see part of Old Chichén Itzá from the gardens, and the hotel has a private walkway into the ruins. All guest rooms
are colonial style and have decorative tiles, air-conditioning, and cable
TV; five suites have hot tubs. Tour buses fill the road in front of the
hotel, so choose a room at the back. The 24 bungalows at the rear of
the hotel are the prettiest (and most expensive) accommodations, with
hammocks out on the wide verandas, bright white tubs, and thatch roofs.
Light meals served poolside and at tables overlooking the garden are
a better choice than the expensive fixed-price meals served in the dining room. Guided horseback tours to Balancanchén are available at
extra cost. ⊠ *Carretera Mérida–Puerto Juárez, Km 120 (reservations: Mayaland Tours, Box 407, Mérida,* ☎ *9/924–2099 or 800/235–4079,* 🖷 *9/924–6290),* ☎ 🖷 *985/1–01–29,* WEB *www.mayaland.com). 24 bun-galows, 67 rooms, 10 suites. 4 restaurants, 2 bars, air-conditioning, minibars, room service, 3 pools, tennis court, shuffleboard, volleyball, meeting rooms, free parking. AE, DC, MC, V.*

$$$ 🏨 **Hacienda Chichén.** A converted 16th-century hacienda, this hotel
★ once served as the home of U.S. Consul General Edward S. Thomp-
son. Later it was the headquarters for the Carnegie expedition to
Chichén Itzá. The rustic cottages have handwoven bedspreads, dehu-
midifiers, and air-conditioning. All rooms, which are simply furnished
in colonial Yucatecan style, have private bathrooms and verandas but
no phones or TVs. There's a color satellite TV in the library. An enor-
mous old pool as well as an old family chapel now used for weddings
sit in the midst of the landscaped gardens. Fairly good meals are served
on the patio overlooking the grounds, and there's an air-conditioned
restaurant; stick with the Yucatecan specialties. ⊠ *Carretera Mérida–Puerto Juárez, Km 120,* ☎ *985/1–00–45, 9/924–2150, or 800/624–8451,* ☎ 🖷 *9/924–5011. 24 rooms, 4 suites. Restaurant, bar, air-con-ditioning, pool, chapel, free parking. AE, DC, MC, V.*

Cave of Balancanchén

⚒ ㉑ *4½ km (3 mi) east of Chichén Itzá.*

The Cave of Balancanchén, a shrine whose Maya name translates as "throne
of the jaguar," remained virtually undisturbed from the time of the con-
quest until its discovery in 1959. Inside is a large collection of artifacts—
mostly vases, jars, and incense burners once filled with offerings. Although
there are seven chambers, only three are open. You walk past tiers of sta-
lactites and stalagmites that form the image of sacred ceiba trees until
you come to an underground lake. The lake is filled with blind fish, and
an altar to the rain god rises above it. In order to explore the shrine you
must take one of the guided tours, which depart almost hourly. You need
to be in fairly good shape for the tour and wear comfortable shoes. Also
at the site is a sound-and-light show that fancifully recounts Maya his-
tory. A small museum at the entrance is very informative. You can catch
a bus or taxi to the caves from Chichén Itzá. 🎟 *$4 (including tour), free Sun.; sound-and-light show $4; parking $2 extra. ☉ Daily 9–5; tours leave daily at 11, 1, 4 (English) and 9, 10, noon (Spanish).*

When you pack your MCI Calling Card, it's like packing your loved ones along too.

Your MCI Calling Card is the easy way to stay in touch when you travel. Use it to call to and from over 125 countries. Plus, every time you call, you can earn frequent flier miles. So wherever your travels take you, call home with your MCI Calling Card. It's even easy to get one. Just visit **www.mci.com/worldphone**.

EASY TO CALL WORLDWIDE

1. Just enter the WorldPhone® access number of the country you're calling from.

2. Enter or give the operator your MCI Calling Card number.

3. Enter or give the number you're calling.

Aruba ✥	800-888-8
Bahamas ✥	1-800-888-8000

Barbados ✥	1-800-888-8000
Bermuda ✥	1-800-888-8000
British Virgin Islands ✥	1-800-888-8000
Canada	1-800-888-8000
Mexico	01-800-021-8000
Puerto Rico	1-800-888-8000
United States	1-800-888-8000
U.S. Virgin Islands	1-800-888-8000

✥ Limited availability.

EARN FREQUENT FLIER MILES

FLIGHTFUND
America West Airlines®

AmericanAirlines®
AAdvantage®

▲Delta
SkyMiles℠

HAWAIIANMILES

MIDWEST EXPRESS AIRLINES
PROGRAM PARTNER

SOUTHWEST AIRLINES
RAPIDREWARDS
A SYMBOL OF FREEDOM®

UNITED
Mileage Plus®

US AIRWAYS
DIVIDEND MILES

SEE THE WORLD
IN FULL COLOR

Fodor's Exploring Guides bring all the great sights vividly to life with hundreds of photographs, fascinating historical background, and colorful anecdotes. Detailed maps and practical information keep you headed in the right direction.

Pair a **Fodor's** Exploring Guide with your trusted Gold Guide for a complete planning package.

Valladolid

② *44½ km (28 mi) east of Chichén Itzá.*

The second-largest city in the State of Yucatán, Valladolid is a picturesque provincial town (pop. 70,000). It has been enjoying growing popularity among travelers en route to or from Chichén Itzá or Río Lagartos who want a change from the more touristy places. Montejo founded Valladolid in 1543 on the site of the Maya town of Sisal. The city suffered during the War of the Castes—when the Maya in revolt killed nearly all Spanish residents—and again during the Mexican Revolution.

Today, however, placidity reigns in this agricultural market town. The center is mostly colonial, although it has many 19th-century structures. The main sights are the colonial churches, principally the large **Catedral de San Servacio** (San Servace Cathedral) on the central square and the 16th-century **Convento y Iglesia de San Bernadino** (San Bernardino Church and Convent) three blocks southwest. Both were pillaged during the War of the Castes. A briny, muddy cenote in the center of town draws only the most resolute swimmers; instead, visit the adjacent **ethnographic museum.** West of the main square and on the old highway to Chichén Itzá, you can swim with the catfish in lovely, mysterious **Cenote Dzitnup,** located in a cave lit by a small natural skylight; admission is $2.

Valladolid is renowned for its cuisine, particularly its sausages; try one of the restaurants within a block of the central square. You can find good buys on sandals, baskets, and the local liqueur, Xtabentún, flavored with honey and anise.

Dining and Lodging

$$ ✕⊡ **El Mesón del Marqués.** On the north side of the main square is this well-preserved, very old hacienda that was built around a lovely courtyard. All rooms have air-conditioning, phones, and cable TV and are attractively furnished with rustic and colonial touches. The 25 junior suites have large bathrooms with bathtubs. The charming restaurant, set under porticos surrounding the courtyard, serves Yucatecan specialties such as pollo pibíl and local sausage served in a variety of ways. It's open 7 AM–11 PM. ⊠ *Calle 39 No. 203, 97780,* ☎ *9/856–2073 or 9/856–3042,* 𝖥𝖠𝖷 *9/856–2280. 58 rooms, 25 suites. Restaurant, bar, air-conditioning, pool. AE.*

$$ ⊡ **Ecotel Quinta Real.** For a little luxury, this attractive salmon-color hotel dressed in Mexican colonial architecture fits the bill. Near a leafy park five blocks from downtown, the pretty rooms have cool tile floors, two double beds, cable TV, air-conditioning, and spacious balconies. You can wander the tree-filled garden and visit the pool, palapa bar, tennis court, or duck pond, or head to the game room for some Ping-Pong or billiards. The restaurant serves regional and some international dishes, but it's a bit more pricey than other places in town. ⊠ *Calle 40 No. 160–A, at Calle 27, 97780,* ☎ *9/856–3472 or 9/856–3473,* 𝖥𝖠𝖷 *9/856–2422,* 𝖶𝖤𝖡 *www.ecotelquintareal.com.mx. 48 rooms. Restaurant, bar, air-conditioning, pool, tennis court, Ping-Pong, travel services, car rental, free parking. MC, V.*

$ ⊡ **María de la Luz.** This main-plaza hotel is built around a shallow, kidney-shape swimming pool surrounded by banana trees. The plain rooms have tile bathrooms, air-conditioning, firm beds, and color cable TV. The street-side restaurant is attractively furnished with high-backed rattan chairs and linen cloths; Mexican dishes are predictable and inexpensive, but tasty. Pollo pibíl is a house specialty. ⊠ *Calle 42 No. 193-C (between Calles 39 and 41), 97780,* ☎ 𝖥𝖠𝖷 *9/856–2071 or 9/856–1181. 70 rooms. Restaurant, bar, air-conditioning, pool, free parking. MC, V.*

Ek Balam

⚓ ㉓ *20 km (12 mi) north of Valladolid, off Rte. 295.*

The site of Ek Balam (Black Jaguar), a powerful city that was driven by a marine economy, opened to the public in 2000. It contains two concentric walls surrounding a main area, a rare configuration in Maya sites, plus 45 structures in the main excavation field. Prominent among them is the stunning **Tower** pyramid, set off by two small temples with staircases; a giant monster mask crowns its summit, which is embedded with marvelous glyphs and friezes. Archaeologists have learned that the Tower was a mausoleum for King Ukit IV. Priceless funerary objects have been uncovered and are under study. Buried with the king were pearls, thousands of perforated seashells, gold, jade, mother-of-pearl pendants, and small bone masks with moveable jaws. Another Ek Balam ruler, Hun-Pik-Tok, was part of a ruling triumvirate of Chichén Itzá in the second phase of development. 🖃 *$1.50, free Sun.* ⊙ *Daily 8–5.*

UXMAL AND THE RUTA PUUC

As soon as you pass through the large Maya town of Uman on Mérida's southern outskirts, you are in one of the least-populated areas of the Yucatán. From the highest point on the peninsula, the 500-ft crest between the present village of Muna and the ruins of ancient Uxmal, an unbroken expanse of low tropical forest reaches all the way to the southern horizon. The highway to Uxmal and Kabah is a fairly traffic-free route through uncultivated woodlands, punctuated here and there by oval thatch-roof huts and roadside stands where women sell hand-embroidered white cotton dresses.

The forest seems to thicken beyond Uxmal, which was in ancient times the largest and most important Puuc city. Raised and cobbled ceremonial roads connected it to a number of smaller ceremonial centers that, despite their apparent subservience to the lords of Uxmal, boasted lofty pyramids and ornate palaces of their own. Several of these satellite sites, including Kabah, Sayil, and Labná, are open to the public; they stand along a side road known as the "Ruta Puuc," which winds eastward and eventually joins busy Route 184, a major highway linking Mérida with Felipe Carrillo Puerto, Quintana Roo, on the Caribbean coast, and serving the largest concentration of present-day Maya agricultural towns on the peninsula. From the east end of the Ruta Puuc near Loltún Caves, it takes motorists less than an hour either to retrace their route back to Uxmal or to return to Mérida on Route 184.

If you don't have your own wheels, a great option for seeing the ruins of the Ruta Puuc is the **ATS** tour (🖂 Calle 69 No. 544, between Calles 68 and 70, ☎ 9/923–2287) that leaves Mérida at 8 AM from the second-class bus station. The tour stops for half an hour each at the ruins of Labná, Xlapac, Sayil, and Kabah, giving you just enough time to scan the plaques, climb a few crumbling steps, and poke your nose into a crevice or two. You get almost two hours at Uxmal before heading back to Mérida at 2:30 PM. The trip costs $8 per person, is unguided, and does not include entrance to the ruins. If you go on Sunday, entrance to all archaeological sites is free.

Uxmal

★ ⚓ ㉔ *78 km (48 mi) south of Mérida on Rte. 261.*

If Chichén Itzá is the most impressive Maya ruin in Yucatán, Uxmal is arguably the most beautiful. Where the former has a Maya Itzá grandeur, the latter seems more understated and elegant—pure Maya.

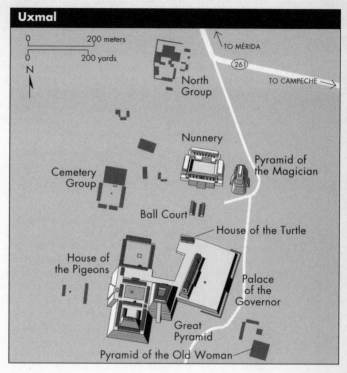

Uxmal

0 — 200 meters
0 — 200 yards
N

TO MÉRIDA
(261)
TO CAMPECHE →

North Group

Nunnery

Pyramid of the Magician

Cemetery Group

Ball Court

House of the Turtle

House of the Pigeons

Palace of the Governor

Great Pyramid

Pyramid of the Old Woman

The architecture reflects the Late Classical renaissance of the 7th–9th centuries and is contemporary with that of Palenque and Tikal, among other great Maya metropolises of the southern highlands. Although the name translates as "thrice built" (referring to the three levels of the Governor's Palace, in which older temples were buried), the site was actually rebuilt, abandoned, and reoccupied in several stages, for reasons still unknown. Itzá invaders briefly occupied Uxmal in the 10th century. The site reemerged as a Maya ceremonial center in the Postclassic era and was deserted for the last time some 90 years before the conquest. When American explorer John Lloyd Stephens came upon Uxmal in 1840, it was owned by a descendant of the same Montejo family that had conquered Yucatán three centuries earlier.

The site is considered the finest and largest example of Puuc architecture, which embraces such details as ornate stone mosaics and friezes on the upper walls, intricate cornices with curled noses, rows of columns, and soaring vaulted arches. Lines are clean and uncluttered, with the horizontal—especially the parallelogram—preferred to the vertical. Many of the flat, low, elongated buildings were built on artificial platforms and laid out in quadrangles. The cult of the rain god, Chaac, who is depicted here with a long curled nose and whose image appears throughout Yucatán, became obsessive in this parched region. But the area lacks cenotes. Though the Maya dug cisterns, called *chultunes*, for collecting rainwater, drought may be the reason that Uxmal was so often occupied and then abandoned. Some phallic figures—important Maya fertility symbols—are found here.

While most of Uxmal hasn't been restored, three buildings in particular merit attention:

At 125 ft high, the **Pyramid of the Magician** is the tallest and most prominent structure at the site. Unlike most other Maya pyramids, which are stepped and angular, it has a strangely round-corner design. Built five times at 52-year sequences to coincide with the ceremony of the new fire, each time over the previous structure, the pyramid has a stairway on its western side that leads through a giant open-mouthed mask of Chaac to two temples at the summit. The mask motif is repeated on one side of the stairs. You get a magnificent panoramic view of Uxmal and the hills by climbing to the top. According to legend, the pyramid derived its name from a dwarf magician who built it overnight. It is especially lovely at night, when its pale beige slope glows in the moonlight.

West of the pyramid lies the **Quadrangle of the Nuns,** considered by some to be the finest part of Uxmal. The name was given to it by the Spanish conquistadors because it reminded them of a convent building in Old Spain. According to recent research, what is called the **Nunnery** was actually the palace and living quarters of a high lord of Uxmal by the name of Chaan Chak, which means "abundance of rain." You can see his carved figure on Stela No. 14, now on exhibit at the museum at the entrance to the site. Chaan Chak also inaugurated the ball court at Uxmal on January 15 and 16, AD 901, inscriptions say. You may enter the four buildings; each comprises a series of low, gracefully repetitive chambers that look onto a central patio. The building on the southern side is broken by a tall corbeled arch that is formed by placing ceiling stones increasingly close to and on top of one another until they meet at a central supporting capstone. Elaborate decoration—stone latticework, masks, geometric patterns reminiscent of ancient Greek ornamentation, representations of the classic Maya thatch hut (*na*), coiling snakes, and some phallic figures—blankets the upper facades, in contrast with the smooth, sheer blocks that face the lower walls. The mosaics that thrust into the upper facade are huge, sometimes surpassing several feet in size.

Continue walking south; you pass the ball court before reaching the **Palace of the Governor,** which archaeologist Victor von Hagen considered the most magnificent building ever erected in the Americas. Interestingly, the palace faces east while the rest of Uxmal faces west. Archaeologists believe this is because the palace was used to sight the planet Venus. Covering 5 acres and rising over an immense acropolis, the palace lies at the heart of what must have been Uxmal's administrative center. Its 320-ft length is divided by three corbeled arches, which create narrow passageways or sanctuaries. Decorating the facade are intricate friezes (along the uppermost section), geometrically patterned carvings overlaid with plumed serpents, stylized Chaac masks, and human faces. These mosaics required more than 20,000 individually cut stones.

First excavated in 1929 by the Danish explorer Franz Blom, Uxmal served in 1841 as home to American explorer John Lloyd Stephens, who wrote of it: "The whole wears an air of architectural symmetry and grandeur. If it stood at this day on its grand artificial terrace in Hyde Park or the Garden of the Tuileries, it would form a new order . . . not unworthy to sit side by side with the remains of Egyptian, Grecian, and Roman art."

Today a sound-and-light show recounts Maya legends, including the kidnaping of an Uxmal princess by a king of Chichén Itzá, and focuses on the people's dependence on rain—thus the cult of Chaac. The artificial colored light brings out details of carvings and mosaics that are easy to miss when the sun is shining—for example, the stone replicas of *nas* (thatch-roof huts), which bear a remarkable resemblance to contemporary huts, on one facade of the nunnery. The show is performed nightly in Spanish; earphones provide an English translation. ✉ *Site and museum $8.50, free Sun.; sound-and-light show $4; parking $2; use of video camera $8.* ☉ *Daily 8–5; sound-and-light show Apr.–Oct., nightly at 8 PM; Nov.–Mar., nightly at 7 PM.*

Dining and Lodging

$ ✕ **Las Palapas.** A great alternative to the area's hotel dining rooms, this family-run restaurant specializes in delicious Yucatecan dishes served with homemade tortillas. When tour groups request it in advance, the owners prepare a traditional feast, roasting the chicken or pork pibíl-style, in a pit in the ground. If you see a tour bus in the parking lot, stop in—you may chance upon a memorable fiesta. ✉ *Hwy. 261, 5 km (3 mi) north of the Uxmal ruins,* ☎ *no phone. No credit cards.*

$$$$ ⊡ **Hacienda Uxmal.** The oldest hotel at the Maya site, built in 1955 and still owned and operated by the Barbachano family, this pleasant colonial-style building has lovely floor tiles, ceramics, and iron grillwork. The rooms—all with ceiling fans, cable TV, and air-conditioning—are tiled and decorated with worn but comfortable furniture. All are fronted with wide, furnished verandas where you can enjoy the fresh air; the large courtyard contains a garden and two pools. The Uxmal ruins are across the road and about 100 yards south. Ask about packages that include free or low-cost car rentals for the nights you spend at Uxmal and at the Mayaland hotel in Chichén Itzá. ✉ *Reservations: Mayaland Tours, Calle 60 between Calles 59 and 61, Mérida,* ☎ *9/924–2099 or 800/235–4079,* ☎ FAX *9/949–4754,* FAX *9/924–6290,* WEB *www.mayaland.com. 78 rooms, 2 suites. 2 restaurants, bar, air-conditioning, fans, room service, 2 pools, Ping-Pong, billiards, free parking. AE, MC, V.*

$$$$ ⊡ **Lodge at Uxmal.** The entrance to the Uxmal ruins is across from this luminous property owned and run by Mayaland Resorts. The rooms are housed in rustic-looking, two-story thatch-roof buildings. They have glossy red-tile floors, lots of carved and polished hardwood, and faux-stained-glass windows as well as cable TV, minibars, air-conditioning, and bathtubs. Simple furnishings and local weavings are used to create a somewhat native ambience in the midst of the luxury amenities. The suites have king-size beds and jet baths. Rocking chairs are placed out on the wide verandas that look out on green lawns or one of the swimming pools. ✉ *Antigua Carretera Mérida–Campeche, Km 78, 97000,* ☎ *9/923–2202, 9/923–0275, or 800/235–4079,* FAX *9/923–4744,* WEB *www.mayaland.com. 30 rooms, 10 suites. 2 restaurants, bar, air-conditioning, 2 pools, free parking. AE, MC, V.*

$$ ⊡ **Villas Arqueológicas Uxmal.** All the rooms at this two-story Club Med down the street from the Uxmal ruins have phones—a departure for this chain. Rooms are small and functional, with wooden furniture that fits the niches nicely and powerful but quiet air conditioners. Half of the rooms have garden views. The French and Continental food served in the restaurant—including niçoise salad, pâté, and filet mignon—can be a delightful change from regional fare. The daily special menu includes appetizer, soup, entrée, dessert, and coffee or tea for under $15. Day-trippers have free use of the pool—towels are provided for those who have a meal or drinks here. ✉ *Carretera Uxmal, Km 76 (Box 449, Mérida 97000),* ☎ *9/976–2018 or 800/258–2633,* FAX *9/976–2018,* WEB *www.clubmed.com. 40 rooms, 3 suites. Restaurant, bar, air-conditioning, pool, tennis court, billiards, library, free parking. AE, MC, V.*

Kabah

⛏ ㉕ *23 km (14 mi) south of Uxmal on Rte. 261.*

Kabah, which experts estimate was first inhabited around 250 BC, was at one point the largest restoration project in the Yucatán. A ceremo-

nial center of soft, almost Grecian beauty, it was once linked to Uxmal
by a sacbé, at the end of which looms a great independent arch—now
across the highway from the main ruins. The 151-ft-long **Codz-Pop** (coiled
mat)—also known as Palace of the Masks—is so called because of its
250 Chaac masks, most without curled noses. To some they resemble
rolled-up straw mats. ☒ *$2.50, free Sun.* ☉ *Daily 8–5.*

Sayil

⚑ ㉖ *9 km (5½ mi) south of Kabah on Rte. 261.*

Sayil, or "home of ants," is the oldest site of the Puuc group: experts
believe the site flourished between AD 800 and AD 1000. It is renowned
primarily for its majestic three-story **palace,** built on a hill and containing more than 90 rooms and a figure of the goddess of fertility. The
structure recalls Palenque in its use of multiple planes, its columned
porticoes and sober cornices, and in the play of its long, graceful horizontal masses. ☒ *$2.50, free Sun.* ☉ *Daily 8–5.*

Labná

⚑ ㉗ *9 km (5½ mi) south of Sayil on Rte. 31 East.*

The striking, monumental structure at Labná ("old house" or "abandoned house") is a fanciful corbeled arch rising high into a near peak,
with elaborate latticework and a small chamber on each side. One theory says the arch was the entrance to an area where religious ceremonies
were staged. The site was used mainly by the military elite and royalty. ☒ *$2.50, free Sun.* ☉ *Daily 8–5.*

Loltún Caves

★ ⚑ ㉘ *18 km (11 mi) northeast of Labná.*

The Loltún ("stone flower" in Maya) is the largest known cave system in the Yucatán. This series of caverns contains wall paintings and
stone artifacts from Maya and pre-Maya times (around 2500 BC), as
well as stalactites and stalagmites. Some of the forms have been given
descriptive names such as Corn Ear and Cathedral. Illuminated pathways wander a little over a kilometer (½ mi) through the caverns. You
can enter the caves only on guided tours, which are run at 9:30, 11,
12:30, 2, 3, and 4. ☒ *$4.50, free Sun.* ☉ *Daily 9–5.*

Ticul

㉙ *27 km (16½ mi) northwest of the Loltún Caves, 28 km (17 mi) east of
Uxmal.*

One of the larger towns in Yucatán, Ticul has a handsome 17th-cen-
tury church and is a good base for exploring the Puuc region. Many
descendants of the Xiu dynasty, which ruled Uxmal until the conquest, still live here. Industries include fabrication of huipiles and
shoes, as well as most of the pottery you see around the Yucatán. **Arte
Maya** (☒ Calle 23 No. 301, ☎ FAX 9/972–1095) is a ceramics workshop that produces museum-quality replicas of archaeological pieces
found throughout Mexico. The workshop, run by master craftsman
Luis Echeverría Villalobos, also produces smaller, souvenir-quality
pieces that are both more affordable and more easily transported than
his more ambitious pieces.

OFF THE
BEATEN PATH
> **MAYAPÁN –** Those who are enamored of Yucatán and the ancient Maya
> may want to take a 49-km (30-mi) detour east from Ticul on Route 18 to
> Mayapán, the last of the great city-states on the peninsula until AD 1450,

when it was demolished by war. It is thought that the city, with an architectural style reminiscent of Uxmal, was as big as Chichén Itzá, and there are more than 4,000 mounds to bear this out. At its height, the population could have been well over 12,000. A half dozen mounds are being vigorously excavated, including the palaces of Maya royalty and the temple of the benign god Kukulcán, where murals in vivid reds and oranges, plus stucco sculptures of Chaac, have been uncovered. The ceremonial structures that were faithfully described in Fray Diego de Landa's writings will look like they have jumped right out of his book when the work is completed. ⊠ *Off road to left before Telchaquillo; follow signs.* ▨ *$2, free Sun.* ⊙ *Daily 8–5.*

Dining and Lodging

$$ ✕ **Los Delfines.** Seafood is the strength of this friendly neighborhood restaurant, which has a high thatch roof and open sides. There's a full bar and a large seafood menu, including seafood cocktails, ceviche, many styles of shrimp, and seafood soup. Delfines also serves chicken, poc chuc, and other regional dishes. A selection of free appetizers is brought to your table soon after you're seated. Guests can use the small octagonal pool in the garden. The place is open daily 11–5. ⊠ *Calle 27 No. 216 (between Calles 28 and 30),* ☎ *9/972–0401. No credit cards. No dinner.*

$ ✕ **Los Almendros.** This restaurant, one of the few in town open until 9 PM, is a decent place to sample regional fare, including poc chuc and cochinita pibíl. Some consider it to be the best regional restaurant around, but Los Almendros is looking rather run-down these days. ⊠ *Calle 23 No. 196,* ☎ *9/972–0021. MC, V.*

$ ▣ **Plaza.** This very pleasant three-story hotel surrounds a large central patio and is just a block from the main plaza. It has clean bathrooms and firm mattresses, hammock hooks, telephones, fans, and local TV. Choose a room with air-conditioning; the price difference is only about $5. ⊠ *Calle 23 No. 202 (between Calles 26 and 26a), 97860,* ☎ *9/972–0484,* FAX *9/972–0026. 21 rooms, 5 suites. Air-conditioning (some), free parking. AE, MC, V (with 6% surcharge).*

Yaxcopoil

㉚ *50 km (31 mi) north of Uxmal, on Rte. 261.*

Yaxcopoil, a restored 17th-century hacienda, makes for a nice change of pace from the ruins. The building, with its distinctive Moorish double arch out front, has been used as a film set and is the best-known henequen plantation in the region. The museum's rooms are fitted with their original European furnishings; the machine room was used in the processing of henequen. The family chapel is in the garden. ⊠ *Km 33, Rte. 261.* ▨ *$2.* ⊙ *Mon.–Sat. 8–sunset, Sun. 9–1.*

Oxkintoc

㉛ *75 km (47 mi) west of Yaxcopoil, off Rte. 184.*

The archaeological site of Oxkintoc is 2 km (1 mi) off Route 180 near the present-day village of Maxcanú and contains the ruins of an important Maya capital that dominated the region from about AD 300 to 1100. Little was known about Oxkintoc until excavations began here in 1987. Bearing a pure Puuc architectural style, structures that have been excavated so far include two tall pyramids, a palace with stone statues of several ancient rulers, and a temple that serves as the entrance to Tzat Tun Tzat, a mysterious subterranean labyrinth. ⊠ *Off Rte. 184, 1½ km (1 mi) west of Rte. 180.* ▨ *$2, free Sun.* ⊙ *Daily 8–5.*

PROGRESO AND THE NORTH COAST

Various routes lead from Mérida to towns along the north coast, which spreads across a distance of 380 km (236 mi). Less-traveled roads dead-end at the forgotten former seaport of Sisal and the laid-back fishing village of Celestún, gateway to a flamingo reserve at the west end of the coast. The busiest route, Highway 261, leads due north from Mérida to the modern shipping port and local beach playground of Progreso. To get to some of the small beach towns east of Progreso, head east on Highway 291 out of Mérida and then cut north on one of many access roads. Wide, white shadeless beaches here are peppered with bathers from Mérida during Holy Week and in summer—but are nearly vacant the rest of the year.

The terrain in this part of the peninsula is absolutely flat. Tall trees are scarce, because the region was almost entirely cleared for coconut palms in the early 19th century and again for henequen in the early 20th century. Local Maya people still tend some of the old fields of henequen, a spike-leaf agave plant, even though there is little profit to be made from the rope fiber it produces. Other former plantation fields have run wild, overgrown with scrub and marked only by the low, white stone walls erected to mark their boundaries. Bird life is abundant in the area, and butterflies swarm in profusion throughout the dry season.

Celestún

③② *90 km (56 mi) west of Mérida.*

This tranquil fishing village, with its air of unpretentiousness and gulf-coast flavor, sits at the end of a spit of land separating the Celestún estuary from the gulf on the western hump of the Yucatán. Celestún is the only point of entry to the **Parque Natural Ría Celestún,** a 100,000-acre wildlife reserve with extensive mangrove forests and salt flats and one of the largest colonies of flamingos in North America. Most of the flamingos took up residence here following Hurricane Gilbert in 1988, abandoning Río Lagartos, which had been badly damaged by the high waters and wind. Clouds of pink wings soar over the pale blue backdrop of the estuary all year, but the best months for seeing them in abundance—as many as 18,000 flamingos at a time—are April through June. This is also the fourth-largest wintering ground for ducks of the gulf-coast region, with more than 200 other species of birds and a large sea-turtle population. Conservation programs sponsored by the United States and Mexico protect not only the birds and endangered hawksbill and loggerhead marine tortoises but species such as the blue crab and crocodiles as well.

Rocks, islets, and white-sand beaches enhance the park's lovely setting. There is good fishing in both the river and the gulf, and if you're really lucky you can see deer and armadillo roaming the surrounding land. Bring your bathing suit if you want to enjoy a swim in one of the cenotes. Most Mérida travel agencies run boat tours of the *ría* (estuary) in the early morning or late afternoon.

Popular with Mexican vacationers, the park's sandy beach is pleasant during the day but tends to get windy in the afternoon, with choppy water and blowing sand. To see the birds, hire a fishing boat at the dock outside town (the boats hang out under the bridge leading into Celestún). A 75-minute tour for up to six people costs about $60, a two-hour tour around $80.

Celestún Expeditions (✉ Calle 10 No. 97, between Calles 9 and 11, ☎ 9/916–2049) is a small company run by two natives of Celestún,

David and Feliciano. They speak English well and are passionate about their work. In addition to the standard flamingo tours, they offer three-hour guided bike tours, jungle walks (day or night), crocodile tours at night, bird-watching excursions, and trips to the Maya ruins and haciendas. Tours range from $20 per person for the bike jaunt to $75 per person for the bird-watching outing. **Mayaland Tours** (⊠ Calle 57 between Calles 58 and 61, ☎ 9/928–3075 or 800/235–4079, ℻ 9/928–3077; ⊠ Fiesta Americana, Calle Colón at Calle 60, ☎℻ 9/924–6290) has a daylong tour out of Mérida that, for about $65 a person, includes all transportation, guide service, a seafood lunch, and time on the beach. (The Mayaland guides tend to be more professional than the ones sometimes subcontracted by the company.)

Dining and Lodging

$ ✕ **La Palapa.** A facade made entirely of conch shells leads you to the best seafood place in town, famous for its *camarones a la palapa* (fried shrimp smothered in a garlic and cream sauce). There's a roofed-in area plus an open-air terrace for lunching and watching the sea. The menu is full of fresh fish such as sea bass and red snapper, plus crab, squid, and other denizens of the deep. The most expensive dish on the menu, a plate of lobster tails and moro crab, is $27 and boosts the price range to $$. La Palapa is usually open 11 AM–7 PM, although it can close at 6 in low season or when business is slow. To the locals, it's overpriced, but seafood restaurants are scarce around here. ⊠ *Calle 12 No. 105, between Calles 11 and 13,* ☎ *9/916–2063. MC, V.*

$$$$ ⌑ **Hotel Eco Paraíso Xixim.** On an old coconut plantation in a nature reserve outside town, this hotel is a cut above the other Yucatán coast lodges. Xixim means "seashells" in Maya—note the thousands of seashells on the beach. Rooms are in thatch-roof bungalows, with porches and hammocks, that stand right on the 5-km-long (3-mi-long) beach. Each small suite has two comfortable queen-size beds, tile floors, and attractive wicker, cedar, and pine furniture, some inlaid with hand-painted tiles. There's also a sitting area and writing desk—but no air-conditioning, TVs, or phones. Bring strong insect repellent, as mosquitoes can be vicious, especially in the rainy season. Room rates include ample breakfasts and dinners at the clubhouse. Special-interest tours to see the flamingos and other birds, old haciendas, and archaeological sites are available for an additional fee, as are mountain-biking tours and excursions to cenotes for swimming; kayaks are available for rent. ⊠ *Camino Viejo a Sisal, Km 10, 97367,* ☎ *9/916–2100 or 888/264–5792,* ℻ *9/916–2111,* WEB *www.mexonline.com/eco-paraiso.htm. 15 cabañas. Restaurant, bar, fans, in-room safes, pool, beach, billiards, library. AE, MC, V.*

$ ⌑ **Hotel Sol y Mar.** Gerardo Vasquez, the friendly owner of this eight-room hotel, also owns the local paint store next door and chose a tasteful combination of gray and rose for the walls and curtains of these cool, spacious units. A half block from the town beach, this is definitely the best hotel of this category around. Rooms are spare but clean, with two double beds, a small table and chairs, tile bathrooms, and either air-conditioning (in three rooms, for $6 more) or overhead fans. There's no restaurant, but the neighborhood has plenty of eateries. ⊠ *Calle 12 No. 104, at Calle 10, 97367,* ☎ *9/916–2166. 8 rooms. Air-conditioning (some), fans (some). No credit cards.*

Sisal

③③ *50 km (31 mi) northwest of Mérida.*

Sisal gave its name to the henequen ("sisal" in English) that was shipped from this port in great quantity during the mid-19th century. With the rise of Progreso, Sisal dwindled into little more than a fisherman's wharf. However, it may take on importance again because of a large, exclusive residential development being built here (albeit slowly) by a Mexican company. The company that created the Continental Plaza Playacar originally planned the development but later shelved it because of near bankruptcy. Sisal livens up in July and August when Meridanos come to swim and dine. Attractions include a **colonial customs house** and the private 1906 **lighthouse.** One of three offshore reefs, **Madagascar Reef** has excellent diving.

Lodging

$　🖼 **Hotel Felicidades.** A few minutes' walk up the beach east of the pier, this somewhat dingy hotel caters to tourists during the vacation months and can be fun when a crowd arrives. ✉ *Calle 8 No. 1004, 97367,* ☎ *no phone. 10 rooms. No credit cards.*

Dzibilchaltún

🔺 ③④ *16 km (10 mi) north of Mérida.*

Dzibilchaltún ("the place where there is writing on flat stones") is a sizeable archaeological site in the north Yucatán area, occupying more than 16 square km (10 square mi) of land cluttered with thousands of mounds, low platforms, piles of rubble, plazas, and stelae. It is also the longest-occupied city of this area, established around 500 BC in the Preclassic era and abandoned only when the conquistadors arrived in the 16th century. Sixteen kilometers (10 miles) from Progreso, it had a marine and coastal economy and was more of an urban center than a ceremonial center.

For now Dzibilchaltún's significance lies in the stucco sculpture and ceramics, from all periods of Maya civilization, that have been unearthed here. The **Temple of the Seven Dolls** (circa AD 500) is one of a half dozen structures excavated on the site to date. Low and trapezoidal, the temple exemplifies the Late Preclassic style, which predates such Puuc sites as Uxmal. The remains of stucco masks adorn each side, and there are vestiges of sculptures of coiled serpents representing Kukulcán. During the spring and fall equinoxes, sunbeams fall at the exact center of two windows opposite each other inside one of the temple rooms, an example of the highly precise mathematical calculations for which the Maya are known. Recent studies have found that a similar phenomena occurs at the full moon between March 20 and April 20. The stone cube atop the temple and the open chapel built by the Spaniards for the Indians are additional points of interest. Twelve sacbéob (or sacbé) lead to various groups of structures. Bones and ceremonial objects unearthed by divers from the National Geographic Society between 1957 and 1959 suggest that the **Xlacah Cenote** was used for ceremonial offerings. These days, it's ideal for taking a dip if you're walking around the ruins in the heat.

An excellent museum called **Pueblo Maya** is at the entrance to the site. It's part of a national program dedicated to establishing museums devoted—and accessible—to the country's native peoples. It's fronted by a long rectangular garden featuring a number of the huge sculptures found on the site plus botanical species common to the area. In the back, two nas let you see how the Maya live today. The museum's collection (marked in English as well as in Spanish) includes figurines, bones, jewelry, and potsherds found in the cenote as well as the seven crude dolls that gave the Temple of the Seven Dolls its name. It also traces the area's Hispanic history and highlights contemporary crafts from the region. An interactive touch-screen area covers the history and other details about the site, but it's only in Spanish. 🖼 *$5.50 (including mu-*

seum), free Sun.; free guided tours, though tips are obligatory (ask at the entrance). ⊙ *Daily 8–5.*

Progreso

㉟ *16 km (10 mi) north of Dzibilchaltún, 32 km (20 mi) north of Mérida.*

Progreso, the waterfront town closest to Mérida, is not particularly historic. It's also not terribly picturesque. On weekdays during most of the year the beaches are deserted, but when school is out (Easter week, July, and August) and on summer weekends it becomes a popular vacation spot for families from Mérida. And more and more retired Canadians are renting apartments here between December and April because of the low prices. Progreso has fine sand and shallow waters that extend quite far out, making for nice walks, although its water is not the tantalizing aquamarine color of that in Caribbean Quintana Roo. Because it is so close to Mérida and because its interest is limited, there is really no reason to spend the night here, unless you want to experience a friendly, nondescript port town. The hotels are for the most part disappointing, but the small town does have a couple of attractions.

Progreso has been the chief port of entry for the peninsula since its founding in 1872, when the shallow port at Sisal, to the southwest, proved inadequate for handling the large ships that were carrying henequen cargo. Since 1989 the 2-km-long (1-mi-long) pier has been extended 9 km (5½ mi) out to sea to accommodate the hoped-for cruise-ship business and to siphon some of the lucrative tourist trade from Cozumel, but only a trickle of cruise ships are berthing here these days.

Progreso's attractions include its **malecón** (waterfront walkway), Calle 19, which is lined with seafood restaurants. Fishermen sell their catch on the beach east of the city between 6 and 8 AM.

Some 120 km (74 mi) offshore, the **Alacranes Reef** is where divers can explore sunken ships. **Pérez Island** is part of Alacranes Reef; it supports a large population of sea turtles and seabirds.

Dining and Lodging

$ ✕ **Le Saint Bonnet.** This thatch-roof restaurant-bar with an open-air terrace on the malecón is *the* place for locals. It gets its pretentious French name from a French partner who has seen to it that all dishes have Gallic monikers, such as the popular shrimp St. Bonnet—jumbo shrimp stuffed with cheese, wrapped with bacon, breaded, fried, and served with crab sauce. Other inventions include *filete à la Normandie* (fish fillet grilled with shrimp, covered with a mushroom-cheese sauce, and sprinkled with bacon bits and walnuts). You can wash it down with a French, German, Italian, Portuguese, or Chilean red or white wine. If you have room for dessert, try caramel crepes and mango or chocolate mousse. A live band plays tropical music daily 12:30–6:30 PM. ⊠ *Av. Malecón 150-D at Calle 78,* ☎ *9/935–2299. AE, MC, V.*

$ ⊡ **Tropical Suites.** The location of this clean but modest Progreso standby, by the ocean, is ideal and the price is right. The tile rooms and suites are spacious; the suites can fit up to four people and have breezy balconies. The sparse decor is nothing to write home about— basic double beds and white plastic chairs. Overhead fans and some air-conditioning (in four rooms) help battle the heat; 10 rooms have kitchenettes. There's a guest terrace-sundeck that takes up half the fourth floor, and numerous eateries are found in the vicinity. ⊠ *Malecón and Calle 70, 97320,* ☎ *9/935–1263,* FAX *9/935–3093. 10 rooms, 10 suites. Air-conditioning (some), fans, kitchenettes (some), free parking. No credit cards.*

Yucalpetén

㊱ *3 km (2 mi) west of Progreso.*

Yucalpetén lies at the end of a narrow, marshy promontory. The harbor here dates only from 1968, when it was built to provide shelter for small fishing boats in hurricane season. Little goes on here other than some activity at the yacht marina, where fishing for grouper, red snapper, dogfish, sea bass, and pompano is popular. Just beyond Yucalpetén, the even tinier village of Chelem has a few beachfront bungalow hotels.

Chicxulub

㊲ *6 km (4 mi) east of Progreso.*

One of the many small beaches strung along the highway east of Progreso, Chicxulub (chick-shoe-*loob*) is a small community where families from Mérida have beachfront weekend homes. A growing number of foreigners are getting wind of the once-inexpensive rentals in the nearby fishing village of Chicxulub Puerto, with its inviting beach and low winter rates. Chicxulub has also gotten press among scientists who theorize that debris raised by an asteroid that landed here some 65 million years ago may have caused the extinction of the dinosaurs.

Dining and Lodging

$ ✕ **Moctezuma.** Those in the know who like really fresh seafood at reasonable prices recommend this unpretentious place. In the middle of the crater caused by the landing of an asteroid millions of years ago, Moctezuma caters mainly to the local gentry who like to look over their fish before sending it into the kitchen. Dine on fresh-caught red snapper, grouper, sea bass, or lobster—grilled, baked, buttered, or breaded and nicely flavored with lime juice, annatto seed, cumin, and pepper. This is country cooking at its best. Tapas are served with beer and mixed drinks before your meal. ✉ *Carretera Chicxulub–Telchac,* ☎ *993/4–12–71. No credit cards.*

$$ ✕▥ **Margarita's Ville.** Owner Margarita Gutierrez has turned her childhood seaside getaway into an inviting hotel. Additions to the original wooden house have been rendered with the same attention to detail, with 1940s and '50s tiles on the floors and screened windows with louvered wood shutters. The effect is comfortable and very classy. Units have custom-made rattan furniture, orthopedic mattresses, quiet air-conditioning, fans, coffeemakers, and balconies shaded by high coconut palms. You can use the stainless-steel kitchen or have Margarita and her staff whip up lunch and dinner for you for $6 a head. A Continental breakfast is included in the room rate. Women's groups are encouraged, and the property is for adults only. You can also come just for a meal; call ahead to make a lunch or dinner reservation. ✉ *Carretera Chicxulub–Telchac,* ☎ 𝖥𝖠𝖷 *99/44–14–34. 2 bungalows, 11 rooms. Restaurant, air-conditioning, fans, pool, beach. No credit cards.*

Xcambo

▲ ㊳ *10 km (6 mi) east of Chicxulub, off the Progreso Hwy. at Xtampu.*

Surrounded by a plantation where disease-resistant coconut trees are being developed, the site is a couple of miles inland following the turnoff for Xtampu. It's also in the hometown of former Gov. Victor Cervera Pacheco, who, it is rumored, had given priority to its excavation. Salt, which was a much-sought-after item of trade, was produced at this ancient city and made it prosperous. Indeed, the bones of 600 former residents discovered in burial plots showed they had been healthier than the average Maya. Two plazas have been restored so far. The tallest temple is the **Pyramid of the Cross,** which is devoid of ornamentation. Ceramics found at the site indicate that the city traded with other Maya groups as far afield as Guatemala, Teotihuácan, and Belize. ⊠ *Turn off the Progreso Hwy. at Xtampu.* ▨ *$1.40.* ◯ *Daily 8–5.*

Telchac Puerto

㊴ *15 km (9 mi) east of Xcambo, 43 km (27 mi) east of Progreso.*

This area is worth visiting for its proximity to Laguna Rosada, where flamingos come to nest, and for its lovely, empty beaches. This isolation may be short-lived, however, as several luxury hotels supposedly are in the planning stages; some 2,500 to 3,500 hotel rooms are slated to be built in the area between Dzilám de Bravo and Telchac Puerto. This coastline has been dubbed the Zona de Nuevo Yucatán, which suggests a rather sudden loss of innocence à la Cancún.

Dining and Lodging

$ ✕ **Bella Mar.** The view from the beach is a knockout as are the daily specials. Owner–chef Veronica Crespo scouts the nearby fishing village for the freshest catch of the day, cooks it herself (nothing frozen here), and adds side dishes of rice, beans, potatoes, or other veggies. Ten palapa-shaded tables line the pretty beach for alfresco dining, and the ocean is inviting enough for a dip before or after lunch. You can even shower here. The local beach-house set have made it their favorite hangout, and Veronica knows the lay of the land if you're looking for a rental. A fish plate costs a reasonable $5, while the most you'll pay is $9 for butterfly shrimp. ⊠ *3 km (2 mi) west of Telchac Puerto on the Telchac–San Crisanto highway,* ☎ *9/991–8274. No credit cards.*

$$$$ ▨ **Reef Yucatán.** This all-inclusive resort is in what is being called the Zona de Nueva Yucatán: the still-primitive beaches of Yucatán's northern coast. The lobby is covered by an enormous, peaked thatch roof, which is repeated on a smaller scale atop the poolside bar. Rooms are pleasantly yet simply decorated and have telephones and cable TV; almost all have balconies with hammocks. A separate children's play area has video games, a basketball and soccer courts, mini theater, painting classes, and a pool and snack shop. The $83 per person rate includes unlimited food and drink (no alcohol is served after 2 AM), as well as nightly variety shows and access to the disco. The rate goes up $5 a person on Friday and Saturday. If you're not staying at the hotel, you can get a day pass for $38 (Sunday through Thursday) or $26 (Friday and Saturday) to use the facilities from 9 to 6; a night pass for the same rates allows visitors access to the facilities from 6 PM to 2 AM. ⊠ *Carretera a Progreso Telchac, Km 32,* ☎ *9/920–4466,* ℻ *9/925–3755,* WEB *www.interclubresorts.com. 122 rooms. 3 restaurants, bar, room service, 2 pools, beach, dance club, nightclub, baby-sitting, children's program (ages 4–12). MC, V.*

Dzilám de Bravo

㊵ *40 km (25 mi) east of Telchac Puerto, 113 km (70 mi) northeast of Mérida.*

The pirate Jean Laffite supposedly lies buried just outside the village of Dzilám de Bravo. At least there's a grave so marked, and two of the 2,000 inhabitants claim to be his descendants. Stop here for a swim in the gentle waters, or hire a boat from a local fisherman to view the seabirds that congregate around the small strip of land offshore about 10 minutes away.

Tizimín

🔴 *108 km (67 mi) southeast of Dzilám de Bravo.*

Tizimín, renowned as the seat of an indigenous messianic movement during the 1840s Caste War, is at the junction of Highways 176 and 295. The town has a 17th-century church dedicated to the Three Wise Men, who are honored here during a festival that is held December 15 to January 15.

If you are driving from Tizimín to Río Lagartos, before you leave town you can stop at the **Oficina del Reserva del Parque Natural Río Lagartos** (Flamingo Reserve Office; ✉ Calle 47 No. 415-A, between Calles 52 and 54, ☎ 9/863–4390), open weekdays 9–2 and 6–9, for park information. (Don't worry if you miss it; there's an information station near the Parque Natural Río Lagartos entrance.)

Parque Natural Río Lagartos

★ 🔴 *52 km (32 mi) north of Tizimín.*

If the thought of a phenomenal flamingo spectacle appeals, don't miss Parque Natural Río Lagartos. Flamingos can be seen year-round here but are particularly abundant from April through June. Actually encompassing a long estuary, the park was developed with ecotourism in mind, though most of the alligators for which it and the village were named have long since been hunted into extinction. In addition to seeing flamingos, birders also can spot snowy and red egrets, white ibis, great white herons, cormorants, pelicans, and even peregrine falcons flying over the murky waters. Fishing is good, too, and the protected hawksbill and green turtles lay their eggs on the beach at night.

Río Lagartos outdoes itself during the annual **Festival of Apostle Santiago** (July 20–26), with folk dances, bullfights, and processions. On the first of June, all the boats get decked out and parade in the lagoon in celebration of **Día de Marina** (Navy Day). To get here, you can drive or take a bus or a tour out of Mérida or elsewhere. Buses leave Mérida and Valladolid regularly from the second-class bus terminals to either Río Lagartos or, 10 km (6 mi) west of the park, San Felipe. A boat tour to see the flamingos is available from either point.

About ½ km (¼ mi) from the entrance to Río Lagartos is an information station (ESTACIÓN is written on it). This is the official reserve entrance. The helpful people who work here can contact a guide with a boat for you. The boat glides up the estuary east of the dock and in 10 minutes is deep into mangrove forests; another hour and the boat is at the flamingo feeding grounds.

Once you walk into the reserve, you don't see any marked paths with signs for bird-watching. If you want a bilingual birding guide ($10–$15 an hour), you must make arrangements at least three days in advance with the reserve office in Tizimín (☎ 9/863–4390). The shortest circuit is a little over 2 km (1 mi) long and goes west along the estuary in a straight line to the ocean.

You can make this a day trip from Valladolid (1¼ hours by road) or Mérida (2½ hours by road) or one of the resorts along the coast west of here, or you can lodge in San Felipe. Río Lagartos itself has just one hotel and few restaurants.

Dining and Lodging

$ ✕ **Isla de Contoy.** Run by an amicable family, this strictly seafood place two blocks from the estuary in Parque Natural Río Lagartos serves generous helpings of fish soup, fried fish fillets, shrimp, squid, and crab.

It's common practice to wash seafood down with a Yucatecan beer. ⊠ *Calle 19 No. 12,* ☎ *9/862–0000. No credit cards.*

$$ ✕🏨 **Hotel San Felipe.** This three-story white hotel in the beach town of San Felipe, 10 km (6 mi) west of Parque Natural Río Lagartos, caters to the growing number of people who want to overnight in the park area. The rooms are pretty basic—white walls with red trim, either with two twin beds or a double bed with a concrete base, overhead fans, reading lamps, and private tile bathrooms with hot and cold water. Some rooms have a TV and a wonderful sea view, but there are no phones. The most expensive room has a private terrace. For $27 a double, with beds and a hammock, you can't go wrong. The restaurant serves only fish and seafood dishes for breakfast and lunch. ⊠ *Calle 9 No. 13, between Calles 14 and 16, 2 blocks from the main square, San Felipe 97720,* ☎ *9/862–2027. 18 rooms. Restaurant, fans, free parking. No credit cards.*

Isla Holbox

43 *141 km (87 mi) northeast of Valladolid.*

The tiny Isla Holbox (25 km [16 mi] long) sits at the eastern end of the Río Lagartos estuary and just across the Quintana Roo state line. A fishing fan's heaven because of the pompano, bass, barracuda, and shark thronging its waters, the island also pleases seekers of tranquillity who don't mind rudimentary accommodations (rooms and hammocks for rent) and simple palapa restaurants. Seabirds fill the air; the long, sandy beach is strewn with seashells; and the swimming is good on the gulf side.

To get here from Río Lagartos, take Route 176 to Kantunilkin and then head north on the unnumbered road for 44 km (27 mi) to Chiquilá. Continue by ferry to the island; schedules vary, but there are normally five crossings a day. The fare is $4 and the trip takes about 35 minutes. A car ferry makes the trip at 11 AM daily, returning at 5 PM. (You can also pay to leave your car in a lot in Chicquilá, in Quintana Roo.)

In addition to Villa Delfines, there are several clean, inexpensive lodgings in town. Right on the zócalo and a block from the beach is **Posada Amapola** (no phone), where you can get a private bath with hot water, air-conditioning, and a hammock (or double bed) for $20. There are several restaurants nearby, and the owners can help you set up a birding expedition.

Dining and Lodging

$$$$ ✕🏨 **Villas Delfines.** This fisherman's lodge is very expensive by island standards. Cabins are simple and have no TV or phone, but you can get your catch grilled in the restaurant, and if you get tired of fishing you can head to the zócalo to arrange for a birding trip. ⊠ *Domicilio Conocido,* ☎ *9/874–4014; 9/884–8606 reservations,* 📠 *9/884–6342. 10 cabins. Restaurant, bar, fans. AE, MC, V.*

MÉRIDA AND THE STATE OF YUCATÁN A TO Z

To research prices, get advice from other travelers, and book travel arrangements, visit www.fodors.com.

AIR TRAVEL

Aeroméxico flies direct to Mérida from Miami with a stop (but no plane change) in Cancún. Mexicana has a connecting flight from Newark via Cancún and a number of other connecting flights from the United

States via Mexico City. Delta has nonstop flights from Atlanta to Mérida and as well as connecting flights via Mexico City. Aerocaribe, a subsidiary of Mexicana, has flights from Cancún, Chetumal, Cozumel, Oaxaca City, Tuxtla Gutiérrez, and Villahermosa, with additional service from Mérida to Veracruz, Monterrey, and Havana. It also offers service from Cozumel, Cancún, and Palenque to Chichén Itzá.

➤ AIRLINES AND CONTACTS: **Aerocaribe** (☎ 9/928–6790). **Aeroméxico** (☎ 9/920–1260 or 9/920–1265). **Mexicana** (☎ 9/946–1332). **Delta** (☎ 800/241–4141).

AIRPORTS

The Mérida airport, Aeropuerto Manuel Crescencio Rejón, is 7 km (4½ mi) west of the city's zócalo, about a 20-minute ride.

A private taxi from the airport costs about $9; collective service, about $4, is only for groups (usually a Volkswagen minibus). For both, you pay the taxi-ticket vendor at the airport, not the driver. The inexpensive but irregular Bus 79 goes from the airport to downtown. If you're driving into town, take the airport exit road, make a right at the four-lane Avenida Itzaes (the continuation of Route 180), and follow it to the one-way Calle 59, just past Parque Zoologico El Centenario. Turn right on Calle 59 and go straight until you reach Calle 62, where you again turn right, and drive a block to the main square. (Parking is difficult here.)

➤ AIRPORT INFORMATION: **Aeropuerto Manuel Crescencio Rejón** (☎ 9/946–1300).

BUS TRAVEL

Mérida's municipal buses run daily 5 AM–midnight, but service is somewhat confusing until you master the system. In the downtown area buses go east on Calle 59 and west on Calle 61, north on Calle 60 and south on Calle 62. You can catch a bus heading north to Progreso on Calle 56. Unfortunately, there is no direct bus service from the hotels around the plaza to the long-distance bus station.

There are many long-distance bus lines, including superdeluxe buses with air-conditioning and spacious seats. Many second-class bus lines now also have air-conditioning. All have at least one round-trip run daily to the main archaeological sites and colonial cities.

Mérida's second-class bus station has service three or four times a day to Chetumal for $16, with stops in Ticul and Oxkutzcab. The TRP line also has frequent service. Autotransportes del Sureste, at the second-class bus station, has the best coverage for out-of-the-way places, with daily service to the Guatemalan border, Palenque, and San Cristóbal de las Casas, and five buses daily to Uxmal.

Mérida's first-class buses, including ADO and UNO, serve Akumal, Cancún, Chichén Itzá, Playa del Carmen, Tulum, Uxmal, Valladolid, and other major Mexican cities from the Camionera Mérida (CAME). ADO also has a branch at the Fiesta Americana hotel (Paseo Montejo).

Several other first-class lines go to CAME, including Super Expreso. ADO has its own terminal next door, the Terminal Unica. These lines have frequent buses to Cancún, Valladolid, and other places east of Mérida.

As its name suggests, the Progreso bus station (Terminal de Autobuses Para Progreso) has departures for Progreso every half hour 6 AM–9 PM. Buses for Dzibilchaltún and Celestún leave regularly from the San Juan park at Calle 41 between Calles 64 and 66. You can also catch a comfortable air-conditioned van to Progreso, on Calle 60 between Calles 65 and 67, for the same price as the bus.

The Nuevos Horizontes travel agency, in the Fiesta Americana hotel in Mérida, sells tickets for deluxe ADO service to Cancún ($20), Campeche City ($11), Tuxtla Gutiérrez ($40), Villahermosa ($38), Playa del Carmen ($22), Mexico City ($80, only in high tourist season), and Palenque ($24). Buses leave from the hotel.

➤ Bus Lines: **ADO** (☎ 9/924–7868; 9/920–0126 or 9/925–0910 in Fiesta Americana). **Autotransportes del Sureste** (ATS; ☎ 9/923–2287 or 9/924–0830). **Super Expreso** (✉ Calle 70 No. 555, at Calle 71, ☎ 9/924–8391; ✉ Fiesta Americana, Av. Colón at Paseo Montejo, ☎ 9/925–0910). **TRP** (☎ 9/923–2287 ext. 3412). **UNO** (☎ 9/924–8391).

➤ Bus Stations: **Camionera Mérida** (CAME; ✉ Calle 70 No. 555, at Calle 71, ☎ 9/924–8391 or 9/924–9263). **Terminal del Autobuses Para Progreso** (Progreso station; ✉ Calle 62 No. 557, between Calles 65 and 67, ☎ 9/928–3965 or 9/924–1858). **Terminal Unica** (✉ Calle 69 No. 544, between Calles 68 and 70, ☎ 9/922–2387 or 9/923–2287).

CAR RENTAL

Mérida has almost 20 car-rental agencies, including Budget, Hertz, National, and Thrifty outlets. Prices are sometimes lower if you arrange your rental in advance of your visit.

➤ Major Agencies: **Budget** (✉ Hyatt Regency, Calle 60 No. 344, at Av. Colón, ☎ 9/942–1226 or 9/925–5453; ✉ Holiday Inn, Av. Colón 498 and Calle 60, ☎ 9/925–5453; ✉ airport, ☎ 9/946–1380). **Hertz** (✉ Fiesta Americana, ☎ 9/925–7595; ✉ Calle 60 between Calles 55 and 57, ☎ 9/924–2834 or 9/984–0028; ✉ airport, ☎ 9/946–1355 or 9/946–2554). **National** (✉ Fiesta Americana, ☎ 9/925–7524; ✉ airport, ☎ 9/946–1394). **Thrifty** (✉ Calle 60 No. 446-C, between Calles 51 and 49, ☎ 9/923–3440; ✉ airport, ☎ 9/946–2515).

CAR TRAVEL

Driving in Mérida can be frustrating because of the one-way streets (many of which are in effect one-lane because of the parked cars) and because traffic is dense. But having your own wheels is the best way to take excursions from the city.

Route 180, the main road along the gulf coast from the Texas border, passes through Mérida en route to Cancún. Mexico City lies 1,550 km (961 mi) west, Cancún 320 km (198 mi) due east.

The *autopista* is a four-lane toll highway between Mérida and Cancún. Beginning at the town of Kantuníl, 55 km (34 mi) southeast of Mérida, it runs somewhat parallel to Route 180 and cuts driving time between Mérida and Cancún—around 4½ hours—by about one hour and bypasses about four dozen villages. Access to the toll highway is off old Highway 180 and is clearly marked. The highway has clearly marked exits for Valladolid and Pisté (Chichén Itzá), as well as rest stops and gas stations. Tolls between Mérida and Cancún total about $24. From Campeche it takes a little more than two hours to reach Mérida on Route 180, which is the fastest route. Another option is the three-hour drive along Route 261 from Campeche, which passes the ruins of Uxmal and other ancient Maya sites as well as present-day Maya villages. From Chetumal, the most direct way—it takes approximately nine hours—is Route 307 to Felipe Carrillo Puerto, then Route 184 to Muna, continuing north on Route 261. These highways are in good condition.

CONSULATES

➤ Contacts: **United Kingdom** (✉ Calle 58 No. 450, at Calle 53, ☎ 9/928–6152). **United States** (✉ Paseo Montejo 453, ☎ 9/925–5011 or 9/925–5409).

CONSUMER PROTECTION

PROFECO is an efficient outfit for resolving tourist complaints on the spot, especially refunds. It's open weekdays 8:30–3:30.

➤ CONTACTS: **PROFECO** (✉ Calle 49 No. 466, at Calle 52, ☎ 9/923–6269 or 9/924–4212).

E-MAIL

Mérida's been sprouting places that offer Internet access (for a fee), especially around the main square. Chandler's Internet and Express Internet have air-conditioning, which can be a treat, and charge about $6 an hour.

➤ SERVICES: **Chandler's Internet** (✉ Pasaje Picheta, Calle 61 No. 501, between Calles 60 and 62, ☎ 9/928–5774 or 9/928–5776). **Express Internet** (✉ Café Express, Calle 60 No. 502, at Calle 59, ☎ 9/928–1691).

EMERGENCIES

➤ DOCTORS AND HOSPITALS: **Clínica Yucatán** (✉ Calle 66 No. 528, at Calle 65, ☎ 9/924–9391). **Red Cross Hospital** (✉ Calle 68 No. 533, between Calles 65 and 67, ☎ 9/928–5391).

➤ EMERGENCY SERVICES: **Fire** (☎ 9/924–9242). **General emergency** (☎ 06). **Police** (☎ 9/925–2555). **Red Cross** (✉ Calle 68 No. 583, at Calle 65, ☎ 9/924–8913).

➤ PHARMACIES: **Farmacia Canto** (San Fernando branch, ✉ Calle 60 at Av. Colón ☎ 9/925–8126; Centro branch, ✉ Calle 60 at Calle 63, ☎ 9/928–5027). **Farmacia Yza** (☎ 9/926–6666 for delivery or nearest branch).

ENGLISH-LANGUAGE MEDIA

Mérida has an English-language library, at Calle 53 No. 523 (between Calles 66 and 68); it's open weekdays 9–1 (plus 4–7 Tuesday, Thursday, and Friday) and Saturday 10–1.

The newsstands under the portals in Plaza Picheta on the main square carry a limited supply of newspapers and magazines from Mexico City and the United States.

MAIL AND SHIPPING

Mérida has only one post office, open weekdays 8–6 and Saturday 9–2. However, you can buy postage stamps at handicrafts shops in town. If you must send mail from Mexico, the Mex Post service can speed delivery a bit, even internationally, for a higher fee than regular mail.

➤ POST OFFICE: ✉ Calle 65 at Calle 56, ☎ 9/928–5404 or 9/924–3590.

MONEY MATTERS

Most banks throughout Mérida are open weekdays 9–5. Banamex has its main offices, open weekdays 9–5 and Saturday 9–1:30, in the handsome Casa de Montejo, on the south side of the main square, with branches at the airport and the Fiesta Americana hotel. All have automatic teller machines that can be accessed with Cirrus, Plus, Master-Card, and Visa bank cards. Several other banks can be found on Calle 65, between Calles 62 and 60, and on Paseo Montejo, and most have the same automatic teller service.

CURRENCY EXCHANGE

There are several exchange houses in Mérida, including Casa de Cambio del Sureste, open weekdays 9–5 and Saturday 9–1; Centro Cambriano Canto, open weekdays 9–1 and 4–7; and two on the ground level of the Fiesta Americana hotel, open weekdays 9–5.

➤ EXCHANGE SERVICES: **Casa de Cambio del Sureste** (✉ Calle 56 at Calle 57, ☎ 9/928–2152). **Centro Cambriano Canto** (✉ Calle 61 No. 468, between Calles 52 and 54, ☎ 9/928–0458).

TAXIS AND CARRIAGES

Taxis charge beach-resort prices, which makes them a little expensive for this region of Mexico. They don't cruise the streets for passengers and instead are available at 13 taxi stands (*sitios*) around the city, or in front of the Hyatt Regency, Holiday Inn, and Fiesta Americana hotels, which are strung out on the same block. The minimum fare is $2. Taxis operate around the clock.

You can hail horse-drawn *calesas* (pony traps) with sad-looking horses along Calle 60. A one-way ride to Saturday's Noche Mexicana, at Paseo Montejo and Calle 47, costs about $7; a round-trip from downtown, along Paseo Montejo and back downtown, is about $14. Bargaining is acceptable.

➤ TAXI COMPANIES: **Sitio Parque de la Madre** (☎ 9/928–5322). **Sitio Mejorada** (☎ 9/928–5589).

TELEPHONES

Larger cities such as Mérida have one-digit area codes followed by seven-digit phone numbers. Smaller towns such as Ticul have three-digit area codes followed by five-digit numbers.

Mérida has many Ladatel phone booths: at the airport, at all bus stations, in the main plaza, at Avenidas Reforma and Colón, Calle 57 at Calle 64, Calle 59 at Calle 62, and Calle 60 between Calles 55 and 53. You can make local and international direct calls at these public phones. Coin-operated phones are history—these take only Ladatel cards, electronic phone cards you can buy at newsstands and pharmacies.

TOURS

Mérida has more than 50 tour operators, who generally go to the same places. What differs is the mode of transportation—and whether or not the vehicle is air-conditioned and insured. Beware the *piratas* (street vendors) who stand outside the offices of reputable tour operators and offer to sell you a cheaper trip. They have been known to take your money and not show up; they also do not carry liability insurance.

A two- to three-hour group tour of the city, including museums, parks, public buildings, and monuments, costs $20 to $55 per person. Or you can pick up an open-air sightseeing bus at Parque de Santa Lucía for $6 (departures are Monday through Saturday at 10, 1, 4, and 7 and Sunday at 10 and 1).

A day trip to Chichén Itzá, with guide, entrance fee, and lunch, costs approximately $53. For about the same price you can see the ruins of Uxmal and Kabah in the Puuc region; for a few more dollars you can add the neighboring sites of Sayil, Labná, and the Loltún Caves. Afternoon departures to Uxmal allow you to take in the sound-and-light show at the ruins and return by 11 PM, for $56 (including dinner). Another option is a tour of Chichén Itzá followed by a drop-off in Cancún, for about $80. Most tour operators take credit cards.

Juergen Kremer, a German anthropologist who worked as a rocket scientist earlier in his life, is one of the best guides to the Maya ruins, including Ek Balam, Chichén Ítza, and Uxmal. He speaks German, English, and Maya and can be contacted via the Casa San Juan.

Diego Nuñez is an outstanding guide who conducts boat tours of Río Lagartos. He charges $42 for a 2½-hour tour, which accommodates five or six people. He usually can be found at the restaurant called Isla de Contoy, which he runs.

Occasionally, Pronatura, a wildlife conservation program, arranges guided one- or two-day trips for groups to Celestún or Río Lagartos accompanied by a bilingual biologist.

➤ Tour Operators: **American Express** (✉ Calle 56 No. 494, between Calles 43 and 45, ☎ 9/942–8200 or 9/924–4326, ℻ 9/942–8270). **Betanzos Internacional** (✉ Calle 60 No. 463, between Calles 53 and 55, Departamento 1, ☎ 9/923–9966 or 9/923–8594, ℻ 9/923–9966). **Carmen Travel Service** (✉ Hotel María del Carmen, Calle 63 No. 550, at Calle 68, ☎ 9/924–1212, ℻ 9/924–1288). **Diego Nuñez** (c/o Isla de Contoy, ✉ Calle 19 No. 12, Tizimín, ☎ 9/862–0000, nune@chichen.com.mx). **Felgueres Tours** (✉ Holiday Inn, Av. Colón 498 and Calle 60, ☎ 9/920–4477 or 9/920–3444, ℻ 9/925–6389). **Juergen Kremer** (☎ c/o Casa San Juan, 9/986–2937 or 9/950–1462, juergenk@altavista.net). **Mayaland Tours** (✉ Calle 57 between Calles 58 and 61, ☎ 9/928–3075 or 800/235–4079, ℻ 9/928–3077; ✉ Fiesta Americana, Calles Colón and 60, ☎ ℻ 9/924–6290); request a Mayaland guide rather than a guide subcontractor. **Pronatura** (✉ Calle 1-D No. 254-A, Campestra, ☎ ℻ 9/925–3787). **Turismo Aviomar** (✉ Calle 58A No. 500-C, Glorieta San Fernando, ☎ 9/920–0444 or 9/920–0443, ℻ 9/925–5064). **Yucatán Trails** (✉ Calle 62 No. 482, at Calle 57, ☎ 9/928–5913 or 9/928–2582, ℻ 9/924–1928).

TRANSPORTATION AROUND MÉRIDA AND THE STATE OF YUCATÁN

Getting around the state is fairly easy, either by public bus or car. There are many bus lines, and all have at least one round-trip run daily to the main archaeological sites and colonial cities. If you're visiting for the first time, a guided tour booked through one of the many Mérida travel agencies provides a good introduction to the city. If you're independent and adventurous, by all means hire a rental car and strike out on your own. Just take plenty of bottled water, fill up the tank whenever you see a station, and don't drive at night.

VISITOR INFORMATION

Mérida has an information kiosk at the airport that's open daily 8–8. The City Tourist Information Center and the kiosk at Calle 39 and Paso de Montejo are open weekdays 8–2 and 5–7. The state tourist center is open daily 8–8.

The tourist office in Progreso is open weekdays 9–2 and 4–7.

➤ Mérida: **City Tourist Information Center** (✉ Calle 59 between Calles 60 and 62, ☎ 9/928–6547). **State Tourist Information Center** (✉ Teatro Peón Contreras, Calle 60 between Calles 57 and 59, ☎ 9/924–9290).

➤ Progreso: **Tourist office** (✉ Calle 80 No. 176, at Calle 37, ☎ 9/935–0104).

6 CAMPECHE

Ruins of fortifications and walls built to fend off pirates who ravaged Yucatán's gulf coast add old-world romance to Campeche City, the capital of this little-explored state. Among the remnants of Maya settlements that dot the rest of intriguing Campeche, Edzná is the best known and most accessible from the capital.

Updated by
Shelagh
McNally

CAMPECHE, THE LEAST-VISITED and most underrated corner of the Yucatán, is the perfect place for adventure. The people here are friendly and welcoming—the colonial cities and towns retain an air of innocence, and protected biospheres, farmland, and jungle traverse the remaining expanse. The forts of Campeche City have 300-year-old cannons pointing across the Gulf of Mexico, relics from pirate days that give the city an aura of romance and history. Beyond its walls, the ancient pyramids and ornate temples of ancient Maya kingdoms—some of the most important discoveries in the Maya empire to date—lie waiting in tropical forests.

The terrain of the State of Campeche varies, from the northeastern flatlands to the rolling mountains of the south. More than 60% of the territory is covered by jungle, which is filled with precious mahogany and cedar. The Gulf Stream keeps temperatures at about 26°C (78°F) year-round, but the humid, tropical climate is eased by evening breezes. Campeche's economy is based on agriculture, fishing, logging, salt, tourism, and, since the 1970s, hydrocarbons—it is the largest producer of oil in Mexico. Currently there are 90 oil platforms dotting the Campeche coast, but most of the oil industry is concentrated at the western end of the state, near Ciudad del Carmen. There was talk of developing more offshore drills at Campeche City, but since it was named a UNESCO World Heritage site in 1999, this is unlikely to happen.

Campeche City's location on the gulf played a pivotal role in its history. Ah-Kin-Pech (Maya for "lord of the serpent tick")—from which the Spanish name of Campeche is derived—was the capital of an Indian chieftainship long before the Spaniards arrived in 1517. Earlier explorers had visited the area, but it was not until 1540 that the conquerors—led by Francisco de Montejo, and later his son—established a real foothold at Campeche (originally called San Francisco de Campeche, using it as a base for their conquest of the peninsula.

Because Campeche City was the only port and shipyard on the gulf, the Spanish ships, loaded with their rich cargoes of plunder from the Maya, Aztec, and other indigenous civilizations, dropped anchor here en route from Veracruz to Cuba, New Orleans, and Spain. News of this wealth spread, and soon the shores were overrun with pirates. From the mid-1500s to the early 1700s, such notorious corsairs as Diego the Mulatto, Lorenzillo, Peg Leg, Henry Morgan, and Barbillas swooped down repeatedly from their base on Tris—or Isla de Términos, as Isla del Carmen was then known—pillaging and burning the city and massacring its people.

Finally, after years of appeals to the Spanish crown, the people received the funds to build a protective wall around the city, with four gates and eight bastions. For some time thereafter, the city thrived on its exports, especially *palo de tinte*—a dyewood used by the nascent European textile industry—but also hardwoods, chicle, salt, and henequen. However, when the port of Sisal on the northern Yucatán coast opened in 1811, Campeche's monopoly of the gulf traffic ended, and its economy fell into decline.

The shape of modern-day Campeche City is still defined by its history. Remnants of the wall and other military structures divide it into two main districts: the historical center (where few people live) and the newer residential areas. Because the city was long preoccupied with defense, colonial architecture is less flamboyant here than elsewhere in Mexico. Churches are more subdued, flagstone streets are narrow because of the confines of the walls, and houses emphasize the practical over the decorative. The face of the city has changed over the centuries: walls were torn down, bastions demolished, and landfill added to make room for expansion. Nonetheless, an aura of antiquity remains. By decree, no more colonial structures are allowed to be destroyed, so the landmarks that still stand are here to stay.

Most of the state's 535,185 residents live in villages and small towns, where Maya traditions still reign. The countryside is dotted with windmills and fields of oranges, tobacco, sugarcane, rice, indigo, maize, and cocoa. Wildlife flourishes here, too: jaguars and deer, tapir, and armadillos roam free, while the sea is rich with shrimp, barracuda, swordfish, and other catch.

The population of Campeche has changed in recent years. Many refugees from Guatemala have returned home, and there has been an influx of Chol Maya homesteaders, relocated from Chiapas after the Zapatista uprising. Many of the newcomers have settled on the southern edge of the Calakmul Biosphere Reserve.

Pleasures and Pastimes

Architecture
Nowhere in the Yucatán does Spanish colonial history feel more immediate than in the city of Campeche. An ongoing project under the direction of the Instituto Nacional de Antropología y Historia (INAH, the National Institute of Anthropology and History), funded by Petroleo Mexico (Pemex, Mexico's government-owned petroleum monopoly), and the municipal, state, and federal governments, has restored the facades of many of the city's 16th- to 19th-century houses and civic and religious buildings. To date, more than 1,600 facades have been rescued and repainted in subtle hues such as butter yellow, dill green, olive green, tan, peach, and blue-gray—usually trimmed in cream or white. Heritage blends easily with pragmatism in the capital; many historical buildings now house hotels, photocopy stores, boutiques, bakeries, and schools. Yet the prevalence of architecture from an earlier era makes this charming city more evocative of its colonial past and much less self-conscious than other preserved historic districts.

Dining
There is nothing fancy about Campeche's restaurants, but the regional cuisine is renowned throughout Mexico—particularly the fish and shellfish stews, cream soups, shrimp cocktails, squid and octopus, crabs' legs, *panuchos* (tortillas covered with refried beans and topped with chopped onion and shredded turkey or chicken), and other specialties. Unusual seafood delicacies include the famous baby shrimp from the coastal town of Champotón; *pan de cazón* (baby shark cooked, shredded, and layered with tortillas, tomato sauce, and black beans); red snapper wrapped in banana leaves; *camarones al coco* (fried shrimp with a crispy layer of coconut, served with applesauce); *pulpo con tinto* (octopus marinated in its own ink); and crayfish claws. Another popular dish is *pollo alcaparrado* (chicken with a sauce of capers, olives, saffron, and chilies). *Botanas* (tapas) include *papadzules* (tortillas stuffed with hard-boiled eggs and covered with a pumpkin and tomato sauce), fruit conserves in syrup with chili peppers, and ceviche.

Fruits are served fresh, added to breads, made into juice and liqueurs, or marinated in rum or vinegar. Look for mango, papaya, *zapote* (sapodilla), *mamey sapote* (a sweet, fleshy fruit the size of a mango), *guanabana* (soursop), tamarind, melon, pineapple, and coconut, to name only a few. Because regional produce is plentiful, most restaurants fall into the $ to $$ price categories. Casual dress—though not always shorts—is fine in restaurants throughout Campeche, and reservations are not required. The ambience may be informal, but the service at restaurants is usually quite attentive.

CATEGORY	COST*
$$$	over $10
$$	$6–$10
$	under $6

*per person for a main course at dinner

Ecotourism

The state of Campeche is quickly becoming the center for ecotourism in the Yucatán, with three ecological reserves. In the northeast is the Reserva Ecologica Peténes, which encompasses the coastline and the archaeological site of Isla Jaina. To the west is the Reserva Ecologica Laguna de Terminos, a large area covering the rivers, lagoons, mangroves, and forest just south of Laguna de Terminos. Southern Campeche contains one of the last primeval rain forests in Mexico, now legally protected under UNESCO's Man and the Biosphere program as the Calakmul Biosphere Reserve. It adjoins the much larger Maya Biosphere Reserve across the Guatemalan border, as well as a smaller reserve in Belize. The deep forest in the heart of the reserve is almost impossible to reach, but the outskirts afford plenty of opportunities to see a wide range of orchids and jungle wildlife, including spider monkeys, peccaries, boa constrictors, and hundreds of species of birds. Thanks to the efforts of the current government, in response to the destruction of certain parts in Campeche by the petroleum industry, the state has emerged as one of most environmentally aware regions of Mexico. Primarily an agricultural society, Campeche hasn't experienced urban sprawl or global commercialization—so it still has something left to preserve. For the most part, the people of Campeche, with cultural traditions of respect for the land still intact, are supportive of ecotourism. The conservation movement is still in its infancy, but already there has been rapid growth—all of the ruins have ecological bathrooms, and many members of the *ejidos* (land collectives) have participated in government-sponsored ecotourism workshops, seminars, and training courses.

Lodging

Hotels in Campeche City tend to be either expensive accommodations along the waterfront, with air-conditioning, restaurants, and other amenities common to high-rise hotels, or small downtown lodgings offering mainly ceiling fans and a no-credit-card policy. The most worthy of those in the latter category are charming little hotels in refurbished Porfiriano buildings, dating from Porfirio Díaz's dictatorship (1876–1911).

CATEGORY	COST*
$$$$	over $150
$$$	$80–$150
$$	$20–$80
$	under $20

*All prices are for a standard double room, excluding service and 15% tax.

Ruins

A thousand years ago, as today, the Maya were a diverse race. Of all the states in the peninsula, Campeche has the most Maya ruins, with several styles completely different from anything found in the state of Yucatán or Quintana Roo. The Chenes style, found in central and southern Campeche, features facades with elaborate geometric patterns and giant masks of jaguars, serpents, crocodiles, and birds. Doorways look like the open mouth of monsters or the god Itzamná. Passing through the jaws of the beast was a symbolic act of rejuvenation; Maya priests entered the doorway to travel through secret underground passageways and staircases that lead to the top of the pyramid. Spectators would watch the priest disappear into the underground and emerge atop the pyramids. The Río Bec style, found in the southern rain forest, incorporates many features of the Chenes style but has a signature characteristic—three towers of equal height. Roof combs and an architectural trick called false perspective make the towers seem larger than they actually are. The Río Bec style also borrowed its large platforms and plazas from the Petén style. The ruins of Calakmul stand alone as a pure version of the Petén style.

While most of the roads have been much improved, visiting the ruins requires driving hundreds of highway miles to the most remote part of the Yucatán Peninsula—not for the faint-hearted but ideal for adventurers. Entrance to all ruins is free Sunday and holidays.

Exploring Campeche

Campeche City, the most accessible place in the state, makes a good hub for exploring other areas, many of which lack more than basic restaurants and primitive lodgings, if any. Bring your Spanish-English dictionary with you, since little English is spoken throughout the state and you need to speak at least rudimentary Spanish. For purposes of exploration, the sights in the state of Campeche are arranged in three distinct regions: the northern interior along Routes 261 and 180, containing the ruins of Edzná and other ancient cities as well as many modern Maya villages that can be visited easily en route between Campeche City and Mérida or Uxmal; the southwestern coast along Route 180— the only part of the Campeche coastline that is accessible by a continuous road—with several small beach resorts and fishing villages that are all but eclipsed by oil industry development; and the southern interior along Route 186, a remote rain-forest area with numerous large Maya ruins that are steadily becoming more user-friendly with better facilities. Route 186 ends in Chetumal, the capital of Quintana Roo. Campeche's ruins are the subject of extensive research, thanks to a 1995 government grant, and a number of excavations at various ruins are under way. The ruins are also more accessible than ever, as an excellent paved, two-lane highway now links southeastern Hopelchén and the Chenes ruins to the Río Bec sites in the south.

Numbers in the text correspond to numbers in the margin and on the State of Campeche and Campeche City maps.

Great Itineraries

While it may sound dauntingly ambitious to accomplish the Campeche City tour in one day, many of the sights described here can be seen in just a few minutes. For a more leisurely approach, schedule two days. Traveling throughout the state of Campeche could take from two to five days, depending on how much you want to explore on and off the beaten path.

IF YOU HAVE 1 DAY

Almost all interesting sights are within the compact historical district. You might want to begin or end your day in Campeche with a tram tour of the city's main sights. Another way to get a historical overview is to begin at the **Baluarte de San Carlos** ⑬ at the southern edge of the Ciudad Viejo for an overview of the history of the port. Then head north into the heart of the old city center and take in its lovely colonial and Porfiriano buildings, ending up at the pretty **Parque Principal** ② for a stop at the **Catedral** ③. Take a break for lunch at one of the small restaurants or cafés close to the **Mercado Municipal.** Everything closes for at least two hours between 2 and 4 for siesta, so you may want to head

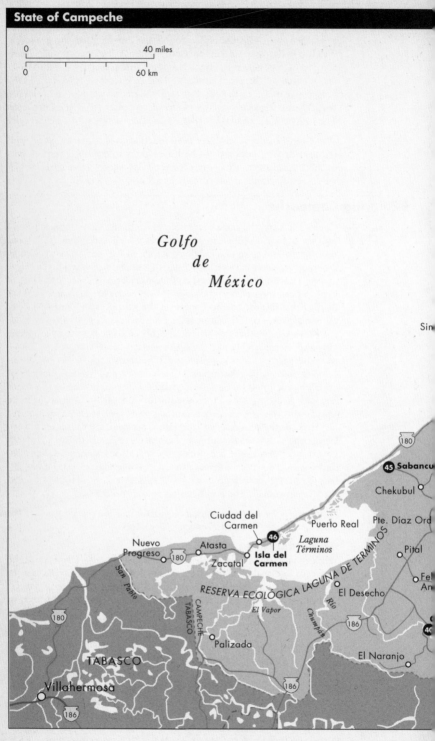

0   40 miles

0   60 km

Golfo
de
México

Sin

180

45 Sabancu

Chekubul

Ciudad del
Carmen

Puerto Real   Pte. Díaz Ord

46

Laguna
Términos

Nuevo
Progreso   180   Atasta

Zacatal   **Isla del**
           Carmen

Pital

Fel
An

San Pablo

RESERVA ECOLÓGICA LAGUNA DE TÉRMINOS

El Desecho

CAMPECHE

TABASCO

El Vapor

Río Champán

186

4C

180

Palizada

TABASCO

El Naranjo

Villahermosa

186

186

back to your hotel and indulge in this fine Mexican tradition or visit the tranquil botanical gardens in the **Baluarte de Santiago** ⑥. After the siesta, when everything, including taxi service, comes to life again, hop in a cab for a late-afternoon visit to the **Fuerte de San Miguel** and its Museum of Maya Culture. On the way back, join the locals on the **malecón** ⑯ and enjoy the sunset or a breezy walk. At 8 o'clock head over to the **Puerta de Tierra** ⑧ and the Baluarte San Juan to view the historical light-and-sound show called "Place of the Sun." Afterward stop for a drink or late dinner on the elegant second-floor balcony of Casa Vieja, a restaurant overlooking the main square.

IF YOU HAVE 3 DAYS

After a day in Campeche City, head inland the next morning to **Edzná** ㉗, a magnificently restored Maya ceremonial center an hour's drive from the city. Return to your Campeche City hotel—aside from a refurbished hacienda, accommodations are nonexistent around Edzná—and set out the next day (early) to the **Hopelchén** ㉘ region, beyond Edzná, where you can explore the little-known Maya temples at **Hochob** ㉜, **Santa Rosa Xtampak** ㉚, and **Dzibilnocac** ㉛, as well as **Las Grutas de Xtacumbilxunaan** ㉙, one of the larger cave systems on the peninsula. From Hopelchén it is as easy to continue north toward Uxmal and Mérida as it is to return to Campeche City.

IF YOU HAVE 7 DAYS

With seven days, you can explore the southern part of the state in addition to the capital and the northern region. From Hopelchén—you can stay overnight in its very basic accommodations if you've spent a day in the area exploring—drive three hours south to **Xpujil** ㉝ and the southern archaeological sites. East along Highway 186, across the base of the Yucatán Peninsula toward Chetumal, are a number of impressive Maya sites. To appreciate the natural beauty of the rain forest and ruins, plan to spend at least two or three days at the one small ecotourism resort in the area. **Balamkú** ㊳, **Becán** ㉞, **Chicanná** ㉟, and **Hormiguero** ㊱ are just off the highway, and you can explore them along with Xpujil in a day and a half. Local guides can take you to more remote sights such as **Río Bec** ㊲ or **Calakmul** ㊴, deep in the forests of the Calakmul Biosphere Reserve. From the Xpujil area it is easy now to return to Campeche City via the Escárcega–Champotón highway, with a stopover at **El Tigre** ㊶, a newly explored ruin one hour south of Escárcega. Or you can just as easily continue to the Caribbean coast, since you are right across the state line from Quintana Roo.

When to Tour Campeche

Both the capital and outlying villages of Campeche state, with their large Maya population, celebrate the Day of the Dead from October 31 to November 2 with special fervor because it corresponds to a similar ancient Maya observance. Colorfully embroidered regional dress, street celebrations, special meals, and altars of offerings to deceased loved ones are typical. If you can't make it to one of the small towns for this celebration, stop in at the main plaza in Campeche City, where altars from different regions of the state are set up for the festival.

An event called Sábadito Alegre (Happy Saturday) was introduced in November 1997 by the tourist office. From 7 to 10:30 on Saturday evening, the streets around the main square are closed to traffic and filled with folk and popular dance performances, singers, comics, handicrafts, and food and drink stands. Don't miss them—the entertainment is often first-rate and always free.

November also marks the end of the rainy season (the strongest rains fall July–September), when the risk of hurricanes is over and the rain forests of the interior are at their most luxuriant. Anytime from November through March is good for traveling, but as elsewhere in Mexico, the Christmas and Holy Week holidays mean extremely crowded hotels and public transportation. The rainy season slows travel down and makes exploring the more remote ruins a bit treacherous.

CAMPECHE CITY

The city of Campeche has a time-weathered and lovely feel to it—no contrived, ultramodern tourist glitz here—just a friendly city by the sea (population 270,000) that is proud of its heritage and welcomes all to share in it. Residents are extremely appreciative of their hometown's transformation from a run-down, poverty-stricken capital to a world-class historical site. The refurbishing of more than 1,600 houses and buildings has left Campeche looking much as it did 350 years ago. With little prompting, locals point out the beauty of the city and ask how you are enjoying your visit. This good-humored, open-minded attitude is described as *campechano,* an adjective that means "easygoing and cheerful." Mexicans still make up the majority of vacationers here. The city's biggest appeal is its history—you can easily imagine pirates attacking. The coastline is cluttered with commercial fishing operations, and there are a few popular public beaches. Though it is easy to take in Campeche in a day or two, a longer stay allows you to absorb the traditional lifestyle—and maybe find a favorite café near the plaza.

Because it has been walled (though not successfully fortified) since 1686, most of the historic downtown is neatly contained in an area measuring just five blocks by nine blocks. Today, for the most part, streets running north–south are even-numbered, and those running east–west are odd-numbered. The city is easily navigable—on foot, that is. With its narrow cobblestone roads and lack of parking spaces, driving here is a frustrating exercise. Walking, on the other hand, is a pleasure, with historical monuments and evocative name plaques above street numbers serving as handy guideposts. Without the large-scale tourism that has sustained Cancún and Mérida, Campeche was hit harder than any other part of the Yucatán by Mexico's 1995 recession (and by subsequent declines in petroleum prices) but is showing definite signs of recovery. People are once again proud of their state and their homes.

On strategic corners surrounding the old city, or Viejo Campeche, stand the seven remaining *baluartes* (bastions) in various stages of disrepair. These were once connected by a 3-km (2-mi) wall in a hexagonal fortification that was built to safeguard the city against the pirates who continually ransacked it. Only short stretches of the wall still stand, and two stone archways—one facing the sea, the other the land—are all that remain of the four gates that once provided the only means of access to Campeche. Although these walls helped protect the residents, it was not until 1771, when Fuerte de San Miguel was built on a hilltop on the outskirts of town, that pirates finally ceased their attacks.

Campeche was one of few walled cities in North or Central America and was built along the traditional lines of defensive Spanish settlements, such as Santo Domingo in the Dominican Republic, Cartagena in Colombia, and Portobello in Panama. The walls also served as a class demarcation. Within them lived the ruling elite. Outside were the barrios of the Indians who aided the conquistadors and whose descendants continued to serve the upper class. The mulattoes brought as slaves from Cuba also lived outside the city walls.

A Good Walk

The Ciudad Viejo, the old city center, is the best place to start a walking tour, beginning with the **Baluarte de la Soledad** ①, which has a small Maya stelae museum. From the nearby **Parque Principal** ②, the city's central plaza, take a stroll across the street to view some of the Yucatán Peninsula's most stately Spanish colonial architecture, including the **Catedral** ③ and the adjacent **Casa Seis** ④. On Calle 8 between Calles 51 and 53 is the **Mansión Carvajal** ⑤; **Baluarte de Santiago** ⑥ is about a block to the north. Head south on Calle 51 to the small, well-fortified **Baluarte de San Pedro** ⑦, at Circuito Baluartes and Av. Gobernadores. Walk west along Calle 18 to **Puerta de Tierra** ⑧ and the Baluarte San Juan, and then take **Calle 59** ⑨ past the beautiful **Iglesia de San Francisquito** ⑩. Proceed west along Calle 8 for a look at the contrasting, modernistic designs of the **Palacio del Gobierno** ⑪ and the **Congreso del Estado** ⑫. A bit farther along Calle 8 past Calle 63 is **Baluarte de San Carlos** ⑬, one of the remaining sections of the Puerta de Tierra. From there, head to the **Ex-Templo de San José** ⑭ and then the **Iglesia de San Román** ⑮. Both are considered masterpieces of colonial religious architecture. Finish the walk along the beachfront **malecón** ⑯.

Sights to See

★ ❶ **Baluarte de la Soledad.** Originally built to protect the **Puerte de Mar** (sea door), one of the four city gates, through which all seafarers were forced to pass, this bastion is on the south side of Parque Principal. Because it stands alone, without any wall to shore it up, it resembles a Roman triumphal arch. The largest of the bastions, this one has comparatively complete parapets and embrasures that offer a sweeping view of the cathedral, municipal buildings, and the 16th- to 19th-century houses along Calle 8. Inside, the **Museo de las Estelas** (Stelae Museum) has artifacts that include a well-preserved sculpture of a man wearing an owl mask, columns from Edzná and Isla Jaina, and 20 well-proportioned Maya stelae from ruins throughout Campeche. ⊠ *Calles 8 and 57,* ☎ *no phone.* ☒ *$2.* ⊙ *Mon. 8–2, Tues.–Sat. 8–8, Sun. 8–6.*

❸ **Baluarte de San Carlos.** Named for Charles II, King of Spain, this bastion, where Calle 8 curves around and becomes Circuito Baluartes, houses the **Sala de las Fortificaciones** (Chamber of the Fortifications), containing scale models of the original defense system and the **Museo de la Ciudad** (City Museum), with photographs and maps of the city as it developed. Don't miss the dungeon inside the bastion (now a gift shop), where captured pirates were jailed, or the rooftop ocean view, especially beautiful at sunset. ⊠ *Calle 8 at Calle 63, Circuito Baluartes,* ☎ *no phone.* ☒ *Donation.* ⊙ *Weekdays 8–8, Sat. 8–2 and 4–8, Sun. 9–1.*

❼ **Baluarte de San Pedro.** Built in 1686 to protect the city from land attacks by pirates, this bastion's thick walls, flanked by watchtowers, now house a handicrafts and souvenir shop and a satellite office for the Secretary of Tourism, where you can book an English tour guide. Many of the tours to ruins such as Calakmul and Edzná leave from this point. ⊠ *Av. Gobernadores and Circuito Baluartes,* ☎ *no phone.* ☒ *Free.* ⊙ *Mon.–Sat. 9–9.*

❻ **Baluarte de Santiago.** The last of the bastions to be built (1704) has been transformed into the **X'much Haltún Botanical Gardens.** More than 200 plant species from the region are house here, including the *ceiba, campeachy,* and *balche* trees. Although the original bastion was demolished at the turn of the 20th century, then rebuilt in the 1950s, architecturally this fort looks much the same as the others in Campeche— a stone fortress with thick walls, watchtowers, and gunnery slits. ⊠ *Calles 8 and 59, Circuito Baluartes,* ☎ *no phone.* ☒ *Donation.* ⊙ *Weekdays 9–4 and 6:30–8:30, Sat. 9–1 and 5–8, Sun. 9–1.*

Campeche City

TO IGLESIA DE
SAN FRANCISCO

TO FUERTE DE SAN JOSÉ

Mercado
Municipal

Puerta
de Mar

TO FUERTE DE SAN MIGUEL,
CENTRO ECOLOGICO

---

⑨ Calle 59. On this city street, between Calles 8 and 18, once stood some
of Campeche's finest homes, many of them two stories high, with the
ground floors serving as warehouses and the upper floors as resi-
dences. The richest inhabitants built as close to the sea as possible, in
case escape became necessary. (Legend has it that beneath the city a
network of tunnels crisscrossed, linking the eight bastions and providing
temporary refuge from the pirates. Although the tunnel network has
never been found, rumors persist that it once existed.) These days, behind the delicate grillwork and lace curtains, you can glimpse genteel
scenes of Campeche life, with faded lithographs on the dun-color walls
and plenty of antique furniture and gilded mirrors. To see the oldest
houses in Campeche, walk south along Calle 10 past Circuito Baluartes to where it meets the malecón the San Roman neighborhood.

★ **④ Casa Seis** (House No. 6). One of the first colonial homes built in
Campeche, this is now the city's Cultural Center. It has been beautifully restored—the rooms are furnished with original antiques and a
few reproductions to create a replica of a typical 19th-century colonial house. The original frescoes bordering the tops of the walls remain,
some dating from 1500. The courtyard has Moorish architecture offset by lovely 18th-century stained-glass windows; it's used as an exhibit area, with displays of various sites in the city. The two largest
bedrooms have been converted into an art gallery and a bookstore.
There's a small restaurant off the original kitchen area that serves excellent local specialities. ⊠ *Calle 57, across from main plaza,* ☎ *9/816–
1782.* ☞ *Free.* ☼ *Daily 9–9.*

★ **③ Catedral.** It took two centuries (from 1650 to 1850) to finish this
grand building, and as a result, it incorporates both neoclassical and
Renaissance elements. The present cathedral occupies the site of Montejo's original church, which was built in 1540 on what is now Calle

55, between Calles 8 and 10. The simple exterior is capped with two bulbous towers rising on each side of the gracefully curved stone entrances, the fluted pilasters echoing those of the towers. Sculptures of saints in niches recall French Gothic cathedrals. The interior is no less impressive, with a single limestone nave, supported by Doric columns set with Corinthian capitals, arching toward the huge octagonal dome above a black-and-white marble floor. The pièce de résistance, however, is the magnificent Holy Sepulchre, carved from ebony and decorated with a multitude of stamped silver angels. ⊠ *North side of the Plaza Principal.* ☉ *Daily 6–noon and 5:30–7.*

☙ **Centro Ecologico de Campeche.** High on a hill near the San Miguel Fort, this combination zoo, botanical gardens, and playground offers guided flora and fauna tours, games and activities for children, and educational lectures. ⊠ *Av. Escénica s/n,* ☎ *9/811–2528.* ☛ *10¢.* ☉ *Tues.–Fri. 9–1, Sat. 9–1 and 4–8, Sun. 9–4.*

⑫ **Congreso del Estado.** A modernistic building resembling a flying saucer, the State Congress building contains the state legislative offices. There's nothing much to see inside. ⊠ *Calle 8, between Calles 61 and 63, across from Tourist Office.*

⑭ **Ex-Templo de San José.** The Jesuits built this fine Baroque structure in 1756, and today it is the most beautiful of the city's churches. It has a block-long facade and a portal that is completely covered with blue-and-yellow Talavera tiles and crowned with seven narrow stone finials that resemble both the roof combs on many Maya temples and the combs Spanish women used to wear as part of their elaborate hairdos. The former convent school next door is now the **Instituto Campechano,** used for cultural events and art exhibitions. Campeche's first lighthouse, built in 1864, sits atop the right tower. Although it's currently not open to the public, the guard at the Instituto Campechano will let you in to see the church interior. Cultural events are held here Tuesday evening starting at 7. ⊠ *Calle 10 at Calle 65.*

☙ **Fuerte de San José "el Alto."** This lofty fortress—*el alto* means "the tall"—at the opposite end of town from Fuerte de San Miguel, is home to the **Museo de Armas y Barcos** (Museum of Arms and Boats). The displays focus on 18th-century weapons of siege and defense used in the many wars fought against the pirates. Also look for scale ships-in-a-bottle, manuscripts, and religious art. The view is terrific from the top of the ramparts, which were used to spot invading ships. ⊠ *Av. Escénica s/n, south of downtown,* ☎ *no phone.* ☛ *$1.70.* ☉ *Tues.–Sun. 8–8.*

Iglesia de San Francisco. Away from the city center, in a residential neighborhood, stands this beautifully restored church, the oldest one in Campeche. It marks the spot where, some say, the first Mass on the North American continent was held in 1517—though the same claim has been made for Veracruz and Cozumel. One of Cortés's grandsons was baptized here, and the baptismal font still stands. ⊠ *Avs. Miguel Alemán and Mariano Escobedo.* ☉ *Daily 8–noon and 5–7.*

☙ **Fuerte de San Miguel.** The scenic Avenida Ruíz Cortínez near the south end of the city winds its way to a hilltop, where this fort commands one of the grandest views overlooking the city and the Gulf of Mexico. Built in 1771, the fort was positioned to bombard enemy ships with cannonballs. But as soon as it was completed, pirates stopped attacking the city. Its impressive cannons were fired only once, in 1842, when General Santa Anna used Fuerte de San Miguel to put down a revolt by Yucatecan separatists seeking independence from Mexico. The fort houses the **Museo de la Cultura Maya,** which was renovated in

2001. The museum has some world-class exhibits that include Maya mummies and funeral masks, as well as jewelry and pottery found at various tombs in the Calakmul ruins. Also noteworthy are funeral vessels, masks, and figurines from Isla Jaina along with stelae and stucco masks from the Río Bec ruins, and an excellent pottery collection. The gift shop sells replicas of artifacts. ⊠ *Av. Francisco Morazán s/n, north of town center,* ☎ *no phone.* ⌖ *$1.70.* ⊙ *Daily 8–8.*

⑩ Iglesia de San Francisquito (Iglesia de San Roque). With its elaborately carved altars, Baroque columns adorned with gold leaf, and carved, wooden pews and creches with statues of San Francisco, this long, narrow church—built as a convent in 1565—adds to historic Calle 59's old-fashioned beauty. The church was originally called Iglesia de San Francisco, but now some know it only as Iglesia de San Roque—a name derived from the neighborhood in which it lies. ⊠ *Calle 12 at Calle 59.* ⊙ *Daily 8:30–noon and 5–7.*

⑮ Iglesia de San Román. Just outside the intramural boundary in the barrio of the same name, at Calles 10 and Bravo, San Román, with its bulbous bell tower typical of other Yucatán churches, was built to house the *naboríos* (Indians brought by the Spaniards to aid in the conquest and later used as household servants). The barrio, like other neighborhoods, grew up around the church. Built in the early part of the 16th century, the church became central to the lives of the Indians when an ebony image of Christ, the "Black Christ," was brought from Italy in about 1575. The Indians had been skeptical about Christianity, but this Christ figure came to be associated with miracles. The legend goes that a ship that refused to carry the tradesman and his precious statue was wrecked, while the ship that did take him on board reached Campeche in record time. To this day, the Feast of San Román—when the black-wood Christ mounted on a silver filigree cross is carried through the streets as part of a colorful and somber procession—is the biggest celebration of its kind in Campeche. ⊠ *Calles 10 y Bravo.* ⊙ *Daily 7–1 and 3–7.*

⑯ Malecón. A broad sidewalk runs the length of Campeche's waterfront boulevard (the *malecón*), from north of the Hotel Debliz to the southern outskirts of town, along Avenida Ruíz Cortínez. Upgraded and expanded in 2000, this popular landscaped boardwalk has sculptures, rest areas, and fountains that are lit up at night with neon colors. It is popular with joggers, strollers, and families enjoying the cool sea breezes and the view at sunset. On weekend nights, students turn the malecón into a party zone. Some of the best restaurants in the city can be found along this walkway.

⑤ Mansión Carvajal. Built in the early 20th century by one of the wealthiest plantation owners in Yucatán, this eclectic mansion did time as the Hotel Señorial before becoming an office for the state-run Delegacíon Integral de Familia (Family Institute), or DIF. The black-and-white tile floor, Art Nouveau staircase with Carrara marble steps and iron balustrade, and blue-and-white Moorish arcades are reminders of city's heyday, when Campeche was the peninsula's only port. ⊠ *Calle 10 No. 584, between Calles 51 and 53,* ☎ *9/816–7644.* ⌖ *Free.* ⊙ *Weekdays 8–1 and 4–7.*

Mercado Municipal. To take in the heart of a true Mexican city, stroll through the market where locals congregate to shop for seafood, produce, and housewares. Beside the market is a small yellow bridge aptly named **Punte de Perro** (Dog Bridge)—four white plaster dogs guard the area. Try to arrive early, before it gets uncomfortably crowded. ⊠ *Av. Baluartes Este, between Calles 51 and 55.* ⊙ *Daily dawn–dusk.*

⓫ Palacio del Gobierno. One block inland from the malecón, on Avenida 16 de Septiembre, the flying saucer–shape Congreso del Estado (legislative building) shares a broad plaza with this much taller building, dubbed El Tocadiscos ("The Jukebox") by locals because of its outlandish facade. The eccentric architecture of these two capital buildings stands in odd contrast to the graceful colonial skyline of the adjacent Ciudad Viejo historic district. ⊠ *Av. 16 de Septiembre y Calle 61.*

❷ Parque Principal. The centerpiece of the old city, this park is also known as the Plaza de la Independencia. It is a focal point for many of the town's events, including concerts and dance performances held on weekends. There is a lovely café under an old-fashioned gazebo in the center where you can watch the city's residents out for an evening stroll. ⊠ *Bounded by Calles 10, 8, 55, and 57.*

★ ☾ **❽ Puerta de Tierra (Land Gate).** Old Campeche ends here, at the only one of the four city gates with its basic structure intact. The walls, arches, and gates were refurbished in 1987. The stone arch intercepts a stretch of the partially crenulated wall, 26 ft high and 10 ft thick, that once encircled the city. You can walk along the full length of the wall to the **Baluarte San Juan,** where there are some excellent views of both the old and new city. The staircase leads down to an old well, underground storage area, and dungeon. There is a two-hour light show offered at Puerta de Tierra in Spanish and English, from Tuesday through Saturday at 8:30 PM, that includes a torchlight walk along the wall and a visit to the underground chambers at Baluarte San Juan. The spectacle is performed by local musicians and dancers and gives an excellent historical overview of Campeche. The schedule is sometimes reduced in low season, so check with the tourist office. ⊠ *Calles 18 and 59.* 🎟 *$1.70.* ☉ *Daily 8–5.*

Dining and Lodging

$$–$$$ ✕ **La Pigua.** A favorite with local professionals lingering over long
★ lunches, La Pigua is arguably the best seafood restaurant in town, with the most pleasant ambience. The restaurant's two long glass walls form a terrarium of trees and plants. A truly ambitious lunch would start with a seafood cocktail or plate of cold crab claws, followed by camarones al coco and, for dessert, local peaches drenched in sweet liqueurs. ⊠ *Av. Miguel Alemán 197-A,* ☎ *9/811–1365. MC, V. No dinner.*

$–$$ ✕ **Casa Vieja.** Look for the hidden stairway on the east side of the plaza next to the Modatela store, and climb to this fabulous nightspot overlooking Campeche's main plaza. Dinner outside on the balcony is a perfect way to enjoy one of the city's savviest eateries. The Cuban owner has created an international menu of pastas, salads, and regional food, and even the music (occasionally live) is modern and international. Delicious desserts are prepared daily. ⊠ *Calle 10 No. 319 (altos), between Calles 57 and 55,* ☎ *9/811–1311. No credit cards. No lunch.*

$–$$ ✕ **Cenaduría los Portales.** Campechano families come here to enjoy a light supper, perhaps a *sandwich claveteado* (honey-flavored ham or turkey sandwich) or panuchos along with a typical drink, *horchata* (cold rice water flavored with cinnamon). The dining area is a colonial courtyard with tables decked out in checkered tablecloths. After eating you can stroll around Plaza San Francisco to walk off your meal. ⊠ *Calle 10 No. 86, at Portales San Francisco, 8 blocks northeast of Plaza Principal,* ☎ *9/816–5298. No credit cards.*

$–$$ ✕ **Chez Fernando.** In an old colonial house, this café-style restaurant
★ offers French-style fresh pastas, salads, fish, chicken, and steak. The lasagna Florentine, pollo Dijon, and fettuccine gambetti are all excellent. The chocolate mousse is the best in the state. The decor, like the

food, is a departure from Campechano tradition—purple walls with watercolor sketches of France and French music in the background. ⊠ *Calle 12, between Calles 51 and 53,* ☎ *9/816–3972. No credit cards.*

$–$$ ✕ **El Guacamayo.** One of the oldest restaurants in Campeche (1947), this eatery is popular with locals and tourists. It serves regional specialties such as *cochinita pibíl* (coconut shrimp) and excellent cream soups on the outdoor patio or indoors in the hacienda-style dining room. After your dinner be sure to visit the mascot—a colorful Guacamayo bird. ⊠ *Av. Miguel Alemán 143,* ☎ *9/816–4636. AE, MC, V.*

$–$$ ✕ **Marganzo.** Traditional Campeche cuisine is served by a tradition-
★ ally attired waitstaff at this colorful and rustic restaurant a half block south of the plaza. Recommended is the *pompano en escabeche* (grilled fish with chilies and orange juice), as well as the fresh shrimp dishes. ⊠ *Calle 8 No. 267, between Calles 57 and 59,* ☎ *9/811–3898. AE, MC, V.*

$ ✕ **Hot Beach Pizza.** The two branches of this restaurant live up to their name: both are close to the beach, and the pizza is hot. Popular pies are the double-cheese with jalapeños or the *campechano* (ham, ham, and more ham). Vegetarians, take heed—all of the pizzas are loaded with meat. Open 7 AM to 11 PM, Hot Beach delivers to your hotel room. ⊠ *Av. Justo Sierra Méndez and malecón,* ☎ *9/816–6006 or 9/811–1133. No credit cards;* ⊠ *Bajos Portals San Francisco, at the Colonial Arc,* ☎ *9/811–3131 or 9/816–5565. No credit cards.*

$ ✕ **Malinches.** Tacos, tortillas, soups, and salads are served at this popular eatery along the malecón. The food is fresh and the prices low. ⊠ *Av. Justo Sierra Méndez and malecón,* ☎ *9/811–3205. No credit cards.*

$ ✕ **La Palapa del Balneario Popular.** One of the few seaside restaurants in Campeche, this place has live music and great ambience. Sit and watch the fishing boats on the gulf or enjoy a drink while the sun sets. Naturally, the fish and seafood cocktails are the freshest in town. ⊠ *Av. Insurgentes, along the malecón,* ☎ *9/816–5918. AE, MC, V.*

$ ✕ **La Parroquia.** The large entrance to La Parroquia, which faces Calle 55, is the best place in town for people-watching. Open 24 hours, this restaurant is a real locals' den—a comfortable family place with plastic tablecloths, a large menu, slow service, and televisions tuned to Mexican soccer. You can feast on inexpensive fried pompano, breaded shrimp, pan de cazón, or spaghetti or just have a sandwich. Beer and tequila are also available. ⊠ *Calle 55 No. 8, between Calles 10 and 12,* ☎ *9/816–8086. No credit cards.*

$ ✕ **Restaurant Campeche.** Since its renovation in 2000, this restaurant directly across from the central plaza has been transformed into a bright, clean eatery offering hearty breakfasts, lunches, and dinners of Mexican and regional dishes. The only downside is the cranky waitstaff left over from older days. ⊠ *Calle 57,* ☎ *no phone. No credit cards.*

$$$ 🏨 **Del Mar Hotel.** Formerly the Ramada Inn, this is the fanciest hotel
★ in town, even if by international standards it is quite average. It has many amenities, including bathtubs. Rooms are fairly large, with tasteful drapes and floor tiles, rattan furniture, color cable TV, and balconies that overlook the pool or the bay across the street. The lobby coffee shop, El Poquito, serves excellent meals, and Lafitte's, the bar-restaurant, offers room service until 2 AM. ⊠ *Av. Ruíz Cortínez 51 (on the waterfront), 24000,* ☎ *9/816–2233,* 𝐅𝐀𝐗 *9/811–1618. 138 rooms, 11 suites. Restaurant, coffee shop, air-conditioning, room service, pool, travel services, free parking. AE, MC, V.*

$$ 🏨 **Baluartes.** Sandwiched between the waterfront malecón and the Puerto del Mar (gateway to the old city), this big, square hotel is much prettier inside than out. Rooms are decorated in cool blue tones, and bathrooms have white tiles. All rooms have air-conditioning, double beds, phones, satellite TV, and ocean views. Baluartes has a huge pool facing the sea and is within walking distance of the historic district. ⊠ *Av. 16 de Septiembre 128, at Av. Ruíz Cortínez, 24000,* ☎ *9/816–3911,* FAX *9/816–2410. 94 rooms, 8 suites. Restaurant, bar, coffee shop, air-conditioning, pool, travel services, free parking. MC, V.*

$$ 🖭 **Debliz.** East of the center, this large hotel caters to tour groups. Although the exterior and lobby look like an office building, the pool and deck area is quite lovely. Rooms are decorated in soft pastels, with two double beds, cable TV, and balconies that look out onto the pool. There's also a decent restaurant and bar. You have to take a cab to the historical center—it's just a bit too far to walk. ⊠ *Av. Las Palmas 55, 24000,* ☎ *9/815–2222,* FAX *9/815–2277. 143 rooms. Restaurant, bar, snack bar, air-conditioning, pool, parking (fee). AE, MC, V.*

$$ 🖭 **Del Paseo.** A block from the ocean, this pretty hotel lies in the quiet neighborhood of San Román. Rooms are tasteful and comfortable, with modern rattan furniture, one double bed, a balcony, and cable TV. A lovely glass-roof atrium with park benches and plants shelters the hotel complex. ⊠ *Calle 8 No. 215, 24000,* ☎ *9/811–0077 or 9/811–0100,* FAX *9/811–0097. 48 rooms, 2 suites. Restaurant, bar, air-conditioning, hair salon, room service, car rental, free parking. AE, MC, V.*

$$ 🖭 **Hotel America.** A converted colonial home, this hotel has three levels of rooms that open onto large corridors with a dramatic black-and-white checked floor, offsetting the white Moorish arches. The rooms all have two double beds, ceiling fans, local television, and bamboo furniture. Rooms facing the street have balconies but are noisier. This is one of the few hotels in the center with parking. ⊠ *Calle 10 No. 252, 24000,* ☎ *9/816–4588,* FAX *9/816–4576. 52 rooms. Fans, parking (fee). AE, MC, V.*

$ 🖭 **Colonial.** The former home of a high-ranking army lieutenant, this
★ building dates back to 1812 but was converted into a hotel in the 1940s, when its wonderful colorful tiles were added. All rooms are delightfully different, as befits a colonial mansion, with ceiling fans or air-conditioning (in four of the rooms), cool cotton bedding, good mattresses, tile bathrooms, and window screens. Most rooms still have the original telephones and antique plumbing (which works quite well), adding to the romance of the hotel. Rooms 16, 18, 27, and 28 have wonderful views of the cathedral and city at night. Public areas include two leafy patios, a small sun roof, and a sitting room on the second floor. ⊠ *Calle 14 No. 122, between Calles 55 and 57, 24000,* ☎ *9/816–2222. 30 rooms. Air-conditioning, fans. No credit cards.*

$ 🖭 **Hotel López.** A pleasant place, and a good choice if you're on a budget, this cheerful little three-story hotel has balconies in an undulating design and smallish standard rooms lit by fluorescent lights with tiny closets, armoires, luggage stands, and easy chairs. Bathrooms are small but clean. The lobby feels like a living room in a private home. ⊠ *Calle 12 No. 189, between Calles 61 and 63, 24000,* ☎ FAX *9/816–3344 or 9/816–3021. 39 rooms. Air-conditioning, fans. No credit cards.*

$ 🖭 **Posada Del Angel.** Directly across from the Catedral is this small 13-room hotel with clean, basic rooms that have one double bed and overhead fans. The staff is friendly and everything is within walking distance. ⊠ *Calle 10 between Calles 53 and 55, 24000,* ☎ *9/816–7718. 13 rooms. Fans. No credit cards.*

$ 🖭 **El Regis.** This seven-room hotel is a good bargain and a mere two blocks from the plaza. Though a bit run-down, the Regis is a lovely old two-story colonial home with a huge wooden front door, high ceilings, and an airy inner atrium. All rooms are spic-and-span, with black-and-white tile floors, two double beds, and a cupboard closet. The low points are an unfriendly staff, tiny bathrooms, poor lighting, and weak air-conditioning. The front doors are locked at 11, but the night watchman will let you in. ⊠ *Calle 12 No. 148, between Calles*

55 and 57, 24000, ☎ *9/816–3175. 7 rooms. Air-conditioning, fans. No credit cards.*

Nightlife and the Arts

Discos

If you're in the mood to dance, try Campeche's discos. **KY8** (✉ Calle 8 between Calles 59 and 61, ☎ no phone) plays dance music popular with locals. The high-tech **Millennium** (✉ Av. Resurgimiento 112, ☎ 9/818–4555) offers laser shows and dance music on Friday and Saturday. The largest dance club in Campeche is **Platform 21** (✉ Av. López Mateos, ☎ no phone), north of the city and open from Wednesday through Saturday nights. You need to take a taxi to get here.

Movies

The smallest of the two major movie theaters in downtown Campeche is **Cine Estelar** (✉ Av. Miguel Alemán and Calle 49-B, ☎ 9/816–5157). **Cinema Hollywood** ✉ Manzana 2, ☎ 9/816–1452) is close to the malecón and has six large screens showing the latest blockbuster movies. Most movies are in English with Spanish subtitles, except for children's movies, which are always dubbed in Spanish.

Outdoor Sports and Activities

Hunting, fishing, and birding are popular throughout the state of Campeche. Contact **Don José Sansores** at the Snook Inn in Champotón (✉ Calle 30 No. 1, ☎ FAX 9/828–0018) to arrange sportfishing or wildlife photo excursions in the Champotón area. **Francisco Javier Hernandez Romero** (✉ La Pigua restaurant, Av. Miguel Alemán 179-A, ☎ 9/811–3365) can arrange boat or fishing trips to the Peténes Ecological Reserve. To enjoy a tour of Campeche Bay and the surrounding area, contact the **Marina Yacht Club** (✉ Av. Resurgimiento 120, ☎ FAX 9/981–1990. The 90-minute tours leave Tuesday–Sunday 9 AM–5 PM.

Shopping

Because Campeche is a seaport, ships-in-a-bottle, tacky statues made of seashells, and mother-of-pearl and black coral jewelry are everywhere. Note that buying black coral is environmentally incorrect, since the harvesting of the coral destroys the reef that takes thousands of years to grow. In recognition of its endangered status, there are some restrictions regarding bringing black coral into the United States. You can find a good selection of basketry, straw hats, embroidered cloth, and clay trinkets.

Local Crafts

In a lovely old mansion, the government-run **Casa de Artesanía Tukulna** (✉ Calle 10 No. 333, between Calles 59 and 61, ☎ 9/816–9098) sells well-made embroidered dresses, blouses, pillow coverings, regional dress for men and women, hammocks, Campeche's famous Panama hats, posters, books on Campeche ecology in Spanish, jewelry, baskets, and stucco reproductions of Maya motifs. The house is beautiful, with arched doorways, black-and-white tile floors, and chandeliers; it's worth a visit if only to admire the interior. The shop is open Monday–Saturday 9–8 and Sunday 10–2. The expensive **Veleros** (✉ Plaza Comercial Ah-Kin-Pech, ☎ 981/1–24–46), closed Sunday, is owned by craftsman David Pérez. It stocks his miniature ships, seashells, furniture with nautical motifs, and jewelry fashioned from sanded and polished bull's horns. The horns look much like tortoiseshell in thickness and color, though not as beautiful. But since it's no longer legal to hunt turtles or to import tortoiseshell to the United States, the horn is a good, legal alternative. Pérez's first shop, **Artesanía Típica Naval** (✉ Calle 8 No. 259, ☎ 9/816–5708), is still thriving, but it's much smaller and more cramped than the mall store. Neither shop accepts credit cards.

Shopping Districts and Malls

Campeche City has two large, modern shopping malls within walking distance of each other. The **Plaza Comercial Ah-Kin-Pech** (✉ Av. Pedro Sainz de Barnada, at Av. Ruíz Cortínez), on the waterfront, has a variety of boutiques, clothing, and souvenir shops. **Plaza Universidad** (✉ Av. Agustín Melgar, at Av. Universidad) has a number of good boutiques. The **Plaza del Mar** (✉ Av. Ruíz Cortínez) is home to San Francisco de Asis, a large grocery store, and a number of specialty stores. Visit the **Municipal Market** (✉ Av. Circuito Baluartes Este, between Calles 51 and 55) for food and crafts items.

ROUTE 180: LA RUTA DE LOS ARTESANOS

The so-called short route to Mérida (192 km, or 119 mi) takes you past several picturesque villages, where many of the artisans in the state produce Campeche's famous handicrafts. For this reason it's been named "The Artists' Route." It's also known as the Camino Real, or "Royal Highway."

San Francisco Koben

㉑ *30 km (19 mi) north of Campeche, along Rte. 180 toward Mérida.*

You can find some real bargains in this small village that has become a roadside market. Hammocks, textiles, hats, clothing, and bottled preserves are sold here. Twenty-nine kilometers (18 miles) north on Route 180 is the picturesque village of **Tenabo.** The town of **Pomuch,** famous for its breads, is north of Tenabo. Be sure to stop and try a cinnamon, anise, vanilla, or cheese loaf.

Hecelchakán

㉒ *60 km (37 mi) north of Campeche, along Rte. 180 toward Mérida.*

A beautiful 15th-century town with a magnificent church, former convent, and school, Hecelchakán is the perfect spot to stop for lunch, watch a small colonial town in action, and stroll around to admire some of the lovely architecture. The area is noted for wonderful tamales as well as its sandals, hammocks, and textiles.

Hecelchakán's primary attraction is the **Museo Arqueológico del Camino Real.** In a 1660 house, the museum has an impressive collection of clay figurines from Isla Jaina and stelae of the Puuc style. It's worth the short detour off the highway to visit. ✉ *Rte. 180, north of Hecelchakán,* ☎ *no phone.* 🎟 *$1.70.* ⊙ *Tues.–Fri. 9–1:30, Sat. 9–1 and 4–8, Sun. 9– noon.*

The only accessible road to **Isla Jaina** (Jaina Island) starts in Hecelchakán. Now part of the **Reserva Ecologica Peténes**, the island, a giant cemetery for the Maya, is off-limits unless you have prior written permission from the National Institute of Anthropology and History (INAH) in Campeche. The tourist office can help arrange a tour, but there's not much to see, as most of the items from the Maya burial grounds have been removed from the island.

On the outskirts of town are a number of old haciendas like **Chunkanán**, and the village of **Dzitbalché**, where the Dzitbalché Verses (descriptions of Maya ceremonies and rituals) were written. Its church dates from 1768.

Calkiní

23 *24 km (17 mi) north of Hecelchakán.*

One of the most important towns along the Camino Real, Calkiní dates from the pre-Colombian Maya Ah-Canul dynasty. According to a local codex, the Ah-Canul chieftainship was founded here in 1443 beneath a ceiba, a tree sacred to the Maya and frequently mentioned in their legends. The Ah-Canul was the most important dynasty at the time of the Conquest, during which the fighters who rebelled against the Spanish leader Montejo were put down in Mérida, dealing a great blow to the Maya spirit. The village of Calkiní is the jumping-off point for exploring the northeastern corner of Campeche.

Calkiní's major attraction is the **Parroquia de San Luis Obispo.** Franciscan friars built this church-fortress-convent between 1548 and 1776, and the Clarisas have used it as a cloistered convent since 1980. You can enter the church (even if the front gate is padlocked) by asking at the office around the right side of the building, but the convent itself is off-limits to tourists. Inside the church is an exquisite carved cedar altarpiece painted in rich gold, red, and black and a handsome pulpit carved with the symbols of the four Evangelists. The portal is Plateresque—a 16th-century Spanish style whose elaborate ornaments suggest silver plate—and the rest of the structure is Baroque. The facade has twin bell towers and a repeated shell motif. ⊠ *Off the town square.* 🎟 *Free.* ⊙ *Wed. and Fri–Mon. 7–noon and 3–9, Thurs. 7 AM–9 PM.*

North of town is the village of **Tepakán,** home of Cal-kin, a ceramics factory. **Cal-kin** (⊠ Carretera Calkiní–Tepakán, Km 1, ☎ 996–102–32) produces the distinctive, hand-painted white, beige, and blue ceramics of Campeche. A four-piece setting starts at $40. The factory has a small store open weekdays 9–5 and Saturday 9–1.

Nunkiní

24 *28 km (15 mi) west of Calkiní, look for the sign for Santa Cruz.*

In this small traditional Maya village, the women weave mats and rugs from the reeds of guano palm, incorporating traditional designs. The colorful church **San Diego Apóstol** is found here.

If you continue going west to the village of Santa Cruz—there is only one road—to where the road curves north for another 15 km (9 mi), you pass the remains of the 18th-century **Santa Cruz** hacienda, and 13 km (8 mi) farther the **Tankuché** hacienda, which, despite efforts of preservation, is in decline. The original machines used to extract dye from Campeche wood are still on site. Fourteen kilometers (9 miles) away is **El Remote,** a wonderful water hole surrounded by sapodilla tress and mangroves. Continuing on the road, you enter the Peténes Ecological Reserve, where you can see flamingos, frigates, herons, and ibis in the mangroves. The final stop is the tiny fishing village of **Isla Arena,** where the birds outnumber humans.

Becal

25 *10 km (6 mi) north of Calkiní.*

The small town of Becal is noted for the famous *jipis* (woven Panama hats). Local residents weave reeds of the guano palm in caves beneath their houses, where the humidity keeps the reeds flexible. As a result, the hats are so pliable that they can be rolled up in a suitcase with no harm done. First produced in the 19th century by the García family, the hats have become a village tradition. It's hard to resist photographing the statue of three giant hats in the center of the town plaza.

The **Sociedad de Artesanas Becaleñas** (✉ Calle 34, between Calles 33 and 35, ☎ no phone), run by Rita Calán, sells fine hats and offers tours of an artisan's workshop. The workshop of Mario Farfán Herrera at **Artesanía Becaleña** (✉ Calle 30 No. 210-A, ☎ 943/1–40–46) has the finest and most expensive hats in town. It also produces jewelry, boxes, and lamp shades—all made from the palms. Buying one of these fine hats direct from the producers helps to sustain this faltering craft and keeps the tradition alive.

Halachó

②⑥ *6 km (4 mi) north of Becal.*

Just across the Yucatán state line from Becal is the village of Halachó. Although not an official part of the Artists' Route, this is a worthwhile stop for those in search of handcrafted baskets, rugs, and bags. Halachó, which means "reed rats," was so named because it was founded on the shores of a lake (long since dried up), where rats once lived in abundance in the reeds along the shore. The centerpiece of Halachó is a magnificent white, 18th-century mission church, **Iglesias Santiago Apóstol,** dedicated to the apostle James, patron saint of the conquistadors. Thousands of standard-bearing pilgrims come to Halachó each year to pay homage at the equestrian statue of the saint, up a flight of stairs behind the altar. The church is open daily 8–noon and 3–8.

ROUTE 261: THE CHENES ROUTE

This is the long way to reach the Yucatán capital of Mérida, passing by the Chenes ruins of southeastern Campeche. Chenes-style temples are easily recognized by their elaborate stucco facades decorated with geometric designs and giant masks of jaguars, and birds. Also characteristic of the style are doorways shaped like the open mouth of a monster. It is a scenic route, leading through green hills with tall dark forests and valleys covered by low scrub, cornfields, and citrus orchards.

Edzná

🔺 **②⑦** *55 km (34 mi) southeast of Campeche City.*

The Maya ruin of Edzná deserves more fame than it has. Archaeologists consider it one of the peninsula's most important ruins because of the crucial transitional role it played among several architectural styles. And as more people discover Campeche, its reputation is growing.

Occupied from around 300 BC to AD 1450, Edzná reached its pinnacle between AD 600 to AD 900. The 6-square-km (2-square-mi) expanse of savanna, broken up only by the occasional tall tree, is situated in a broad valley prone to flooding and flanked by low hills. Surrounding the site are vast networks of irrigation canals, the remnants of a highly sophisticated hydraulic system that channeled rainwater and water from the Champotón River into human-made *chultunes,* or wells. Over the course of several hundred years, Edzná grew from a humble agricultural settlement into a major political-religious center. It's now known that Edzná was the collection point for agricultural products grown in the region. Some products were sent to the Peté in Guatemala in exchange for hand-carved ritual objects and adornments for the site.

Commanding center stage in the **Great Acropolis** (Gran Acrópolis) is the **Five-Story Pyramid** (Pirámide de los Cinco Pisos), which rises 102 ft. The structure consists of five levels, each narrower than the one below it, terminating in a tiny temple crowned by a roof comb. Hieroglyphs have been carved into the vertical face of the 15 steps between each level, and numerous stelae depict the opulent attire and adornment of the ruling class—quetzal feathers, jade pectorals, and skirts of jaguar skin. The **House of the Moon, Southwest Temple, Northwest Temple, Temezcal** (steam bath), and **Puuc Courtyard** are within this complex. Also found here is the **Platform of the Knives,** a 264-ft edifice, which has 20 rooms with vaulted roofs; a number of flint knives were found here during a 1970 archaeological exploration.

In 1992 Campeche archaeologist Antonio Benavides discovered that the Five-Story Pyramid was so constructed that, during certain dates of the year, the setting sun would illuminate the mask of the sun god, Itzamná, inside one of the pyramid's rooms. This happens annually on May 1, 2, and 3, the beginning of the planting season for the Maya—then and now—when they invoke the god to bring rain. It also occurs on August 7, 8, and 9, the days of harvesting and thanking the god for his help. A local anthropologist, Elvira del Carmen Tello, stages an ancient Maya production at Edzná each May. Check with the tourist office in Campeche City (☞ Visitor Information *in* Campeche A to Z, *below*) for information.

South of the Great Acropolis lies the **Small Acropolis,** whose four buildings each face a cardinal point in the compass. The heaviest looking is the **Temple of the Stairway with Reliefs,** which has a stairway decorated with crude reliefs showing seated figures, faces, and jaguars. The architectural style of this complex is derived from the Petén and Puuc schools; the structures were built between AD 800 and AD 1000.

Carved into the **Temple of the Masks (Building 414),** adjacent to the Small Acropolis, are some masks of the sun god with huge protruding eye sockets and crossed eyes, the effect of which is enhanced by the oversize tongues extending from the upper lips. Local lore holds that Edzná, which can be translated as "the house of the gestures (or grimaces)," might have been named for these images. More recent theories claim the name means "home of the echo" and refers to the acoustic effect between the main buildings of the site. Yet others say that it means "home of the Itzáes." Itzá is the name of a Maya group native to southwest Campeche—as well as a common Maya surname.

A variety of architectural styles have been discerned at this site. The Petén style of northern Guatemala and Chiapas is reflected in the use of acropoli as bases for pyramids; of low-lying structures that contrast handsomely with soaring temples; and of corbeled arch roofs, richly ornamented stucco facades, and roof combs. The Río Bec style, which dominated much of Campeche, can be seen in the slender columns, high towers, and exuberant stone mosaics. The multistory edifices, arched passageways, stone causeways, and hieroglyph-adorned stairways are representative of both the Chenes and Puuc styles.

If you're not driving, consider taking one of the inexpensive day trips offered by most travel agencies in Campeche; this is far easier than trying to get to Edzná by municipal buses. **Servicios Turísticos Picazh** (✉ Calle 16 No. 348, between Calles 57 and 59, ☎ 9/816–4426) offers transportation only or guided service to Edzná at reasonable prices. ✉ *Rte. 261 east from Campeche City for 44 km (27 mi) to Cayal, then Rte. 188 southeast for 18 km (11 mi),* ☎ *no phone.* 🎟 *$2, free Sun.* ☉ *Daily 8–5.*

Lodging

$$$$ ⌖ **Hacienda Uayamón.** In the past, this elegant 1792 hacienda was, among other things, an ice factory. Abandoned since 1905, it was rescued in 1999 by the Vanwetswinkel-Zalduá family. The estate is now a luxury hotel, with guest rooms in the original workers' cabanas. Each cabana has its own private garden, hot tub, and bathroom as well as a cozy bedroom. The machine shop is now a pool, the old hospital has been converted into suites, and the main house is a restaurant-bar. The original architecture and decor have been carefully preserved, so staying here is reminiscent of living in a colonial hacienda. ⌧ *9 km (5½ mi) north of Edzná,* ☎ *9/981–9033 in Merida,* FAX *9/944–8484. 30 rooms, 2 suites. Restaurant, bar, air-conditioning, fans, pool, hot tub, travel services, convention center. AE, MC, V.*

Hopelchén

28 *41 km (25 mi) north of the Edzná turnoff on Rte. 261, 153 km (95 mi) north of Xpujil.*

Since 1985 Hopelchén has been home to an immigrant colony of blond-haired, blue-eyed Mennonites who came from northern Mexico looking for arable land. These people are very tradition-bound, and they still speak a Dutch-German dialect, although those who do business with outsiders learn Spanish. The Campeche group makes and sells Mennonite cheese, and they can be seen hawking it on the streets and in restaurants in Campeche City.

Otherwise, Hopelchén—the name means "place of the five wells"—is a traditional Maya town noted for the lovely **Iglesia de San Francisco** built in honor of St. Francis of Padua in 1667. Corn, beans, tobacco, fruit, squash, and *henequen* (sisal hemp) are cultivated in this rich agricultural center. If you want an ice cream cone, a magazine, or an old-fashioned treadle sewing machine, check out the **Escalante Heredia Hermanas** right on the town square—it's also the place to make long-distance phone calls.

Lodging

$ ⌖ **Los Arcos.** Those who want to stay the night and explore the area can check into this charming hostelry. Named for the arches that span the front of the hotel, Los Arcos is clean and bright, with basic rooms facing a traditional colonial-style courtyard. There is a small restaurant in the lobby. ⌧ *Calle 17 s/n, Col. Centro,* ☎ *982/2–01–23. 24 rooms. Fans, free parking. No credit cards.*

Las Grutas de Xtacumbilxunaan

29 *34 km (21 mi) north of Hopelchén.*

Just short of the state line between Campeche and Yucatán and a few miles before Bolonchén de Rejón are the Grutas de Xtacumbilxunaan ("shta-*cum*-bil-shu-nan"), the "caverns of the hidden women" in Spanish and Maya—where legend says a Maya girl disappeared after going for water. In ancient times, cenotes (sinkholes) deep in the extensive cave system provided an emergency water source during droughts. Only a few chambers are open to the public, because the rock surfaces are dangerously slippery and the depth of the caverns is 240 ft. In the upper part of the caves you can admire the delicate limestone formations, which have been given whimsical names such as "Witch's Ball" and "Devil's Bridge." You should book the two-hour tour through the tourist office in Campeche or in Hopelchén; there are sometimes guides at the site, but don't count on it. ⌸ *$1.50.* ◷ *Daily 8–5.*

Santa Rosa Xtampak

🏛 ⓷⓪ *25 km (16 mi) east of Hopelchén, 10 km (6 mi) south of Las Grutas de Xtacumbilxunaan.*

It's a trek through the forest to get to these interesting ruins, believed to be the political center of the Chenes empire. Although Xtampak was discovered in 1842, excavation didn't begin until 1995. It's believed there are 100 structures in the area, although only 12 have been cleared. The most exciting find was the colossal **Palacio** (Palace), in the western plaza. Inside are two inner staircases running the length of the structure, each with openings that lead to different levels and ending in subterranean chambers. This combination is extremely rare in Maya temples. The **House of the Serpent's Mouth** is noteworthy for its perfectly preserved and integrated zoomorphic entrance. The mouth of the sacred earth monster, sometimes referred to as the god Itzamná, stretches wide to reveal a perfectly proportioned inner chamber. Work is ongoing at the site, giving you the feel of being at an archaeological dig. It's certainly worth the effort to reach it. ⊠ *East of Hopelchén on Dzibalchén–Chencho road, watch for sign,* ☎ *no phone.* 🖾 *Donation.* ☉ *Daily 8–5.*

Dzibilnocac

🏛 ⓷⓵ *18 km (11 mi) northeast of Dzibalchén, 69 km (43 mi) northeast of Hopelchén.*

To get to the rarely visited archaeological site of Dzibilnocac, you must first reach the village of Dzibalchén by traveling south on Route 261. From there you proceed north on a small side road to Vincente Guerrero, also known as Iturbide, a farming community 19 km (11½ mi) north—literally at the end of the road. Each corner of the town square has a small stone guardhouse built in 1850 during the War of the Castes, and the road around them eventually turns into a dirt path passing houses and ending at the ruins. Dzibilnocac was a fair-size ceremonial center between AD 250 and AD 900. Although there are at least seven temple pyramids here, the only one that has been partially excavated is the **Palacio Principal,** a palace with three separate towers, combining elements of the Puuc and Chenes architectural styles. Only one of the towers has been cleared, revealing a one-room, square temple at the top with beautifully executed carvings of Chaac on the outside walls. The middle tower, partially cleared on top, has two small underground chambers accessed through a Maya arch. The farthest tower has a roof comb sticking up from a mound of grass, trees, and stones—an incongruous sight. ⊠ *South to Dzibalchén and then north to Vincente Guerrera,* ☎ *no phone.* 🖾 *Free.* ☉ *Daily 8–5.*

Hochob

🏛 ⓷⓶ *55 km (34 mi) southwest of Hopelchén, 15 km (9 mi) west of Dzibilnocac.*

The small Maya ruin of Hochob is an excellent example of the Chenes architectural style, which flowered in the Classic period from about AD 200 to AD 900. Most of the ruins in this area (central and southeastern Campeche) were built on the highest possible elevation to prevent flooding during the rainy season, and Hochob is no exception. It rests high on a hill overlooking the surrounding valleys. Another indication that these are Chenes ruins is the number of wells, or *chultunes,* found in the area. Since work began at Hochob in the early 1980s, four temples and palaces have been excavated at the site, including two that have been brought back to their original grandeur. **Structure III** has wonderfully preserved stucco carvings that are perfect examples of the intricate geometric designs of the Chenes style. Ask the guide to show you the series of natural and man-made chultunes that extend back into the forest. ⊠ *Southwest of Hopelchén on Dzibalchén–Chencho road,* ☎ *no phone.* ▣ *Free.* ⊘ *Daily 8–5.*

ROUTE 186 TOWARD CHETUMAL

Campeche's archaeological sites, particularly those near the Quintana Roo border, are attracting more attention from scientists and travelers alike. Secluded yet accessible ruins are surrounded by tropical jungle—and for the most part are devoid of tourists. The vestiges of at least 10 little-known Maya cities lie hidden off Route 186 between Francisco Escárcega and Chetumal. Becán and the neighboring sites of Chicanná, Xpujil, Hormiguero, and Balamkú are just off Highway 186 near the Quintana Roo border. The road to Calakmul, near the Guatemala border south of Xpujil, has been paved, making parts of the biosphere more accessible. Río Bec, on the other hand, is more difficult to reach.

You can easily see Xpujil, Becán, Hormiguero, and Chicanná in a day if you're en route between Escárcega and Chetumal. If you want to include Balamkú and Calakmul you should plan for another day and stay overnight at one of the hotels in the area. Add another full day to your itinerary if you want to include Río Bec; it requires a full-day guided tour through the jungle at the edge of the Calakmul Biosphere Reserve.

Southern Campeche is an area with genuine ecotourism. As late as 1950, the region was unoccupied. Then the Mexican government began colonizing the area with Maya settlers from Tabasco whose land had been seized by cattle barons. Later immigrants—also victims of the cattle industry—came from Veracruz, and when the Chicosen volcano erupted in Chiapas in the early 1980s, another wave of farmers appeared. The local people live a marginal existence in isolated communities, with only two schools serving them. About 25 communities of between 4,000 and 5,000 people live inside the Calakmul reserve, and another 2,500–3,000 people live just outside it. Their slash-and-burn technique of farming, which requires that sections of precious forests be burned down to make way for crops, is probably the most dangerous threat to the reserve. In an attempt to protect the land, alternative means of making a living, like beekeeping and pig farming, have been introduced to the farmers. They also have been taught organic farming methods that result in higher crop yields, so that more land need not be cleared for agriculture. Another important alternative being offered is the state tourism program, which trains local people to act as guides to the various ruins and for special excursions into the biosphere. As a result, the area offers excellent guides trained in environmental education, Maya culture, ecotourism, basic English, and local flora and fauna. Hiring a local guide not only enhances your visit to the ruins but gives economic support to the local community and helps preserve the area. Arrangements for English-speaking guides must be made through the tourist office in Campeche City.

The well-maintained Route 269 runs north from Xpujil, connecting to Hopelchén, west of Campeche City. Travelers can now continue north from Xpujil to visit several Chene-style ruins, from there returning to Campeche City or continuing north toward Yucatán state. Xpujil's tiny bus station has at least one bus per day to Escárcega, Hopelchén, Chetumal, Campeche, and Cancún.

Xpujil

🔺 ㉝ *300 km (186 mi) southeast of Campeche, 130 km (81 mi) south of Dz-ibilnocac, 125 km (78 mi) west of Chetumal.*

Xpujil (literally "cat's tail," pronounced ish-*poo*-hil), comprises three large towers in one structure overlooking the jungle, along with several other building groups that have not yet been excavated. The site, which can be seen clearly from the highway, blends architectural elements of both the Chenes style and the Río Bec style. The elaborately carved facades and doorways fashioned like a monster's mouth reflect the Chenes style, while the Río Bec style is seen in the three adjacent pyramid-towers, which are connected by a long platform. All three towers have false roofs, and at the front of each are the remains of four vaulted rooms (for a total of 12) thought to have been used by priests and royalty. On the back side of the central tower is a huge mask of the rain god Chaac. It's believed this was the ceremonial center for the Río Bec region. 🔳 *$1.70.* 🕙 *Daily 8–5.*

Lodging

$$$ 🏨 **Chicanná Ecovillage Resort.** Rooms in this classy, comfortable jungle lodge are in two-story stucco duplexes with thatch roofs. Each of the large units has one king-size or two double beds, an overhead fan, a large bathroom, screened windows, and a porch or balcony with a table and chairs. Solar energy heats the water, and there's a small pool surrounded by banana trees and flowering plants. There is no phone or fax at the hotel, although public long-distance telephones and fax service are available in the tiny village of Xpujil. For reservations, contact the Del Mar Hotel in Campeche City. ⊠ *Carretera Escárcega–Chetumal, Km 144, 9 km (5 mi) north of village of Xpujil,* ☎ *9/816–2233 reservations. 32 rooms. Restaurant, bar, fans, pool, library. AE, MC, V.*

$$ 🏨 **Hotel Calakmul.** Señora María Cabrera is the owner of this charming hotel offering double or single rooms and small wooden cabanas. The rooms are comfortable and large but extremely basic, with bright coral-color walls, white tile floors, double beds, overhead fans, and bathrooms with hot water. The original wooden cabins are a bit cramped and have shared bathrooms. A restaurant, renovated in early 2001, offers delicious meals of meat or fish or *mole poblano* (a turkey leg topped with rich, spicy chocolate sauce). ⊠ *Carretera Escárcega–Chetumal, Km 153, Xpujil ,* ☎ *987/1–60–06. 13 rooms, 9 cabanas. Restaurant, fans. No credit cards.*

Becán

🔺 ㉞ *7 km (4½ mi) west of Xpujil.*

Becán ("road of the serpent") is thought to have been a political and military center as early as AD 250, judging from the age of its defensive moat. The moat, ½ km (¼ mi) long and ½ km (¼ mi) deep, surrounds the ruins and provided the first clue that the site was a military post. Recent investigations of the fortified walls have established that Becán was often under siege—more than likely from neighboring Calakmul. However, the constant skirmishes didn't seem to hinder the construction of the more than 84 main buildings between AD 600 and AD 900. The most exciting building is **Structure VIII**, which has underground passages that go on for miles. The passages lead to small subterranean rooms and to a concealed staircase leading to the top of the temple. Do hire a guide to explore these ruins; Miguel Perez Cortés, better known locally as "Zapata," is considered the best around. 🔳 *$2.* 🕙 *Daily 8–5.*

Chicanná

🏛 ③⑤ *3 km (2 mi) east of Becán.*

Thought to have been the commercial center for Xpujil and the larger, fortified city of Becán, Chicanná ("house of the serpent's mouth") also dates from the Late Classic period. **Structure II,** the main temple at this intimate site, has well-preserved sculpted reliefs and faces with long twisted noses, symbols of Chaac, adorning its facade. Beside them are carved masks representing the god Itzamná and, in the center, the typical earth-monster doorway with protruding tongue and fierce fangs. 🎟 *$1.70.* ⊙ *Daily 8–5.*

Hormiguero

🏛 ③⑥ *19 km (12 mi) southeast of Xpujil.*

Hormiguero is Spanish for "anthill," referring both to the looters' tunnels that honeycombed the ruins when archaeologists discovered them and to the number of large anthills in the area. The buildings here were constructed roughly between 400 BC and AD 1100 in the Río Bec style, with lateral towers and ornamental stairways. The site has five temples, two of which have been excavated to reveal ornate facades covered with zoomorphic figures whose mouths are the doorways. **Structure II** was an important find because of its size (it is the largest structure on the site) as well as its beautifully preserved carved facade, rounded corners, and simulated staircases. **Structure V** has some admirable Chaac masks arranged in a cascade atop a pyramid. The road into the ruin is passable only with a small vehicle; passengers on buses have to get out and walk about 1 km (½ mi). 🎟 *Free.* ⊙ *Daily 8–5.*

Río Bec

🏛 ③⑦ *15 km (9 mi) south of Xpujil; same distance east of Hormiguero.*

The sprawling Río Bec archaeological zone covers nearly 78 square km (30 square mi) along the banks of the river of the same name. The zone includes five major ceremonial centers and 15 smaller temple groups, but although archaeologists have done extensive surveys of the area, little clearing or excavation has been done. The only structure that has been completely excavated and restored, known as **Río Bec B,** is a 55-ft-tall temple with two false-pyramid towers at opposite edges of a long, low building whose front entrance is the mouth of a serpent. Seeing all the main ceremonial centers at Río Bec requires an all-day trip with an experienced guide arranged through the tourist office in Campeche (☎ 981/6–55–93) or at Rancho Encantado at Bacalar, Quintana Roo. 🎟 *Free.* ⊙ *Daily 8–5.*

Balamkú

🏛 ③⑧ *25 km (15 mi) north of Calakmul, 20 km (12 mi) northwest of Río Bec.*

The easternmost ruin on the Río Bec route, Balamkú (temple of the jaguar) is famous for the stunning fresco discovered here in 1995. Believed to have been created in the Early Classic period (300–600 AD), the work is 55½ ft long and 5¾ ft high and is composed of four adjacent carvings, two of a frog and two of a crocodile. On each rests the figure of the king wearing the mask of the sun god. Interspersed are carvings of jaguars and in the middle is a tomb. The original red and black paint can be seen in places. The fresco recently was enclosed to protect it from the elements, and flash cameras are prohibited. There are other structures here, but they're anticlimactic after the impressive fresco. ▧ *$2.* ☉ *Daily 8–5.*

Calakmul Biosphere Reserve

🔺 ㊴ *70 km (43 mi) southwest of Xpujil.*

Remote Calakmul ("twin towers") is in the isolated region near the Guatemala border. The area surrounding the ancient Maya city was declared a protected biosphere reserve in 1989; covering 1.8 million acres, Calakmul is the second-largest reserve of its kind on the continent, next to Sian Ka'an. Within its borders there are numerous species of flora and fauna, including some that are endangered. Among them are wildcats (jaguar, puma, ocelot), spider and howler monkeys, 329 different kinds of birds—Calakmul is perfect for birding—and 120 varieties of orchids, including a species of black orchid.

The Escárcega–Chetumal highway runs right through the reserve. Lying just south of the highway is the reserve's archaeological zone. Although structures will be excavated, the dense jungle surrounding them is being left in its natural state. Extensive information on the site's ecosystem is presented in tours conducted by local guides. Arrangements for an English-speaking tour guide must be made beforehand with the Campeche City tourist office.

Archaeologists and anthropologists estimate that the region may once have been inhabited by more than 50,000 Maya and have thus far mapped more than 6,250 structures of all sizes, including what may be the largest Maya building on the peninsula. More than 180 stelae have been found, as have twin pyramids that face each other across a plaza, similar to those at Tikal in Guatemala. However, Calakmul's towering, early Petén–style temples, with their long, sloping sides, are a bit bulky compared to Tikal's graceful pyramids.

Perhaps the most monumental discovery so far at Calakmul is a 1,000-year-old individual, found wrapped in animal skins (but not embalmed) and locked away in a royal tomb. The 1994 find is the first known example of this type of burial in the Maya world to date, and the remains are under study at the government's anthropology institute in Mexico City. Other items from the site—including a mummy and jade funeral masks—are on display at the Fuerte de San Miguel's Museum of the Maya in Campeche City.

Calakmul was a formidable military power in its time. It was first estimated to have been settled around 1500 BC, but now experts agree it was founded no earlier than 1000 BC. Historians believe it was probably the capital city of the mighty Serpent Head dynasty. The glyph with this symbol has been found on stelae in other cities of the ancient Maya empire, suggesting that Calakmul dominated a large number of tributary city-states. It reached the pinnacle of its power in the Late Classic period, when it held sway over Palenque in Chiapas and the superpowers Tikal in Guatemala and Caracol in Belize. Stelae under study also indicate that the new heads of tributary cities were obligated to journey to Calakmul to be formally consecrated in their new duties by the leader of the Serpent Head lineage. Epigraphists also have discovered inscriptions relating the defeat of Calakmul's most famous ruler, Jaguar Paw, at the hands of arch rival Tikal in AD 695. The city-state went into decline after this.

From the entrance gate, it is a 60-km (37-mi) drive along a paved road to the parking area. It's at least a 20-minute hike from there to the first building. The site is shrouded in thick rain forest, but paths with signposts lead to various temples. You can see only about a half dozen structures, including **Temple II** and **Temple VII**—twin pyramids separated by an immense plaza. Temple II, at 175 ft, is the tallest structure found here so far. Getting to the top involves climbing up a ragged rock incline, as the steps have not been completely restored yet. It's worth the effort, though, because the view from the top of the surrounding canopy of rain forest is spectacular. A stone mask was uncovered on the facade of Temple II in 1997 and is currently under study.

The facade and steps of slightly smaller Temple I have been restored, so it's easier to climb. A pair of royal tombs has been extracted from here, one of a female regent. There's a stela at the base of the pyramid overlooking the plaza. Parts of temples are scattered around one of the rain forest paths—a state likely attributable to grave robbers who got away with the choice pieces. It's hard to thwart these criminals, since to do so would require a large corps of guards at the site, and there is no budget available for hiring them.

Upon entry to Calakmul, you must register yourself and your vehicle, paying an entrance fee for both at the gate. There is a module with rest rooms and a bookstore on site, but you have to bring your own food and water. *97 km (60 mi) east of Escárcega to the turnoff at Cohuas, then 65 km (40 mi) south to Calakmul.* ☒ *$4 per car (more for larger vehicles), plus $2 per person.* ☉ *Daily 8–5.*

Lodging

$$ ☷ **Calakmul Cabañas.** These are the very best accommodations in the
★   area. Designed and built by a master woodworker and architect, the rustic cabanas are tucked away in the forest on the edge of the Calakmul biosphere and ruins. Built with natural wood and stone from the area, each has been decorated individually with jungle colors and has inlaid stone floors, large showers, wooden tables, comfortable beds with overhead fans, and screened-in porches. Small ponds and sitting areas complete the Garden of Eden atmosphere, and nearby trails allow for hiking in the woods. A trailer park and campgrounds closer to the highway are under the same management. ☒ *Carretera Escárcega–Chetumal 186, Km 98.5, by the entrance to the Calakmul ruins,* ☎ *981/80–74–44. 15 cabanas, 8 trailer sites, 10 tents. Restaurant, pool. No credit cards.*

Candelaria

▲ ④ *95 km (59 mi) west of Calakmul Biosphere Reserve.*

Bird-watching, hunting, and fly-fishing in Lake Salsipuedes and Vieja Lagoon in the Candelaria River basin are what make this spot an increasingly popular destination. Primarily an agricultural hub producing wheat, corn, and sugarcane, Candelaria is also the starting-off point for a visit to the ruins of El Tigre.

Lodging

$$ ☷ **Autel Jardines.** Equipped with a number of amenities, offering the most comfortable lodgings in town, this hotel is an unexpected surprise. Rooms are spacious and have two double beds, large bathrooms, and cable TV, and each is decorated in the style of a different country. The two suites have kitchenettes. The owner, Manuel Valladares Hernández, can make arrangements for a tour to El Tigre or for fly-fishing in the area. ☒ *Calle 27 No. 1, Col. Acalán,* ☎ *982/6–00–64,* FAX *981/6–00–75, mvalladb@etzna.com. 20 rooms, 2 suites. Restaurant, bar, air-conditioning, kitchenettes (some), pool, gym, dance club, laundry service. AE.*

El Tigre

⚔ ④ *18 km (11 mi) south of Candelaria.*

With a new road from the village of Candelaria, El Tigre has become quite accessible. Right next to the Candelaria River, this commercial center is thought to have been the site of Postclassic Itzankanac, capital of the province of Acalán, where Spanish conquistador Cortés supposedly hanged Cuauhtémoc, the last Aztec emperor. El Tigre comprises a 656-ft-long ceremonial plaza where stucco masks, some with and some without zoomorphic features, and dating from 400 BC, were found. Two large *sacbéob* (ceremonial roads) that lead down to the river and a landing site have recently been discovered. It's a long drive to reach the site, so you may need to stay overnight in the nearby village of Candelaria. Admission to El Tigre is $1.70.

ROUTE 180 TO VILLAHERMOSA

Heading southwest from Campeche, Route 180 hugs the coast, offering a wonderful view of the Gulf of Mexico. The deep green sea is so shallow that the continental shelf is almost visible at low tide. Because waves are rare and the current runs at a nearly imperceptible 0.3 knots, the gulf resembles a lake more than the vast body of water that it is.

Lerma

④ *13 km (8 mi) southwest of Campeche City.*

Playa Bonita, the first beach southwest of Campeche City, is in this rural village. Public buses to Lerma depart daily 6 AM–11 PM from the market in Campeche City (✉ Circuito Baluartes, between Calles 53 and 55). The unmarked beach has lockers, changing rooms, showers, and a snack bar. It is lovely during weekdays, but crowded on weekends, and litter is a problem.

Seybaplaya

④ *About 7 km (4 mi) southwest of Lerma.*

Dozens of identical, turquoise-and-white fiberglass motor launches line the beach at the traditional fishing port of Seybaplaya. Its palm-fringed setting is the prettiest seascape on the Campeche coast. Snorkeling is good here, as a number of large coral heads are just offshore, along with an underwater cemetery for boats. The local church is an unusual combination of white and blue geometric patterns—unusual for this area. Visitors looking for a challenge may want to climb the huge staircase that juts up the mountain, ending at the giant statue of Jesus with his arms outstretched. The view is incredible, but it is quite a hike. A couple of miles north via Highway 180 is **Payucán**—a beach with fine white sand and lots of herons, sandpipers, pelicans, and other seabirds—and **Punta del Morro** ("point of the nose"), a huge seaside cavern created by centuries of erosion. The sound of the crashing waves echoes off the walls, adding to the drama of the place.

About 9 km (5½ mi) southwest is **Siho Playa,** the old home of the pirate Henry Morgan. Here the beach is quite calm and stays shallow for about 10 yards. Three kilometers (2 miles) southwest is the beautiful **Costa Blanca** beach, with lots of shells, birds, and smooth surf.

Champotón

44 *35 km (22 mi) southwest of Seybaplaya.*

The highway curves through a hilly region before reaching Champotón's immensely satisfying vista of open seas. Champotón is a charming little town with a bridge, *palapas* (thatch-roof huts) on the water, and plenty of swimmers and launches in sight. The Spaniards dubbed the outlying bay the Bahía de la Mala Pelea, or Bay of the Evil Battle, because it was here that the troops of the Spanish conqueror and explorer Hernández de Córdoba were trounced for the first time in Mexico, in 1517, by pugnacious Indians armed with arrows, slingshots, and darts. The famous battle is commemorated with a parade and fair on March 21.

The 17th-century church of **Nuestra Señora de las Mercedes** is the site for the large Virgin of Guadaloupe feast that begins on November 28 and ends on December 18. In the middle of town also stand the ruins of the **Fortín de San Antonio** (Small Fort of San Antonio). Champotón is ideal for bird-watching, fishing, and hunting. More than 37 kinds of fish, including shad, snook, and bass, live in Río Champotón; on land there are deer, wild boar, doves, and quail. The mangroves and swamps are home to a variety of cranes and other waterfowl. The town is primarily an agricultural hub—its most important exports are the world-famous Champotón baby shrimp, along with water coconut, sugarcane, bananas, avocados, corn, and beans.

About a dozen small seafood restaurants make up **Los Cockteleros,** an area 5 km (3 mi) north of the center of Champotón. This is where campechanos head on weekends to munch fried fish or slurp down a variety of seafood cocktails, some with the famous sweet, spicy salsa. The open-air palapa eateries are near the beach and are open daily during daylight hours.

Approximately 15 km (9 mi) southwest of Champotón is another beautiful beach called **Punta Xen.** It's a long stretch of deserted sand interrupted only by birds and seashells. Across the highway are a few restaurants serving basic food.

Dining and Lodging

$ ✕ **Las Brisas.** A favorite with locals, this is the best place in town for fresh fish, shrimp, and octopus. It is on the main street by the water and looks out onto the bay. ⊠ *Av. Eugenio Echeverría Castellot s/n,* ☎ *982/8–05–15. No credit cards.*

$$ ☐ **Geminis.** On a hill overlooking the bay, this cute white hotel is the most modern in the village. Most rooms have air-conditioning, TV sets, and spacious double beds with colorful bedspreads. The restaurant, La Casona, serves delicious local specialties. ⊠ *Calle 30 No. 10,* ☎ *982/8–00–08,* FAX *982/8–00–94. 32 rooms. Restaurant, bar, air-conditioning, fans. MC, V.*

$$ ☐ **Snook Inn.** The walls that enclose this hotel give it an unassuming appearance. The extremely clean pool is surrounded by a garden, and the deck has comfortable chairs and tables. Rooms are simple, with tile floors, unadorned walls, so-so beds, and hammock hooks in the walls (bring your own hammock). The hotel is mainly the domain of serious anglers who come for fishing and hunting trips with hotel owner Don José Sansores and his son Fernando. ⊠ *Calle 30 No. 1,* ☎ FAX *982/8–00–18. 20 rooms. Pool, free parking. No credit cards.*

Sabancuy

45 *47 km (29 mi) west of Champotón.*

The launching point for exploring the **Laguna de Terminos** and its many estuaries and mangroves, Sabancuy is the final village before high-tension lines start to follow the coastal highway and oil country starts. The pretty beach here is not part of the village, which is actually off the main highway. Plan tours of this area ahead of time with the tourist office in Campeche City, since little English is spoken here. The secondary highway (pitted with potholes in various spots, which makes for slow going at times) leads to the ruins of El Tigre.

Dining and Lodging

$$ ✕ **Viaductoplaya Restaurant Bar Turistico.** The catch of the day might include shrimp, squid, or fish at this beachside restaurant. Mexican favorites such as panuchos and grilled chicken are on the menu as well. Beer, wine, and liquor are available. ⊠ *Carretera Carmen–Champotón, Km 77.50,* ☎ *982/5–00–08. No credit cards.*

$ ▥ **Posada Bellavista.** The only hotel in town, this small, colonial-style hostelry has sparsely decorated but clean rooms equipped with the basics—two single beds, fans, and hot water. It's in front of the park adjacent to the municipal palace. It operates on a cash-only basis. ⊠ *Calle Marina y J. Ortiz Avila,* ☎ *no phone. 10 rooms. Fans. No credit cards.*

Isla del Carmen

46 *147 km (91 mi) south of Champotón.*

It was on this barrier island protecting the lagoon from the gulf that the pirates who raided Campeche hid from 1663 until their expulsion in 1717. The island has served as a depot for everything from dyewoods and textiles to hardwoods, chicle, shrimp, and (for more than 20 years) oil.

Chances are, you will at least pass through **Ciudad del Carmen** in your travels through Campeche. A major hub and the second largest city in Campeche, Ciudad is actually not on the island but on the adjoining peninsula's east end. The island is connected by east and west bridges to the mainland.

Ciudad del Carmen has some charming historic attractions that are worth a look, but the modern, commercialized sections of the city are a sad example of what happens when an oil company is given free rein. Parts of the bay are polluted, and the city is battling problems like prostitution and alcoholism, which is reflected in the cheap, ugly motels advertised as "men's clubs." Be prepared to pay higher prices than in Cancún for a safe hotel room. A new civic pride campaign is slowly making the city more tourist-friendly by cleaning up the streets and restoring historic buildings.

Isla del Carmen has some fine white-sand beaches such as **Playa Norte** and **Playa Caracol,** though you should watch out for oil spills. On the outskirts of town the best beaches for swimming are **El Playón** and **Playa Benjamín.** They are pretty, but the string of unsightly high-power tension lines mars the scenery.

Sights to See

Museo de la Ciudad (City Museum). In the building of the old hospital (Victoriano Nieves), this museum has displays about the pirates and the history of the city. ⊠ *Calle 22,* ☎ *no phone.* ✹ *Wed.–Sun. 10–8.*

La Parroquia de la Virgen del Carmen. Two towers, each with a domed roof, grace this 1856 church. Inside is a gray-and-white marble altar dedicated to the Virgin of Carmen. ✉ *Av. López Mateos and Calle 47,* ☎ *no phone.* ⊙ *Daily 8–2 and 5–7.*

Dining and Lodging

$$ ✕ **El Cactus.** Meaty entrées welcome carnivorous appetites here, where dishes include succulent rib eye and a large filet mignon. The bone-marrow soup and the cheese pie are recommended. The restaurant's exterior resembles an adobe house with—you guessed it—cacti growing at the doorway. Inside are whitewashed stucco walls, wood furnishings, and quiet romantic background music. ✉ *Calle 31 No. 132, Col. Cuauhtémoc (next to Hotel Lino), Ciudad del Carmen,* ☎ *938/ 2–49–86. AE, MC, V.*

$$$ ✕🏨 **Eurohotel.** Geared toward Mexican business travelers, this contemporary, upscale hotel is close to the center of town. It provides lots of after-work relaxation options, including a gambling club. Modern rooms done in gray, blue, and cream colors have king-size beds, cable TV, room safes, and phones. Junior suites have a separate living area and separate bathtubs. The restaurant, Piamonte, serves some of Ciudad del Carmen's finest fare. ✉ *Calle 22 No. 208, Ciudad del Carmen,* ☎ *938/2–30–44,* ⓕ*AX 938/2–30–21. 80 rooms, 12 suites. Restaurant, bar, in-room safes, pool, business services, meeting rooms. AE, DC, MC, V.*

$$$ ✕🏨 **Holiday Inn.** All the amenities one has come to expect from a Holiday Inn can be found at this small hotel. The lobby is intimate, with bamboo furniture and Mexican accents. Rooms have king-size beds and small patios or terraces. The figure-8 pool, gymnasium, and restaurant are quite nice, and there is an on-site golf course. ✉ *Calle 31 No. 273, Ciudad del Carmen,* ☎ *938/2–08–90,* ⓕAX *938/2–05–20,* ⓦEB *www.holiday-inn.com. 20 rooms, 2 suites. Restaurant, bar, pool, 18-hole golf course, gym. AE, DC, MC, V.*

CAMPECHE A TO Z

To research prices, get advice from other travelers, and book travel arrangements, visit www.fodors.com.

AIR TRAVEL

Aeroméxico has one flight daily from Mexico City to Campeche City. ➤ AIRLINES AND CONTACTS: **Aeroméxico** (☎ 981/6–56–78).

BUS TRAVEL

ADO, a first-class line, runs buses to Campeche City from Mérida almost every hour, and to Ciudad del Carmen, Mexico City, Tampico, Veracruz, and Villahermosa regularly, but less frequently. Adjacent to the ADO station, the second-class bus station has service on Autobuses del Sur to intermediate points throughout the Yucatán Peninsula, as well as less desirable service to Chetumal, Ciudad del Carmen, Escárcega, Mérida, Palenque, Tuxtla Gutiérrez, and Villahermosa. A half block from the ADO station is the office of the Nuevos Horizontes bus company, which offers first-class service at least once a day to Mérida, Ciudad del Carmen, Mexico City, Veracruz, Cancún, Jalapa, Puebla, and Villahermosa.

Try to book your bus tickets to avoid an extended stopover in Escárcega, along Route 261. Though the government has beefed up security—Escárcega was an unsafe spot for tourists, with bus passengers the targets of robberies and assaults—and things have calmed down quite a bit, it is still not a place to linger.

Within Campeche City, buses run along Avenida Ruíz Cortínez and cost the equivalent of about 30¢.

➤ Bus Information: **ADO** (✉ Av. Gobernadores 289, at Calle 45, along Rte. 261 to Mérida, ☎ 981/1–43–34 or 981/6–34–45). **Autobuses del Sur** (✉ Av. Gobernadores 575, between Calles 15 and 17, ☎ 981/6–34–45 or 981/6–28–02 ext. 2405). **Nuevos Horizontes** (✉ Av. Gobernadores 575, between Calles 15 and 17, ☎ 981/1–02–61).

CAR RENTAL

Reliable rental agencies are AutoRent—which charges $45 a day including insurance and allows 200 km (120 mi) per day—and the slightly more expensive Maya Rent a Car, which rents small Chevys for $59 a day, including insurance and unlimited mileage.

➤ Major Agencies: **AutoRent** (✉ Hotel del Paseo, Calle 8 No. 215, ☎ 981/1–01–00). **Maya Rent a Car** (✉ Del Mar Hotel, Av. Ruíz Cortínez, at Calle 59, ☎ 981/6–22–33, FAX 981/1–16–18).

CAR TRAVEL

Campeche City is about 1½ hours from Mérida along the 160-km (99-mi) *via corta* (short way), Route 180. The alternative route, the 250-km (155-mi) *via larga* (long way), Route 261, takes at least six hours but passes the major Maya ruins of Uxmal, Kabah, and Sayil. From Chetumal, take Route 186 west to Francisco Escárcega, where you pick up Route 261 north; the drive takes about seven hours. Villahermosa is about six hours away if you drive inland via the town of Francisco Escárcega but longer if you hug the gulf and cross the bridge at Ciudad del Carmen. A four-lane toll road runs from Campeche City to Champotón. One-way costs $3 and it shaves 20 km (12 mi) off the 68-km (42-mi) road. Look for the 180 CUOTA sign when leaving the city for the coast. (The bridge toll is another $2.60 each way to Ciudad del Carmen.) A paved, two-lane highway south from Hopelchén to Xpujil is the continuation of Route 269 south, which takes you to the Río Bec area and Calakmul much faster from Mérida (hooks up with Route 261 north) and more easily from Campeche City if you want to bypass the coastal region.

E-MAIL

In Campeche City, get on-line at En Red Cibercafé sucursal Universidad, open Monday–Saturday 10–10, or Cybercafé Campeche, open Monday–Saturday 9–9. Both places charge $1–$2 per hour.

➤ Services: **Cybercafé Campeche** (✉ Calle 61 No. 19-A, between Calles 10 and 12) **En Red Cibercafé sucursal Universidad** (✉ Av. Agustín Melgar 12).

EMERGENCIES

Las Ángeles Verdes (the Green Angels), an organization funded by the government, patrols the highways on a regular basis and offers emergency roadside assistance. Basic medical care is available at the government-funded Social Security Clinic.

➤ Doctors: **Social Security Clinic** (✉ Av. López Mateos y Av. Talamantes, ☎ 981/6–18–55 or 981/6–52–02).

➤ Emergency Services: **Emergencies** (☎ 06). **Green Angels** (☎ 981/6–09–34 or 981/1–25–44). **Police** (✉ Av. Resurgimiento 77, Col. Lazareto, ☎ 981/6–23–09). **Red Cross** (✉ Av. Las Palmas, at Ah-Kim-Pech s/n, Campeche City, ☎ 981/5–24–11).

➤ Hospitals: **Hospital General** (✉ Av. Central, at Circuito Baluartes, ☎ 981/6–09–20 or 981/6–42–33).

➤ 24-Hour Pharmacies: **Clínica Campeche** (✉ Av. Central 65, near the Social Security Clinic, Campeche City, ☎ 981/6–56–12).

MAIL AND SHIPPING

The post office (*correos*) in Campeche City is open weekdays 8–8, Saturday 9–1.

➤ SERVICES: **Post Office** (✉ Av. 16 de Septiembre, between Calles 53 and 55, ☎ 981/62134).

MONEY MATTERS

Campeche City banks are open weekdays 9–1. Those where you can exchange money include Banamex and Bancomer.

➤ BANKS: **Banamex** (✉ Calle 53 No. 15, at Calle 10, ☎ 981/6–52–51). **Bancomer** (✉ Av. 16 de Septiembre 120, ☎ 981/6–66–22).

TAXIS

Taxis can be hailed on the street in Campeche City or, more reliably, commissioned from the main taxi stand, or at stands by the bus stations and market. Because of the scarcity of taxis, it's quite common to share them with other people headed in the same direction—rarely will you have a cab to yourself, and drivers will not ask your permission to pick up another fare. To get picked up, just wait for one to slow down near you. A shared cab ride costs under $1. If you have one to yourself, it's $1.50–$3.

➤ TAXI COMPANIES: **Sitio de Taxis** (✉ Calle 8, between Calles 55 and 53, ☎ 981/5–30–36).

TELEPHONES

LONG-DISTANCE CALLS

TELMEX phones that take the electronic Ladatel cards are found throughout the city. Intertel has phone booths for long-distance calls. Another *larga distancia* (long-distance) store can be found at the corner of Calle 10 and Calle 59.

➤ SERVICES: **Intertel** (✉ Calle 57 No. 1, ☎ 981/6–68–63, FAX 981/6–73–34).

TOURS

Trolley tours of Campeche City leave from the Plaza Principal daily at 9:30, 6, and 8. The one-hour, bilingual tour costs 70¢. On weekends there is an additional tour at 7 PM. You can buy tickets on board the trolley, or ahead of time in the municipal tourist office right next to the cathedral, also on the plaza. One route takes you through the city and another goes to the forts—check to see which route is being offered before boarding.

Corazón Maya arranges tours to the Calakmul Biosphere Reserve. Camping trips and tours of the biosphere can also be arranged through Fernando Sastré Méndez at Aventura Máxima. The Secretaría de Turismo can arrange most tours throughout the state, with English-speaking guides if necessary, and is especially helpful in making arrangements for the tours offered by the ejido communities near Calakmul. The sponsor of the Calakmul project—a private conservation group called Pronatura that receives support from several prestigious international conservation funds—acts as a coordinator of tours to the reserve (receiving a percentage of the booking revenue) and occasionally leads shorter overnight group trips to Calakmul. These trips require advance reservations and a donation.

➤ FEES AND SCHEDULES: **Aventura Máxima** (✉ Zoh Laguna, Xpujil, ☎ 987/1–60–10, FAX 987/1–60–35). **Corazón Maya** (✉ Baluarte de San Pedro, Calle 18 No. 51, ☎ FAX 982/1–58–37). **Pronatura** (✉ Calle 1-D No. 254-A, Campestra, ☎ FAX 99/44–33–90 or 99/44–35–80). **Secretaría de Turismo** (✉ Plaza Moch Couoh, Av. Ruíz Cortínez s/n, ☎ 981/6–55–93 or 981/6–73–64, FAX 981/6–67–67).

TRAVEL AGENCIES

➤ LOCAL AGENTS: **American Express/VIPs** (✉ Prolongación Calle 59, Edificio Belmar, Depto. 5, ☎ 981/1–10–10 or 981/1–10–00, FAX 981/6–83–33). **Destinos Maya** (✉ Av. Miguel Alemán 162 [altos], Locale 106, ☎ 981/1–09–34; 713/440–0291 in the U.S., FAX 981/1–09–34). **Viajes Campeche** (✉ Calle 10 No. 329, between Calles 61 and 63, ☎ 981/6–52–33, FAX 981/6–28–44).

VISITOR INFORMATION

The Secretaría de Turismo (Tourism Office) is open daily 9–3 and 5–8. On weekends a guard hands out maps and literature but has little knowledge. The *oficina de turismo de municipio* (municipal tourism office) is open daily 8–2:30 and 4–8. The staff speaks very little English, but you can pick up a map. City trolley tours are booked here.
➤ TOURIST INFORMATION: **Oficina de turismo de municipio** (✉ Calle 55, west of the cathedral, ☎ 981/1–39–89 or 981/1–39–90). **Secretaría de Turismo** (✉ Av. Ruíz Cortínez s/n, Plaza Moch Couoh, across the street from the Palacio del Gobierno, ☎ 981/6–55–93, ☎ FAX 981/6–67–67).

7 BACKGROUND AND ESSENTIALS

Portrait of the Yucatán

Chronology

Map of Yucatán Peninsula

Map of Mexico

Smart Travel Tips A to Z

Spanish Vocabulary

A PLACE APART

The Yucatán Peninsula has captivated travelers since the early Spanish explorations. "A place of white towers, whose glint could be seen from the ships . . . temples rising tier on tier, with sculptured cornices" is how the expeditions' chroniclers described the peninsula, then thought to be an island. Rumors of a mainland 10 days west of Cuba were known to Columbus, who obstinately hoped to find "a very populated land," and one that was richer than any he had yet discovered. Subsequent explorers and conquistadors met with more resistance there than in almost any other part of the New World, and this resistance continued for centuries.

Largely because of their geographic isolation, Yucatecans tend to preserve ancient traditions more than many other indigenous groups in the country. This can be seen in such areas as housing (the use of the ancient Maya thatch hut, or *na*); dress (*huipiles* have been made and worn by Maya women for centuries); occupation (most modern-day Maya are farmers, just as their ancestors were); language (while the Maya language has evolved considerably, basically it is very similar to that spoken at least 500 years ago); and religion (ancient deities persist, particularly in the form of gods associated with agriculture, such as the Chacmools, or rain gods, and festivals to honor the seasons and benefactor spirits maintain the traditions of old).

This vast peninsula encompasses 113,000 square km (43,630 square mi) of a flat limestone table covered with sparse topsoil and scrubby jungle growth. Geographically, it comprises the states of Yucatán, Campeche, and Quintana Roo, as well as Belize and a part of Guatemala (these two countries are not discussed in this book). Long isolated from the rest of Mexico and still one of the least

Hispanicized (or Mexicanized) regions of the country, Yucatán catapulted into the tourist's vocabulary with the creation of its most precious man-made asset, Cancún.

Mexico's most popular resort destination owes its success to its location on the superb eastern coastline of Yucatán, which is washed by the exquisitely colored and translucent waters of the Caribbean and endowed with a semitropical climate, unbroken stretches of beach, and the world's second-longest barrier reef, which separates the mainland from Cozumel. Cancún, along with Cozumel and to a lesser extent Isla Mujeres and Playa del Carmen, incarnates the success formula for sun-and-sand tourism: luxury hotels, sandy beaches, water sports, nightlife, and restaurants that specialize in international fare.

Although Cancún is no longer less expensive than its Caribbean neighbors, it can be reached via more nonstop flights and it offers a far richer culture. With the advent of Cancún, the peninsula's Maya ruins—long a mecca for archaeology enthusiasts—have become virtual satellites of that glittering star. The proximity of such compelling sites as Chichén Itzá, Uxmal, and Tulum allows Cancún's visitors to explore the vestiges of one of the most brilliant civilizations in the ancient world without having to journey too far from their base.

Yucatán offers a breathtaking diversity of other charms, too. The waters of the Mexican Caribbean are clearer and more turquoise than those of the Pacific; many of the beaches are unrivaled. Scuba diving (in natural sinkholes and along the barrier reefs), snorkeling, deep-sea fishing, and other water sports attract growing numbers of tourists. They can also go birding, kayaking, bicycling, and camping, and shop for Yucatán's splendid handicrafts. There is a broad spectrum of settings and accommodations to choose from: the high-rise, pricey strip of hotels along Cancún's Boulevard Kukulcán; the less showy properties on Cozumel, beloved by scuba divers; and the relaxed ambience of Isla Mujeres, where most lodgings consist of rustic bungalows with ceiling fans and hammocks.

There are also the cities of Yucatán. Foremost is Mérida, where Moorish-inspired, colonnaded colonial architecture blends handsomely with turn-of-the-20th-century pomposity. In Mérida, café life remains an art, and the Maya still live proudly as Maya. Campeche, one of the few walled cities in North America, possesses an eccentric charm; it is slightly out of step with the rest of the country and not the least bothered by the fact. Down on the border with Belize stands Chetumal, an eclectic mix of wood-frame houses and brightly colored buildings that hosts a hybrid culture of coastal Central America and Mexico. Progreso, at the other end of the peninsula on the Gulf of Mexico, is Chetumal's northern counterpart, an overgrown fishing village turned commercial port. Hotels in these towns, while for the most part not as luxurious as the beach resort properties, range from the respectable if plain 1970s commercial buildings to the undated fleabags so popular with detective novelists (one thinks especially of Raymond Chandler) and filmmakers.

Wildlife is another of Yucatán's riches. Iguanas, lizards, tapirs, deer, snakes, armadillos, and wild boars thrive on this alternately parched and densely foliated plain. Flamingos and herons, manatees and sea turtles, their once-dwindling numbers now rising in response to Mexico's newly awakened ecological consciousness, find idyllic watery habitats in and above the coastline's mangrove swamps, lagoons, and sandbars, acres of which have been made into national parks. Both Río Lagartos and the coast's Sian Ka'an Biosphere Reserve sparkle with Yucatán's natural beauty. Orchids, bougainvillea, and poinciana are ubiquitous; dazzling reds and

pinks and oranges and whites spill into countless courtyards—effortless hothouses. And while immense palm groves and forests of precious hardwood trees slowly succumb to fire and disease, the region's edible tropical flora—coconuts, papaya, bananas, and oranges—remains a succulent ancillary to the celebrated Yucatecan cuisine.

But perhaps it is the colors of Yucatán that are most remarkable. From the stark white, sun-bleached sand, the sea stretches out like some immense canvas painted in bands of celadon greens, pale aquas, and deep dusty blues. At dusk the sea and the horizon meld in the sumptuous glow of a lavender sunset, the sky just barely tinged with periwinkle and violet. Inland, the beige, gray, and amber stones of ruined temples are set off by riotous greenery. The colors of newer structures are equally intoxicating: tawny, gray-brown thatch roofs sit atop white oval huts. Colonial mansions favor creamy pastels of bisque, salmon, and coral tones, again highlighted by elegant white: white arches, white balustrades, white rococo porticos. Brilliant colors glimmer in carved hardwood doors, variegated tile floors, brown and green pottery and rugs affixed to walls, and snatches of bougainvillea rushing down the sides of buildings.

Yucatán's color extends beyond the physical to the historical. From the conquistadors' first landfall off Cape Catoche in 1517 to the bloody skirmishes that wiped out most of the Indians to the razing of Maya temples and burning of their sacred books, the peninsula was a battlefield. Pirates wreaked havoc off the coast of Campeche for centuries. Half the Indian population was killed during the 19th-century uprising known as the War of the Castes, when the enslaved indigenous population rose up and massacred thousands of Europeans; Yucatán was attempting to secede from Mexico, and dictator Porfirio Díaz sent in his troops. These events, like the towering Maya civilization, have left their mark throughout the peninsula: in its archaeological museums, its colonial monuments, and the opulent mansions of the hacienda owners who enslaved the natives to cultivate their henequen.

Today this remains a land of paradox, where you quickly can move from the lavish luxury of an all-inclusive resort to the simplicity of a Maya home with a thatch roof and no electricity. The economic crisis triggered by the late-1994 peso devaluation resulted in increased purchasing power for foreigners, who have bought homes and hotels throughout the region, creating a diverse international population that lives alongside the Maya.

But despite the past's violent conflicts with foreigners, the people of Yucatán treat today's visitors with genuine hospitality and friendliness, especially outside the beach resorts. If you learn a few words of Spanish or Maya, you will be rewarded with an even warmer welcome.

— Erica Meltzer and Shelagh McNally

Portrait

THE MAYA AND YUCATÁN AT A GLANCE

11,000 BC   Hunters and gatherers settle in Yucatán.

Preclassic Period: 2000 BC–AD 200

2,000 BC   Maya ancestors in Guatemala begin to cultivate corn and build permanent dwellings.

1500–900 BC   The powerful and sophisticated Olmec civilization develops along the Gulf of Mexico in the present-day states of Veracruz and Tabasco.

Primitive farming communities develop in Yucatán.

900–300 BC   Olmec iconography and social institutions strongly influence the Maya populations in neighboring areas. The Maya adopt the Olmecs' concepts of tribal confederacies and small kingships as they move across the lowlands.

600 BC   Edzná is settled. It will be inhabited for nearly 900 years before the construction of the large temples and palaces found there today.

400 BC– AD 100   Dzibilchaltún develops as an important center in Komchen, an ancient state north of present-day Mérida. Becán, in southern Campeche, is also settled.

300 BC   Major construction begins in the Maya lowlands as the civilization begins to flourish.

300 BC– AD 200   New architectural elements, including the corbeled arch and roof comb, develop in neighboring Guatemala and gradually spread into the Yucatán.

300 BC– AD 900   Edzná becomes a city; increasingly large temple–pyramids are built.

AD 200   A small temple is built on the island of Cancún.

Classic Period: 200–900

The calendar and the written word are among the achievements that mark the beginning of the Classic period. The architectural highlight of the period is large, stepped pyramids with frontal stairways topped by limestone and masonry temples, arranged around plazas and decorated with stelae (stone monuments), bas-reliefs, and frescoes. Each Maya city is painted a single bright color, often red or yellow.

200–600   Economy and trade flourish. Maya culture achieves new levels of scientific sophistication and some groups become warlike.

250–300   A defensive fortification ditch and earthworks are built at Becán.

300   The first structures are built at San Gervasio on Cozumel.

300–600   Kohunlich rises to dominate the forests of southern Quintana Roo.

400–1100	Cobá grows to be the largest city in the eastern Yucatán.
432	The first settlement is established at Chichén Itzá.
6th Century	Influenced by the Toltec civilization of Teotihuacán in Central Mexico, larger and more elaborate palaces, temples, ball courts, roads, and fortifications are built in southern Maya cities, including Becán, Xpujil, and Chicanná in Campeche.
600–900	Northern Yucatán ceremonial centers become increasingly important as centers farther south reach and pass developmental climax; the influence of Teotihuacán wanes. Three new Maya architectural styles develop: Puuc (exemplified by Chichén Itzá and Edzná is the dominant style; Chenes (in northern Campeche, between the Puuc hills and the Río Bec area) is characterized by ornamental facades with serpent masks; and Río Bec (at Río Bec and Becán) features small palaces with high towers exuberantly decorated with serpent masks.
850–950	The largest pyramids and palaces of Uxmal are built. By 975, however, Uxmal and most other Puuc sites are abandoned.

Post-Classic Period: 900–1541

900–1050	The great Classic Maya centers of Guatemala, Honduras, and southern Yucatán are abandoned. The reason for their fall remains one of archaeology's greatest mysteries.
circa 920	The Itzá, a Maya tribe from the Petén rain forest in Guatemala, establish themselves at Champotón and then at Chichén Itzá.
987–1007	The Xiu, a Maya clan from the southwest, settle near ruins of Uxmal.
1224	An Itzá dynasty known as Cocomes emerges as a dominant group in northern Yucatán, building their capital at Mayapán.
1263–1440	Mayapán, under the rule of Cocomes aided by Canul mercenaries from Tabasco, becomes the most powerful city–state in Yucatán. The league of Mayapán—including the key cities of Uxmal, Chichén Itzá, and Mayapán—is formed in northern Yucatán. Peace reigns for almost two centuries. To guarantee the peace, the rulers of Mayapán hold members of other Maya royal families as lifelong hostages.
1441	Maya cities under Xiu rulers sack Mayapán, ending centralized rule of the peninsula. Yucatán henceforth is governed as 18 petty provinces, with constant internecine strife. The Itzá return to Lake Petén Itzá in Guatemala and establish their capital at Tayasal (modern-day Flores), one of the last un-Christianized Maya capitals, which will not be conquered by the Spanish until 1692.
15th Century	The last ceremonial center on Cancún island is abandoned. Other Maya communities are developing along the Caribbean coast.
1502	A Maya canoe is spotted during Columbus's fourth voyage.

1511 Spanish sailors Jerónimo de Aguilar and Gonzalo Guerrero are shipwrecked off Yucatán's Caribbean coast and taken to a Maya village on Cozumel.

1517 Fernández de Córdoba discovers Isla Mujeres.

Trying to sail around Yucatán, which he believes to be an island, Córdoba lands at Campeche, marking first Spanish landfall on the mainland. He is defeated by the Maya at Champotón.

1518 Juan de Grijalva sights the island of Cozumel but does not land there.

1519 Hernán Cortés lands at Cozumel, where he rescues Aguilar. Guerrero chooses to remain on the island with his Maya family.

1527, 1531 Unsuccessful Spanish attempts to conquer Yucatán.

1540 Francisco de Montejo founds Campeche, the first Spanish settlement in Yucatán.

1541 Another unsuccessful attempt by the Spanish to defeat Yucatán.

Colonial Period: 1541–1821

1542 Maya chieftains surrender to Montejo at T'ho; 500,000 Indians are killed during the conquest of Yucatán. Indians are forced into labor under the *encomienda* system, by which conquistadors are charged with their subjugation and Christianization. The Franciscans contribute to this process.

Mérida is founded on the ruins of T'ho.

1543 Valladolid is founded on the ruins of Zací.

1546 A Maya group attacks Mérida, resulting in a five-month-long rebellion.

1562 Bishop Diego de Landa burns Maya codices at Maní.

1600 Cozumel is abandoned after smallpox decimates the population.

1686 Campeche's city walls are built for defense against pirates.

1700 182,500 Indians account for 98% of Yucatán's population.

1736 Indian population of Yucatán declines to 127,000.

1761 The Cocom uprising near Sotuta leads to the death of 600 Maya.

1771 The Fuerte (fort) de San Miguel is completed on a hill above Campeche, ending the pirates' reign of terror.

1810 Port of Sisal opens, ending Campeche's ancient monopoly on peninsular trade and its economic prosperity.

Postcolonial/Modern Period: 1821–Present

1821 Mexico wins independence from Spain by diplomatic means. Various juntas vie for control of the new nation, resulting in frequent military coups.

1823 Yucatán becomes a Mexican state encompassing the entire peninsula.

1839–42 American explorer John Lloyd Stephens visits Yucatán's Maya ruins and describes them in two best-selling books.

1840–42 Yucatecan separatists revolt in an attempt to secede from Mexico. The Mexican government quells the rebellion, reduces the state of Yucatán to one-third its previous size, creates the federal territories of Quintana Roo and Campeche, and recruits Maya soldiers into a militia to prevent further disturbance.

1846 Following years of oppression, violent clashes between Maya militiamen and residents of Valladolid launch the War of the Castes. The entire non-Indian population of Valladolid is massacred.

1848 Rebels from the Caste War settle in the forests of Quintana Roo, creating a secret city named Chan Santa Cruz. An additional 20 refugee families settle in Cozumel, which has been almost uninhabited for centuries. By 1890 Cozumel's population numbers 500, Santa Cruz's 10,000.

1850 Following the end of the Mexican War with the United States in 1849, the Mexican army moves into the Yucatán to end the Indian uprising. The Maya flee into the unexplored forests of Quintana Roo. Military attacks, disease, and starvation reduce the Maya population of the Yucatán Peninsula to less than 10,000.

1863 Campeche achieves statehood.

1872 The city of Progreso is founded.

1880–1914 Yucatán's monopoly on henequen, enhanced by plantation owner's exploitation of Maya peasants, leads to its Golden Age as one of the wealthiest states in Mexico. Prosperity will last until the beginning of World War II.

Waves of Middle Eastern immigrants arrive in Yucatán and become successful in commerce, restaurants, cattle ranching, and tourism.

Payo Obispo (present-day Chetumal) is founded on the site of a long-abandoned Spanish colonial outpost.

1901 The Cult of the Talking Cross reaches the height of its popularity in Chan Santa Cruz (later renamed Felipe Carrollo Puerto). The Cruzob Indians continue to resist the Mexican army.

U.S. Consul Edward Thompson buys Chichén Itzá for $500 and spends the next three years dredging the Sacred Cenote for artifacts.

1902 Mexican President Porfirio Díaz asserts federal jurisdiction over the Territory of Quintana Roo to isolate rebellious pockets of Indians and increase his hold on regional resources.

1915 The War of the Castes reaches an uneasy truce after the Mexican Army leaves the Cruzob Indians to rule Quintana Roo as an independent territory.

1915–24 Felipe Carrillo Puerto, Socialist governor of Yucatán, institutes major reforms in land distribution, labor, women's rights, and education during Mexican Revolution.

Chronology

1923–48 A Carnegie Institute team led by archaeologist Sylvanus Moreley restores the ruins of Chichén Itzá.

1934–40 President Lázaro Cárdenas implements significant agrarian reforms in Yucatán.

1935 Chan Santa Cruz rebels in Quintana Roo relinquish Tulum and sign a peace treaty.

1940–70 With collapse of the world henequen markets, Yucatán gradually becomes one of the poorest states in Mexico.

1968 The Mexican government selects Cancún as the site of the country's largest tourist resort.

1974 Quintana Roo achieves statehood. The first resort hotels at Cancún open for business.

1988 Hurricane Gilbert shuts down Cancún hotels and devastates the north coast of the Yucatán. The reconstruction is immediate. Within three years, the number of hotels on Isla Cancún triples.

1993 Under the guise of an environmentalist platform, Quintana Roo's newly elected governor Mario Villanueva begins systematically selling off state parks and federally owned land to developers.

1994 Mexico joins the United States and Canada in NAFTA (North American Free Trade Association), which will phase out tariffs over a 15-year period.

Popular Partido Revolucionario Institucional (PRI) presidential candidate Luis Donaldo Colosio is assassinated while campaigning in Tijuana. Ernesto Zedillo, generally thought to be more of a technocrat and "old boy"–style PRI politician, replaces him and wins the election.

Zedillo, blaming the economic policies of his predecessor, devalues the peso in December.

1995 Recession sets in as a result of the peso devaluation. The former administration is rocked by scandals surrounding the assassinations of Colosio and another high-ranking government official; ex-President Carlos Salinas de Gortari moves to the United States.

Quintana Roo governor Mario Villanueva is suspected of using his office to smuggle drugs into the state.

1996 Mexico's economy, bolstered by a $28 billion bailout led by the United States, turns around, but the recovery is fragile. The opposition National Action Party (PAN), which is committed to conservative economic policies, gains strength. New details emerge of scandals within the former administration.

1997 Mexico's top antidrug official is arrested on bribery charges. Nonetheless, the United States recertifies Mexico as a partner in the war on drugs. Party elections are scheduled for midyear. When Mexican environmentalists discover that Villanueva has sold the turtle sanctuary on Xcacel beach to a Spanish hotel chain, they begin an international campaign to save the site; Greenpeace stages a protest on the beach.

1998 Mexican author Octavio Paz dies.

U.S. Congress demands an investigation into the office of Mario Villanueva. Villanueva is refused entry into the United States when the DEA reveals that it has an open file on his activities.

1999 Raúl Salinas, brother of former Mexican president Carlos Salinas di Gortari (in exile in Ireland), is sentenced for the murder of a PRI leader.

Joaquin Hendricks, a retired military officer, is elected the new governor of Quintana Roo. Although he is thought to be an enemy of Mario Villanueva, the ex-governor sanctions Hendricks's rise to power. The Mexican government decides to arrest Villanueva on drug charges; Villanueva disappears.

2000 Spurning long-ruling PRI, Mexicans elect opposition candidate Vicente Fox president. Villanueva remains at large.

Chronology

Golfo de México

Dzilam
de Bravo

Chicxulub
Progreso   Xcambó   Dzilan
Yucalpetén   González
Sisal   Tekantó
        Dzibilchaltún   Motul
Punta Baz
                              Citilcúm   Izan
        Parque   80
        Natural   Mérida ✈
Celestún Celestún   S. José   Hoctún
        281   Umán   Tzal   Holca
Punta Nimun   180
Chuncucmil   Mayapán   18
        Maxcanú
                    Muna   YUCA
Santa Cruz   Uxmal   Ticul
                                      184   Oxkutzcab
                          Kabah
                                      Tzucacab
                          Sayil
                          Labná
        Tenabó   261
Campeche   Tinúm   Becanchén
180 ✈
Punta Seybaplaya   261
                    Hopelchén
                                Dzilibnocac
                    Edzná
                          Dzibalchén
        La Joya   Hochol
Champotón

        CAMPECHE
Sabancuy   Río Champotón
180

Escárcega
        186   Xpujil
                                      186
            CALAKMUL
            BIOSPHERE RESERVE   Río Bec
186 ↓

Q

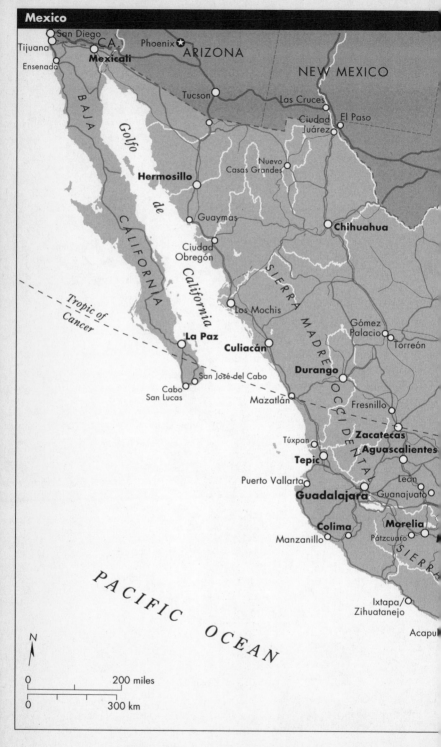

Mexico

San Diego
Tijuana
Mexicali
Ensenada
Phoenix
ARIZONA
NEW MEXICO

BAJA

Golfo

Tucson
Las Cruces
Ciudad
Juárez
El Paso

de

Hermosillo
Nuevo
Casas Grandes

Guaymas
Ciudad
Obregón

CALIFORNIA
California

Chihuahua

SIERRA MADRE

Los Mochis

Tropic of
Cancer

La Paz
Culiacán

San José del Cabo
Cabo
San Lucas
Mazatlán

Gómez
Palacio
Torreón

Durango

Fresnillo

OCCIDENTAL

Túxpan
Tepic
Puerto Vallarta

Zacatecas
Aguascalientes

León
Guadalajara
Guanajuato

Colima
Manzanillo
Morelia
Pátzcuaro

SIERRA

PACIFIC OCEAN

Ixtapa/
Zihuatanejo
Acapu

N

0   200 miles

0   300 km

Oklahoma City

OKLAHOMA   ARKANSAS   TENN.

Memphis

Little Rock

MISS.

Dallas

Fort Worth

Jackson

TEXAS

ALA.

Austin

LOUISIANA   Mobile

San
Antonio

Baton
Rouge

New Orleans

Rio Grande

Monterrey

Brownsville

Reynosa

Saltillo

Matamoros

Gulf of Mexico

SIERRA MADRE ORIENTE

Ciudad Victoria

Ciudad Mante

San Luis
Potosí

Tampico

Tropic of Cancer

Isla
Mujeres

San Miguel
de Allende

Querétaro

Poza Rica

El Tajín

Mérida

Cancún

Tula

Teotihuacán

Chichén Itzá

Tizimín

Cozumel

Mexico City

Veracruz

Uxmal

Cobá

Xel-Há

Toluca

Puebla

Campeche

YUCATAN

Tulum

Cuernavaca

Bahía de Campeche

MADRE DEL SUR

Chilpancingo

Ciudad del
Carmen

Chetumal

Coatzacoalcos

Monte Albán

Minatitlán

Villahermosa

Caribbean Sea

Oaxaca

Palenque

Tuxtla
Gutiérrez

BELIZE

Tehuantepec

San Cristóbal
de las Casas

Bonampak

Huatulco

Comitán

Golfo de
Tehuantepec

GUATEMALA

HONDURAS

Tapachula

ESSENTIAL INFORMATION

ADDRESSES

The Mexican method of naming streets can be exasperatingly arbitrary, so **be patient when searching for street addresses.** Streets in the centers of many colonial cities (those built by the Spanish) are laid out in a grid surrounding the *zócalo* (main square) and often change names on different sides of the square. Other streets simply acquire a new name after a certain number of blocks. Numbered streets are usually designated *norte/sur* (north/south) or *oriente/poniente* (east/west) on either side of a central avenue. Three of these are abbreviated: Nte., Ote., and Pte. Sur is spelled out.

In many cities, streets that have proper names change names when they cross some other street—and only a map will show where one begins and the other ends. Blocks are often labeled numerically, according to distance from a chosen starting point, as in "la Calle de Pachuca," "2a Calle de Pachuca," etc.

Many Mexican addresses have "s/n" for *sin número* (no number) after the street name. This is common in small towns where there aren't many buildings on a block. A *carretera* is a main highway.

Abbreviations used in addresses include the following: Av. (*avenida,* or avenue); Calz. (*calzada,* or road); Fracc. (*fraccionamiento,* residential complex or development); and Int. (*interior,* which is the same in English). "Sm" stands for Super Manzana (*manzana* alone means block), or neighborhood; each may have its own park or square. Super Manzanas in Cancún and in other cities and towns are labeled with an Sm number (Sm 23, Sm 25, etc.).

Addresses in Mexico are written with the street name first, followed by the street number. A five-digit *código postal* (postal code) precedes the name of the city, followed by the state. Apartado Postal, abbreviated as Apdo. Postal or A.P., means post-office box.

AIR TRAVEL

Almost all flights to Cancún have stopovers at hub airports (Houston, Dallas, Miami, Chicago, Los Angeles, or Washington D.C.), where you must change planes and transfer luggage. Some flights go to Mexico City, where you must pass through customs before transferring to a domestic flight to Cancún. This applies to air travel from the United States, United Kingdom, Australia, and New Zealand.

BOOKING

When you book **look for nonstop flights** and **remember that "direct" flights stop at least once.** Try to avoid connecting flights, which require a change of plane. For more booking tips and to check prices and make online flight reservations, log on to www.fodors.com.

CARRIERS

You can reach the Yucatán by U.S., Mexican, or regional carriers. The most convenient flight from the United States is a nonstop one on a domestic or Mexican airline. Booking a carrier with stopovers adds several hours to your travel time. Flying within the Yucatán, although not cost efficient, saves you precious time if you are on a tight schedule. A flight from Cancún to Mérida, for example, can cost as much as one from Mexico City to Cancún. Select your hub city for exploring before making your reservation from abroad.

All the major airlines listed here fly to Cancún. Aeroméxico, American, Continental, and Mexicana also fly to Cozumel. Aeroméxico, Delta, and Mexicana fly to Mérida.

Within the Yucatán, Aerocaribe serves Cancún, Cozumel, Mérida, Chichén Itzá, Palenque, Chetumal, and Playa del Carmen. Aeroméxico flies to Campeche and Ciudad del Carmen from Mexico City. Aviacsa serves Cancún, Chetumal, and Mérida.

➤ MAJOR AIRLINES: **Aeroméxico** (☎ 800/237–6639). **American** (☎ 800/433–7300). **Continental** (☎ 800/231–0856). **Delta** (☎ 800/241–4141). **Lacsa** (☎ 800/225–2272). **Mexicana** (☎ 800/531–7921). **TWA** (☎ 800/892–4141). **US Airways** (☎ 800/428–4322).

➤ WITHIN THE YUCATÁN: **Aerocaribe** (through Mexicana, ☎ 800/531–7921). **Aeroméxico** (☎ 800/237–6639). **Aviacsa** (☎ 5448–8900 in Mexico City).

CHECK-IN & BOARDING

Assuming that not everyone with a ticket will show up, airlines routinely overbook planes. When everyone does, airlines ask for volunteers to give up their seats. In return, these volunteers usually get a certificate for a free flight and are rebooked on the next flight out. If there are not enough volunteers, the airline must choose who will be denied boarding. The first to get bumped are passengers who checked in late and those flying on discounted tickets, so **get to the gate and check in as early as possible,** especially during peak periods.

Always **bring a government-issued photo ID to the airport** (even when it's not required, a passport is best). You may be asked to show it before you are allowed to check in.

CUTTING COSTS

The least expensive airfares to the Yucatán Peninsula must usually be purchased in advance and are non-refundable. It's smart to **call a number of airlines, and when you are quoted a good price, book it on the spot**—the same fare may not be available the next day. Always **check different routings** and look into using different airports. Travel agents, especially low-fare specialists (☞ Discounts & Deals, *below*), are helpful.

Consolidators are another good source. They buy tickets for scheduled international flights at reduced rates from the airlines, then sell them at prices that beat the best fare available directly from the airlines, usually without restrictions. Sometimes you can even get your money back if you need to return the ticket. Carefully read the fine print detailing penalties for changes and cancellations, and **confirm your consolidator reservation with the airline.**

➤ CONSOLIDATORS: **Cheap Tickets** (☎ 800/377–1000). **Discount Airline Ticket Service** (☎ 800/576–1600). **Unitravel** (☎ 800/325–2222). **Up & Away Travel** (☎ 212/889–2345). **World Travel Network** (☎ 800/409–6753).

ENJOYING THE FLIGHT

For more legroom, **request an emergency-aisle seat.** Don't sit in the row in front of the emergency aisle or in front of a bulkhead, where seats may not recline. If you have dietary concerns, **ask for special meals when booking.** These can be vegetarian, low-cholesterol, or kosher, for example. On long flights, try to maintain a normal routine, to help fight jet lag. At night, **get some sleep.** By day, **eat light meals, drink water** (not alcohol), and **move around the cabin** to stretch your legs. For additional jet-lag tips consult *Fodor's FYI: Travel Fit & Healthy* (available at bookstores everywhere).

Many of the larger U.S. airlines no longer offer meals on flights to the Yucatán Peninsula. The flights are considered short-haul flights because there is a stopover at a hub airport (where you can purchase your own overpriced meals). The snacks provided on such flights are measly at best, so you may want to **bring food on board** with you.

FLYING TIMES

Cancún is 3½ hours from New York and Chicago, 4½ hours from Los Angeles, 3 hours from Dallas, 11¾ hours from London, and 18 hours from Sydney. Your actual travel time may be more if you must change planes at one of the hub airports and have a long layover. Flights to

Cozumel and Mérida are comparable in length.

HOW TO COMPLAIN

If your baggage goes astray or your flight goes awry, complain right away. Most carriers require that you **file a claim immediately.**

➤ AIRLINE COMPLAINTS: U.S. Department of Transportation **Aviation Consumer Protection Division** (✉ C-75, Room 4107, Washington, DC 20590, ☎ 202/366–2220, WEB www.dot.gov/airconsumer). **Federal Aviation Administration Consumer Hotline** (☎ 800/322–7873).

RECONFIRMING

Call the airline to reconfirm your flight at least 24 hours in advance. Reconfirming is especially important when flying with charter airlines, which often have long delays and cancellations.

AIRPORTS

Cancún Airport (CUN) and **Cozumel Airport** (ZZM) are the area's major gateways. The inland **Hector José Navarrette Muñoz Airport** (MID), in Mérida, is good-sized and closest to the major Maya ruins. Campeche, Chetumal, and Playa del Carmen have smaller airports served primarily by domestic carriers. The ruins at Palenque and Chichén Itzá also have airstrips that handle small planes.

Fly into the airport closest to where you'll be doing most of your travel. Airfares to Cancún, Mérida, and Cozumel don't differ much and the airports serving these three are no more than 20 minutes from downtown. Car rentals are a bit less expensive in Mérida than in Cancún and Cozumel, but not enough to warrant a four-hour drive to Cancún if it's your hub.

➤ AIRPORT INFORMATION: **Cancún Airport** (☎ 9/886–0500). **Cozumel Airport** (☎ 9/872–0485). **Navarrette Muñoz Airport** (☎ 9/943–1340).

DUTY-FREE SHOPPING

Cancún and Cozumel are duty-free shopping zones with more variety and better prices than the duty-free shops at the airports.

BIKE TRAVEL

Bicycling in Mexico is a rough-and-ready proposition. Most roads lack shoulders, and drivers are not used to accommodating cyclists. Bikes are especially useful for travel off the beaten track. In the Yucatán, where bikes are the primary form of transportation for locals, every small town has a bike-repair shop. Be sure to **carry plenty of water and everything you might need to repair your bike.** Pack extra patch kits; shards of glass often litter the roads. If you can take your bike apart and fold it up, buses will allow you to store it in the cargo space.

Your hotel can direct you to local rental agents. You may get a new mountain bike, but it is more likely that you'll get an ordinary bicycle, nothing glamorous or high-tech. Rentals start at about $30 per day. Helmets are not widely worn or available.

Pemex and Guía Roji maps are available at *papelerias* (stationery stores), bookstores, newspaper stands, and department stores in Mexico.

BIKES IN FLIGHT

U.S. airlines charge extra for bikes. For bike boxes, often free at bike shops, you pay about $20, for bags, $10, and for the bike itself, $75. This goes for international as well as domestic flights. Canadian airlines allow you to substitute a bike for a piece of checked luggage at no charge; otherwise, the cost is more than $100.

BIKING RESOURCES

Latin America by Bike (Mountaineer Books), by Walter Sienko, provides information on biking opportunities in Mexico as well as Central and South America. *Bicycling Mexico* (Hunter Publishing Inc.), by Ericka Weisbroth and Eric Ellman, is the bible of bicyclists, complete with maps, color photos, historical information, and a kilometer-by-kilometer breakdown of every route possible. For a list of companies that run organized bike tours of Mexico, *see* Tours & Packages, *below.*

BOAT & FERRY TRAVEL

The Yucatán is served by a number of ferries and boats, ranging from the efficient hydrofoils (motorized catamarans) between Playa del Carmen and Cozumel to the more modest launches between Puerto Juárez, Punta Sam, and Isla Mujeres.

FARES & SCHEDULES

Most carriers follow schedules, with the exception of boats going to the smaller, less-visited islands. However, departure times can vary with the weather and the number of passengers.

For specific fares and schedules, *see* the A to Z sections in each chapter.

BUS TRAVEL

The Mexican bus network is extensive and also the best means of getting around since passenger trains have just about become obsolete. Service is frequent and tickets can be purchased on the spot (except during holidays and on long weekends, when advance purchase is crucial). **Bring something to eat on long trips** in case you don't like the restaurant where the bus stops; **bring toilet tissue;** and **wear a sweater,** as the air-conditioning is often set on high. Most buses play videos or television continually until midnight, so if you are bothered by noise **bring earplugs.** Smoking is prohibited on a growing number of Mexican buses, though the rule is occasionally ignored.

CLASSES

Buses range from comfortable, fast, air-conditioned coaches with bathrooms, televisions, and complimentary beverages (*especial,* deluxe, and first-class) to dilapidated "vintage" buses (second-class) on which everyone rides, including pigs and chickens, and which stop at every small village along the way. A second-class bus ride can be interesting if you're not in a hurry and want to see the sights and experience the local culture. The fare is usually at least 20% cheaper. For comfort's sake alone, travelers planning a long-distance haul are advised to **buy first-class or especial tickets.** Several truly first-class bus companies offer service connecting Mexico's major cities.

ADO (Autobuses del Oriente) is the Yucatán's principal first-class bus company.

For additional city-specific bus travel information, *see* Bus Travel *in* the A to Z sections in each chapter.

FARES & SCHEDULES

Bus travel in the Yucatán, as throughout Mexico, is inexpensive by U.S. standards, with rates averaging $2–$5 per hour depending on the level of luxury (or not). Schedules are posted at bus stations; the bus leaves more or less around the listed time.

➤ BUS INFORMATION: **ADO** (☎ 01–800/702–8000; 9/884–5542; 9/884–4804 in Cancún; 9/925–0910 in Mérida).

RESERVATIONS

Most bus tickets, including first-class or *especial* and second-class, can be reserved in advance in person at ticket offices.

BUSINESS HOURS

In well-traveled places such as Cancún, Mérida, and Cozumel, businesses generally are open during posted hours. In more off-the-beaten-path areas, neighbors can tell you when the owner will return.

BANKS & OFFICES

Banks are open weekdays 9–5. Some banks open on Saturday mornings. Most businesses are open weekdays 9–2 and 4–7.

GAS STATIONS

Most gas stations are open 24 hours.

MUSEUMS & SIGHTS

Most museums throughout Mexico are closed on Monday and open 8–5 the rest of the week. But it's best to call ahead or ask at your hotel. Hours of sights and attractions in this book are denoted by a clock icon, ☉ .

PHARMACIES

Pharmacies in Cancún and Cozumel are usually open 8 AM–10 PM and stay open through the afternoon. More and more pharmacies in Campeche and the Yucatán are staying open during lunch. The big cities have at least one 24-hour pharmacy.

SHOPS

Stores in the tourist areas such as Cancún and Cozumel are usually open 10–9 Monday through Saturday. Some open on Sunday afternoon as well. Shops in more traditional areas, such as Campeche and the Yucatán, are generally closed Sunday. With the exception of Mérida, during the rest of the week they close between 1 and 4 PM, opening again in the evening.

CAMERAS & PHOTOGRAPHY

Don't snap pictures of military or high-security installations anywhere in the country. It's forbidden. Ask permission before taking pictures of indigenous people. Don't miss photos of the ruins at Tulum and Chichén Itza.

For tips, check out the *Kodak Guide to Shooting Great Travel Pictures* (available at bookstores everywhere).

➤ PHOTO HELP: **Kodak Information Center** (☎ 800/242–2424).

EQUIPMENT PRECAUTIONS

Try to **keep sand out of your camera. Don't pack film and equipment in checked luggage,** where it is much more susceptible to damage. X-ray machines used to view checked luggage are becoming much more powerful and therefore are much more likely to ruin your film. Always **keep film and tape out of the sun.** Carry an extra supply of batteries, and **be prepared to turn on your camera or camcorder** to prove to security personnel that the device is real. Always **ask for hand inspection of film,** which becomes clouded after repeated exposure to airport X-ray machines, and **keep videotapes away from metal detectors.**

FILM & DEVELOPING

Film is widely available in Cancún, Cozumel, Playa del Carmen, Campeche City, and Mérida, and all have one-hour photo development places. (Check to see that all the negatives were developed into pictures; sometimes a few are missed.) Prices are a bit more expensive than those in the United States.

CAR RENTAL

An economy car with no air-conditioning, manual transmission, and unlimited mileage begins at $50 a day or about $300 a week in Cancún; in Mérida, rates are about $35 a day or $210 a week; and in Campeche, $30 a day or $200 a week. Count on about $10 a day more with air-conditioning and automatic transmission. This does not include tax, which is 10% in Cancún and on the Caribbean coast and 15% elsewhere. The most common and least-expensive brand of car here is the Volkswagen Beetle.

➤ MAJOR AGENCIES: **Alamo** (☎ 800/522–9696; 020/8759–6200 in the U.K., WEB www.alamo.com). **Avis** (☎ 800/331–1084; 800/879–2847 in Canada; 02/9353–9000 in Australia; 09/525–1982 in New Zealand; 0870/606–0100 in the U.K., WEB www.avis.com). **Budget** (☎ 800/527–0700; 0870/156–5656 in the U.K., WEB www.budget.com). **Dollar** (☎ 800/800–6000; 0124/622–0111 in the U.K., where it's affiliated with Sixt; 02/9223–1444 in Australia, WEB www.dollar.com). **Hertz** (☎ 800/654–3001; 800/263–0600 in Canada; 020/8897–2072 in the U.K.; 02/9669–2444 in Australia; 09/256–8690 in New Zealand, WEB www.hertz.com). **National Car Rental** (☎ 800/227–7368; 020/8680–4800 in the U.K., WEB www.nationalcar.com).

CUTTING COSTS

To get the best deal, **book through a travel agent who shops around.** Also **price local car-rental companies,** although the service and maintenance may not be as good as those of a major player. Remember to ask about required deposits, cancellation penalties, and drop-off charges if you're planning to pick up the car in one city and leave it in another. If you're traveling during a holiday period, also make sure that a confirmed reservation guarantees you a car.

Do **look into wholesalers,** companies that do not own fleets but rent in bulk from those that do and often offer better rates than traditional car-rental operations. Payment must be made before you leave home.

> WHOLESALERS: **Kemwel Holiday Autos** (☎ 800/678–0678, FAX 914/825–3160, WEB www.kemwel.com).

INSURANCE

When driving a rented car you generally are responsible for any damage to or loss of the vehicle as well as for any property damage or personal injury that you may cause. Before you rent, see what coverage your personal auto-insurance policy and credit cards provide.

Regardless of any coverage afforded to you by your credit-card company, you must **obtain Mexican auto-liability insurance.** This is usually sold by car-rental agencies and included in the cost of the car. Be sure that you have been provided with proof of such insurance; if you drive without it, you are not only liable for damages, but you're also breaking the law. If you are in a car accident and you don't have insurance, you may be placed in jail until you are proven innocent.

REQUIREMENTS & RESTRICTIONS

In Mexico your own driver's license is acceptable, but an International Driver's Permit is a good idea. It's available from the American and Canadian automobile associations, and, in the United Kingdom, from the Automobile Association or Royal Automobile Club. These international permits are universally recognized, and having one may save you a problem with the local authorities.

SURCHARGES

Before you pick up a car in one city and leave it in another, **ask about drop-off charges or one-way service fees,** which can be substantial. Note, too, that some rental agencies charge extra if you return the car before the time specified in your contract. To avoid a hefty refueling fee, **fill the tank just before you turn in the car,** but be aware that gas stations near the rental outlet may overcharge.

CAR TRAVEL

Though convenient, cars are not a necessity in this part of Mexico. Cancún offers excellent bus and taxi service; Isla Mujeres is too small to make a car practical. Cars are not needed in Playa del Carmen because the downtown area is quite small and the main street is blocked off to vehicles. They're actually a burden in Mérida and Campeche City because of the narrow cobbled streets and the lack of parking spaces. Driving is the easiest way to explore other areas of the region, especially those off the beaten track. But even then a car is not absolutely necessary, as there is good bus service.

Before setting out on any car trip, **check your vehicle's fuel, oil, fluids, tires, and lights.** Gas stations and mechanics can be hard to find, especially in more remote areas. Consult a map and have your route in mind as you drive. Be aware that there is no formal driver's education in Mexico. This makes for many bad drivers on the roads who think nothing of tailgating, speeding, and weaving in and out of traffic. **Drive defensively** and keep your cool. When stopped for traffic or at a red light, always **leave sufficient room between your car and the one ahead** so you can maneuver to safety if necessary.

EMERGENCY SERVICES

The Mexican Tourism Ministry operates a fleet of some 350 pickup trucks, known as Los Angeles Verdes, or the Green Angels, to render assistance to motorists on the major highways. The bilingual drivers provide mechanical help, first aid, radio-telephone communication, basic supplies and small parts, towing, and tourist information. Services are free, and spare parts, fuel, and lubricants are provided at cost. Tips are always appreciated.

The Green Angels patrol fixed sections of the major highways twice daily 8–8, later on holiday weekends. If your car breaks down, **pull as far as possible off the road,** lift the hood, hail a passing vehicle, and ask the driver to **notify the patrol.** Most bus and truck drivers will be quite helpful. Do not accept rides from strangers. If you witness an accident, do not stop to help but instead find the nearest official.

> CONTACTS: **Green Angels** (☎ 9/928–6003; 5250–8221; 5250–8555, ext. 314).

GASOLINE

Pemex, Mexico's government-owned petroleum monopoly, franchises all gas stations, so prices throughout the Yucatán are the same. Prices tend to be about 30% higher than those in the United States; some stations in Mexico accept U.S. dollars and credit cards. Unleaded fuel, known as Magna Premio and Magna Sin (lower octane), is available at most Pemex stations. There are no self-service stations in Mexico. When you have your tank filled, **ask for a specific amount in pesos** to avoid being overcharged. Check to make sure that the attendant has set the meter back to zero and that the price is shown. Watch the attendant check the oil as well—to make sure you actually need it—and watch while he pours it into your car. **Never pay before** the gas is pumped, even if the attendant asks you to. Always **tip your attendant** a few pesos. Finally, **keep your gas tank full,** because gas stations are not plentiful in this area. If you run out of gas in a small village and there's no gas station for miles, ask if there is a local store that sells gas from containers.

PARKING

Always **park your car in a parking lot,** or at least in a populated area. Never leave anything of value in an unattended car.

ROAD CONDITIONS

The road system in the Yucatán Peninsula is extensive and generally in good repair. Route 307 parallels most of the Caribbean coast from Punta Sam, north of Cancún, to Tulum; here it turns inward for a stretch before returning to the coast at Chetumal and the Belize border. Route 180 runs west from Cancún to Valladolid, Chichén Itzá, and Mérida, then turns southwest to Campeche, Isla del Carmen, and on to Villahermosa. From Mérida, the winding, more scenic Route 261 also leads to some of the more off-the-beaten-track archaeological sites on the way south to Campeche and Francisco Escárcega, where it joins Route 186 going east to Chetumal. These highways are two-lane roads. Route 295 (from the north coast to Valladolid and Felipe Carrillo Puerto) is also a good two-lane road.

The *autopista,* or *carretera de cuota,* an eight-lane toll highway between Cancún and Mérida, was completed in 1993. It runs roughly parallel to Route 180 and cuts driving time between Cancún and Mérida—otherwise about 4½ hours—by about one hour. Tolls between Mérida and Cancún can run as high as $24 one way, and the stretches between highway exits are long.

Many secondary roads are in bad condition—unpaved, unmarked, and full of potholes. If you must take one of these roads, the best course is to **allow plenty of daylight hours and never travel at night.** Slow down when approaching towns and villages—which you are forced to do by the *topes* (speed bumps)—because small children and animals are everywhere. Children selling oranges, nuts, or other food will almost certainly approach your car. Some people feel that it's best not to buy from them, reasoning that if the children can make money this way, they will not go to school. Others choose to buy from them on the theory that they would probably go to school if they could afford it and need the meager profits to survive. Judge for yourself.

ROAD MAPS

Maps published by Pemex are available in bookstores and *papelerias* (stationery stores), but gas stations don't sell them.

RULES OF THE ROAD

Mileage and speed limits are given in kilometers. One kilometer is approximately ⁶⁄₁₀ mile. In small towns, observe the posted speed limits, which can be as low as 20 kph (12 mph). To make a left turn on the highway, move over to the right shoulder of the road, turn your left blinker on, wait for all the traffic to pass you, and then make your turn. Be aware that drunk driving is not a crime in Mexico. **Do not drive late at night even on good roads.**

If you are stopped for speeding or other traffic violations, the police officer will say he wants to take your license or license plates to hold until you pay a fine at the local police station. This is only a ploy that involves a time-wasting trip to the station. What he really wants is to have you pay the "fine" on the spot. This is actually a small bribe, called a *mordida* (literally, "a bite"); police salaries are quite low in Mexico and this is how many officers support themselves. If you are in a hurry, pay the fine, which may be as little as $10 to $20. If you decide to dispute the charge, do so with a smile (getting angry only makes things worse) and say that you'd like to give the fine to the police captain. The officer is likely to let you go rather than go to the station.

CHILDREN IN THE YUCATÁN PENINSULA

Traveling with children opens doors in Mexico that often remain closed to single travelers. If they enjoy travel in general, your children will do well throughout the Yucatán. If you are renting a car, don't forget to **arrange for a car seat** when you reserve.

FLYING

If your children are two or older, **ask about children's airfares.** As a general rule, infants under two not occupying a seat fly at greatly reduced fares or even for free. When booking, **confirm carry-on allowances** if you're traveling with infants. In general, for babies charged 10% of the adult fare you are allowed one carry-on bag and a collapsible stroller; if the flight is full, the stroller may have to be checked or you may be limited to less.

Experts agree that it's a good idea to use safety seats aloft for children weighing less than 40 pounds. Airlines set their own policies: U.S. carriers usually require that the child be ticketed, even if he or she is young enough to ride free, since the seats must be strapped into regular seats. Do check your airline's policy about using safety seats during takeoff and landing. And since safety seats are not allowed everywhere in the plane, get your seat assignments early.

When reserving, **request children's meals or a freestanding bassinet** if you need them. But note that bulkhead seats, where you must sit to use the bassinet, may lack an overhead bin or storage space on the floor.

FOOD

The more-populated areas, such as Cancún, Mérida, Campeche City, Cozumel, and Playa del Carmen, have U.S. fast-food outlets, and most restaurants that serve tourists have a special children's menu with the usual chicken fingers, hot dogs, and spaghetti. It's common for parents to share a plate with their children, so no one will look twice if you order one meal with two plates.

LODGING

Most hotels in the Yucatán Peninsula allow children under 12 to stay in their parents' room at no extra charge, but others charge for them as extra adults; be sure to **find out the cutoff age for children's discounts.** Most of the chain hotels offer services that make it easier to travel with children. These include connecting family rooms, wading pools and playgrounds, and kid's clubs with special activities and outings. Check with your hotel before booking to see if the price includes the services you're interested in.

➤ GOOD CHOICES: **Fiesta Americana Mérida** (✉ Av. Colón 451, at Paseo Montejo, Mérida 97000, ☎ 9/942–1111 or 800/343–7821, WEB www.fiestaamerican.com). **Reef Club** (✉ Carretera a Progreso Telchac, Km 32, Telchac Puerto 97320, ☎ 9/920–4466, WEB www.interclubresorts.com).

PRECAUTIONS

Mexico has one of the strictest policies about children entering the country. All children up to 18 years of age, including infants, are considered minors and must have proof of citizenship. If the child is traveling alone, he or she must have a notarized consent form signed by both parents. Airlines also require the name, address, and telephone number of the person meeting the unaccompanied minor upon arrival in Mexico. Children traveling with one parent must also have a notarized letter from the other parent stating that the child has his or her permission to leave the home country. If the other parent is deceased or the child has only one legal parent, a notarized statement to this effect must be presented. Parents must fill out a tourist card for each child over 10 years of age traveling with them.

Since children are particularly prone to diarrhea, be especially careful with their food and beverages. Infants and young children may be bothered by the heat and sun; make sure they drink plenty of fluids, wear sunscreen, and stay out of the sun at midday (☞ Health, *below*).

SIGHTS & ATTRACTIONS

The larger tourist areas have plenty of activities for children, including museums, zoos, aquariums, and theme parks. Places that are especially appealing to children are indicated by a rubber-duckie icon (🦆) in the margin.

SUPPLIES & EQUIPMENT

Fresh milk is hard to find—most of the milk sold here is reconstituted. Most other necessities, including *pañales desechables* (disposable diapers) and *fórmula infantil* (infant formula), can be found in almost every small town.

COMPUTERS ON THE ROAD

Before you plug in your computer in Mexico, invest in a Mexican surge protector, available at most electronics stores for about $45. The country experiences frequent surges and brown-outs (periods of diminished electrical power), and surge protectors used in the United States and in Canada are not effective here.

CONSUMER PROTECTION

Whenever shopping or buying travel services in the Yucatán, **pay with a major credit card,** if possible, so you can cancel payment or get reimbursed if there's a problem. If you're doing business with a particular company for the first time, **contact your local Better Business Bureau and the attorney general's offices** in your state and (for U.S. businesses) the company's home state as well. Have any complaints been filed? Finally, if you're buying a package or tour, always **consider travel insurance** that includes default coverage (☞ Insurance, *below*).

➤ BBBs: **Council of Better Business Bureaus** (✉ 4200 Wilson Blvd., Suite 800, Arlington, VA 22203, ☎ 703/

276–0100, FAX 703/525–8277, WEB www.bbb.org).

CRUISE TRAVEL

Cozumel and Playa del Carmen have become increasingly popular ports for Caribbean cruises. Royal Caribbean and Norwegian cruise lines depart from Miami. Lines with Caribbean cruises stopping in the Yucatán from other Florida ports (principally Fort Lauderdale, Port Manatee, and Tampa) include Cunard, Norwegian, Princess, and Regal. Holland America departs from New Orleans; Royal Olympic leaves from Galveston, Texas.

To learn how to plan, choose, and book a cruise-ship voyage, consult *Fodor's FYI: Plan & Enjoy Your Cruise* (available in bookstores everywhere).

➤ CRUISE LINES: **Cunard** (☎ 800/221–4770). **Holland America** (☎ 800/426–0327). **Norwegian** (☎ 800/327–7030). **Princess** (☎ 800/421–0522). **Regal** (☎ 800/270–7245). **Royal Caribbean** (☎ 800/327–6700). **Royal Olympic** (☎ 800/872–6400).

DISCOUNT CRUISES

Usually, the best deals on cruise bookings can be found by consulting a cruise-only travel agency.

➤ AGENCY: **National Association of Cruise Oriented Agencies** (NACOA; ✉ 7600 Red Rd., Suite 128, South Miami, FL 33143, ☎ 305/663–5626, FAX 305/663–5625).

CUSTOMS & DUTIES

When shopping, **keep receipts** for all purchases. Upon reentering the country, **be ready to show customs officials what you've bought.** If you feel a duty is incorrect or object to the way your clearance was handled, note the inspector's badge number and ask to see a supervisor. If the problem isn't resolved, write to the appropriate authorities, beginning with the port director at your point of entry.

It is illegal to bring tortoiseshell into the United States and several other countries. There are also some restrictions regarding black coral; to bring it into the United States you must present a certificate that shows it was purchased from a recognized dealer.

IN THE YUCATÁN PENINSULA

Entering Mexico, you may bring in personal items needed for your stay, along with: 400 cigarettes or 50 cigars (if you are over 18); one photographic camera and one nonprofessional film or video camera and 12 rolls of film for each; up to 20 cassettes or CDs; medicine for personal use; one personal laptop computer; and gift items not exceeding a combined value of $300. You are not allowed to bring meat, vegetables, plants, fruit, or flowers into the country.

IN AUSTRALIA

Australian residents who are 18 or older may bring home A$400 worth of souvenirs and gifts (including jewelry), 250 cigarettes or 250 grams of tobacco, and 1,125 ml of alcohol (including wine, beer, and spirits). Residents under 18 may bring back $A200 worth of goods. Prohibited items include meat products. Seeds, plants, and fruits need to be declared upon arrival.

➤ INFORMATION: **Australian Customs Service** (Regional Director, ✉ Box 8, Sydney, NSW 2001, Australia, ☎ 02/9213–2000, FAX 02/9213–4000, WEB www.customs.gov.au).

IN CANADA

Canadian residents who have been out of Canada for at least seven days may bring home C$750 worth of goods duty-free. If you've been away fewer than seven days but more than 48 hours, the duty-free allowance drops to C$200; if your trip lasts 24–48 hours, the allowance is C$50. You may not pool allowances with family members. Goods claimed under the C$750 exemption may follow you by mail; those claimed under the lesser exemptions must accompany you. Alcohol and tobacco products may be included in the seven-day and 48-hour exemptions but not in the 24-hour exemption. If you meet the age requirements of the province or territory through which you reenter Canada, you may bring in, duty-free, 1.14 liters (40 imperial ounces) of wine or liquor *or* 24 12-ounce cans or bottles of beer or ale. If you are 19 or older you may bring in, duty-free,

200 cigarettes and 50 cigars. Check ahead of time with the Canada Customs Revenue Agency or the Department of Agriculture for policies regarding meat products, seeds, plants, and fruits.

You may send an unlimited number of gifts worth up to C$60 each duty-free to Canada. Label the package UNSOLICITED GIFT—VALUE UNDER $60. Alcohol and tobacco are excluded.

➤ INFORMATION: **Canada Customs Revenue Agency** (✉ 2265 St. Laurent Blvd. S, Ottawa, Ontario K1G 4K3, Canada, ☎ 204/983–3500 or 506/636–5064; 800/461–9999 in Canada, FAX 613/991–4126, WEB www.ccra-adrc.gc.ca).

IN NEW ZEALAND

Homeward-bound residents 17 or older may bring back NZ$700 worth of souvenirs and gifts. Your duty-free allowance also includes 4.5 liters of wine or beer; one 1,125-ml bottle of spirits; and either 200 cigarettes, 250 grams of tobacco, 50 cigars, or a combination of the three up to 250 grams. Prohibited items include meat products, seeds, plants, and fruits.

➤ INFORMATION: **New Zealand Customs** (Custom House, ✉ 50 Anzac Ave., Box 29, Auckland, New Zealand, ☎ 09/300–5399, FAX 09/359–6730, WEB www.customs.govt.nz).

IN THE U.K.

From countries outside the European Union, including Mexico, you may bring home, duty-free, 200 cigarettes or 50 cigars; 1 liter of spirits or 2 liters of fortified or sparkling wine or liqueurs; 2 liters of still table wine; 60 ml of perfume; 250 ml of toilet water; plus £145 worth of other goods, including gifts and souvenirs. If returning from outside the EU, prohibited items include meat products, seeds, plants, and fruits.

➤ INFORMATION: **HM Customs and Excise** (✉ Dorset House, Stamford St., Bromley, Kent BR1 1XX, U.K., ☎ 020/7202–4227, WEB www.hmce.gov.uk).

IN THE U.S.

U.S. residents 21 and older may bring back 1 liter of alcohol duty-free. In addition, regardless of your age, you are allowed 200 cigarettes and 100 non-Cuban cigars. Antiques, which the U.S. Customs Service defines as objects more than 100 years old, enter duty-free, as do original works of art done entirely by hand, including paintings, drawings, and sculptures.

You may also mail or ship packages home duty-free: up to $200 worth of goods for personal use, with a limit of one parcel per addressee per day (except alcohol or tobacco products or perfume worth more than $5); label the package PERSONAL USE and attach a list of its contents and their retail value. Do not label the package UNSOLICITED GIFT or your duty-free exemption will drop to $100. Mailed items do not affect your duty-free allowance on your return.

➤ INFORMATION: **U.S. Customs Service** (✉ 1300 Pennsylvania Ave. NW, Washington, DC 20229, WEB www. customs.gov; inquiries ☎ 202/354–1000; complaints c/o ✉ 1300 Pennsylvania Ave. NW, Room 5.4D, Washington, DC 20229; registration of equipment c/o ✉ Office of Passenger Programs, ☎ 202/927–0530).

DINING

Eating breakfast or having cocktails in a variety of hotels is a good way of getting to know different properties. For lunch and dinner in Cancún, it's generally best to stay away from restaurants in the large chain hotels because prices tend to be exorbitant. (That said, some of the best restaurants may be located in such hotels; they are reviewed when that's the case.) The restaurants we list are the cream of the crop in each price category. Because it's impossible to evaluate the more makeshift places, when buying fish from beachside and roadside *palapas* (thatch-roof stands), examine the facilities as best you can for signs of unsanitary conditions, so you don't get food poisoning. Be especially careful with shellfish and chicken if there is no refrigeration.

MEALS & SPECIALTIES

Desayuno can be either a breakfast sweet roll and coffee or milk or a full breakfast of an egg dish such as *huevos a la mexicana* (scrambled eggs with chopped tomato, onion, and chilies), *huevos rancheros* (fried eggs on a tortilla covered with tomato sauce), or *huevos con jamón* (scrambled eggs with ham), plus juice and tortillas. Lunch is called *comida* or *almuerzo* and is the biggest meal of the day. Traditional businesses close down between 2 PM and 4 PM for this meal. It usually includes soup, a main dish, and dessert. Regional specialties include *pan de cazón* (baby shark shredded and layered with tortilla and tomato sauce), in Campeche; *pollo pibíl* (chicken marinated in sour orange and baked in banana leaves), in Mérida; and *tikinchic* (fish in a sour-orange sauce), on the coast. Restaurants in tourist areas also serve American-style food such as hamburgers, pizza, and pasta. The lighter evening meal is called *cena*.

MEALTIMES

Most restaurants are open daily for lunch and dinner during high season (December through April), but hours tend to be more erratic during the rest of the year. It's always a good idea to **phone ahead.** Unless otherwise noted, the restaurants listed in this guide are open daily for lunch and dinner.

PAYING

Most small restaurants do not accept credit cards. Larger chain restaurants and those catering to tourists take credit cards, but their prices reflect the fee placed on all credit-card transactions.

RESERVATIONS & DRESS

Reservations are always a good idea: we mention them only when they're essential or not accepted. Book as far ahead as you can, and reconfirm as soon as you arrive. We mention dress only when men are required to wear a jacket or a jacket and tie. For the most part, however, Yucatán restaurants, including those in hotels, are casual.

WINE, BEER & SPIRITS

Almost all restaurants in the region serve beer and some also offer wine. Larger restaurants have beer, wine, and spirits. You pay more for imported liquor such as vodka, brandy, and whiskey; tequila and rum are less expensive. Small lunch places called *loncherias* don't sell liquor, but you can bring your own as long as you are discreet. Almost all corner stores sell beer and tequila; grocery stores carry all brands of beer, wine, and spirits. Liquor stores are rare and usually carry specialty items. You must be 18 to buy liquor, but this rule is often overlooked.

DISABILITIES & ACCESSIBILITY

For people with disabilities, traveling in the Yucatán can be both challenging and rewarding. Travelers with mobility impairments used to venturing out on their own should not be surprised if locals try to prevent them from doing things. This is mainly out of concern; most Mexican families take complete care of relatives who use wheelchairs, so the general public is not accustomed to such independence. Additionally, very few places in the Yucatán have handrails, let alone special facilities and means of access. Although some of the newer hotels are accessible to wheelchairs, not even Cancún offers wheelchair-accessible transportation. Knowing how to ask for assistance is extremely important. If you are not fluent in Spanish, be sure to **take along a pocket dictionary.** Travelers with vision impairments who have no knowledge of Spanish probably need a translator; people with hearing impairments who are comfortable using body language usually get along very well.

LODGING

Le Meridien in Cancún, the Presidente Inter-Continental Cozumel, and the Fiesta Americana Mérida are the only truly wheelchair-accessible hotels in the region. Individual arrangements must be made with other hotels.

➤ GOOD OPTIONS: **Fiesta Americana Mérida** (⊠ Av. Colón 451, at Paseo Montejo, Mérida, Yucatán 97000, ☎ 9/942–1111 or 800/343–7821, ᴡᴇʙ www.fiestaamericana.com). **Le Meridien** (⊠ Retorno Del Rey Lote 37, Cancún, Quintana Roo 77500, ☎ 9/881–2200 or 800/225–5843, ᴡᴇʙ www.meridiencancun.com.mx). **Presidente Inter-Continental Cozumel** (⊠ Carretera Chankanaab, Km 6.5, Cozumel, Quintana Roo 77600,

☎ 9/872–0322 or 800/327–0200, ᴡᴇʙ www.interconti.com).

RESERVATIONS

When discussing accessibility with an operator or reservations agent, **ask hard questions.** Are there any stairs, inside *or* out? Are there grab bars next to the toilet *and* in the shower/tub? How wide is the doorway to the room? To the bathroom? For the most extensive facilities meeting the latest legal specifications, **opt for newer accommodations.**

SIGHTS & ATTRACTIONS

Few beaches, ruins, and sites around the Yucatán are accessible for people who use wheelchairs. The most accessible museums are found in Cancún. Xcaret is wheelchair accessible; special transport is available but must be arranged in advance.

TRANSPORTATION

There isn't any special transportation for travelers who use wheelchairs. Public buses are simply out of the question, there are no special buses, and some taxi drivers are not comfortable helping travelers with disabilities. Have your hotel arrange for a cab.

➤ COMPLAINTS: **Aviation Consumer Protection Division** (☞ Air Travel, *above*) for airline-related problems. **Civil Rights Office** (⊠ U.S. Department of Transportation, Departmental Office of Civil Rights, S-30, 400 7th St. SW, Room 10215, Washington, DC 20590, ☎ 202/366–4648, ꜰᴀx 202/366–9371, ᴡᴇʙ www.dot.gov/ost/docr/index.htm) for problems with surface transportation. **Disability Rights Section** (⊠ U.S. Department of Justice, Civil Rights Division, Box 66738, Washington, DC 20035-6738, ☎ 202/514–0301 or 800/514–0301; 202/514–0383 TTY; 800/514–0383 TTY, ꜰᴀx 202/307–1198, ᴡᴇʙ www.usdoj.gov/crt/ada/adahom1.htm) for general complaints.

TRAVEL AGENCIES

In the United States, the Americans with Disabilities Act requires that travel firms serve the needs of all travelers. Some agencies specialize in working with people with disabilities.

> TRAVELERS WITH MOBILITY PROBLEMS: **Access Adventures** (✉ 206 Chestnut Ridge Rd., Scottsville, NY 14624, ☎ 716/889–9096, dltravel@ prodigy.net), run by a former physical-rehabilitation counselor. **CareVacations** (✉ No. 5, 5110–50 Ave., Leduc, Alberta T9E 6V4, Canada, ☎ 780/ 986–6404 or 877/478–7827, FAX 780/ 986–8332, WEB www.carevacations. com), for group tours and cruise vacations. **Flying Wheels Travel** (✉ 143 W. Bridge St., Box 382, Owatonna, MN 55060, ☎ 507/451– 5005 or 800/535–6790, FAX 507/451– 1685, WEB www.flyingwheelstravel. com).

DISCOUNTS & DEALS

Be a smart shopper and **compare all your options** before making decisions. A plane ticket bought with a promotional coupon from travel clubs, coupon books, and direct-mail offers or on the Internet may not be cheaper than the least expensive fare from a discount ticket agency. And always keep in mind that what you get is just as important as what you save.

DISCOUNT RESERVATIONS

To save money, **look into discount reservations services** with toll-free numbers, which use their buying power to get a better price on hotels, airline tickets, even car rentals. When booking a room, always **call the hotel's local toll-free number** (if one is available) rather than the central reservations number—you'll often get a better price. Always ask about special packages or corporate rates.

When shopping for the best deal on hotels and car rentals, **look for guaranteed exchange rates,** which protect you against a falling dollar. With your rate locked in, you won't pay more, even if the price goes up in the local currency.

> AIRLINE TICKETS: ☎ **800/FLY– ASAP.**

> HOTEL ROOMS: **Players Express Vacations** (☎ 800/458–6161, WEB www.playersexpress.com). **Turbotrip. com** (☎ 800/473–7829, WEB www. turbotrip.com).

PACKAGE DEALS

Don't confuse packages and guided tours. When you buy a package, you travel on your own, just as though you had planned the trip yourself. Fly-drive packages, which combine airfare and car rental, are often a good deal.

ECOTOURISM

Turtle-nesting beaches in Cozumel, Isla Mujeres, and along the Caribbean coast are protected areas during July and August, when the females come ashore to lay their eggs. Always, when camping, be considerate of the environment by packing up your garbage, burying your waste, and following the rules as you would in your native country.

ELECTRICITY

Mexico operates on the 60-cycle, 120-volt system; however, many outlets have not been updated to accommodate three-prong and polarized plugs (those with one larger prong), so **bring an adapter.** When in Mexico **purchase a surge protector** for valuable electronic equipment such as computers and stereos.

EMBASSIES

> AUSTRALIA: **Australian Embassy** (✉ Rubén Darío 55, Col. Polanco, 11560 Mexico City, ☎ 5531–5225 information; 5407–1698 emergencies).

> CANADA: **Canadian Embassy** (✉ Calle Schiller 529, Col. Polanco, 11560 Mexico City, ☎ 5724–7900, FAX 5724–7982).

> NEW ZEALAND: **New Zealand Embassy** (✉ José Luis Lagrange, Col. Polanco, 11510 Mexico City, ☎ 5281–5486, FAX 5281–5212).

> UNITED KINGDOM: **U.K. Embassy** (✉ Río Lerma 71, Col. Cuauhtémoc, 06500 Mexico City, ☎ 5207–2089 or 5207–2449, FAX 5207–7672).

> UNITED STATES: **U.S. Embassy** (✉ Paseo de la Reforma 305, Col. Cuauhtémoc, 06500 Mexico City, ☎ 5511–9980 or 5209–9100, FAX 5511–9980).

EMERGENCIES

It's helpful, albeit daunting, to know ahead of time that you're not protected by the laws of your native land once you're on Mexican soil. However, if you get into a scrape with the law, you can call the Citizens' Emergency Center in the United States. In Mexico, you can also call the 24-hour English-speaking hot line of the Mexican Ministry of Tourism (SEC-TUR). The hot line can provide immediate assistance as well as general, nonemergency guidance. **In an emergency, call 06 from any phone.**

➤ CONTACTS: **Air Ambulance America of Mexico** (☎ 01–800/222–3564). **Air Evac** (☎ 619/278–3822), in the United States. **Citizens' Emergency Center** (☎ 202/647–5225 or 202/634–3600), in the United States. **Mexican Ministry of Tourism** (SEC-TUR; ☎ 01–800/903–9200 or 800/482–9832). **Procuraduría de Protección al Turista** (Attorney General for the Protection of Tourists; ☎ 514–2166 or 514–0155), in Mexico City.

ENGLISH-LANGUAGE MEDIA

BOOKS

There are very few English-language bookstores in the region, but Puerto Morelos and Isla Mujeres have some. Mérida has bookstores with small sections in English plus an English-language library. English-language books and magazines can be found at the bookstores and also at some of the larger grocery stores, but the publications are expensive.

NEWSPAPERS & MAGAZINES

Mexico has two major English-language newspapers, the *Mexico City Times* and the *News*. The latter is the larger of the two and contains the most complete coverage of local and international news, sports, and cultural events. Both are rather conservative in their politics. The *Miami Herald* publishes a Cancún edition that includes a few news stories from the United States.

RADIO & TELEVISION

There are no English-language radio stations except those picked up by shortwave radio. But Mexico is well served by cable and satellite TV; for example, Direct TV offers more than 500 (mostly English-language) stations.

ETIQUETTE & BEHAVIOR

In the United States, being direct, efficient, and succinct are highly valued traits. In Mexico, where communication tends to be more diplomatic and subtle, this style is often perceived as rude and aggressive. People will be far less helpful if you lose your temper and/or complain loudly, as such behavior is considered impolite. Remember that things move at a much slower rate here. There is no stigma attached to being late. Try to accept this pace gracefully. Learning basic phrases such as *por favor* (please) and *gracias* (thank you) in Spanish will make a big difference.

BUSINESS ETIQUETTE

Business etiquette is much more formal and traditional in Mexico than in the United States. Personal relationships always come first, so developing rapport and trust is essential. A handshake is an appropriate greeting, along with a friendly inquiry about family members. With established clients, do not be surprised if you are welcomed with a kiss on the check or full hug with a pat on the back. Mexicans love business cards—be sure to present yours in any business situation. Without a business card you may have trouble being taken seriously. In public always be respectful of colleagues and keep confrontations private. Meetings may or may not start on time, so remain patient with delays. When invited to dinner at the home of a customer or business associate, it's not necessary to bring a gift.

GAY & LESBIAN TRAVEL

Gender roles in Mexico are rigidly defined, especially in rural areas. Openly gay couples are a rare sight, and two people of the same gender may have trouble getting a *cama matrimonial* (double bed) at hotels. All travelers, regardless of sexual orientation, should be extra cautious when frequenting gay-friendly venues, as police sometimes violently crash these clubs, and there's little recourse or sympathy available to victims. The companies below can help answer your questions about safety and travel to the Yucatán.

➤ GAY- & LESBIAN-FRIENDLY TRAVEL AGENCIES: **Different Roads Travel** (✉ 8383 Wilshire Blvd., Suite 902, Beverly Hills, CA 90211, ☎ 323/651–5557 or 800/429–8747, FAX 323/651–3678, lgernert@tzell.com). **Kennedy Travel** (✉ 314 Jericho Turnpike, Floral Park, NY 11001, ☎ 516/352–4888 or 800/237–7433, FAX 516/354–8849, WEB www.kennedytravel.com). **Now Voyager** (✉ 4406 18th St., San Francisco, CA 94114, ☎ 415/626–1169 or 800/255–6951, FAX 415/626–8626, WEB www.nowvoyager.com). **Skylink Travel and Tour** (✉ 1006 Mendocino Ave., Santa Rosa, CA 95401, ☎ 707/546–9888 or 800/225–5759, FAX 707/546–9891, WEB www.skylinktravel.com), serving lesbian travelers.

HEALTH

Medical clinics in all the main tourist areas have English-speaking personnel. Many of the doctors in Cancún have studied in Miami and speak English fluently. Campeche and the more rural areas have few doctors who speak English.

DIVERS' ALERT

Do not fly within 24 hours of scuba diving.

FOOD & DRINK

In the Yucatán, the major health risk is posed by the contamination of drinking water, fresh fruit, and vegetables by fecal matter, which causes the intestinal ailment known as *turista,* or traveler's diarrhea. Bad shellfish can also be a culprit. To prevent such unpleasant interruptions to your vacation, **watch what you eat** and **always wash your hands before eating.** Stay away from ice, uncooked food, seafood that may not have been refrigerated, and unpasteurized milk and milk products, and **drink only bottled water or water that has been boiled** for several minutes. When ordering cold drinks at untouristed establishments, skip the ice—ask for your beverage *sin hielo.* (You can usually identify ice made commercially from purified water by its uniform shape and the hole in the center.) Hotels with water-purification systems post signs to that effect in the rooms. For mild cases of *turista,* try Pepto-Bismol. Drink plenty of puri-

fied water or tea; chamomile tea (*te de manzanilla,* which is readily available in restaurants throughout Mexico) is a good folk remedy for soothing the stomach. Try the BRAT diet (bananas, rice, applesauce, and dry toast). In severe cases, rehydrate yourself with a Gatorade drink or a salt–sugar solution. For children there is a special rehydrating formula available at all pharmacies. If you suspect food poisoning, see a local doctor immediately. If diarrhea persists for more than two days, see one of the local doctors. Take Lomotil or Imodium (loperamide), an antidiarrheal agent that dulls or eliminates abdominal cramps, if you must travel. Otherwise, it's often better to let the illness run its course.

MEDICAL PLANS

No one plans to get sick while traveling, but it happens, so **consider signing up with a medical-assistance company.** Members get doctor referrals, emergency evacuation or repatriation, hot lines for medical consultation, cash for emergencies, and other assistance.

➤ MEDICAL-ASSISTANCE COMPANIES: **International SOS Assistance** (WEB www.internationalsos.com; ✉ 8 Neshaminy Interplex, Suite 207, Trevose, PA 19053, ☎ 215/245–4707 or 800/523–6586, FAX 215/244–9617; ✉ 12 Chemin Riantbosson, 1217 Meyrin 1, Geneva, Switzerland, ☎ 4122/785–6464, FAX 4122/785–6424; ✉ 331 N. Bridge Rd., 17-00, Odeon Towers, Singapore 188720, ☎ 65/338–7800, FAX 65/338–7611).

OVER-THE-COUNTER REMEDIES

U.S. brands of acetaminophen, ibuprofen, aspirin, and other popular medications are readily available in Mexico (as is Pepto-Bismol). Most pharmacies have a blue book that lists generic and Mexican drug names. Get the generic name of your prescription drugs before your trip. Sunscreen is available at large supermarkets, pharmacies, and department stores. Prices are slightly higher than in the United States.

PESTS & OTHER HAZARDS

It's best to be cautious and go indoors at dusk (called the "mosquito hour" by locals). An excellent brand of *repellente de insectos* (insect repellent) called Autan is readily available; do not use it on children under age 2. If you want to bring a mosquito repellent from home, make sure it has at least 10% DEET or it won't be effective. If you're hiking in the jungle, wear repellent and long pants and sleeves; if you're camping in the jungle use a mosquito net and invest in a package of mosquito coils (sold in most stores). Another local flying pest is the deer fly, which resembles a common household fly with yellow stripes. Some people swell up after being bitten, but taking an antihistamine can help. Scorpions also live in the region; their sting is similar to a bee sting. Again, antihistamines help. Clean all cuts carefully as the rate of infection is much higher here.

Other hazards to travelers in Mexico are sunburn and heat exhaustion. The sun is strong here; it takes fewer than 20 minutes to get a serious sunburn. Avoid the sun between 11 AM and 3 PM all year round. Wear a hat and use sunscreen. You should **drink more fluid than you do at home**—Mexico is probably hotter than what you're used to and you will perspire more. Rest in the afternoons and stay out of the sun to avoid heat exhaustion. The first signs of dehydration and heat exhaustion are dizziness, extreme irritability, and fatigue.

SHOTS & MEDICATIONS

According to the U.S. government's National Centers for Disease Control and Prevention (CDC) there is a limited risk of malaria and dengue fever in certain rural areas of the Yucatán Peninsula, especially the states of Campeche and Quintana Roo. Travelers in mostly urban or easily accessible areas need not worry. However, if you plan to visit remote regions or stay for more than six weeks, **check with the CDC's International Travelers Hotline.** In areas where mosquito-borne diseases like malaria and dengue are prevalent, use mosquito nets, wear clothing that covers the body, apply repellent containing DEET, and use spray for flying insects in living and sleeping areas. You might **consider taking antimalarial pills,** but the side effects are quite strong and the current strain of Mexican malaria can be cured with the right medication. There is no vaccine to combat dengue, although it is not a life-threatening disease.

➤ HEALTH WARNINGS: **National Centers for Disease Control and Prevention** (CDC; National Center for Infectious Diseases, Division of Quarantine, Traveler's Health Section, ✉ 1600 Clifton Rd. NE, M/S E-03, Atlanta, GA 30333, ☎ 888/232–3228 or 877/394–8747, 𝙵𝙰𝚇 888/232–3299, 𝚆𝙴𝙱 www.cdc.gov).

HOLIDAYS

The lively celebration of holidays in Mexico interrupts most daily business, including banks, government offices, and many shops and services, so plan your trip accordingly: January 1, New Year's Day; February 5, Constitution Day; May 5, Anniversary of the Battle of Puebla; September 1, the State of the Union Address; September 16, Independence Day; October 12, Día de la Raza; November 1, Día de los Muertos (Day of the Dead); November 20, Revolution Day; and December 25, Christmas Day.

Banks and government offices close during Holy Week (the Sunday before Easter until Easter Sunday), especially the Thursday and Friday before Easter Sunday. Some private offices close from Christmas to New Year's Day; government offices usually have reduced hours and staff.

INSURANCE

The most useful travel-insurance plan is a comprehensive policy that includes coverage for trip cancellation and interruption, default, trip delay, and medical expenses (with a waiver for preexisting conditions).

Without insurance you will lose all or most of your money if you cancel your trip, regardless of the reason. Default insurance covers you if your tour operator, airline, or cruise line goes out of business. Trip-delay covers expenses that arise because of bad weather or mechanical delays. Study the fine print when comparing policies.

If you're traveling internationally, a key component of travel insurance is coverage for medical bills incurred if you get sick on the road. Such expenses are not generally covered by Medicare or private policies. U.K. residents can buy a travel-insurance policy valid for most vacations taken during the year in which it's purchased (but check preexisting-condition coverage). British and Australian citizens need extra medical coverage when traveling overseas.

Always **buy travel policies directly from the insurance company**; if you buy them from a cruise line, airline, or tour operator that goes out of business you probably will not be covered for the agency or operator's default, a major risk. Before making any purchase, **review your existing health and home-owner's policies** to find what they cover away from home.

➤ TRAVEL INSURERS: In the United States: **Access America** (✉ 6600 W. Broad St., Richmond, VA 23230, ☎ 800/284–8300, FAX 804/673–1491, WEB www.etravelprotection.com), **Travel Guard International** (✉ 1145 Clark St., Stevens Point, WI 54481, ☎ 715/345–0505 or 800/826–1300, FAX 800/955–8785, WEB www. noelgroup.com).

➤ INSURANCE INFORMATION: In the United Kingdom: **Association of British Insurers** (✉ 51–55 Gresham St., London EC2V 7HQ, U.K., ☎ 020/7600–3333, FAX 020/7696–8999, WEB www.abi.org.uk). In Canada: **Voyager Insurance** (✉ 44 Peel Center Dr., Brampton, Ontario L6T 4M8, Canada, ☎ 905/791–8700, 800/668–4342 in Canada). In Australia: **Insurance Council of Australia** (✉ Level 3, 56 Pitt St., Sydney NSW 2000, ☎ 02/9253–5100, FAX 02/9253–5111, WEB www.ica.com.au). In New Zealand: **Insurance Council of New Zealand** (✉ Box 474, Wellington, New Zealand, ☎ 04/472–5230, FAX 04/473–3011, WEB www.icnz.org.nz).

LANGUAGE

Spanish is the official language of Mexico, although Indian languages are spoken by approximately 20% of the population, many of whom speak no Spanish at all. In the beach resorts of Cancún and Cozumel, English is understood by most people employed in tourism; at the very least, shopkeepers know numbers in English for bargaining purposes. Mexicans welcome even the most halting attempts to use their language; in Mérida, you may even be introduced to a few Maya words and phrases. For a rudimentary vocabulary of terms that travelers are likely to encounter in the Yucatán, **review the Spanish vocabulary at the end of this book.**

The Spanish that most U.S. and Canadian citizens learn in high school is based on Castilian Spanish, which is different from Latin American Spanish. In terms of grammar, Mexican Spanish ignores the *vosotros* form of the second person plural, using the more formal *ustedes* in its place. As for pronunciation, the lisped Castilian "c" or "z" is dismissed in Mexico as a sign of affectation. The most obvious differences are in vocabulary: Mexican Spanish has thousands of indigenous words and uses *¿mande?* instead of *¿cómo?* (excuse me?). Words or phrases that are harmless or commonplace in one Spanish-speaking country can take on salacious or otherwise offensive meanings in another. Unless you are lucky enough to be briefed on these nuances by a native coach, the only way to learn is by trial and error.

LANGUAGE-STUDY PROGRAMS

Intensive Spanish classes for foreigners are offered by two schools in Mérida: Centro de Idiomas and the slightly more expensive Academia de Cultura e Idiomas de Mérida. Classes last a minimum of two weeks; advanced classes in special areas of study are available. Students stay with local families or in hotels. There is also a recommended Spanish-language study center in Playa del Carmen. Students can stay at the center or lodge with a local family.

➤ PROGRAMS: **Academia de Cultura e Idiomas de Mérida** (✉ Calle 13 No. 23, at Calle 10, Prado Nte., 97137 Mérida, Yucatán, ☎ 9/944–3148). **Centro de Idiomas** (✉ Calle 57 at Calle 66, Altos, Ed. Alejandria, 97000 Mérida, Yucatán, ☎ 9/923–0954 or 9/926–1156). **Playalingua del Caribe** (✉ Calle 20 Nte. between Avs.

5a and 10a, Playa del Carmen, ☎ 9/
873–3876, WEB www.playalingua.
com).

LANGUAGES FOR TRAVELERS

A phrase book and language-tape set
can help get you started. *Fodor's
Spanish for Travelers* (available at
bookstores everywhere) is excellent.

LODGING

You have a variety of accommodations to choose from if you plan to
stay in Cancún or Cozumel. Here,
luxurious and expensive internationally affiliated properties, with lots of
restaurants, cafés, and bars, have the
latest room amenities, boutiques, and
sports facilities. These beach resorts
also have more-modest accommodations—usually a short walk or a
shuttle ride from the water. Of course,
as you get into the less-populated and
-visited areas of the Yucatán, accommodations tend to be simpler and
more typically Mexican: inexpensive
bungalows, campsites, and beachside
places to hang a hammock. The
lodgings and facilities we list are the
cream of the crop in each price category. When pricing accommodations,
always ask what's included and what
costs extra.

Assume that hotels operate on the
European Plan (EP, with no meals)
unless we specify that they use either
the **Continental Plan** (CP, with a
Continental breakfast) or the **Modi-
fied American Plan** (MAP, with
breakfast and dinner) or are **all-
inclusive** (including all meals and
most activities).

APARTMENT & VILLA RENTALS

➤ INTERNATIONAL AGENTS: **Hide-
aways International** (✉ 767 Islington
St., Portsmouth, NH 03801, ☎ 603/
430–4433 or 800/843–4433, FAX 603/
430–4444, WEB www.hideaways.com;
membership $129). **Vacation Home
Rentals Worldwide** (✉ 235 Kensing-
ton Ave., Norwood, NJ 07648,
☎ 201/767–9393 or 800/633–3284,
FAX 201/767–5510, WEB www.
vhrww.com). **Villas International**
(✉ 950 Northgate Dr., Suite 206, San
Rafael, CA 94903, ☎ 415/499–9490
or 800/221–2260, FAX 415/499–9491,
WEB www.villasintl.com).

➤ LOCAL AGENTS: **Mundaca Travel**
(✉ Av. Hidalgo, 77400 Isla Mujeres,
Quintana Roo, ☎ 9/877–0025 or 9/
877–0026, FAX 9/877–0076, WEB www.
mundaca.com). **Vicki Sharp** (☎ FAX 9/
871–0112), in Puerto Morelos.

HOME EXCHANGES

If you would like to exchange your
home for someone else's, **join a home-
exchange organization,** which will
send you its updated listings of available exchanges for a year and will
include your own listing in at least
one of them. It's up to you to make
specific arrangements.

➤ EXCHANGE CLUBS: **HomeLink
International** (✉ Box 47747, Tampa,
FL 33647, ☎ 813/975–9825 or 800/
638–3841, FAX 813/910–8144, WEB
www.homelink.org; $98 per year).

HOTELS

In the off-season, Cancún hotels can
cost one-third to one-half what they
cost during peak season. Keep in
mind, however, that this is also the
time that many hotels undergo necessary repairs or renovations.

All hotels listed have private bath
unless otherwise noted.

➤ TOLL-FREE NUMBERS: **Best Western**
(☎ 800/528–1234, WEB www.best-
western.com). **Choice** (☎ 800/221–
2222, WEB www.hotelchoice.com).
Doubletree and Red Lion Hotels
(☎ 800/222–8733, WEB www.
doubletree.com). **Forte** (☎ 800/225–
5843, WEB www.forte-hotels.com).
Hilton (☎ 800/445–8667, WEB www.
hilton.com). **Holiday Inn** (☎ 800/
465–4329, WEB www.basshotels.com).
Howard Johnson (☎ 800/654–4656,
WEB www.hojo.com). **Hyatt Hotels &
Resorts** (☎ 800/233–1234, WEB www.
hyatt.com). **Inter-Continental**
(☎ 800/327–0200, WEB www.
interconti.com). **Marriott** (☎ 800/
228–9290, WEB www.marriott.com).
Le Meridien (☎ 800/543–4300, WEB
www.lemeridien-hotels.com). **Omni**
(☎ 800/843–6664, WEB www.
omnihotels.com). **Ritz-Carlton**
(☎ 800/241–3333, WEB www.
ritzcarlton.com). **Sheraton** (☎ 800/
325–3535, WEB www.starwood.com).
Westin Hotels & Resorts (☎ 800/
228–3000, WEB www.westin.com).

MAIL & SHIPPING

Mail can be sent from your hotel or the local post office. Be forewarned, however, that mail service to, within, and from Mexico is notoriously slow and can take anywhere from 10 days to six weeks. **Never send anything of value to or from Mexico via the mail,** including checks or credit-card numbers.

POSTAL RATES

It costs a minimum of 6 pesos to mail a postcard or letter weighing fewer than 20 grams to the United States or Canada; the cost to Great Britain is 8 pesos.

RECEIVING MAIL

Mail can be sent either to your hotel, to the post office, or, if you are an American Express card member, to the local branch of American Express. There are American Express offices in Campeche City, Mérida, Cancún, and Cozumel. Another option is the Mexican postal service's *lista de correos* service. To use this service, you must first register with the local post office where you wish to receive your mail. Mail should be addressed to: your name; a/c Lista de Correos; town name; state, postal code; Mexico. Mail is held at post offices for 10 days, and a list of recipients is posted daily. Postal codes for the main Yucatán destinations are as follows: Cancún, 77500; Isla Mujeres, 77400; Cozumel, 77600; Campeche, 24000; Mérida, 97000.

SHIPPING PARCELS

Hotel concierges can recommend international carriers, such as DHL, Estafeta, UPS, or Federal Express, which give your package a tracking number and ensure its arrival back home.

MONEY MATTERS

Prices in this book are quoted most often in U.S. dollars. This is because the value of the peso fluctuates considerably and what costs 90 pesos today might cost 120 pesos in six months.

Mexico has a reputation for being inexpensive, particularly compared with other North American vacation spots, such as the Caribbean; peso devaluations have made this especially true, though prices of the large chain hotels, calculated in dollars, have not gone down, and most restaurant owners and merchants have raised their prices to compensate for the devaluation. In general, costs vary with the when, where, and how of your travel. If you are not wedded to standardized creature comforts, you can spend as little as $30 a day on room, board, and local transportation. Speaking Spanish is also helpful in bargaining situations and when asking for dining recommendations. As a rule, region by region, costs decrease as the amount of English that people speak decreases.

Cancún is one of the most expensive destinations in Mexico. Cozumel is a bit less costly than Cancún, and Isla Mujeres in turn is slightly less expensive than Cozumel. You're likely to get the best value for your money in Mérida and the other Yucatán cities less frequented by visitors, like Campeche. For obvious reasons, if you stay at international chain hotels and eat at restaurants designed with tourists in mind (especially hotel restaurants), you may not find the Yucatán such a bargain.

Peak-season sample costs: cup of coffee, 10–20 pesos; bottle of beer, 20–50 pesos; plate of tacos with trimmings, 25–60 pesos; grilled fish platter at a tourist restaurant, 35–80 pesos; 2-km (1-mi) taxi ride, 20 pesos.

Prices throughout this guide are given for adults. Substantially reduced fees are almost always available for children, students, and senior citizens. For information on taxes, *see* Taxes, *below.*

ATMS

Cirrus and Plus are the most commonly found networks in Mexico. Many big hotels and all but the smallest Mexican towns have major banks with 24-hour ATMs. If your transaction cannot be completed—an annoyingly common occurrence—chances are that the computer lines are busy or being serviced and you'll have to try again later. If it's a holiday, it's possible that the machine has run out of money.

Many Mexican ATMs accept only personal identification numbers (PINs) of four or fewer digits. If your PIN is longer, ask your bank about changing it before you go; it sometimes takes a few weeks to process the change.

For cash advances, plan to use your Visa and MasterCard, as many Mexican ATMs don't accept American Express. The ATMs at Banamex, one of the oldest and perhaps the strongest of the nationwide banks, tend to be the most reliable, and generally give you an excellent exchange rate. Bancomer is another bank with many *cajero automatico* (ATM) locations, but they generally provide only cash withdrawals (rather than credit-card advances). The Serfín banks have reliable ATMs that accept credit cards as well as Plus and Cirrus bank cards.

CREDIT CARDS

Large hotels, restaurants, and department stores accept credit cards readily. Most of the smaller, less expensive restaurants and shops take cash only. Credit cards are generally not accepted in small towns and villages, except in the larger hotels. When shopping, you can usually get better prices if you **pay with cash.** But if you need to rely on your credit cards, it's wise to **make sure that "pesos" is clearly marked on all credit-card receipts** to avoid fraud. Keep good, accurate records of all transactions to avoid paying for fraudulent charges that might be put through by unscrupulous hotel employees.

Throughout this guide, the following abbreviations are used: **AE,** American Express; **D,** Discover; **DC,** Diners Club; **MC,** MasterCard; and **V,** Visa.

➤ REPORTING LOST CARDS: **American Express** (☎ 301/214–8228; call collect from Mexico). **Diners Club** ☎ 5258–3220 or, for collect calls from Mexico, 303/799–1504). **MasterCard** (☎ 800/307–7309; call collect from Mexico). **Visa** (☎ 800/847–2911 or 410/581–9994; call collect from Mexico).

CURRENCY

At press time, the exchange rate was 9.27 pesos to the U.S. dollar, 6.04 pesos to the Canadian dollar, 13.30 pesos to the pound sterling, 5.85 pesos to the Australian dollar, 4.80 pesos to the New Zealand dollar, and 10.50 pesos to the Irish punt. Because the market and prices continue to adjust, **check with your bank or the financial pages of your local newspaper for current exchange rates.** Prices in this book were calculated using a rate of 10 pesos to $1.

Pesos come in denominations of 10, 20, 50, 100, 200, and 500 pesos. Coins come in denominations of 20, 10, 5, 2 and 1 pesos and 50, 20 and 10 *centavos* (100 centavos equal one peso). Some denominations of bills and coins are very similar, so check carefully.

U.S. dollar bills, but not coins, are widely accepted in the Yucatán, particularly in Cancún, Cozumel, and Playa del Carmen. Many hotels, shops, and market vendors, as well as virtually all hotel service personnel, take them, too. Dollar bills are particularly welcome tips.

CURRENCY EXCHANGE

For the most favorable rates, **change money through banks.** Although ATM transaction fees may be higher abroad than at home, ATM rates are excellent because they are based on wholesale rates offered only by major banks. You won't do as well at exchange booths in airports or rail and bus stations, in hotels, in restaurants, or in stores. To avoid lines at airport exchange booths, **get a bit of local currency before you leave home.**

Most banks only change money on weekdays until 1 (though they stay open until 5), while *casas de cambio* (private exchange offices) generally stay open until 6 or 9 and often operate on weekends. Bank rates are regulated by the federal government and are therefore invariable, while casas de cambio have slightly more variable rates. Some hotels also exchange money, but for providing you with this convenience, they help themselves to a bigger commission than banks.

When changing money, count your bills before leaving the bank, and don't accept any partially torn, ink-marked, or taped-together bills; they will not be accepted anywhere. Also, many shop and restaurant owners are unable to make change for large bills. Enough of these encounters may compel you to request *billetes chicos* (small bills) when you exchange money.

➤ EXCHANGE SERVICES: **International Currency Express** (☎ 888/278–6628 for orders, WEB www.foreignmoney. com).

TRAVELER'S CHECKS

Do you need traveler's checks? It depends on where you're headed. If you're going to rural areas and small towns, go with cash; traveler's checks are best used in cities. Lost or stolen checks can usually be replaced within 24 hours. To ensure a speedy refund, buy your own traveler's checks—don't let someone else pay for them: irregularities like this can cause delays. The person who bought the checks should make the call to request a refund.

OUTDOORS & SPORTS

Water activities such as scuba diving, snorkeling, and deep-sea fishing are the main sports in the Yucatán. Scuba diving is synonymous with Cozumel, and with good reason. It's lauded as one of the best dive sites in the world. Divers also favor several spots along the Caribbean coast, which is blessed with abundant reefs. Isla Mujeres is best known for snorkeling, Cancún and Cozumel for deep-sea fishing. You can bring your own equipment or rent it at the myriad rental shops. Those bound for the elusive marlin or other billfish can find boat rentals with captain, crew, and equipment readily available; Cozumel has a billfishing tournament each spring.

Cancún has several world-class golf courses and Mérida has an 18-hole golf course on the outskirts of town.

Biking is one of the newer sports attracting a loyal following, but rental places are few and far between.

PACKING

Pack light, because you may want to save space for purchases: the Yucatán is filled with bargains on clothing, leather goods, jewelry, pottery, and other crafts.

Bring lightweight clothes, sundresses, bathing suits, sun hats or visors, and cover-ups for the Caribbean beach towns, but also pack a jacket or sweater to wear in the chilly, air-conditioned restaurants, or to tide you over during a rainstorm or an unusual cool spell. For trips to rural areas or Mérida, where dress is typically more conservative and shorts are considered inappropriate, women may want to pack one longer skirt. If you plan to visit any ruins, **bring comfortable walking shoes** with rubber soles. Lightweight rain gear is a good idea during the rainy season. Cancún is the dressiest spot on the peninsula, but even fancy restaurants don't require men to wear jackets.

Pack insect repellent, sunscreen, sunglasses, and umbrellas for the Yucatán. Other handy items—especially if you are traveling on your own or camping—include toilet paper, facial tissues, a plastic water bottle, and a flashlight (for occasional power outages or use at campsites). Snorkelers should consider bringing their own equipment unless traveling light is a priority; shoes with rubber soles for rocky underwater surfaces are also advised. For long-term stays in remote rural areas, *see* Health, *above*.

In your carry-on luggage, **pack an extra pair of eyeglasses or contact lenses** and **enough of any medication you take** to last the entire trip. You may also ask your doctor to write a spare prescription using the drug's generic name, since brand names may vary from country to country. In luggage to be checked, **never pack prescription drugs or valuables.** To avoid customs delays, carry medications in their original packaging. And don't forget to carry with you the addresses of offices that handle refunds of lost traveler's checks. Check *Fodor's How to Pack* (available in bookstores everywhere) for more tips.

CHECKING LUGGAGE

How many carry-on bags you can bring with you to the airline. Most allow two, but not always, so make sure that everything you carry aboard will fit under your seat or in the overhead bin, and get to the gate early. Note that if you have a seat at the back of the plane, you'll probably board first, while the overhead bins are still empty.

If you are flying internationally, note that baggage allowances may be determined not by piece but by weight—generally 88 pounds (40 kilograms) in first class, 66 pounds (30 kilograms) in business class, and 44 pounds (20 kilograms) in economy.

Airline liability for baggage is limited to $1,250 per person on flights within the United States. On international flights it amounts to $9.07 per pound or $20 per kilogram for checked baggage (roughly $640 per 70-pound bag) and $400 per passenger for unchecked baggage. You can buy additional coverage at check-in for about $10 per $1,000 of coverage, but it excludes a rather extensive list of items, shown on your airline ticket.

Before departure, **itemize your bags' contents** and their worth, and label the bags with your name, address, and phone number. (If you use your home address, cover it so potential thieves can't see it readily.) Inside each bag, **pack a copy of your itinerary**. At check-in, **make sure that each bag is correctly tagged** with the destination airport's three-letter code. If your bags arrive damaged or fail to arrive at all, file a written report with the airline before leaving the airport.

PASSPORTS & VISAS

When traveling internationally, **carry your passport** and **make two photocopies of the data page** (one for someone at home and another for you, carried separately from your passport). If you lose your passport, promptly call the nearest embassy or consulate and the local police.

ENTERING THE YUCATÁN PENINSULA

Citizens of the United States and Canada need only a valid piece of identification (passport, certified copy of a birth certificate, or a voter registration card) for stays of 180 days. British citizens need only a valid passport, and residents of Australia and New Zealand require a multiple-entry visa to the United States in addition to a valid passport. If you are flying into the state of Quintana Roo you will be issued a 30-day tourist visa. Your entry fee is included in the price of your airline ticket. If you drive into Mexico, you are given a 30- to 180-day tourist visa depending on the mood of the official. Ask for 180 days up front if that's what you want.

PASSPORT OFFICES

The best time to apply for a passport or to renew is in fall and winter. Before any trip, check your passport's expiration date and, if necessary, renew it as soon as possible.

➤ AUSTRALIAN CITIZENS: **Australian Passport Office** (☎ 131–232, WEB www.dfat.gov.au/passports).

➤ CANADIAN CITIZENS: **Passport Office** (☎ 819/994–3500; 800/567–6868 in Canada, WEB www.dfait-maeci.gc.ca/passport).

➤ NEW ZEALAND CITIZENS: **New Zealand Passport Office** (☎ 04/494–0700, WEB www.passports.govt.nz).

➤ U.K. CITIZENS: **London Passport Office** (☎ 0870/521–0410, WEB www.ukpa.gov.uk) for fees and documentation requirements and to request an emergency passport.

➤ U.S. CITIZENS: **National Passport Information Center** (☎ 900/225–5674; calls are 35¢ per minute for automated service, $1.05 per minute for operator service; WEB www.travel.state.gov/npicinfo.html).

REST ROOMS

Tourist destinations such as Cancún, Cozumel, Playa del Carmen, and Mérida generally have U.S.-style facilities with clean flush toilets, toilet paper, soap, and running water. Other places have simple but clean toilets. The more primitive rest rooms, usually in public areas with little tourist traffic, have no toilet paper and at times no water and no toilet seats. Some public places, like bus stations, charge 1 or 2 pesos to use the facility, but toilet paper is included in the fee. Because the Yucatán Peninsula is actually a limestone shelf, the whole area operates on a septic system that can't handle toilet paper. Standard procedure is to place the paper in a basket by the toilet. It's always a good idea to carry some tissue or toilet paper with you.

SAFETY

When visiting the Yucatán, even in such resort areas as Cancún and Cozumel, use common sense. Wear a money belt, make use of hotel safes when available, and carry your own baggage whenever possible unless you are checking into a hotel. Leave expensive jewelry and other valuables in the hotel safe when you go on sightseeing excursions. Reporting a crime to the police is often a frustrating experience unless you speak excellent Spanish and have a great deal of patience.

WOMEN IN THE YUCATÁN PENINSULA

Women traveling alone (especially blond women) are likely to be subjected to catcalls, although this is less true in the Yucatán than in other parts of Mexico. Avoid direct eye contact with men on the streets—it invites further acquaintance. It's best not to enter into a discussion with harassers, even if you speak Spanish. Say "no" to whatever is said, walk briskly, and leave immediately for a safe place, such as a nearby store. Dressing conservatively may help; clothing that seems innocuous to you, such as brief tops or Bermuda shorts, may be inappropriate in more conservative rural areas. **Never go topless on the beach** unless it is a recognized nude beach with lots of other people.

SENIOR-CITIZEN TRAVEL

To qualify for age-related discounts, **mention your senior-citizen status up front** when booking hotel reservations (not when checking out) and before you're seated in restaurants (not when paying the bill). When renting a car, ask about promotional car-rental discounts, which can be cheaper than senior-citizen rates.

➤ EDUCATIONAL PROGRAMS: **Elderhostel** (✉ 11 Ave. de Lafayette, Boston, MA 02111-1746, ☎ 877/426–8056, FAX 877/426–2166, WEB www.elderhostel.org). **Interhostel** (✉ University of New Hampshire, 6 Garrison Ave., Durham, NH 03824, ☎ 603/862–1147 or 800/733–9753, FAX 603/862–1113, WEB www.learn.unh.edu).

SHOPPING

Shopping is convenient in Cancún and Cozumel, but often you pay top peso for items that you can find in smaller towns for less money. Bargaining is widely accepted in the markets, but keep in mind that in many small towns residents earn their livelihoods from the tourist trade. Rarely are the prices outrageous. If you feel the price quoted is too high, start off by offering no more than half the asking price and then slowly go up, usually to about 70% of the original price. Bargaining is not accepted in most shops, except at times when you are paying cash instead of using a credit card.

It is illegal to take out of the country pre-Hispanic artifacts and paintings by such Mexican masters as Diego Rivera and Frida Kahlo, which are defined as part of the national patrimony.

STUDENTS IN THE YUCATÁN PENINSULA

➤ IDs & SERVICES: **Council Travel** (CIEE; ✉ 205 E. 42nd St., 15th floor, New York, NY 10017, ☎ 212/822–2700 or 888/268–6245, FAX 212/822–2699, WEB www.councilexchanges.org) for mail orders only, in the United States. **Travel Cuts** (✉ 187 College St., Toronto, Ontario M5T 1P7, Canada, ☎ 416/979–2406 or 800/667–2887 in Canada, FAX 416/979–8167, WEB www.travelcuts.com).

TAXES

AIRPORT TAXES

An air-departure tax of $18 or the peso equivalent must be paid at the airport for international flights from Mexico. For domestic flights the departure tax is around $10. It's important that you save a little cash for this transaction, as traveler's checks and credit cards are not accepted.

HOTELS

Hotels in the state of Quintana Roo charge a 12% lodging tax; in Yucatán and Campeche, expect a 17% lodging tax.

VALUE-ADDED TAX (VAT)

Mexico has a value-added tax (VAT), or IVA (*impuesto de valor agregado*), of 15% (10% along the Cancún–Chetumal corridor). Many establishments already include the I.V.A. in the quoted price. Occasionally (and illegally) it may be waived for cash purchases.

TELEPHONES

AREA & COUNTRY CODES

The country code for Mexico is 52. When dialing a Mexico number from abroad, drop the initial 0 from the local area code.

COLLECT CALLS

To place a collect or person-to-person international call, first **dial 09** and wait (sometimes a very long time) for the bilingual long-distance operator to pick up. Then give the operator the number you want to call and your name or card number, as appropriate.

Collect calls can also sometimes be placed from *casetas de larga distancia*, a telephone service usually operated out of a store, for a fee; look for the phone symbol on the door. Casetas may cost more to use than pay phones, but you have a better chance of immediate success. To make a direct long-distance call from a caseta, tell the person on duty the number you'd like to call, and he or she will give you a rate and dial for you. Casetas generally charge 50¢–$1.50 to place a collect call (some charge by the minute); it's usually better to **call *por cobrar* (collect) from a pay phone.**

DIRECTORY & OPERATOR ASSISTANCE

Throughout Mexico, you can **dial 040 for information.**

INTERNATIONAL CALLS

International phone calls can be made from many hotels, but excessive taxes and surcharges—on the order of 60% to 70%—usually apply. It's better to buy a phone card to use in one of the many TELMEX phones. Other types of phones charge exorbitant rates.

When calling direct to the United States or Canada, **dial 001** before the area code and phone number (the country code for the United States and Canada is 1). When calling Europe, Latin America, or Japan, dial 00 before the country and city codes. (The country for Australia is 61; it's 64 for New Zealand and 44 for the United Kingdom.) For long-distance calls within Mexico, **dial 01,** then the area code and the local number.

LOCAL CALLS

To place a local call, dial only the local number, without the area code. At the end of 1999, a restructuring of the area's telephone numbering system began. Prefixes (in most cases, the last two numbers of the area code) are being added to local telephone numbers for most of Cancún, the Caribbean coast, and Mérida, which means that you must dial those extra numbers when placing local calls.

Throughout the book, toll-free numbers that work in the United States are simply listed as 800/123–4567; those that work in Mexico only appear as 01–800/123–4567.

LONG-DISTANCE SERVICES

AT&T, MCI, and Sprint access codes make calling long distance relatively convenient, but you may find the local access number blocked in many hotel rooms. First ask the hotel operator to connect you. If the hotel operator balks, ask for an international operator, or dial the international operator yourself. One way to improve your odds of getting connected to your long-distance carrier is to travel with more than one company's calling card (a hotel may block Sprint, for example, but not MCI). If all else fails, call from a pay phone.

➤ ACCESS CODES: AT&T Direct (☎ 01–800/288–2872 or 800/462–4240). MCI WorldPhone (☎ 800/674–7000). Sprint International Access (☎ 800/877–8000).

PHONE CARDS

Public telephones are operated by TELMEX and accept prepaid phone cards, called Ladatel cards, sold in blocks of 30, 50, 100, and 200 pesos (about $3, $5, $10, and $20, respectively) at newsstands and pharmacies. Many pay phones accept only these cards, and coin-only pay phones are usually broken. To use a Ladatel card, simply insert it in the slot of the phone, dial 001 (for calls to the States and Canada) or 01 (for long-distance calls in Mexico), followed by the area code and number you're trying to reach. Credit is deleted from the card as you use it, and your balance is displayed on the phone's small screen.

TIME

Mexico has two time zones. The west coast and middle states are on Pacific Standard Time. The rest of the country is on Central Standard Time, which is one hour ahead of Pacific Time.

TIPPING

At restaurants it's customary to leave a 10%–15% tip (make sure, however, that a service charge hasn't already been added to your bill). Give bellhops and porters $1 to $2; hotel maids, $1 to $2 per day, per room. Tour guides should get $1 per person for a half-day tour and $2 for a full day. Tour-bus drivers should receive $1 per person per day. Car watchers and windshield washers (usually young boys), as well as gas-station attendants and theater ushers, should be satisfied with 3 to 5 pesos. Taxi drivers and shoe shiners do not expect tips, although a few pesos are always appreciated.

TOURS & PACKAGES

Because everything is prearranged on a prepackaged tour or independent vacation, you spend less time planning—and often get it all at a good price.

BOOKING WITH AN AGENT

Travel agents are excellent resources. But it's a good idea to collect brochures from several agencies, as some agents' suggestions may be influenced by relationships with tour and package firms that reward them for volume sales. If you have a special interest, **find an agent with expertise in that area**; ASTA (☞ Travel Agencies, *below*) has a database of specialists worldwide.

Make sure your travel agent knows the accommodations and other services of the place being recommended. Ask about the hotel's

location, room size, beds, and whether it has a pool, room service, or programs for children, if you care about these. Has your agent been there in person or sent others whom you can contact?

Do some homework on your own, too: local tourism boards can provide information about lesser-known and small-niche operators, some of which may sell only direct.

BUYER BEWARE

Each year consumers are stranded or lose their money when tour operators—even large ones with excellent reputations—go out of business. So **check out the operator.** Ask several travel agents about its reputation, and try to **book with a company that has a consumer-protection program.** (Look for information in the company's brochure.) In the United States, members of the National Tour Association and the United States Tour Operators Association are required to set aside funds to cover your payments and travel arrangements in the event that the company defaults. It's also a good idea to choose a company that participates in the American Society of Travel Agents' Tour Operator Program (TOP); ASTA will act as mediator in any disputes between you and your tour operator.

Remember that the more your package or tour includes the better you can predict the ultimate cost of your vacation. Make sure you know exactly what is covered, and **beware of hidden costs.** Are taxes, tips, and transfers included? Entertainment and excursions? These can add up.

➤ TOUR-OPERATOR RECOMMENDATIONS: **American Society of Travel Agents** (☞ Travel Agencies, *below*). **National Tour Association** (NTA; ✉ 546 E. Main St., Lexington, KY 40508, ☎ 859/226–4444 or 800/ 682–8886, WEB www.ntaonline.com). **United States Tour Operators Association** (USTOA; ✉ 342 Madison Ave., Suite 1522, New York, NY 10173, ☎ 212/599–6599 or 800/468–7862, FAX 212/599–6744, WEB www.ustoa. com).

THEME TRIPS

➤ ADVENTURE: **TrekAmerica** (✉ Box 189, Rockaway, NJ 07866, ☎ 973/983–1144 or 800/221–0596, FAX 973/983–8551, WEB www.trekamerica.com).

➤ ART AND ARCHAEOLOGY IN THE YUCATÁN: **Ceiba Adventures** (✉ Box 2274, Flagstaff, AZ 86003, ☎ 520/527–0171, FAX 520/527–8127). **Destino Maya** (✉ Av. Miguel Alemán 162, Altos 106, 24000 Campeche, ☎ 9/811–0934, FAX 9/811–0934). **Far Horizons Archaeological & Cultural Trips** (✉ Box 91900, Albuquerque, NM 87199-1900, ☎ 505/343–9400 or 800/552–4575, FAX 505/343–8076, WEB www.farhorizon.com). **Maya-Caribe Travel** (✉ 7 Davenport Ave., 3F, New Rochelle, NY 10805, ☎ 914/235–2221). **Sanborn's Viva Tours** (✉ 2015 S. 10th St., McAllen, TX 78505, ☎ 956/682–9872 or 800/395–8482, FAX 956/682–0016, WEB www.sanborns.com). From the United Kingdom: **Journey Latin America** (✉ 16 Devonshire Rd., Chiswick, London W4 2HD, ☎ 020/8747–8315, FAX 020/8742–1312).

➤ BICYCLING: **Aventuras Tropicales de Sian** (✉ 37 S. Clearwater Rd., Grand Marais, MN 55604, ☎ 218/388–9455 or 800/649–4166). **Backroads** (✉ 801 Cedar St., Berkeley, CA 94710-1800, ☎ 510/527–1555 or 800/462–2848, FAX 510/527–1444, WEB www.backroads.com).

➤ ECOTOURISM: **Ecoturismo Yucatán** (✉ Calle 3 No. 235, between Calles 32A and 34, Col. Pensiones, 97219 Mérida, ☎ 9/925–2187, FAX 9/925–9047). **Emerald Planet** (✉ 4076 Crystal Court, Boulder, CO 80304, ☎ 919/401–9593 or 800/883–3260, FAX 303/541–9683, WEB www.emerald-planet.com).

➤ FISHING: **Costa de Cocos** (✉ 2 km [1 mi] outside of Xcalak, Quintana Roo, ☎ FAX 983/10–110, ☎ 800/555–8842 in the U.S.). **Cutting Loose Expeditions** (✉ Box 447, Winter Park, FL 32790, ☎ 407/629–4700 or 800/533–4746). **Fishing International** (✉ Box 2132, Santa Rosa, CA 95405, ☎ 707/539–3366 or 800/950–4242, FAX 707/539–1320). **Rod & Reel Adventures** (✉ 566 Thomson La., Copperopolis, CA 95228, ☎ 209/785–0444, FAX 209/785–0447, WEB rodreeladventures.com).

➤ SPAS: **Spa-Finders** (✉ 91 5th Ave., Suite 301, New York, NY 10003-3039, ☎ 212/924–6800 or 800/255–7727).

TRAIN TRAVEL

Trains in southeast Mexico have a somewhat bad reputation—they're notoriously run-down, late, and a haven for thieves.

TRANSPORTATION AROUND THE YUCATÁN

Forget train travel. Buses are efficient and cheap and go to just about every location in the Yucatán. Traveling by car gives you lots of freedom and flexibility; primary roads are excellent throughout the region, and most secondary roads are in good condition (with some potholes). Short-distance flights are offered by a variety of companies, and while more expensive than ground transportation, they can be a good alternative for those with limited time.

TRAVEL AGENCIES

A good travel agent puts your needs first. Look for an agency that has been in business at least five years, emphasizes customer service, and has someone on staff who specializes in your destination. In addition, **make sure the agency belongs to a professional trade organization.** The American Society of Travel Agents (ASTA), with more than 26,000 members in some 170 countries, is the largest and most influential in the field. Operating under the motto "Without a travel agent, you're on your own," it maintains and enforces a strict code of ethics and will step in to help mediate any agent-client disputes if necessary. ASTA also maintains a Web site that includes a directory of agents. (If a travel agency is also acting as your tour operator, *see* Buyer Beware *in* Tours & Packages, *above*.)

➤ LOCAL AGENT REFERRALS: **American Society of Travel Agents** (ASTA; ☎ 800/965–2782 24-hr hot line, FAX 703/739–7642, WEB www.astanet.com). **Association of British Travel Agents** (✉ 68–71 Newman St., London W1T 3AH, U.K., ☎ 020/7637–2444, 𝖥𝖠𝖷 020/7637–0713, 𝖶𝖤𝖡 www.abtanet.com). **Association of Canadian Travel Agents** (✉ 130 Albert St., Ste. 1705, Ottawa, Ontario K1P 5G4, Canada, ☎ 613/237–3657, 𝖥𝖠𝖷 613/237–7052, 𝖶𝖤𝖡 www.acta.net). **Australian Federation of Travel Agents** (✉ Level 3, 309 Pitt St., Sydney NSW 2000, Australia, ☎ 02/9264–3299, 𝖥𝖠𝖷 02/9264–1085, 𝖶𝖤𝖡 www.afta.com.au). **Travel Agents' Association of New Zealand** (✉ Level 5, Paxus House, 79 Boulcott St., Box 1888, Wellington 10033, New Zealand, ☎ 04/499–0104, 𝖥𝖠𝖷 04/499–0827, 𝖶𝖤𝖡 www.taanz.org.nz).

VISITOR INFORMATION

➤ IN THE UNITED STATES: **Mexican Government Tourist Office** (MGTO; ☎ 800/446–3942; ✉ 21 E. 63rd St., 3rd fl., New York, NY 10021, ☎ 212/821–0314, 𝖥𝖠𝖷 212/821–0367; ✉ 300 N. Michigan Ave., 4th fl., Chicago, IL 60601, ☎ 312/606–9252, 𝖥𝖠𝖷 312/606–9012; ✉ 2401 W. 6th St., 5th fl., Los Angeles, CA 90057, ☎ 213/351–2075, 𝖥𝖠𝖷 213/351–2074; ✉ 10103 Fondren St., Suite 555, Houston, TX 77042, ☎ 713/772–2581, 𝖥𝖠𝖷 713/772–6058); ✉ 1200 NW 78th St., Miami, FL 33126, ☎ 305/718–4098, 𝖥𝖠𝖷 305/718–4091).

➤ IN CANADA: **Mexican Government Tourist Office** (MGTO; ✉ 1 Pl. Ville Marie, Suite 1510, Montréal, Québec H3B 2B5, ☎ 514/871–1052, 𝖥𝖠𝖷 514/871–3825; ✉ 2 Bloor St. W, Suite 1502, Toronto, Ontario M4W 3E2, ☎ 416/925–0704, 𝖥𝖠𝖷 416/925–6061; ✉ 999 W. Hastings St., Suite 1610, Vancouver, British Columbia V6C 2WC, ☎ 604/669–2845, 𝖥𝖠𝖷 604/669–3498).

➤ IN THE U.K.: **Mexican Government Tourist Office** (MGTO; ✉ 42 Hert Ford St., Mayfair, London WIY7TF, ☎ 171/499–8586, 𝖥𝖠𝖷 171/495–4035).

➤ U.S. GOVERNMENT ADVISORIES: **U.S. Department of State** (✉ Overseas Citizens Services Office, Room 4811 N.S., 2201 C St. NW, Washington, DC 20520, ☎ 202/647–5225 for interactive hot line, 𝖶𝖤𝖡 travel.state.gov/travel/html); enclose a self-addressed, stamped, business-size envelope.

WEB SITES

Do check out the World Wide Web when planning your trip. You'll find everything from weather forecasts to virtual tours of famous cities. Be sure to **visit Fodors.com** (www.fodors.com), a complete travel-planning site. You can research prices and book plane tickets, hotel rooms, rental cars, vacation packages, and more. In addition, you can post your pressing questions in the Travel Talk section and, in the site's Rants & Raves section, read comments about some of the restaurants and hotels in this book—and chime in yourself. Other planning tools include a currency converter and weather reports, and there are loads of links to travel resources.

The official Web site for Mexico is www.mexico-travel.com. If you would like to get a feel for the country's political climate, check out the president's site at world.presidencia.gob.mx. For more information specifically on the Yucatán Peninsula, try www.mayan-riviera.com or www.cancunsouth.com. These are fairly comprehensive sites with information on nightlife, archaeological sites, area history, and other useful information for travelers. Other Web sites, including www.rivieramaya.com, offer listings of hotels, activities, rentals, services, and maps.

WHEN TO GO

High season along the Mexican Caribbean runs from mid-December through the week after Easter. The most popular vacation times are Semana Santa (Holy Week, the week leading up to Easter) and the week from Christmas to New Year's. Most hotels are booked well in advance for these holiday periods, when prices are at their highest and armies of travelers swarm popular attractions. Resorts popular with college students (i.e., any place with a beach) tend to fill up in the summer months and during spring break season (generally March through April).

Off-season price changes are considerable at the beach resorts but are less pronounced in Mérida, Campeche, and other inland regions. To avoid crowds, and high prices, the best times to go are October and March through May.

CLIMATE

December to May is usually pleasant along the coast, although you may experience some afternoon rain and winds; in autumn, storms are common. The steamiest times of year both on the coast and inland are late spring and in July and August and early September, just before the rainy season. What follows are the average daily maximum and minimum temperatures for Cancún; the rest of the Yucatán follows the same general pattern.

➤ FORECASTS: **Weather Channel Connection** (☎ 900/932–8437), *95¢* per minute from a Touch-Tone phone.

Climate in Cancún

Jan.	84F	29C	May	91F	33C	Sept.	87F	31C
	66	19		73	23		75	24
Feb.	85F	29C	June	92F	33C	Oct.	87F	31C
	68	20		75	24		73	23
Mar.	88F	31C	July	91F	33C	Nov.	86F	30C
	69	21		73	23		71	22
Apr.	88F	31C	Aug.	91F	33C	Dec.	84F	29C
	71	22		75	24		66	19

FESTIVALS AND SEASONAL EVENTS

➤ JAN. 1: **New Year's Day.**

➤ JAN. 6: **El Día de Los Reyes** (Three Kings' Day/Feast of the Epiphany) is the day Mexican children receive gifts brought by the three kings (the Mexican version of Santa Claus). It also coincides with **Día de la Fundación de Mérida** (Founding Day), the anniversary of the 1542 founding of Mérida. There, traditional gift-giving is combined with parades, fireworks, and outdoor parties.

➤ FEB. 2: **La Candeleria** is the date of the final Christmas fiesta, hosted by whoever got the small plastic doll called *El Niño* (literally "the child," for Baby Jesus) in his or her piece of *Rosca de Reyes* (Kings' Ring) cake on January 6.

➤ FEB.–MAR.: **Carnival** festivities take place the week before Lent, with parades, floats, outdoor dancing, music, and fireworks; they're especially spirited in Mérida, Cozumel, Isla Mujeres, Campeche, and Chetumal.

➤ EASTER WEEK: Easter is the most important holiday in Mexico. Fiestas, parades, visits to the family, and numerous religious processions and services mark the event.

➤ MAR. 21: **Aniversario de Benito Juárez** (Benito Juárez's Birthday) is the celebration of the birthday of one of Mexico's greatest heroes; parades are held on this national holiday. On the **Equinoxes** (Mar. 21 and Sept. 21), shadows on the steps of the temple at Chichén Itzá create a snake that appears to be slithering down to earth.

➤ APR. 28–MAY 3: **Fiestas de la Cruz Sagrada** (Holy Cross Fiestas) in Chumayel, Celestún, and Hopelchén—all in Yucatán state—include cockfights, dances, and fireworks.

➤ LATE APR.–EARLY MAY.: The **Sol a Sol International Regatta,** launched from St. Petersburg, Florida, arrives in Isla Mujeres, sparking regional dances and a general air of festivity.

➤ LATE APR.–JUNE: **Billfish tournaments** take place in Cozumel, Puerto Aventuras, Puerto Morelos, and Cancún.

➤ MAY 1: **Día del Trabajo** (Day of Work) is celebrated with a big parade.

➤ MAY 20–27: **Hammock Festival,** hailing the furnishing that originated here, is held in Tecoh, on the southern outskirts of Mérida.

➤ MEMORIAL DAY WEEKEND: The **Cancún Jazz Festival,** an annual event since 1991, has featured such top musicians as Wynton Marsalis and Gato Barbieri.

➤ AUG. 18–24: **Día de la Fundación de Cozumel** (Founder's Day) celebrates the founding of Cozumel with a week of races, folk dances, music, and regional cuisine.

➤ SEPT. 14: *Vaquerías* (traditional cattle-branding feasts) attract aficionados to rural towns for bullfights, fireworks, and music.

➤ SEPT. 14–28: **Fiesta de San Román** attracts 50,000 people to Campeche to view the procession carrying the Black Christ of San Román—the city's most sacred patron saint—through the streets.

➤ SEPT. 15–16: **Día de la Independencia** (Independence Day), the commemoration of a historic speech, known as the *grito* (shout), by Independence leader Padre Miguel Hidalgo, is celebrated throughout Mexico with fireworks and parties.

➤ SEPT. 27: **Fiesta de Cristo de las Ampollas** (Feast of Our Lord of the Blisters) begins two weeks or more of religious events and processions in Mérida; dances, bullfights, and fireworks take place in Ticul and other small villages.

➤ OCT. 18–25: **Fiesta de Cristo de Sitilpech** (Feast of Our Lord of Sitilpech) in Izamal, an hour from Mérida, heralds a week of daily processions in which the image of Christ is carried from Sitilpech village to Izamal; dances and fireworks accompany the walks.

➤ NOV. 1–2: On the **Día de los Muertos** (Day of the Dead), or All Saints' or All Souls' Day, Mexicans all over the country visit cemeteries to construct marigold-strewn altars on the graves of loved ones and ancestors and to symbolically share a meal with them by leaving offerings and having graveside picnics. Bakers herald the annual return of the departed from the spirit world with pastry skulls and candy.

➤ NOV. 29–DEC. 8: **Fiesta de Isla Mujeres** honors the island's patron saint, the Virgin of the Immaculate Conception, as members of various guilds stage processions, dances, and bullfights.

➤ NOV. 30–DEC. 8: The **Fiesta de Nuestra Señora de la Concepción** (Feast of the Virgin of the Conception) is held each year in Champotón, Campeche.

➤ EARLY DEC.: The **Feria de Cancún** (Cancún Fair) serves as a nostalgia trip for provincials who now live along the Caribbean shore but still remember the small-town fiestas back home.

➤ DEC. 3–9: **Fiesta de la Imaculada Concepción** (Feast of the Immaculate Conception) is observed for six days in the villages across Quintana Roo, with processions, folkloric dances, fireworks, and bullfights.

➤ DEC. 8–12: The **Aquatic Procession** highlights festivities at the fishing village of Celestún, west of Mérida.

➤ DEC. 12: **Fiesta de Nuestra Señora de Guadalupe** (Feast of Our Lady of Guadalupe) is celebrated throughout Mexico. Pilgrims who journeyed to the Basilica of the Virgin of Guadalupe in Mexico City return home via bicycles or on foot in time for a midnight Mass followed by dance performances and fiestas.

➤ DEC. 16–25: Christmas, or **Navidad,** is celebrated in the Yucatán villages with processions culminating in the breaking of candy-filled piñatas. The most important day of the holiday season is December 24, **Nochebuena** (Holy Night), when families gather to eat a traditional midnight dinner.

WORDS AND PHRASES

English	Spanish	Pronunciation
Basics		
Yes/no	Sí/no	see/no
Please	Por favor	pohr fah-**vohr**
May I?	¿Me permite?	meh pehr-**mee**-teh
Thank you (very much)	(Muchas) gracias	(**moo**-chas) **grah**-see-as
You're welcome	De nada	deh **nah**-dah
Excuse me	Con permiso/perdón	con pehr-**mee**-so/ pehr-**dohn**
Pardon me/ what did you say?	¿Perdón?/Mande?	pehr-**dohn/mahn**-deh
Could you tell me . . . ?	¿Podría decirme . . . ?	po-**dree**-ah deh-**seer**-meh
I'm sorry	Lo siento	lo see-**en**-to
Good morning!	¡Buenos días!	**bway**-nohs **dee**-ahs
Good afternoon!	¡Buenas tardes!	**bway**-nahs **tar**-dess
Good evening!	¡Buenas noches!	**bway**-nahs **no**-chess
Goodbye!	¡Adiós!/ ¡Hasta luego!	ah-dee-**ohss/ ah**-stah-**lwe**-go
Mr./Mrs.	Señor/Señora	sen-**yor**/sen-**yohr**-ah
Miss	Señorita	sen-yo-**ree**-tah
Pleased to meet you	Mucho gusto	**moo**-cho **goose**-to
How are you?	¿Cómo está usted?	**ko**-mo es-**tah** oo-**sted**
Very well, thank you.	Muy bien, gracias.	**moo**-ee bee-**en**, **grah**-see-as
And you?	¿Y usted?	ee oos-**ted**
Hello (on the phone)	Diga	**dee**-gah
Numbers		
1	un, uno	oon, **oo**-no
2	dos	dohs
3	tres	tress
4	cuatro	**kwah**-tro
5	cinco	**sink**-oh
6	seis	saice
7	siete	see-**et**-eh
8	ocho	**o**-cho
9	nueve	new-**eh**-veh
10	diez	dee-**es**

11	once	**ohn**-seh
12	doce	**doh**-seh
13	trece	**treh**-seh
14	catorce	ka-**tohr**-seh
15	quince	**keen**-seh
16	dieciséis	dee-**es**-ee-**saice**
17	diecisiete	dee-**es**-ee-see-**et**-eh
18	dieciocho	dee-**es**-ee-**o**-cho
19	diecinueve	dee-**es**-ee-new-**ev**-eh
20	veinte	**vain**-teh
21	veinte y uno/ veintiuno	**vain**-te-oo-noh
30	treinta	**train**-tah
32	treinta y dos	train-tay-**dohs**
40	cuarenta	kwah-**ren**-tah
50	cincuenta	seen-**kwen**-tah
60	sesenta	sess-**en**-tah
70	setenta	set-**en**-tah
80	ochenta	oh-**chen**-tah
90	noventa	no-**ven**-tah
100	cien	see-**en**
200	doscientos	doh-see-**en**-tohss
500	quinientos	keen-**yen**-tohss
1,000	mil	meel
2,000	dos mil	dohs meel

Days of the Week

Sunday	domingo	doh-**meen**-goh
Monday	lunes	**loo**-ness
Tuesday	martes	**mahr**-tess
Wednesday	miércoles	me-**air**-koh-less
Thursday	jueves	hoo-**ev**-ess
Friday	viernes	vee-**air**-ness
Saturday	sábado	**sah**-bah-doh

Useful Phrases

Do you speak English?	¿Habla usted inglés?	**ah**-blah oos-**ted** in-**glehs**
I don't speak Spanish	No hablo español	no **ah**-bloh es-pahn-**yol**
I don't understand (you)	No entiendo	no en-tee-**en**-doh
I understand (you)	Entiendo	en-tee-**en**-doh
I don't know	No sé	no seh
I am American/ British	Soy americano (americana)/ inglés(a)	soy ah-meh-ree-**kah**-no (ah-meh-ree-**kah**-nah)/in-**glehs**(ah)
My name is . . .	Me llamo . . .	meh **yah**-moh
Yes, please/ No, thank you	Sí, por favor/ No, gracias	**see** pohr fah-**vor**/ no **grah**-see-ahs
Yesterday/today/ tomorrow	Ayer/hoy/mañana	ah-**yehr**/oy/mahn-**yah**-nah
This morning/ afternoon	Esta mañana/tarde	**es**-tah mahn-**yah**-nah/**tar**-deh

Tonight	Esta noche	**es**-tah **no**-cheh
This/Next week	Esta semana/ la semana que entra	**es**-tah seh-**mah**-nah/lah seh-**mah**-nah keh **en**-trah
This/Next month	Este mes/el próximo mes	**es**-teh mehs/el **prok**-see-moh mehs
How?	¿Cómo?	**koh**-mo
When?	¿Cuándo?	**kwahn**-doh
What?	¿Qué?	keh
What is this?	¿Qué es esto?	keh es **es**-toh
Why?	¿Por qué?	por **keh**
Who?	¿Quién?	kee-**yen**
Where is . . . ?	¿Dónde está . . . ?	**dohn**-deh es-**tah**
the train station?	la estación del tren?	la es-tah-see-**on** del **train**
the subway station?	la estación del metro?	la es-ta-see-**on** del **meh**-tro
the bus stop?	la parada del autobus?	la pah-**rah**-dah del oh-toh-**boos**
the bank?	el banco?	el **bahn**-koh
the hotel?	el hotel?	el oh-**tel**
the post office?	la oficina de correos?	la oh-fee-**see**-nah deh-koh-**reh**-os
the museum?	el museo?	el moo-**seh**-oh
the hospital?	el hospital?	el ohss-pee-**tal**
the bathroom?	el baño?	el **bahn**-yoh
Here/there	Aquí/allá	ah-**key**/ah-**yah**
Open/closed	Abierto/cerrado	ah-bee-**er**-toh/ ser-**ah**-doh
Left/right	Izquierda/derecha	iss-key-**er**-dah/ dare-**eh**-chah
Straight ahead	Todo recto	**toh**-doh-**rec**-toh
Is it near/far?	¿Está cerca/lejos?	es-**tah sehr**-kah/ **leh**-hoss
I'd like . . .	Quisiera . . .	kee-see-**ehr**-ah
a room	una habitación	**oo**-nah ah-bee-tah-see-**on**
the key	la llave	lah **yah**-veh
a newspaper	un periódico	oon pehr-ee-**oh**-dee-koh
a stamp	un sello	**say**-oh
How much is this?	¿Cuánto cuesta?	**kwahn**-toh **kwes**-tah
A little/a lot	Un poquito/ mucho	oon poh-**kee**-toh/ **moo**-choh
More/less	Más/menos	mahss/**men**-ohss
I am ill	Estoy enfermo(a)	es-**toy** en-**fehr**-moh(mah)
Please call a doctor	Por favor llame un medico	pohr fah-**vor ya**-meh oon **med**-ee-koh
Help!	¡Ayuda!	ah-**yoo**-dah

On the Road

Avenue	Avenida	ah-ven-**ee**-dah
Broad, tree-lined boulevard	Paseo	pah-**seh**-oh
Highway	Carretera	car-reh-**ter**-ah
Port; mountain pass	Puerto	poo-**ehr**-toh
Street	Calle	**cah**-yeh
Waterfront promenade	Paseo marítimo	pah-**seh**-oh mahr-**ee**-tee-moh

In Town

Cathedral	Catedral	cah-teh-**dral**
Church	Iglesia	**tem**-plo/ee-**glehs**-see-ah
City hall, town hall	Ayuntamiento	ah-yoon-tah-me-**yen**-toh
Door, gate	Puerta	poo-**ehr**-tah
Main square	Plaza Mayor	plah-thah mah-**yohr**
Market	Mercado	mer-**kah**-doh
Neighborhood	Barrio	**bahr**-ree-o
Tavern, rustic restaurant	Mesón	meh-**sohn**
Traffic circle, roundabout	Glorieta	glor-ee-**eh**-tah
Wine cellar, wine bar, wine shop	Bodega	boh-**deh**-gah

Dining Out

A bottle of . . .	Una bottella de . . .	**oo**-nah bo-**teh**-yah deh
A glass of . . .	Un vaso de . . .	oon **vah**-so deh
Bill/check	La cuenta	lah **kwen**-tah
Breakfast	El desayuno	el deh-sah-**yoon**-oh
Dinner	La cena	lah **seh**-nah
Menu of the day	Menú del día	meh-**noo** del **dee**-ah
Fork	El tenedor	ehl ten-eh-**dor**
Is the tip included?	¿Está incluida la propina?	es-**tah** in-cloo-**ee**-dah lah pro-**pee**-nah
Knife	El cuchillo	el koo-**chee**-yo
Large portion of tapas	Ración	rah-see-**ohn**
Lunch	La comida	lah koh-**mee**-dah
Menu	La carta, el menú	lah **cart**-ah, el meh-**noo**
Napkin	La servilleta	lah sehr-vee-**yet**-ah
Please give me . . .	Por favor déme . . .	pohr fah-**vor** **deh**-meh
Spoon	Una cuchara	**oo**-nah koo-**chah**-rah

INDEX

FODOR'S CANCÚN, COZUMEL, YUCATÁN PENINSULA

EDITOR: Chris Swiac

Editorial Contributors: Patricia Alisau, Jane Driesen, Jennifer Kasoff, Shannon Kelly, Julie Mazur, Shelagh McNally, Helayne Schiff

Editorial Production: Stacey Kulig

Maps: David Lindroth, *cartographer;* Rebecca Baer and Robert Blake, *map editors*

Design: Fabrizio La Rocca, *creative director;* Guido Caroti, *art director;* Jolie Novak, *senior picture editor;* Melanie Marin, *photo editor*

Cover Design: Pentagram

Production/Manufacturing: Colleen Ziemba

IMPORTANT TIP

Although all prices, opening times, and other details in this book are based on information supplied to us at press time, changes occur all the time in the travel world, and Fodor's cannot accept responsibility for facts that become outdated or for inadvertent errors or omissions. So **always confirm information when it matters,** especially if you're making a detour to visit a specific place.

SPECIAL SALES

Fodor's Travel Publications are available at special discounts for bulk purchases for sales promotions or premiums. Special editions, including personalized covers, excerpts of existing guides, and corporate imprints, can be created in large quantities for special needs. For more information, contact your local bookseller or write to Special Markets, Fodor's Travel Publications, 280 Park Avenue, New York, NY 10017. Inquiries from Canada should be directed to your local Canadian bookseller or sent to Random House of Canada, Ltd., Marketing Department, 2775 Matheson Boulevard East, Mississauga, Ontario L4W 4P7. Inquiries from the United Kingdom should be sent to Fodor's Travel Publications, 20 Vauxhall Bridge Road, London SW1V 2SA, England.

PRINTED IN THE UNITED STATES OF AMERICA

10 9 8 7 6 5 4 3 2 1

PHOTOGRAPHY

The Image Bank: Andrea Pistolesi, cover (Izamal convent).

Amigos de Sian Ka'an, 14B.

Campeche Tourism, 2 top left, 2 bottom left, 2 bottom right, 3 bottom right, 13A, 13B, 13C, 13D.

Cancun Convention & Visitors Bureau: José A. Granados, 2 bottom center. Jesús Moltalvo, 14D. Stefano Morini, 2 top right, 6A, 8C.

Club de Golf Pok Ta Pok Cancun: Eduardo Lopez Mustaros, 3 top right.

Club Med, 3 bottom left.

Corbis: 4–5. Gary Braasch, 11D. Richard A. Cooke, 14G. Danny Lehman, 14F. Kevin R. Morris, 14E. Gian Berto Vanni, 10A.

Fundacion de Parques y Museos de Cozumel, 3 top left, 9C, 9D.

Blaine Harrington III, 7D.

Bruce Herman, 6 top left inset, 8B, 16.

Robert Holmes, 1, 14H.

Hotel Camino Real Cancun, 14I.

Houserstock: Jan Butchofsky-Houser, 10B. Michael J. Pettypool, 11C.

The Image Bank: Angelo Cavalli, 7C, 7E. David W. Hamilton, 14J.

Bob Krist, 6B, 9B, 11E, 12B.

Liaison International: George Swain, 8A.

Na Balam Beach Hotel, 14A.

The Ritz-Carlton Resorts of the Caribbean, 14C.

Stone: Demetrio Carrasco, 12C. Cosmo Condino, 12A. Mark Lewis, 9A.

ABOUT OUR WRITERS

The more you know before you go, the better your trip will be. Cancún's loveliest beach (or most creative restaurant) could be just around the corner from your hotel, but if you don't know it's there, it might as well be on the other side of the globe. That's where this book comes in. It's a great step toward making sure your next trip lives up to your expectations. As you plan, check out the Web as well. Guidebooks have been helping smart travelers find the special places for years; the Web is one more tool. Whatever reference you consult, be savvy about what you read, and always consider the source. Images and language can be massaged to make places appear better than they are. And one traveler's quaint is another's grimy. Here at Fodor's, and at our on-line arm, Fodors.com, our focus is on providing you with information that's not only useful but accurate and on target. Every day Fodor's editors put enormous effort into getting things right, beginning with the search for the right contributors—people who have objective judgment, broad travel experience, and the writing ability to put their insights into words. There's no substitute for advice from a like-minded friend who has just come back from where you're going, but our writers, having seen all corners of Cancún and the Yucatán Peninsula, are the next best thing. They're the kind of people you'd poll for tips yourself if you knew them.

Patricia Alisau, who updated the Mérida and the State of Yucatán chapter and the Smart Travel Tips, is a psychologist-turned-journalist who was so drawn to the surrealism of Mexico that she moved to the capital. What began as a one-week vacation turned into a 20-year-plus sojourn. She's explored just about every nook and cranny of this marvelous country many times over and has credits as a foreign correspondent, war correspondent (in Nicaragua), and restaurant and food editor for many publications abroad. Her favorite pursuit is researching the Maya culture and scaling its lofty pyramids in near and far places of the ancient empire.

Journalist–turned–travel writer **Shelagh McNally** has lived on the Yucatán Peninsula with her young daughter since 1987, when she left her native Canada for a four-month Mexican vacation that turned into a major life change. She has covered Cancún, Cozumel, Campeche, Isla Mujeres, and elsewhere on the Caribbean coast for Fodor's and also has written for the *Miami Herald, Mundo Maya Magazine,* and other publications in Mexico, Canada, and the United States.

Don't Forget to Write

Your experiences—positive and negative—matter to us. If we have missed or misstated something, we want to hear about it. We follow up on all suggestions. Contact the Cancún editor at editors@fodors.com or c/o Fodor's, 280 Park Avenue, New York, NY 10017. And have a fabulous trip!

Karen Cure
Editorial Director